STAGED ACTION

STAGED ACTION

Six Plays from the American Workers' Theatre

Edited by **Lee Papa**

ILR PRESS
an imprint of
Cornell University Press
Ithaca and London

First published 2009 by Cornell University Press

Printed in the United States of America
First printing, Cornell Paperbacks, 2009

Library of Congress Cataloging-in-Publication Data

Staged action : six plays from the American workers' theatre / edited by Lee Papa.
p. cm.
Includes bibliographical references.
ISBN 978-0-8014-4688-7 (cloth : alk. paper)
ISBN 978-0-8014-7523-8 (pbk. : alk. paper)
1. Workers' theater—United States. 2. American drama—20th century. I. Papa, Lee. II. Title.
PN3306.S73 2009
792.02′2—dc22 2008052546

Cornell University Press strives to use environmentally responsible suppliers and materials to the fullest extent possible in the publishing of its books. Such materials include vegetable-based, low-VOC inks and acid-free papers that are recycled, totally chlorine-free, or partly composed of nonwood fibers. For further information, visit our website at www.cornellpress.cornell.edu.

Cloth printing 10 9 8 7 6 5 4 3 2 1

Paperback printing 10 9 8 7 6 5 4 3 2 1

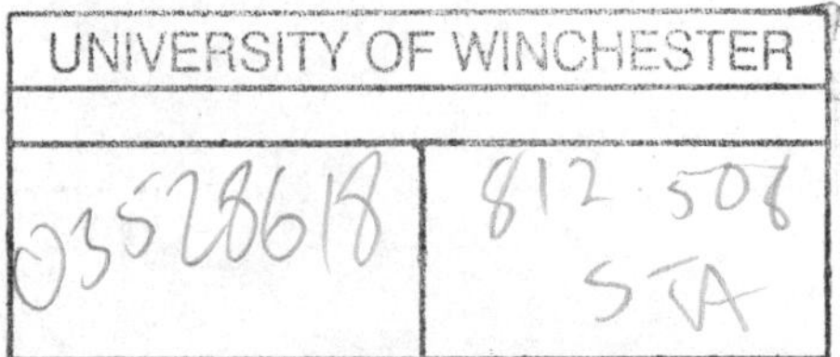

Contents

Introduction
vii

The 1920s: Workers In (and Out of) Jail
1

Processional
John Howard Lawson
9

Singing Jailbirds
Upton Sinclair
83

***The Miners* and *Mill Shadows*: Labor College Productions**
151

The Miners
Bonchi Friedman
159

Mill Shadows
Tom Tippett
185

Plays from the ILGWU:
In Union There Is Strength
and *Pins and Needles*
231

In Union There Is Strength
IRWIN SWERDLOW AND FANNIA COHN
237

Pins and Needles
HAROLD ROME ET AL.
249

Works Cited
287

Acknowledgments
290

Introduction

> "It is theatre which provides one of the most valuable means through which communities understand themselves and become understood by others. . . . [I]mages and imagination are . . . the means through which the material needs of communities and their mental aspirations form and disperse, at each point allowing a break with past dogmas and the expression of intangible possibilities."
>
> —Alan Read, *Theatre and Everyday Life: An Ethics of Performance* (93)

This collection is an attempt to restore and revitalize interest in a largely forgotten American theatrical genre, the workers' theatre movement. "Workers' theatre" is a term that is used broadly to define theatre from the working class or theatre about working-class people. Here it refers to a unique and specific movement in the American theatre of the 1920s and 1930s to employ the stage to address issues concerning the worker and the workers' movement. A simple definition was given by Hollace Ransdell of the Affiliated Schools for Workers in 1936: a workers' theatre play "deals truthfully with the lives and problems of the masses of the people, directly or suggestively, in a way that workers can understand and appreciate" (2). These plays need not be written by workers themselves, and, in fact, many were written by figures sympathetic to the labor movement. The plays themselves are a series of fascinating, moving, occasionally frustrating dramas that often passionately explore the possibilities of the workers' movement. Even during the Great Depression, these plays never displayed the pessimistic images of the future as reflected in the contemporary fiction of Steinbeck and Dos Passos. Instead, the plays of the American workers' theatre clung tightly to stirring, utopian visions, as was hoped for in the early writings that formed a basis for the movement.

In *Left-Wing Dramatic Theory in the American Theatre,* Ira Levine cites the common characteristics of pre-World War I theories concerning the social function of dramatic art. First was an "insistence on the independence of political and artistic practice"; art and politics existed on equal planes, and neither could avoid the other. Second, "ideas and artistic perception had power in themselves to hasten the momentum and affect the direction of social change." Third, theatre was seen as "the best artistic medium for the presentation of social ills and discontents" (2). One can assume that the appeal to left-wing thinkers was the immediacy and intimacy of theatre, as well as the ability of theatre to bring large groups to a common understanding of an issue. In his 1917 "Valedictory to a Theatrical Season," *Seven Arts* theatre critic Waldo Frank railed against "unreal" theatre and "love theme dramatic parades." He called for the "dawning of a theatre of populous America" against the "present danger of America [so that] the citizen will find no clearer picture of our condition than within the world of the stage" (363).

For radicals in publications like *The Masses* and *Seven Arts,* drama appeared to be the most viable means for the dissemination of a revolutionary ideology. In her 1914 *The Social Significance of Modern Drama,* anarchist and activist Emma Goldman attempted to set down a theory of the drama in the wake of the spread of realism and other dramatic innovations. She argued that American theatre was in its "infancy," explaining, "We in America have so far looked upon the theatre as a place of amusement only, exclusive of ideas and inspiration" (5). At the same time, Goldman found modern drama universal, because it "mirrors the complex struggle of life, the struggle which . . . has its roots in the depth of human nature and social environment" (6). She therefore believed drama was the necessary medium to link intellectuals with the "common" people, who were the persecuted ones in the United States. Only drama could succeed in making intellectuals "realize their relation to the people, to the social unrest permeating the atmosphere," because drama reflects "every phase of life and embraces every strata of society" (7). Goldman hoped that her book, with its detailed analysis of the revolutionary nature of modern European drama from Ibsen and Chekhov to non-realists like Maeterlinck and Yeats, would lead the way to a revolutionary drama in the United States: "[The social drama] is the dynamite which undermines superstition, shakes the social pillars, and prepares men and women for reconstruction" (8).

The climax of the early part of the established workers' theatre movement was the Paterson Silk Strike Pageant of 1913. Influenced by German expressionistic theatre and the pageant/parade tradition in the United States, journalist John Reed, among other intellectuals supportive of the labor movement, collaborated with the Industrial Workers of the World to bring to New York City a staged version of an ongoing strike against silk mills in Paterson, New Jersey. Before an audience of over fifteen thousand in Madison Square Garden, workers and sympathizers enacted the closing of the mills, the rallies, and the violence of the strike. Ultimately, the Pageant, which was supposed to be a fundraiser for the IWW, was a financial failure, and the IWW's leaders later blamed the distraction of the Pageant for union's loss in the strike. However, the Pageant would prove to be a launch point for the entire movement that came after.

In her autobiographical appreciation of the period, *The Road to the Tem-*

ple, author Susan Glaspell called the Pageant "the first labor play" (368). The most stirring summation of the meaning of the Paterson Silk Strike Pageant would come from John Howard Lawson, author of *Processional,* included here. In his introduction to a 1967 edition of Reed's chronicle of the Bolshevik revolution, *Ten Days That Shook the World,* Lawson attributes to the Pageant the roots of "audience participation, living newspaper, working-class point of view," stating further that it "foreshadowed Mayakovsky and Meyerhold in the Soviet Union and Brecht and Piscator in Germany, as well as the New Playwrights' Theater in New York and the social drama of the 1930s" (x). The Paterson Pageant thus demonstrated that drama and the labor stage could be used as a weapon in the struggles of workers.

Few full-length studies of the workers' theatre movement have been done, though notable is *Staging Strikes: Workers' Theatre and the American Labor Movement* by Colette Hyman (1997). Jay Williams' *Stage Left* (1974) takes a look at the American theatre companies that produced social dramas; it concentrates on the Group Theatre, the Theatre Guild, and the Federal Theatre Project. *The Political Stage: American Drama and the Great Depression* by Malcolm Goldstein (1974) provides a strong overview of the labor drama movement from 1926 to 1940. Mostly, the workers' theatre movement shows up in larger discussions of leftist or Communist culture in the 1930s, for example, in *The Cultural Front: The Laboring of American Culture in the Twentieth Century* by Michael Denning (1998) and *The Work of Dance: Labor, Movement, and Identity in the 1930s* by Mark Franko (2002). An interesting (if a bit anomalous) study is the red-baiting *Drama Was a Weapon* by Morgan Himmelstein (1963), which investigates how the left-wing stage was used to propagate Communist ideology.

Most plays of the American workers' theatre movement of the first part of the twentieth century are available only as typewritten manuscripts in scattered collections and archives across the United States. These works are an untapped, obscure source of material from a movement that at one point in the 1930s had over four hundred companies nationwide, several successful plays on Broadway, and courses at major universities like Vassar and Bryn Mawr that were devoted to its continuation. The plays themselves are fascinating not just as historical documents, but as theatre. They range in quality from the purely didactic sketches of the International Ladies' Garment Workers' Union to absorbing explorations of class and gender. For example, Bonchi Friedman's 1928 play *The Miners* combines expressionism and realism in a drama about a violent strike that has a female union leader as its hero, willing to risk life and limb for the union.

The large number of plays could fill many different kinds of anthologies; a volume could be devoted to plays about the Sacco and Vanzetti case, like Maxwell Anderson and Harold Hickerson's *Gods of the Lightning* and Peter Yrondy's *Seven Years of Agony;* another volume could be devoted to plays just about the coal mining industry, and still another volume to the plethora of plays about the case of the Scottsboro boys, such as Langston Hughes' *Scottsboro, Unlimited* (1933) and John Wexley's 1934 play, *They Shall Not Die*.

Rather than being an isolated sub-genre left in the past, the plays of the workers' theatre movement had an influence on American drama that continues until today. Indeed, these plays provide a key to a transformation in American literature and culture, through drama and theatre, in the representation of workers' lives. It is not overstating the case to say that works by Arthur Miller and Eugene O'Neill are direct results of the movement. *All My Sons, Death of a Salesman, The Hairy Ape,* and *The Iceman Cometh* have some of their origins in their creators' interactions with the workers' theatre.

While the dramas of August Wilson and David Mamet carry on that influence, workers' theatre in its more direct form remains in action in the work of Vermont's Bread and Puppet Theatre and California's El Teatro Campesino. In 2006, writer Kim Bent and the Lost Nation Theatre of Vermont produced *Stone,* a play based on a 1930s oral history of granite quarry workers and their families. *The Line* by Michael Gordon and Milwaukee's now-defunct Theatre X, about meatpacking workers who went on strike against Hormel in the mid-1980s, is a stunning piece of documentary theatre that weaves monologues taken from interviews with workers into the drama of the strike. These groups have created ensemble works and performed them in much the same fashion as the theatre groups of the early 20th century. In a more mainstream vein, the work of Anna Deavere Smith, as well as *The Laramie Project* by Moises Kaufman and the Tectonic Theatre Company, continue the project of the workers' theatre movement through labor dramas: to represent the voice of the working class on stage by staging the working class and its concerns.

Given the enormously rich and varied amount of material, the most difficult part has been whittling *Staged Action* down to a publishable length. My file cabinets alone have nearly a hundred plays, copied from archives at the ILR library at Cornell, the Wisconsin State Historical Society, the Billy Rose Theatre Collection at the New York Library of the Performing Arts, the Highlander Center in Tennessee, and the University of Indiana, as well as from libraries and collections at activist centers elsewhere. However, I used a few basic criteria as a way to select the texts for the anthology:

(1) Importance to the Movement. Each play in *Staged Action* was considered integral and influential to some part of the workers' theatre movement, as discussed by the labor press and other media. For example, *Processional* by John Howard Lawson is constantly cited by writers in the 1920s and 1930s as an example of the best work of the movement (and Lawson himself was a strong proponent of the workers' theatre). Bonchi

Friedman's *The Miners* was one of the most performed plays from a labor college; Irwin Swerdlow's *In Union There Is Strength* was performed for years by the ILGWU and other unions.

(2) Availability in Print. None of the texts in *Staged Action* are in print. Two of the plays, *The Miners* and *Pins and Needles,* are only available as typewritten manuscripts from archives. While the score for *Pins and Needles* is partially available, the script is not. Another pair of the plays, *Mill Shadows* and *In Union There Is Strength,* were only printed contemporaneously by the organizations involved at the time of their performance. The remaining two, *Processional* and *Singing Jailbirds,* while published in the 1920s, have long been out of print. This criterion allows the anthology to concentrate on "lost" scripts, and it necessitates leaving out two canonical works from the workers' theatre: *The Hairy Ape* by Eugene O'Neill and *Waiting For Lefty* by Clifford Odets. Both of these plays are widely available.

(3) Quality and Interest to a Wide Audience. To be frank and subjective, many of the plays from the workers' theatre are just not very good. They are overly didactic, mannered, and clichéd. Yet each one is fascinating as a historical document. However, in considering the selection, I included works that had been well-received in their time and works that were not simply recruiting tools for unions, although *In Union There Is Strength* remains as the most potent example of this kind of pure agit-prop drama. Instead, I sought to bring together works that are artistically fascinating and very much alive and relevant. In addition to labor issues, the plays included in the anthology address racial and ethnic disparities, treatment of prisoners, the effects of violence against women, and the destruction of the working class community. Also, the plays range in style from expressionism to realism.

Since this anthology may be one of the first occasions in which readers will have encountered this genre, I wanted to present a selection of the strongest work that crossed multiple areas of interest. Therefore, the book can appeal to a broad range of general readers, scholars, and students. I also considered which plays might be most readily produced by theatre companies, especially those that concentrate on older or "forgotten" works of the American stage.

(4) Exclusion of Federal Theatre Project Plays. I have not included any plays from the Federal Theatre Project. During its existence from 1935–1939, the FTP was a Works Progress Administration program that sought to give employment to artists during the Great Depression. In addition to many productions of Shakespeare and Shaw, as well as puppet shows and circuses, the FTP staged new plays that considered issues such as the threat of fascism, the treatment of workers, and workers' rights. The FTP existed more or less side by side with the workers' theatre movement; in fact, many of the artists active in the workers' theatre believed that because it was

funded by the federal government, the FTP delegitimized the political impact of its productions (although others worked in both FTP and non-FTP productions). Federal Theatre Project plays exist under a readily definable and distinct umbrella, and, as such, I believe they should be published as a volume separately, a project I hope to develop in the future.

LEE PAPA

New York

STAGED ACTION

The 1920s

Workers In (and Out of) Jail

Produced during the nadir of the labor movement in the 1920s, plays by John Howard Lawson and Upton Sinclair reflect the historic reality of the American government's crackdown on union activity—the large-scale arrests of strikers and union organizers—during and after the First World War. The image of the jailed laborer became a popular archetype that perhaps had its origins in the response to the imprisonment of Eugene Debs, the labor organizer and socialist who ran for president from jail in 1920 and garnered almost a million votes. Debs's popularity grew in large part because of his willingness to be jailed after disobeying court orders against strikes. Leading a Pullman strike in Chicago in 1893, Debs was one of seven hundred arrested in the violent clashes with police. In his two years in jail, Debs was radicalized and became a socialist; by the end of his term, he had become something of a folk hero, and one hundred thousand people cheered him when he was released from jail in 1895 (Feuerlicht 25–27). Debs helped organize the Industrial Workers of the World, or the Wobblies, which actively recruited groups that other unions rejected—unskilled laborers, minorities, immigrants, farmworkers (30).

Perhaps seeing the possibilities of this heroic stance, the IWW fostered the image of the brave worker unjustly imprisoned. When Wobbly leader "Big" Bill Haywood was imprisoned in Chicago in 1917, he wrote:

> A prison cell is the heritage we gain for the blood and lives our forefathers gave; they fought for religious freedom and left us with minds free from superstitious cant and dogma; they waged war for political justice; they carried on the struggle against chattel-slavery—these were the titanic battles that were fought, bringing us to the threshold of the greatest of all wars—the class war—in which we are enlisted as workers. (334)

The cell, then, became a part of the history of the struggle for socio-economic freedom. Such inspirational language established the jailed worker, more often than not represented as a Wobbly, as the rallying point for the labor community. For instance, in a drawing in a newspaper of the IWW, *Solidarity* (August 4, 1917), one can see the stern face of a man staring between bars of a prison window, his hands clasping the bars. The caption reads: "Fellow workers: Remember! We are in here for you; you are out there for us" (qtd. in Kornbluh 220). In other words, in order to succeed, the labor movement needed its martyrs. And imprisonment, by fair or unfair methods, was one quick path to martyrdom. Haywood and Debs both knew the power of the prison in drawing new members to their causes. But often the strongest rallying for the cause surrounded martyrs with no grounds for their imprisonment.

This picture of jail-as-community is historically accurate; in fact, jail-time was often viewed as an additional opportunity to organize workers. Haywood called imprisonment "a period of improvement," and the workers used the opportunity to recruit new Wobblies (334). According to a Wobbly prisoner in 1909 in Spokane, Washington:

> In the jail we held rousing meetings and in order to do it systematically we elected a secretary and chairman and set aside Sunday night for propaganda meetings and Wednesday night for business meetings. . . . [W]e established rules and regulations of all kinds . . . Needless to say, these . . . were scrupulously obeyed by the IWW members, and also by many of the ordinary prisoners, who fell under the magic spirit of the well known IWW discipline. (qtd. in Kornbluh 64)

The organized workers in the jail fought against cruel treatment by guards and went on hunger strikes for better conditions, often with great success (66).

This martyrdom and its role in the labor movement may be best exemplified by two cases from 1916. In the famous case of Tom Mooney, the imprisonment became a cause célèbre because of the obvious injustice involved. During a parade in San Francisco, an explosion killed eight people. Despite the fact that Mooney, a popular union agitator, was a mile away on his own roof at the time, witnesses placed Mooney at the scene. The jury heard conflicting testimony from prosecution witnesses yet convicted Mooney and sentenced him to be hanged. Upon appeal, the defense showed that a key government witness had been paid to give false testimony. However, not only were perjury charges never filed against the witness, but Mooney was kept in jail for twenty-two years for a crime he did not commit before being pardoned by a less hysterical state government. Even the involvement of Woodrow Wilson and the federal government failed to cause any change of heart on the part of the California Supreme Court, which refused to overturn Mooney's conviction on writ of error. Writer I. J. Golden wrote a 1931 play about the Mooney case as a way to agitate for Mooney's release. Upon Mooney's release in 1938, a parade was held in San Francisco in which tens of thousands of workers marched with him.[1] Mooney's belief in the labor movement remained undaunted throughout his time in prison, and after his release he lectured for the rest of his life in support of union causes and to make a living.

Another injustice occurred in the case of Frank Little, an executive member of the IWW. Little, who had been jailed several times for union activities, was taken out of a lodging house in Butte, Montana, in 1917 and hanged by a group later identified as the "Montana Vigilantes." The DA of the region called the act "unwise," yet no one was ever arrested for the crime (Dubofsky 391–92).

The United States government, under the guise of national security during World War I, systematically destroyed the IWW. Woodrow Wilson, not heeding advice to the contrary by his secretaries of War and Labor, believed the IWW was "worthy of being suppressed" (Johnson 93). Wilson's fear was that if the IWW called a strike, the resulting industrial shutdown could slow the war effort. A bill essentially directed at outlawing the IWW was introduced by Senator Thomas Walsh of Montana, who called the Wobblies "public enemies" (Johnson 98). The bill passed the Senate but failed in the House in 1918.[2] In the end, nothing could persuade the Wilson administration not to crush the IWW, not the fact that the unions of the AFL took part in over five hundred strikes in the first six months of the war versus the IWW's three, not even the fact that the National Civil Liberties Bureau, created by the federal government, demanded that Wilson end the prosecutions against the union (Johnson 101). With the Espionage Act of 1917 and the Sedition Act of 1918, the final nails were placed in the coffin of the free speech for which the Wobblies had fought so hard in the previous ten years. Under these acts, it was illegal to say or write anything "disloyal . . . or abusive about the government, the Constitution, the flag, or the army and navy uniform" (Feuerlicht 36). These laws were interpreted loosely in the ensuing years: in the first year after their passage, almost one thousand people were prosecuted under the Espionage and Sedition Acts, and half of these were IWW members from Sacramento to Chicago (*American Labor Year Book, 1919–1920* 92).

Despite the fact that the IWW did not endorse violence, the popular mis-

1. The information on Mooney is taken from *The Gentle Dynamiter* by Estolv Ethan Ward (Palo Alto, CA: Ramparts Press, 1983).

2. After the Palmer Raids in 1921, when any suspicious immigrants were rounded up and arrested under the orders of the Attorney General, Walsh became a "staunch civil libertarian" (Johnson 98).

interpretation of the union's ambivalence about the First World War and the public's reaction against the Russian Revolution led to the perception that the union might be a vehicle for the violent overthrow of the American government. An editorial cartoon showing the devil manipulating his two bestial servants, a Bolshevik and a Wobbly and other similar images in the press bolstered the misconception (Feuerlicht 61). The representation of the union man in popular culture was almost always a violent Wobbly. In the cinema, before and during the war, despite several films that were sympathetic to the labor movement, union workers were overwhelmingly portrayed as unclean, shady, Eastern European types, easily mesmerized by a leader with ulterior motives. Films such as *The Dynamiters* (1911) and *Bill Joins the WWW* (1916) never offered even the most cursory examination of the workers' grievances; instead, the audience was supposed to cheer as workers were clubbed by police and jailed (Ross 339).

The major labor dramas of the 1920s tended to focus on the persecution and trials of the Wobblies, which were the most enduring images of the labor movement. As the government attempted to crush the effort to form a labor community and further alienated and separated the radical union male from society, the artistic response attempted both to explain the original source of the worker's alienation and to offer rejoinders to the popular perceptions of the Wobbly male.

In *Processional* by John Howard Lawson, produced by the Theatre Guild on January 12, 1925, the jailed worker not only has a place to belong, but he needs to belong in order for the workers to unite. Lawson's play is perhaps the most accomplished of all labor dramas. It combines elements that will be picked up in later labor drama, such as the "dangerous" worker, the eventual demeaning of the worker, and the need for the worker community to come together for the sake of the jailed worker.

Lawson combines several techniques to create what he considers a new kind of drama. In his preface to the play (not reproduced here), Lawson explains that he wants to merge straight drama with vaudevillian slapstick, shtick, and song and dance, using as his model jazz music with its "staccato, burlesque" rhythm ("Preface" ix). In doing so, he presents, without apology, stereotypes in every character, from a Steppinfetchit-type black worker to a kvetching Jewish storekeeper, with names that immediately identify the characters: Dynamite Jim, Boob, Slop. The strikers are a jazz band that periodically marches through the audience, bringing the viewers into "the American processional" (ix) Lawson hopes to present. The sets for the original production, designed by Mordecai Gorelik, were satirical, cartoonish representations, with, for example, an exaggeratedly large jail cell with a single window or the Labor Temple with grotesque statues at its front. The reasons for this technique seem obvious: if the writer is creating, for the widest possible audience, a drama that is ultimately about "industrial peace," as a character says at the end (see page 80 in this volume), then one efficient method of presentation is to reflect the message through the popular culture of the day, using easily identifiable characters. However, Lawson also satirizes the very popular culture that he uses to create his play; in taking every character to its extreme, he uses grotesques to expose the mythology of American history and capitalism. To subvert the play's ebullience, Lawson gives the play a protagonist, Dynamite Bill, whose purpose is to revel in the undercurrent of violence beneath the gaudiness and spectacle of the play.

Contemporary critics noted Lawson's technique with varying degrees of praise. Joseph Wood Krutch, in *The Nation,* found that the expressionistic drama with a realistic tragic hero "suggests the wild disorder of contemporary life," that the play was "grotesque yet veracious," and that its "emotional effects could not be duplicated by any drama of conventional structure" ("Drama" 99). While Krutch approved of this, he also noted that "large parts of the audience were puzzled or contemptuous" (100). Stark Young, in *The New Republic,* belonged in the latter category for the most part. He was sarcastic about the "comico-realistic expressionism" and "social comment expressionism" throughout the play and also derided it for being "formed by a theory and cursed by an excess of seriousness." He did, however, find *Processional* a "thoroughly American play" that "adds to [the tradition of] plays of curiosity and uneasiness of Americans about themselves" (281).

Other reviews were much more effusive. R. Dana Skinner, in the *Independent,* who found the play "a really splendid achievement," believed that the identity of the nation was wrapped up in the play. Watching the play, he said, is "as if you are in a cathedral and you hear the noise of elevated trains, a Salvation Army choir, the riveting of a new building, and a jazz band outside," with all sounds commingling to create an image of "how American life treats us at our moments of crisis" (114). Barrett Clark also identified something uniquely American in the fact that the play is "about our fear of radicalism." Clark went further than the other critics, saying that "*Processional* will in the years to come be regarded as marking an epoch in American drama" (130).

Upton Sinclair's *Singing Jailbirds* moves away from a depiction of the labor community outside the cage to focus on the community of workers inside the jail cell. *Singing Jailbirds,* which had its American premiere at the New Playwrights' Theatre on December 4, 1928, keeps its action confined to the cell, other than within the mind of "Red" Adams, the Wobbly hero of the play.

Few other plays so starkly lay out the issues of a union community and the meaning of being divorced from it. Red is constantly attempting a communion with the other workers. His last deed before being thrown into jail is to rush to the window of the DA's office and shout, "Solidarity for the workers!" (see page 000 in this volume—), an act that elicits cheers from the workers below. Inside the jail exists a community of caged men of similar types and ethnic groups as seen on the outside in other plays. Even in jail, Sinclair says, where one is presumably completely alienated, the worker will try to create a community. Here, with the other jailed workers, Red becomes a historian of sorts, telling the workers what stories to recount when they are released from their cells. The workers even get their own religion in the person of the Dominie, who brings faith into the community of workers by calling Christ "the First Wobbly of the World." The singing also helps to create community: as long as they sing, the prisoners do not fight among themselves; they simply attempt to show the most unified face possible for their community.

According to Brooks Atkinson, the jail scene was the most stunningly designed of the play: "The cage-full of militant migrant malcontents, figuring for the occasion as striking dock workers, was impressive both as a simulated spectacle of man's notorious inhumanity to man and as an example of skillful organization and direction in the art of stage make-believe" ("*Singing*" 4). Atkinson perhaps reveals his prejudices when he adds that "if it was not convincing . . . it was because the idea of the manual laborer as an oppressed creature in this tenth year after the Great War in these United States is . . . patently absurd" (4). Among other events, in the ninth year after the Great War, a mob in Walsenberg, Colorado, led by the mayor of the town, wrecked the IWW headquarters when the Wobblies threatened a miners' strike. In January 1928, a U.S. Senate committee issued a report pointing out that, in Pittsburgh, employers were regularly using hired thugs to beat any union agitators in the coal industry (Taft and Ross 218).

Atkinson draws attention to a strange moment in the play when the audience is forced to look through bars to see the prisoners, who have formed a tidy community in their cage where all work together to give everyone an equal position in the cell (they rotate to allow those in the rear a chance for fresh air). In designing the scene with the bars in front, and a united labor community outside, Sinclair also places bars in front of the viewers; he, in essence, cages the audience. The audience is invited to join in the singing in order to join the community of workers inside the cage. With the bars caging the audience, those in the audience themselves become "singing jailbirds." As a result, the prisoners inside the cell are no longer distinct from those outside the cell; all are part of the same community.

Sinclair presents a stark lesson concerning the need for community within and without the workers' world; the two refrains of the play are, after all, the Wobbly preamble, "We are forming the new society within the shell of the old," and the words of the Joe Hill song, echoed in that flyer mentioned earlier, "Remember you're outside for us / while we're in here for you," which is inverted whenever the crowd outside the prison is heard to sing. The singing demonstrates a direct bond between the separated workers' communities. Sinclair asserts that the workers' community is in fact the community of all people, that the people inside the cages are exactly like the people outside, and that "One Big Union," the goal of the IWW, is in fact the entire nation.

Both of these plays portray tumult of one kind or another. That tumult includes the failures of institutional American society to offer the worker-community any kind of redress for abuses against it. Within that tumult the labor movement would shift from the radical Wobbly stance to the more conciliatory stand of the more mainstream AFL. The labor drama would also shift during the late 1920s and early 1930s, from the romantic Wobbly model to a drama which sought to educate and indoctrinate. With the dream of the One Big Union all but dead, labor drama became more particularized and, while even more popular, perhaps less universal.

In these plays, we see the results of the dissolution of the labor communities of the first part of the century, before World War I, before industrialization affected all aspects of the lives of workers, before "the industrialist's power became legitimized" by establishing itself firmly in city government and institutions (Gutman 259). The labor plays discussed here anticipate the plays of the 1930s, which place the labor community firmly in the center rather than focusing on just an individual necessary to the success or defeat of the community as a whole.

Processional

JOHN HOWARD LAWSON

Cast of Characters

BOOB ELKINS
ISACC COHEN
SADIE COHEN
JAKE PSINSKI
POP PRATT
MACCARTHY
BILL
PHILLPOTS
THE SHERIFF
A MAN IN A SILK HAT
OLD MAGGIE
MRS. EUPHERMIA STEWART FLIMMINS
DYNAMITE JIM
RASTUS
SLOP
SMITH
FIRST SOLDIER
SECOND SOLDIER
THIRD SOLDIER
FOURTH SOLDIER

Place: Outskirts of a large town in the West Virginia coal fields during a strike.
Time: The present.

Processional

ACT 1

On the Fourth of July

A drop curtain, like those used in the older vaudeville theatres, represents a town street painted with brick buildings, signs of Central Hotel, Palace Movie, Quick Lunch, etc. In center of curtain is the door of Cohen's General Store, with show window painted on curtain and this sign: Isaac Cohen the Cut-Rate Store, Green-Grocer, Antiseptic Barber, Kosher Delicatessen, Mining Tools. Above the door is a small practicable window in the curtain. The tone is that of the usual vaudeville drop, except that it is more startlingly crude, vigorous in color contrast, blaringly American.

A broad, uniform row of steps leads up to the stage.

Stage and auditorium brilliantly lighted.

Down the aisle of theatre comes a newsboy selling papers, shouting as he comes. BOOB ELKINS *is a thin, pimply lad of sixteen, with bright eyes and a hoarse voice.*

BOOB: Extry! Extry! Trouble in West Virginia! Charleston paper! Jazzin' up the big strike! (*By this time he is on the stage, still shouting.*) Extry! Extry!

(COHEN *sticks his head out from square window in curtain. A middle-aged merchant with a lisp that makes his caressing voice a little ridiculous. A kindly man, puzzled and worried by the violent labor dispute going on around him. The vaudeville type of Yiddish figure. He has just gotten out of bed, his sleepy head surmounted by an absurd nightcap.*)

COHEN: Say, just lay one on the doorstep, will you? Here's a nickel.

(*He throws the coin.* BOOB *catches it adroitly. Boob throws newspaper on doorstep. The head above disappears.*)

BOOB: (*Shouting*) Extry! Soldiers an' miners clash! Threats thrill throngs!

(*He exits left. Enter right* SADIE COHEN, *a sallow-faced girl of seventeen, all dressed up in white with short skirts and frills calculated to fill out her childish figure. Her hair in two neat pigtails. Sometimes she sticks her finger in her mouth. She often stands on one leg and giggles.*)

SADIE: (*As she runs in breathless with news*) Popper . . . Popper . . . (*She stands on one leg for a moment waiting, then louder.*) Hey . . . Popper!

(COHEN *sticks his head out of square window again with nightcap as before.*)

COHEN: Well, who's dead now?

SADIE: Nobuddy yet, but they're gonna kill lots a' people, oo . . . lots a' people!

COHEN: Come indoors then, you li'l devil you, before you get shot. Can't I get no sleep on a holiday?

SADIE: They got a lot a' soldiers an' they got martial law.

COHEN: Never heard of him.

SADIE: (*More and more breathless*) The Governor a' West Virginia has made a big paper sayin' it's martial law an' everybody can be kilt . . . an' the soldiers has taken the mines an' the strikers has got music an' they're marchin' an' they're marchin' . . .

COHEN: Is that a fact? There it is for the Fourth a' July . . . Coal dust an' blood . . . oi, there's no money in it! I'll be right down; come indoors,

Sadie. (*He disappears from window*)

(THE JAZZ MINERS *come through the audience playing the jazz march which forms a background throughout the play,* "Yankee Doodle Blues." *The band is a group of nine men in tattered blue overalls, playing on an incongruous assortment of instruments ranging from Jew's harps to bassoons. These do not keep time or tune very well but the effect is lively. The men are rugged types, hardened mine workers of the mountain region.* The Jazz Band: *(1) The leader,* SLOP, *is thin, with a long, glum face, playing on an old-fashioned flute. (2)* JAKE PSINSKI, *a Pole, with fiery wild eyes and a starved face, blows a long trumpet. (3)* RASTUS JOLLY *is a Negro, his torn overalls hung up by a string over his muscular back. He plays a banjo and sings most of the time for good measure. (4) A big Soiled Man with a beard which looks as if chickens might roost in it manipulates the slide trombone. (5) He is followed by a little, middle-aged, anaemic man who makes a ghostly effort to manage a badly dented French horn. The feeble players of this feeble instrument is known as* FELIX. *(6)* ALEXANDER GORE, *a man of the hayseed type, straw-colored hair and beard, red face, red bandana handkerchief tied around his scrawny neck, blows on the big bassoon. (7)* DAGO JOE, *a sleek, greasy Italian has an accordion. (8)* WAYNE WHIFFLEHAGEN, *a man with a curious face, plays a harmonica. (9)* SMITH, *young and serious, brings up the rear with the big drum banging methodically. This group makes its noisy eruption into the theatre, marches around stage and lines up still playing.* SLOP, *the glum man with the flute, stands a step below, leading them, waving his arms.* SADIE *stands on one leg at edge of stage.*)

SLOP: (*Pointing the flute at* PSINSKI, *shouts angrily*) Hey . . . you! (*The band stops in a straggling manner. Slop approaches* PSINSKI *angrily.*) You with the face, what you trying to hog it all for?

PSINSKI: (*Taking* SLOP *by the arm*) My friend, we make the jazz today for the glory of the working class.

SMITH: (*Bored*) Speech . . . speech . . .

PSINSKI: Each man make the big noise what he can. (PSINSKI *is evidently a man of education, slight foreign accent.*)

DAGO JOE: (*Pleased*) Sure, maka da beeg noise!

SLOP: Aw, say it with flowers—I'm a musician, that's what I am; I can sing too, that's my nature. This bunch a' tin-horn mechanics is rotten!

(*He sits down top step wearily.* SADIE *walks in front of the* Jazz Band, *looking curiously at instruments, finger in mouth.*)

GORE: (*Poking Smith*) Who's the skirt?

SMITH: Store-keeper's daughter.

WAYNE: She's a li'l lady, y'know what I mean.

SMITH: A clean, square li'l girl.

(*Seeing that there is a halt,* RASTUS *has seated himself on steps at extreme left, lazily twanging banjo.*)

SLOP: I wish Jim Flimmins was here; he's the guy got music inside him comes out natural like the foam off beer.

SMITH: Well, Jim's in jail, where we'll all be before long.

RASTUS: No, sir!

PSINSKI: We do not go to jail, we got rights, we are class-conscious workmen—

GORE: (*Scratching himself uncomfortably*) I ain't conscious a' nuthin' except an itch an' a thirst.

SLOP: Now, if Jim was here, he'd blow a horn like it would make the cows shimmy.

SADIE: (*Who has been listening to the conversation, eager and scared*) I can shimmy!

RASTUS: Wanna join the coal town jazz, kid? Wanna step along in the big parade with us guys?

SADIE: I'd be scared.

GORE: (*Offering* SADIE *his bassoon*) Wanna play, kid?

SADIE: (*Looks down it*) What's in it?

GORE: Noise.

(SADIE *turns to Soiled Man with the trombone, who is pulling it in and out sadly.*)

SADIE: I like this one 'cause it slides so funny.

WAYNE: Aw, give it to her. (*Soiled Man looks puzzled, wipes the mouthpiece carefully and hands it to her.*) Gentlemen, lemme introduce Miss Sadie Cohen, about to tickle the slide trombone.

(SADIE *tries to play, when* COHEN *reappears at window in his undershirt.*)

COHEN: Sadie, what's that in your hand?

SADIE: Look, Pop.

COHEN: Lay it down.

WAYNE: Just a slide trombone—

COHEN: Oi, a lot a' musical rippers, they don't do you no good with their slide trombones! Get in the house for once, will you? I'm comin' down.

(*He disappears from window.*)

SADIE: (*Giving back the trombone*) I don't do nuthin' I hadn't oughter, but Popper's always got the blues, he's always scoldin'.

(*Down aisle of theatre comes* POP PRATT, *hobbling on a stick, a typical Civil War veteran, wizened and unbelievably old in his tattered blue uniform. He has one wooden leg. He carries a faded American flag.*)

POP PRATT: (*Calling as he comes, in a plaintive, cracked voice*) Hey, boys, wait for me; I wanna march along in this procession—

WAYNE: He can't march, he ain't a member a' the Union.

POP PRATT: What's that?

WAYNE: A back number.

SMITH: A hot sketch.

SLOP: You ain't in, that's all, you're out.

POP PRATT: Try the other ear. I don't hear very good.

SLOP: You tell him.

(SADIE *sits down at foot of steps center practically in the audience looking up at group of men.*)

WAYNE: (*To* POP PRATT): Where you goin' with a face like the newspapers was writ on it?

SMITH: What's eatin' you, old man?

GORE: (*Pulling him the other way*) What for you wave the old flag?

(RASTUS *continues throughout to twang the banjo in lazy accompaniment to the scene, now and then breaking into song.*)

RASTUS: (*Sings*)

"He's got them Yankee Doodle Blues . . .
He's ninety an' he's spry,
With them never-say-die,
Them historic blues . . .
Yankee Doodle Blues . . ."

POP PRATT: Eh?

SMITH: (*Loudly, pointing to flag*) Them stars is states, stars in that flag.

POP PRATT: Oh . . . (*Scratching head*) I quit countin' year Amanda died: Mandy died in '93 . . . now it don't seem like she could be dead, her with her yaller curls.

WAYNE: I bet you seen lots of 'em die.

POP PRATT: (*Not heeding him, pounds stick on ground and chuckles*) That girl was a devil . . . yes, sir. Yaller-haired girls die quicker—they uses their strength dancin'.

WAYNE: Ain't that the cat's knuckles? Ninety years a' drums a-ratllin', he's seen wars an' deaths an' the makin' a' states an' yet he won't die.

RASTUS: (*Continues his accompaniment*)

"He's got them Yankee Doodle . . .
Yes, sir . . . Blues."

POP PRATT: They don't make girls the same no more, ain't got the same shape now. I seen shapes change—

PSINSKI: (*Pushing the others aside importantly*) This is somethin' you ain't never seen, this is industrial, savvy—there's men marchin', men in a sweat an' their flag is the black smoke in the sky, 'cause they dig coal from the ground—

(PRATT *has not heard a word.*)

SLOP: Listen, then.

(*He cocks the old man's hand over ear, then he beats a lively volley on the drum.*)

POP PRATT: (*Puts his hat on and salutes*) I hear the drums a-rattlin' across Gettysburg.

WAYNE: Don't it beat hell the way they walk aroun' rememberin'?

(RASTUS *sings low as* PRATT *continues.*)

POP PRATT: (*Looking very much alive*) Yes, friends, in them days sinful pride leaped up an' we fought our brothers, American blood to water American earth . . . (*Tapping wooden leg with stick*) That's what my flesh done; fertilizer. My leg went to make the flowers grow in Gettysburg. We fought our brothers, we did . . .

PSINSKI: (*Shouts at* PRATT) All men are brothers!

POP PRATT: (*Turning and wiggling his finger in his ear*) Try the other ear.

(COHEN, *dressed, has come out of store, carrying a large wooden board which he sets up beside door, on it written in big letters: "Headquarters for Guns—Wholesale Prices." He pushes through the men to* SADIE, *who stands up.*)

COHEN: Sadie . . . Sadie . . . Did I tell you to get in the house, or are you deaf already, is it?

SADIE: I wanna hear the music, Pop.

COHEN: Ain't you got a swell victrola? Didn't I tell you them fellers mean you no good? (*Turning to the* JAZZ BAND) Get away from the front a' my store an' leave my daughter alone.

SMITH: We ain't said a word to her.

WAYNE: She's just been settin' there, an' that's the truth.

COHEN: (*His arm affectionately around his daughter*) A child raised for sassiety, understand . . . a flower, I am here to say it, a rosebud, a tulip, a forget-me-not, a regular Madonnis! . . . What else? A lady. . . . Have I spoken? (JAZZ BAND *is impressed.* COHEN *looks them over.*) Oi, what a bunch this is!

PSINSKI: This is the Industrial Jazz chosen for their music talent, every mother's son.

POP PRATT: (*Coming between them, trying to hear*) What's that?

COHEN: (*Peering down the bassoon*) Have you got a bomb in that thing?

PSINSKI: (*Catching* COHEN *by arm and swinging him around*) Bourgeois!

COHEN: You dirty little foreigner.

SMITH: (*Swinging* COHEN *around the other way*) Who the hell's a foreigner? What are you yourself?

COHEN: What's your name?

SMITH: Smith.

COHEN: Mine's Cohen, you an' me is Americans. Shake. (SMITH *turns away from him.* COHEN *shakes his own hand.*) It's just the same by me—half a' these birds can't even talk in U.S.A.

DAGO JOE: Me savvy all linguagio, sail on da sea, walk on da land, see all da place, me clever wop, speaka Sensen wid Chinese girl, speaka Spearmint wid Eskimo girl, see all da place!

SLOP: Line up, boys, it's your turn to show 'em.

FELIX: Peerade—

WAYNE: March—

SMITH: Procession—

SLOP: An' for Christ's sake, sugar it!

COHEN: (*As* Jazz Band *forms in line*) Play the music, make a little music, murder an' starve—rights . . . rights . . . wave the flag an' play a little jazz . . .

(*Music starts with a bang and they march off right, led by* SLOP. *Music continues in distance off stage.* PRATT, COHEN *and* SADIE *remain.*)

POP PRATT: (*Hand cocked over ear*) Why, don't them boys make a noise, eh . . . music, eh?

COHEN: You got luck an' you don't know it. Come on, Sadie.

(*He exits into shop.* SADIE *is at door of shop when* BOOB *returns, still shouting.*)

BOOB: Extry! Extry! Threats thrill throngs!

POP PRATT: Here y'are, boy.

(PRATT *buys a paper.* BOOB *turns to* SADIE.)

BOOB: Hello, Sadie.

SADIE: Good mornin'.

BOOB: Give us a kiss, will you?

SADIE: (*Pointing to* PRATT) Huh, the old man.

BOOB: When you gonna give me the other garter off your leg?

SADIE: I can't . . . I got nuthin' to keep my stockings up.

BOOB: I'll give you a new pair with diamond buckles.

SADIE: You're kiddin', you ain't got the money—

BOOB: I'd steal for you! Give us a kiss for the Fourth a' July.

SADIE: I don't want to.

BOOB: (*Produces a pile of firecrackers from pocket*) I'll give you a firecracker if you do.

SADIE: (*Hesitating, finger in mouth*) Well . . . no, I don't want to.

BOOB: I thought you was my girl.

SADIE: I ain't nobuddy's girl. I'm free, I'm a suffragette, I don't care!

(*She goes into shop.*)

BOOB: Aw, listen, Sadie.

(*He follows her into shop, but only for an instant, then he is projected out head first, falling on the ground.* COHEN *appears in door.*)

COHEN: Out an' stay out, a boy that's no good, a thief, a loafer, I don't want to soil the hands on you again. (COHEN *disappears.* BOOB *picks himself up, produces firecracker, lights it and throws it into shop. A small explosion is heard inside.* COHEN*'s head appears at door.*) That's how boys learn to be gunmen an' murderers. You will end in a big jail.

(*He disappears again.* PRATT *limps forward.*)

POP PRATT: What you doin' with them things?

BOOB: (*Hopping around*) Celebratin' my country 'tis of thee . . . it makes people dance! (*He lights the pack, throws it under* PRATT *and runs off, shouting.*) Extry! Threats thrill throngs!

(BOOB *has gone. The firecrackers explode with bangs and puffs of smoke. The old man loses his balance, waves his stick wildly and then goes flat on the ground. Enter on either side of stage simultaneously a soldier fully armed. The soldiers stand at either side, worried as if they were attacking an enemy trench.* MACCARTHY, *muscular and grizzled, hard-boiled, with dirty red hair, whispers loudly.*)

MACCARTHY: D'ye hear it, Bill?

BILL: (*A young city boy, tough, but easily frightened.*) I heard shootin'.

(*They approach* PRATT *on the ground.*)

MACCARTHY: They've done for the old man.

POP PRATT: (*Angrily*) Help me up, bloomin' fools!

MACCARTHY: Where'd it get you?

POP PRATT: My ear—(MACCARTHY *and* BILL *look at each other.*) Louder.

MACCARTHY: (*Shouts*) What was it?

POP PRATT: Rheumatism.

MACCARTHY: He ain't hurt.

(*They help him up.*)

BILL: Handle him careful, he's a veteran.

MACCARTHY: No, he ain't. Where's his American Legion button?

BILL: Sh . . . the other war . . . the Civil . . .

(COHEN *comes out of shop with a bunch of American flags on a stand which he hangs by the door, on it a sign, "Your Country's Flag. Special Sale." He bustles forward.*)

COHEN: Good mornin', gentleman, nice mornin', can I sell you anything?

BILL: Say, you remind me of Second Avenue.

COHEN: A New York boy?

BILL: No, Jersey City.

COHEN: Keep your eye out, Sammy, this is a tough place.

MACCARTHY: That's the bunk, tie it outside.

COHEN: They got what they call industrial warfare here—

MACCARTHY: (*Slapping chest*) We been in a real war; what about Argonne?

COHEN: Well, what about it?

MACCARTHY: Ever hear of Chateau Thierry? There was blood in the woods that day, a stinkin' lot a' blood.

BILL: Shut your head, I cough up every time I think a' that.

MACCARTHY: Uncle Sam's gonna keep order here. Any guy doubts it goes underground with lead in him, that's the law an' order program, savvy, 'cause the place is lousy with foreigners that don't understand American freedom—

(*Enter* PSINSKI, *a bullet wound in shoulder, shirt torn open shows a red scar.*)

BILL: What's a' matter with him?

PSINSKI: Some guy didn't like the music—just a flesh wound, it's nuthin'.

MACCARTHY: Hurry up, Bill, we better go look. (*Turning to* COHEN) Send the old man home, he'll get hurt. Come on, Bill.

BILL: (*Whining as they go*) I don't half like it.

(*Exit* MACCARTHY *and* BILL. *Off stage the recurrent rhythm of marching feet and music.*)

PSINSKI: (*Center*) Hear them feet a-shufflin' . . . the feet go clippety-clop an' the music make a splash like dynamite!

COHEN: (*To* POP PRATT) Better go home, Pop; looks like trouble here.

POP PRATT: (*Listening intently*) What's that about beer?

COHEN: (*Shouting angrily in* PRATT'*s ear*) Trouble, disorder, riots, fighting . . .

(*Enter* PHILLPOTS, *young, amiable, brisk, neat made-to-order clothes, straw hat, nasal voice, folding Kodak slung over shoulder, a very* GEORGE M. COHAN *sort of newspaper man.*)

PHILLPOTS: Who said trouble? Riots, masses, poisonous gas, I'm for it!

POP PRATT: (*To* COHEN) Did you say there was gonna be another war?

PHILLPOTS: Sure, why not?

COHEN: Stranger here?

PHILLPOTS: I belong everywhere.

COHEN: Well, you look like you thought you was a devil with the women.

PHILLPOTS: Confidentially, I am.

COHEN: A newspaper feller!

PSINSKI: Treat him good, he owns us all, the guy that holds the wires . . . he laughs, he makes death, he telegraphs—

COHEN: Umph!

PHILLPOTS: That's me, Hiram, the History Kid. (*Inside the house* SADIE *has started the phonograph, a nasal voice singing. "There's no land so grand as my land from California to Manhattan Isle."* PHILLPOTS *continues to speak.*) Say, I've covered the map—steamers, trams, aeroplanes, camels, round and round in the path of war and all the time I had . . . (*The phonograph goes on. "Make me lose those . . . Yankee Doodle Blues."* PHILLPOTS *joins in, singing.*)

"I had those, yes I had those . . .
Yankee Doodle Blues . . ."

(*The phonograph starts again at the beginning,* SADIE *dances out of store clapping her hands.*)

SADIE: I was makin' music an' I heard a voice that answered, heard a stranger's voice.

(PHILLPOTS *and* SADIE *look at each other smiling, stepping in time to the music.*)

PHILLPOTS: Is this my dance?

(*He and* SADIE *dance.* POP PRATT *delighted, pounds stick and jigs in a circle.*)

COHEN: Here . . . here! (*He tries to stop them. The first time he fails, but on next round succeeds in separating them.*) Enough is too much, young man. That's my daughter an' you ain't been introduced.

PHILLPOTS: She sure knows how to dance.

COHEN: She goes out now an' then to a social party where they dance genteel with a fox-trot an' a rabbit run, but no fightin' or pushin'—a social time, would you believe it.

(*The phonograph ends in a cracked wheeze.*)

PHILLPOTS: Are you one of the debutantes here?

SADIE: No, sir, I'm a good girl.

PHILLPOTS: You can't kid me, little girl, my mother was Jewish . . .

COHEN: Welcome.

PHILLPOTS: And my father was Irish.

COHEN: (*Suspiciously*) Oh ho, is that so?

PHILLPOTS: Yes, sir.

SADIE: What you doin' in a coal town, stranger?

PHILLPOTS: What sort of place is this?

COHEN: Oh, there you ask somethin'. It's rotten! Look at me: I come up here from Charleston when the mines opened. It looked like a million dollars, an' I tumble into a valley where Death lives.

PSINSKI: Go up that big hill, see all the graves a' men died sweatin' in the mines, little stones standin' like an army, but there on the other side a' town a temple built by a rich man with statues an' all—but go look at them graves!

PHILLPOTS: I don't care about the dead ones, but the live ones!—

COHEN: A live town, a coal center, ain't it? . . . (He points to the picture on curtain.) With a movie palace an' a rotary club an' a Ku Klux Klan—but out here on the outskirts a' town the hell a' coal begins, all these little black valleys full up with mines.

PHILLPOTS: Out of this the soul of America rises in a pillar of smoke. It warms the heart of the U.S.A. all right.

SADIE: (*Stands on one leg looking at* PHILLPOTS, *gaping with admiration*) Ain't he got the silver tongue, though?

PHILLPOTS: Little girl, rose of the coal dust with olive skin, were you born of smoke?

COHEN: Not on your life, she ain't, I'm here to say it, an' don't you go give her no such ideas. What a place for a girl among all these foreigners an' rippers!

SADIE: What's a ripper, Pop?

COHEN: A feller pulls the clothes off your back.

SADIE: Oo . . . I'd like that!

COHEN: Innocent, ain't it? She's all I got in the world. I got money saved to send her to correspondence school, some swell place, y'know what I mean.

PSINSKI: (*Comes up to* PHILLPOTS, *looks him over thoughtfully.*) Looking for trouble, are you?

PHILLPOTS: If I don't find it I'll make it. What do I care for guns! I'm going to raise the lid off this strike, make it a national issue, put it on the front page, put it before Congress, put it—

(*While he has been speaking, all his hearers have suddenly taken cover, made signs of fright and disappeared.* PSINSKI *to left, followed by* POP PRATT, COHEN *and* SADIE *into shop.* SADIE *peeks out once and retires as a big, dangerous-looking man enters right.* CONNER, *the* SHERIFF, *carries two large pistols, dressed in half Buffalo Bill style, high boots, black whiskers, a very big badge on his chest. He twirls the pistols in each hands in a way to terrify any onlooker.* PHILLPOTS *sees him and his voice dies.*)

SHERIFF: (*Roaring*) Out a' my path, stranger!

(PHILLPOTS *dives into Cohen's store.* SHERIFF *walks up and down dangerously, trying to intimidate the audience. Enter right a tall* MAN IN A SILK HAT *and immaculate afternoon clothes, white kid gloves, followed by* BILL *and* MACCARTHY *marching stiffly, guns on shoulder.* SHERIFF *swings fiercely on the newcomer. His manner immediately changes to cringing civility. He salutes.*) Yes, sir.

MAN IN SILK HAT: (*Has a deep, ringing voice*) I wish to announce . . . (*He clears his throat.*) Sheriff, I have arranged to have the strictest cooperation between your deputies and the army. The Colonel is sending his men out on police duty.

SHERIFF and TWO SOLDIERS: (*In chorus*) Yes, sir, yes, sir.

MAN IN SILK HAT: Another point, Sheriff. I am informed loose women are hanging around the camp making propositions to the soldiers. People take advantage of these periods of disorder to commit nuisances. (*Off stage the distant discord of the Jazz Band is heard again like a derisive echo.*) What's that?

MACCARTHY: It's them musical miners.

BILL: It's that strikers' jazz.

MAN IN SILK HAT: Gratuitous effrontery—

(*A shot off stage, and the silk hat flies off into wings, disclosing a shiny bald head.*)

MACCARTHY: What was that?

BILL: Where was it?

SHERIFF: You get the hat, you chase whoever done it.

(*The soldiers hurry off, one on either side.*)

MAN IN SILK HAT: (*Clapping hands to head*) Did it hit my head? . . . No, no, I think not.

SHERIFF: (*Cheerfully*) Why sure, that's nuthin'.

MAN IN SILK HAT: (*Muttering*) I wish to announce . . . (*Looking at watch*) That is, I think I'll just be going, Sheriff, I have a meeting . . .

(*He is so nervous that he leaves watch hanging on its gold chain.* BILL *returns with silk hat and a handsome gray wig.*)

BILL: I found this, too.

SHERIFF: Excuse me.

(*He takes wig and brushes it. It is very dusty.* MAN IN SILK HAT *claps it sideways on head.*)

MAN IN SILK HAT: Yes, I have a meeting . . . Law and order, Sheriff . . .

(*He hurries off nervously.* PHILLPOTS *runs out of Cohen's shop.*)

PHILLPOTS: Who was that?

SHERIFF: That's the President a' the Law an' Order League. (PHILLPOTS *laughs.* SHERIFF *produces both guns.*) Do you prefer to be tarred an' feathered or run out on a rail?

PHILLPOTS: Don't make me laugh!

SHERIFF: You're under martial law. We can investigate, search, enter an' strip you.

PHILLPOTS: Oh, Sheriff!

SHERIFF: (*To* BILL) Search him, boy.

PHILLPOTS: Don't search me. Here it is.

(*He produces large silver flask and hands it to* SHERIFF, *who smells it and takes a long drink.*)

SHERIFF: (*With manner of a connoisseur*) Not bad.

PHILLPOTS: Johnnie Walker. (*He takes a drink himself.*) I want to get to know you better, Sheriff.

SHERIFF: (*Pointing to camera*) What you doin' with that picture machine?

PHILLPOTS: Do you a big service, put your physiogonomy on the front page in fourteen cities, badge and all.

(*He takes out handkerchief and polishes the Sheriff's badge.*)

SHERIFF: (*At once becoming very civil*) That's different. What paper do you represent?

PHILLPOTS: The best . . .

(*He unfolds copy of* New York Evening Journal. *The soldiers salute.*)

SHERIFF: The open hand to friends an' a short gun for strangers. Shake. (*They shake hands.*) They call me the Big Sheriff with the Big Heart.

PHILLPOTS: (*Opening camera*) Good, now look pleasant, point your gun—not at me, point it at him.

(*He indicates* BILL. SHERIFF *has struck a very funny attitude. As* PHILLPOTS *is about to take the picture,* MACCARTHY *drags in* PSINSKI.)

MACCARTHY: (*Roughly*) I found this, Sheriff. I think mebbe he shot the silk hat.

(*He throws* PSINSKI *down in front of* SHERIFF, *who, with great presence of mind, strikes an even better attitude, glowering on the man at his feet.*)

SHERIFF: Go right ahead with the picture.

PHILLPOTS: (*Smiling*) Oh, Sheriff. (*He clicks camera and comes forward.*) What's this man done?

MACCARTHY: He took a pot shot at the Law an' Order League.

PSINSKI: (*Starting to get up*) It's a lie, I got no gun, I do not shoot!

SHERIFF: Go on, speak up.

PSINSKI: I believe in the brotherhood of man.

SHERIFF: Knock him down, boys.

MACCARTHY: (*Bored*) All right.

(*He does so, using butt end of rifle expertly.*)

PHILLPOTS: Say, is this legal?

SHERIFF: Certainly. (SHERIFF *produces large pair of spectacles and sheaf of legal-looking papers with the air of a magician taking rabbits out of a hat.*) Search him, boys, in the name a' the Law. (BILL *proceeds to investigate* PSINSKI'*s pockets.* Sheriff *fingers papers, reading.*) "Search an' Entry" . . . no that's not it. . . . "Summary action . . . can be applied to any person who talks, speaks, addresses, writes, advertises, states by word a' mouth by posted notice or placard"—well, you see how it is, we can make anythin' legal here!

BILL: (*Producing things from* PSINSKI'*s pockets*) Here's a queer-lookin' book.

PSINSKI: That's the Rubaiyat of Omar Khayyam.

SHERIFF: (*Taking it*) One a' them Armenian Bolcheviks. We keep it for evidence.

PSINSKI: (*To the soldiers*) You soldiers are work men, too, what for you come here to shoot down your brothers?

MACCARTHY: Hear him, Sheriff?

BILL: (*Holding up objects he finds on* PSINSKI) One dime . . . first naturalization papers in state of Colorado . . . a letter in Chinee . . .

PSINSKI.: That's Polish.

SHERIFF: Well, it's good evidence, 'cause no one can read it.

(BILL *passes a picture to* MACCARTHY.)

MACCARTHY: Here's a picture of an old girl.

PHILLPOTS: (*Looking over* MACCARTHY'S *shoulder*) That would be his mother.

BILL. (*Scratching his head*) Even this dirty Pole got a mother, don't it beat all?

MACCARTHY: Looks like the mother of all time.

PSINSKI: (*Fiercely*) Gimme the picture!

BILL: That's all, Sheriff, except he's tattooed all over with crescents an' crosses.

SHERIFF: I reckon he ain't worth hangin'.

(*Off stage the distant tooting of the* JAZZ BAND *breaks in again.*)

MACCARTHY: There's that noise, Sheriff . . . well, I guess we better break it up.

PSINSKI: The music goes on.

SHERIFF: That ain't music. I guess I know music when I hear it.

PSINSKI: It goes on, while there's a man left, they blow them horns!

SHERIFF: (*To soldiers*) Come on, boys, we'll see about that. (*To* PSINSKI) You know what's healthy for you, better leave town in just about two hours, get me . . . I know your kind, this ain't a health resort for Bolcheviki—where's that music?

(*The persistent rhythm of the* JAZZ BAND *off stage grows louder. The men begin to sway in spite of themselves.*)

BILL: It's here.

MACCARTHY: (*Pointing the other way*) It's there.

BILL: Here an' there.

MACCARTHY: It's everywhere.

SHERIFF: (*To* PHILLPOTS) You tell the world we keep order here.

(*Exit* SHERIFF *with* BILL *and* MACCARTHY. *The off-stage music dies down gradually.*)

PHILLPOTS: (*Coming to* PSINSKI *with friendly interest*) Are you going to get out of town?

PSINSKI: No.

PHILLPOTS: Why not? What's going to happen? I want the news.

PSINSKI: People in a sweat marchin' under a lot a' flags—it is news that?

PHILLPOTS: No, they're always doing it.

PSINSKI: An' fellers like you always lookin' on.

PHILLPOTS: (*Waving newspaper*) That's my job.

PSINSKI: You got a newspaper soul.

PHILLPOTS: Never mind about my soul.

PSINSKI: City feller, ain't you?

PHILLPOTS: Well, in a way.

PSINSKI: A fool that walks on asphalt among electric lights, what can you know about people born in the dark, a lonely bitter people in the mountains, an' to them come a stream of mystic foreigners—the Pole, the Greek, the Italian—

PHILLPOTS: That's all right, but they all turn into Americans.

PSINSKI: They turn into dirt, the earth is their mother an' she calls 'em.

(*Enter* OLD MAGGIE, *hobbling along energetically, a bent hag's body and bruised, wrinkled face.*)

PHILLPOTS: There's Mother Earth now.

PSINSKI: That's Old Maggie that they call the daughter a' God 'cause she tells everyone they're goin' to hell. Say, Maggie, tell us about God. Does He wear a silk hat; does He smoke a big cigar?

OLD MAGGIE: (*Simply*) No, he don't, but the lightnin' is his sword.

PSINSKI: Don't that beat hell?

OLD MAGGIE: Yes, it beats hell.

PSINSKI: God, don't frighten me!

OLD MAGGIE: There's a black time comin'. I'm old an' my eyes is sore, but I can see things yet.

PSINSKI: What you see?

OLD MAGGIE: Ruins an' a Bible as big as a baseball field spread over the ruins to cover 'em like a mustard plaster.

PSINSKI: Some say she can read the future in clouds an' the inside a' dead cows—

OLD MAGGIE: Fools!

PSINSKI: (*To* OLD MAGGIE) Don't you see a new light comin', a new sun risin'?

PHILLPOTS: What's that?

PSINSKI: The Proletariat.

PHILLPOTS: You don't expect me to fall for that bunk.

PSINSKI: I could convince you, you got some intelligence, come with me, I'll take you to a workers' meetin', show you the serious side.

OLD MAGGIE: Fools, fools!

PHILLPOTS: The old woman is wiser than you are.

OLD MAGGIE: I ain't so all-fired proud. I just walk in the fields a-diggin' roots.

PHILLPOTS: Are you alone in the world?

OLD MAGGIE: Ain't we all alone, walkin' wherever we walk?

PHILLPOTS: No, no, I mean family, men folks?

OLD MAGGIE: There's been men I reared. But some died in the stinkin' mines, some choked off the coal dust, others kilt in some war a long ways off . . . only Jim's left an' he ain't so much, sittin' in the jail-house.

PSINSKI: She's got a daughter she lives with an' one grandson, Jim Flimmins, in jail—

PHILLPOTS: On account of the strike?

PSINSKI: For the Proletariat—

OLD MAGGIE: (*Screaming*) I'll go mad hearin' them words!

PSINSKI: She don't know what it's all about, she just lives by boilin' up things that cure fever an' make dreams.

PHILLPOTS: A witch.

OLD MAGGIE: (*Standing huddled in her shawl, center*) I known this soil since I was yaller-haired. I raised men out of it an' buried 'em. Why wouldn't I know what the green grass hides!

PSINSKI: Hides graves, that's what.

OLD MAGGIE: An' flowers spring where the flesh rots.

PSINSKI: (*To* PHILLPOTS) Come with me, I'll convince you, show you the tent colonies, show you where they live in pigsties an' barns . . .

(*He and* PHILLPOTS *exit together,* PSINSKI *talking eagerly.*)

OLD MAGGIE: (*Alone, pulling shawl closer around her*) Fools . . . well, I'll be gettin' on. (*The lights fade,* OLD MAGGIE *in a blue spotlight huddled in shawl; shaking her head.*) There's a black time comin' . . .

(*Blackness covers her. In the dark a single blare of discordant music.*)

CURTAIN

ACT 2

The Same Evening

Scene 1. DYNAMITE JIM

A dark curtain, in which is a square window with bars five feet above the ground. From the window a red glow. Pale light and a shaft of moonlight center. An oblong box, evidently a coffin, lying on ground under window center.

Enter MRS. FLIMMINS *and* OLD MAGGIE *left.* MRS. FLIMMINS *is a woman under forty, tall and bony in her loose dress. She has an odd, regal beauty, lines of age beginning to appear in her lean, noble face. Her hair is frowsy. A sugary, cracked voice, from which tense emotion flashes now and then like sparks.*

MRS. FLIMMINS: Come on, it's late, you walk so slowly.

OLD MAGGIE: Can't no wise help it, dearie.

MRS. FLIMMINS: This is his window . . . Jim . . . Jim . . . (JIM FLIMMINS *appears behind bars at window, a tall man with rough-hewn face and muscles like granite. He stares fixedly through the bars.*) It's your mammy, Jim. Are you all right?

JIM: Who's there with you?

MRS. FLIMMINS: It's your granny I brung to see you.

OLD MAGGIE: I hope you got peace, Jim.

JIM: All I need is a chew a' tobacco.

MRS. FLIMMINS: Mebbe I can bring you tobacco tomorrow.

OLD MAGGIE: You'd oughter pray!

JIM: I sit here watchin' the rats. A rat is a friendly kind a' animal, got a funny way a' scratchin' behind the ear, diff'rent from a dawg, ever notice it?

MRS. FLIMMINS: You reckon they'll let you out?

JIM: They want me to rot here—but mebbe I'll take these bars an' twist 'em like wire in my two hands.

OLD MAGGIE: Better set still an' pray, Jimmie.

MRS. FLIMMINS: They got soldiers here thick as flies, soldiers come from Washington train after train, they got guns with knives on the end, they'd stick you like a pig.

JIM: If I had some shootin' irons an' a bottle a' hooch I'd fight the army with one hand tied behind my back.

OLD MAGGIE: You couldn't no wise hold a gun an' a bottle with one hand tied.

MRS. FLIMMINS: He shoots his face but he don't mean nuthin', there's no harm in Jimmie.

OLD MAGGIE: It's sinful pride, God help him.

MRS. FLIMMINS: There may be trouble tonight, they been paradin' roun' an' threatenin' an' talkin' big.

JIM: I'd like to be in a fight.

MRS. FLIMMINS: Never mind, Jim. When the strike's over they'll let you out an' we'll go to Philadelphia or New York.

JIM: Where do you reckon to git money for that?

MRS. FLIMMINS: I'll manage.

JIM: When you an' the old girl ain't got no food for your face nor a roof in the rain.

MRS. FLIMMINS: We're right comfortable, Jim, in that old barn on Mullins' hill.

JIM: A pigsty, that's what it is.

MRS. FLIMMINS: I cleaned it up kind a' neat.

JIM: Rain comes in, don't it?

MRS. FLIMMINS: There's cracks where the sun shines through an' the moon—

JIM: That's no place for a man's mother.

OLD MAGGIE: Home is where the heart is.

JIM: God help us!

MRS. FLIMMINS. Some day you'll be rich in New York, Jim.

JIM: I won't never see New York, I won't never see nuthin' but these dirty walls no bigger'n the sides of a grave.

OLD MAGGIE: I brung men an' wimmim into the world till my old sides was sore, an' they died, exceptin' only you . . . you stand there lookin' out into the night.

MRS. FLIMMINS: It don't do no good to cry about it. I'll get you tobacco tomorrow, Jim.

JIM: Mebbe I won't be here tomorrow.

MRS. FLIMMINS: What you mean?

JIM: I dunno, never mind.

MRS. FLIMMINS: What you so hot about?

OLD MAGGIE: Better pray, Jim.

MRS. FLIMMINS: Go home, Ma, an' pray yourself, I got errands to do.

OLD MAGGIE: You better come home with me, Euphemia.

MRS. FLIMMINS: I got other business—

OLD MAGGIE: I'm afraid.

MRS. FLIMMINS: You ain't scared a' the dark, are you?

OLD MAGGIE: T'ain't that, it's people makin' mischief in the night, monkey-doin's, sin an' capers . . . they call, "Yoohoo, yoohoo" in the shadows—why ain't men got nuthin' better to do but kill an' drink an' chase wimmin folk?

MRS. FLIMMINS: They've always done that.

OLD MAGGIE. What makes 'em do it?

MRS. FLIMMINS: The moon, I guess.

JIM: Yes, an' corn liquor.

OLD MAGGIE: An' if they get to fightin' . . .

MRS. FLIMMINS: You just head straight for home an' nobuddy will touch you. Toddle along, Ma.

OLD MAGGIE: Don't be late like you been these last nights. I don't like to think a' you out alone.

MRS. FLIMMINS: Oh, I guess I can take care a' myself.

OLD MAGGIE: (*As she goes*) I'm goin' then, but try to come home quick, Euphemia.

(OLD MAGGIE *exits.*)

MRS. FLIMMINS: (*Starts to leave, and turns back*) Good night, Jim.

JIM: Good night, Ma.

MRS. FLIMMINS: Your granny's a terror. She's too old, always talkin'.

JIM. She'll die soon.

MRS. FLIMMINS: Might be better.

(*Exit* MRS. FLIMMINS. JIM *makes sure no one is outside his window, then he starts to file at the bars, a regular grating noise. Enter left* RASTUS *with his banjo, singing. The rasping sound stops.*)

RASTUS: (*Stands, against the curtain crooning the unvarying blues tune*)

"I got them Bow Wow Blues
'Cause they treats me like a dawg . . ."

(*He howls like a dog.*)

JIM: Who's there?

RASTUS: (*Continuing to thrum banjo*) One lonesome nigger, Boss, wid a heart full a' care an' desecration.

JIM: What you doin' roun' this jail?

RASTUS: I wants to get in, wants to lay me on a prison bed.

JIM: What's a' matter?

RASTUS: Ma woman done me wrong, she went to Alabama wid a Pullman porter man.

JIM: Always wimmin; hell with wimmin!

RASTUS: Was it a woman put you in the jail-house, brudder?

JIM: No, it was like this . . . a bunch a' soldiers a-comin' down a road, with a big flag—

RASTUS. (Strumming banjo)

"Wid dem Yankee Doodle Blues . . ."

JIM: Me standin' in the road, can you picture it?—"Come on," they says. (*He shakes his fist.*) So I come on an' they lowers the flag in my face. I was lousy with liquor, understan', first thing I knows I was in the flag like a net on a fish spittin' an' kickin' under them stars an' stripes, down in the mud. I seen black, couldn't see nuthin' else. I tore the guts out a' them stars I did—but it weren't wavin' in the sky that's the point. I says, "Hell, Judge," I says; but the Judge says, "Silence," he says—

RASTUS: (*Singing*)

"An' now you got those, yes, you got those
Yankee Doodle Blues . . ."

JIM: That's how I got in but you ain't heard yet how I'm gonna get out.

RASTUS: You ain't a' gonna get out.

(JIM *reaches one arm through bars and grabs* RASTUS *in iron grip.*)

JIM. Ain't I, nigger?

RASTUS. No, you ain't—

JIM: (*Shaking him*) Wait'll you see me walkin' free.

RASTUS: Leggo me.

JIM: Ain't I gonna get out?

RASTUS: Mebbe you is. (*Shaking himself free from* JIM'*s grip*) Say, brudder, you got that strangle grip.

(*He exits left. His voice off stage singing:*)

"I got no girl neither white nor black
Ma woman's gonna hell in Alabama
An' she ain't comin' back . . ."

(JIM *starts methodically to file again. Then, with a mighty effort of his arms he twists out two of the bars. With the movement of a cat he reaches the ground in one jump. He looks around ready to run. He pulls a piece of sacking out of the coffin and hides in coffin, throwing sacking over himself, as* BILL *and* MACCARTHY *enter right.*)

BILL: (*Whining*) I don't half like it . . . that bunch a' miners is drunk an' you can't tell what they do next.

MACCARTHY: They got no guns.

BILL: Mebbe they got guns hid somewheres, just waitin' for a sign to raise the lid off hell.

MACCARTHY: No, no, these guys is good guys, y'know wot I mean, I was talkin' to one a' these miners.

BILL: What'd he say?

MACCARTHY: A good guy, said his name was Smith, he gimme a drink. I reckon if them an' us could get together with some booze there wouldn't be no more strike.

BILL: Mebbe that's so—

MACCARTHY: (*Seeing broken bars of window*) Look a' that window, some guy has broke jail!

BILL: Hello inside, who's there?

MACCARTHY: A man busted loose.

BILL: Where would he be?

MACCARTHY: (*Knocks coffin with gun*) What's this?

BILL: Just a box for some feller rotted in prison. What'll we do?

MACCARTHY: Get the Sheriff. I'll go roun' the house this way. Make it snappy, now. (*He goes off right.* BILL *runs off left.* MACCARTHY's *voice off stage right.*) Help! Man busted loose . . .

(*Enter* RASTUS *left lounging along the wall of prison. Confused noise of voices and shouting off stage.*)

RASTUS: Say, brudder, lonesome brudder in the jailhouse . . .

(*He looks around to see the figure with sacking rise from coffin.*)

JIM: Yes.

RASTUS: (*Trembles, and goes down on his knees*) I'm a good nigger an' I done no wrong, I paid ma dues an' I done no wrong, I kilt ma mother-in-law but I done no wrong . . .

(JIM *ducks down again. Enter left* BILL *with sheriff.*)

SHERIFF: What's that nigger doin'?

BILL: He's prayin' to his black God.

SHERIFF: Get up, you.

RASTUS: I can't right well 'cause ma laigs says no.

SHERIFF: You see anybuddy?

RASTUS: Ain't seen nobuddy livin'.

(*Enter* MACCARTHY *right.*)

MACCARTHY: What was it, Sheriff?

SHERIFF: Jim Flimmins is out.

MACCARTHY: Say, what sort a' guy was this?

SHERIFF: Dynamite Jim, that's what he is.

BILL: Dynamite?

SHERIFF: A rip-roarin' son of a gun, a gun-totin' son of a bitch.

BILL: Is he a Wobbly?

SHERIFF: He ain't a Democrat, that's all I aim to know about a man.

MACCARTHY: We'll get him dead or alive.

SHERIFF: It would do my heart sweet to see six feet a' him layin' here.

(*Off stage distant blowing of discordant horns.* The Jazz Band *is at it again. It sounds slow and funereal.*)

MACCARTHY: What's that?

BILL: It's them.

MACCARTHY: At it again.

SHERIFF: They that music.

BILL: Sounds drunk.

SHERIFF: They got away from us this mornin', hid down in a mine. I reckon we'll make Dynamite Jim dance to that music.

MACCARTHY: Them fellers don't mean no harm, Sheriff, they just like to jazz her up same as any man.

SHERIFF: I make my jazz with a gun, understan'.

MACCARTHY: Bill an' me will go hunt for this bird.

BILL: I don't half like it.

SHERIFF: You boys go down the road there under the hill; keep a watch to each side. I'll give the alarm an' then I'll join you.

MACCARTHY: Come on, Bill.

SHERIFF: Y'know how coal gas is, one spark can set a whole mine to blazin'!

(SHERIFF *exits right,* BILL *and* MACCARTHY *left.* RASTUS *rises from ground still trembling.* JIM, *stepping out of coffin, tap* RASTUS *on shoulder.* RASTUS *tries to move away but his legs are rooted to the ground. He tickles banjo nervously.*)

RASTUS: Seems like somethin' ghost-like jus' brushed ma shoulder.

JIM: Come with me.

RASTUS: I ain't so friendly wid the ghosts.

JIM: I ain't a ghost . . . yet.

RASTUS: Ain't you?

(*Enter* PSINSKI *right.*)

PSINSKI: So, you used the file I give you.

JIM: Thanks . . . thanks . . .

PSINSKI: Now you are free, be a man, don't let 'em get you.

JIM: Pretty near tuk me. "Who's there," they says. I pretty near says, "No one," I says—but I kept my jaw shut tight.

PSINSKI: If they catch you they string you up.

JIM: Help me then.

PSINSKI: You an' me is pals; stick with me an' you will be safe.

JIM: That's a go.

PSINSKI: (*To* RASTUS) You help us.

RASTUS: I ain't helpin' nobuddy.

JIM: If I could get home to my ma she'd mebbe hide me.

PSINSKI: Don't be a fool; that's the first place they look.

JIM: What do we do then?

PSINSKI: Y'know that big stone house on the hill that a rich man built?

JIM: The Labor Temple?

PSINSKI: Nobuddy'd ever go look there; we go hide in that.

JIM: Them soldiers is wantin' me.

PSINSKI: Which way they go?

JIM: That there road under the hill, but they wouldn't never think a' goin' up to the top a' the hill.

PSINSKI: Surely no; what's this?

(*He points at coffin.*)

RASTUS: We all know what that is.

PSINSKI: Who's it for?

RASTUS: Ma name ain't writ on it.

JIM: (*Pulling coffin forward*) I'll get in this; you an' him carry this, understan', up the hill to that stone house.

RASTUS: Come again?

PSINSKI: Carry it, you an' me.

RASTUS: I ain't gonna carry no coffin.

JIM: You're gonna come, understan'?

PSINSKI: If anybody sees us they won't ever say a word.

RASTUS: I ain't comin'.

JIM: (*Grabbing him, firmly*) You is, or I wring your neck!

RASTUS: (*Weakening*) I might be.

PSINSKI: If you was in trouble, you'd want help. What you scared of?

RASTUS: I ain't scared, just thoughtful, that's all.

JIM: Come on then.

(*Gets in coffin*)

PSINSKI: (*To* RASTUS) Come on.

JIM: If you meet any one, make 'em take off their hats.

(*Off stage ghostly music continues a funereal sound, slow and painful rendering of the Bow Wow Blues converted to a funeral march. They start to move slowly with coffin. Lights go out. Stage is black.*)

RASTUS' VOICE: Ain't it dark, though?

JIM'S VOICE: Keep right on movin'.

RASTUS: What's that?

JIM: That's me.

RASTUS: I thought somebuddy else was you.

PSINSKI: Come on, everything's all right.

RASTUS: Where are we now?

PSINSKI: Never mind.

(*In total darkness the distant music sounds dimly. Then two other men's voices take the place of those of* PSINSKI *and* RASTUS.)

Scene 2. The Labor Temple

(*In the dark, men's voices*)

BILL'S VOICE: Oh, God, if we only had some light.

MACCARTHY'S VOICE: What you doin'?

BILL: Never mind.

MACCARTHY: A man's got no chance against black night; might as well look for a cross-eyes canary in an African jungle.

BILL: What's that about a cross-eyed canary? (*No answer.* BILL *calls out loudly.*) Help, help. (*Pause*) Oh, God, where's that moon?

(*Stage lights up as the moon comes out. Drop curtain represents a marble temple with columns and two slightly grotesque statues painted on the canvas. A large door in this temple center. Elaborately carved inscriptions across top and under statues. Behind it the shadowy blue of the sky. Then a bright spot of moonlight falls front center. Music stops.* BILL *and* MACCARTHY *at edge of stage right.*)

MACCARTHY: Who called for help? . . . Hey, Bill . . . Bill . . .

BILL: Must a' walked off this way.

MACCARTHY: Weren't it dark jus' then?

BILL: I don't like the dark.

MACCARTHY: We got the ole moon now.

BILL: Wonder where the feller went to.

MACCARTHY: They say he eats the stuff.

BILL: What?

MACCARTHY: Dynamite.

BILL: What's this place?

MACCARTHY: We're way up the hill.

BILL: Is this a church? (*He approaches it, examining lettering on wall.*) Got writin' on it. "To the Spirit of American Industry, Coal . . . Steel . . . Oil . . ."

MACCARTHY: Banana Oil!

BILL: One a' these here statues is Capital an' the other one is Labor. "American Manhood" it says.

MACCARTHY: Don't kid me.

BILL: That is a queer place; let's beat it.

MACCARTHY: Here's the Sheriff.

(*Enter* SHERIFF. *He stalks boldly into bright ray of light center.*)

SHERIFF: Well, boys. (*They come to either side of him.*) Seen anybuddy?

BILL: Them trees throw funny shadows.

MACCARTHY: What's this white house here?

SHERIFF: That's no White House, that's the Labor Temple. Darius Swindleweight that was Governor a' West Virginia in 1908, he built that.

BILL: I'll say he got himself a swell house.

SHERIFF: A farmer, a hard guy like he was, too, that found coal where plowed, so he figgered he'd like a swell white monument-like, to what coal could do. Now let's us get busy: you boys look over that side a' the hill, I got a posse beatin' through the woods.

MACCARTHY: We'll look over the whole damn place.

BILL: I don't half like it.

MACCARTHY: My friend's a little scared, Sheriff.

BILL: I seen some eyes lookin' out from them dirty shadows.

MACCARTHY: Cats.

BILL: (*Relieved*) Cats.

SHERIFF: You're a soldier, ain't you?

BILL: Yes, but I can't help it. Say, I just think I'll put the bayonet in my gun, might be handy if I meet this dynamite child face to face, wouldn't like to hurt him but . . .

(*He puts bayonet in gun.*)

MACCARTHY: Aw, you don't need that.

BILL: Can't tell . . .

SHERIFF: You got whistles, ain't you? If anythin' happens, whistle.

MACCARTHY: Rely on us.

(*The three exit,* SHERIFF *right,* MACCARTHY *and* BILL *left. Off stage a distant note of derisive music. Then enter right* PHILLPOTS *and* SADIE *walking leisurely admiring the moonlight. They stop center. Off stage sound of languorous jazz continues.*)

PHILLPOTS: It's not often I get a chance to go walking with a pretty girl and the moon shining.

SADIE: I shouldn't a' come. I stole the key off'n Poppers vest. Popper would kill me if he knew I was out.

PHILLPOTS: Don't you worry, little girl. I shouldn't be here either, ought to be studying this strike.

SADIE: What do you care about the strike?

PHILLPOTS: Are you interested in the labor question?

SADIE: Only when they get to shootin'; then it makes thrills up an' down your spine.

PHILLPOTS: There's a good deal of shooting going on in town, but it's all serene here.

SADIE: Oh, it's quiet up here! Folks often comes along this hill to talk . . . an' . . . well, you know, talk. (*Approaching him flirtatiously*) You think kind a' slow for a city boy.

PHILLPOTS: I don't get you, kid.

SADIE: Oh, talk . . . an' spoon . . .

PHILLPOTS: Well, is that so?

SADIE: I don't even know your name.

PHILLPOTS: Call me Mr. Zip.

SADIE: Ain't the moonlight silvery shivery?

PHILLPOTS: You've caught a little of it in each eye, just a streak of moon!

SADIE: You got a jimjam line a' talk, Mr. Zip . . . Zip . . . Zip!

PHILLPOTS: Sadie Cohen—

SADIE: Call me Desdemona . . . why do you laugh?

PHILLPOTS: A great big black man killed her. Is that what will happen to you, little Desdemona, daughter of the smoke?

SADIE: Say, you're a real gent.

PHILLPOTS: Yes, that's my trouble.

SADIE: If you want me, try an' catch me!

(*She suddenly runs off left.*)

PHILLPOTS: (*Annoyed, muttering*) Oh, they're all the same. Now I'll break a leg on one of these tree stumps!

(*He follows her left. Off stage the jazz rhythm changes completely, becomes funereal blues. Enter* RASTUS *and* PSINSKI *right carrying the coffin. They stop center.*)

RASTUS: Say, is this coffin made a' lead?

PSINSKI: Sure, lead to keep the dead from dancin' in the cold ground.

(*They set down the coffin left rear in shadows.*)

RASTUS: Why don' we throw the box in a river an' be done wid it?

JIM: (*His head appears in coffin.*) Don't throw me in no river.

PSINSKI: This is the place I was talkin' about.

JIM: Sure there's nobuddy aroun'?

RASTUS: That voice out a' the ghost box gimme nervous indigestion.

PSINSKI: You black fellers is always afraid.

RASTUS: I dunno; it just comes on.

PSINSKI: Guess it's in the blood; I can see your ancestors . . .

RASTUS: (*Trembling*) Where? Where?

PSINSKI: A people that ain't had a fair chance, black—

RASTUS: Hush yo' mouth; some day we git a chance.

PSINSKI: Sure you will, the whole future belongs to you.

RASTUS: A black future: mebbe the coons'll be kings, mebbe yet you see a black President a' the United States—

PSINSKI: Sure . . . sure . . .

RASTUS: A cultured nigger wid a good speakin' an' singin' voice!

JIM: (*Standing up*) What's them ghost noises?

PSINSKI: We ain't alone here, there's voices somewhere.

JIM: If I could get in a good fight I wouldn't mind so much.

PSINSKI: Sit tight, the time ain't come for an open fight, you understand?

JIM: Not so much.

PSINSKI: You're a workman.

JIM: If I knew what it was about, I'd take a gun an' fight the world.

RASTUS: Who, you?

JIM: Me alone.

RASTUS: I don't much mind a daylight fight wid a razor—

PSINSKI: Wait an' learn. You must hide here.

(PSINSKI *turns to door of monument. From within comes noise of a woman singing raucously.*)

"Runnin' Wild . . . Lost control . . .
Runnin' Wild . . . Mighty bold . . ."

PSINSKI: There's someone inside there.

JIM: Who in hell would be in that place this time a' night? (*Men's rough laughter heard from rear inside the monument.*) Some fellers drunk in there.

PSINSKI: Huh, I hear men's voices.

JIM: I could do with a short swig a' liquor myself.

PSINSKI: It's probably soldiers.

JIM: We better get away from here quick.

PSINSKI: Can't now; may be other soldiers in any a' them shadows: lay low.

RASTUS: Oh, Lawd!

PSINSKI: What's a' matter now?

RASTUS: Red-hot ghost jus' passed through me.

JIM: If I had some shootin' irons!

PSINSKI: Stay right here; lay low, I'm goin' round, see what we can do.

RASTUS: Don't bestir yourself, I'll go see.

(*He exits hurriedly.*)

PSINSKI: He won't stop till he hits Kelly's Pool Parlor. (*Whispering to* JIM) Some one comin' . . . lay quiet . . . I'll be back . . .

(*Exit* PSINSKI *left.* JIM *lies down out of sight covered with sacking as* BILL *and* MACCARTHY *re-enter right.*)

MACCARTHY: I ain't gonna worry no more about chasin' nobuddy. The Sheriff's gone in the woods, let him worry . . . I'd like to get a drink in me, y'know what I mean.

BILL: But we're on duty—

MACCARTHY: That's the bunk, tie it outside. When officers ain't aroun' one man's as good as another.

BILL: I hear funny noises.

MACCARTHY: It's them drunks playin' music. The soldiers is drunk an' the miners is drunk!

BILL: I don't see so much harm in it.

MACCARTHY: No harm . . . it ain't a crime to play music, not yet it ain't—let's go see them miners . . . when a guy's as strewed as them he's everybuddy's friend. This is a good town.

BILL: It's a tough place.

MACCARTHY: (*Strutting up and down*) Well, I'm tough, ain't I? (BILL *nods sadly.*) What's the use a' bein' in the army excep' it leaves a guy free sometimes to raise cain when he feels it comin' on?

BILL: What's it get you?

MACCARTHY: I like the life, makes me feel proud.

BILL: I had enough, I have, what are we here for? Shoot down other Americans; ain't they as good as we are?

MACCARTHY: Can that talk, a soldier's got no right to think.

BILL: Makes you think, this stuff.

MACCARTHY: Better write a letter to Congress.

BILL: They gassed me in the Argonne, they jailed me for bein' drunk in Haiti, got sick off'n a woman in Texas, I got a weak stomach—it's salute an' shoulder arms an' they kick you aroun'—

MACCARTHY: That's seein' the world with Uncle Sam.

BILL: I don't wanna march no more in no dust, I don' wanna carry no flag, I ain't a pack-horse, I'm a man!

MACCARTHY: Stand back while we see who's this.

(*They stand aside right as* FIRST SOLDIER *enters doing a clog step.*)

BILL: It's one a' the boys.

MACCARTHY: Hey feller, where you goin'?

FIRST SOLDIER: (*Still doing a little dance*) I'm off duty.

MACCARTHY: (*To* BILL) Y'see, he's full a' corn liquor.

FIRST SOLDIER: Why wouldn't I be?

BILL: Listen, you ain't seen a dynamite-eatin' baby that busted out a' jail tonight?

FIRST SOLDIER: (*Dancing*) Ain't seen nuthin' but my own shadow, but I gotta date with frien's. She ain't so much in the face, but the shape!

(*He exits into monument center.*)

MACCARTHY: He's gone inside that monument.

BILL: (*Reading from front of monument*) "Labor . . . Industry . . . American Manhood." (*Scratching head*) No, I don' understand it at all.

(*Enter a* SECOND SOLDIER *in a great hurry.*)

MACCARTHY: Hey, you!

SECOND SOLDIER: (*Staccato*) Good-bye . . . don't stop me . . . I'll be back . . . Just gotta finish a piece a' business.

BILL: What business?

SECOND SOLDIER: Monkey business . . . There's a skirt in there!

(*He starts toward door of monument.*)

MACCARTHY: Say, I'm in on that.

BILL: (*Urgently*) Listen to me, you fellers is all wrong, you should be ashamed a' yourselves.

MACCARTHY: You'd oughter be a preacher, you ought!

BILL: No, 'tain't that, but I had experience, an' I love my mother.

(*Enter a* THIRD SOLDIER, *a big hulk of a man chewing tobacco.*)

MACCARTHY: Hello, Hank.

THIRD SOLDIER: Jus' goin' to see a party a' frien's.

BILL: You boys has got the wrong dope: don't you know ev'ry time you drink an' cut loose, you do wrong to your mother? Each guy got a mother livin' or dead, ain't he?

MACCARTHY: Dead ones don't count.

BILL: Even in hell a guy's mother's what made him out a' flesh an' sorrow, ain't she?

SECOND SOLDIER: (*Touched, sings*)

> "You are a wonderful mother . . .
> Dear old mother a' mine . . ."

MACCARTHY: Banana Oil! One woman's just like another, jus' a bag a' bones!

BILL: Are you callin' my mother a bag a' bones? I'll fix you for that!

(*He tries to attack* MACCARTHY. SECOND *and* THIRD SOLDIER*s hold them back.*)

SECOND SOLDIER: Now, that's enough.

THIRD SOLDIER: You're pals, ain't you?

BILL: (*Shamefacedly*) Sure, he's my buddy.

SECOND SOLDIER: Shake, then . . . pals got no cause to fight over wimmin.

MACCARTHY: Aw, s'all right, I was jus' thinkin' a' my Ma an' how the ole man threw her out a' the house—good reason he had too!

SECOND SOLDIER: (*Continues to sing*)

> "Wonderful mother a' mine . . ."

THIRD SOLDIER: Boys, we'd oughter be better men than we are . . . I'm gonna take the pledge.

BILL: Why don't you take the pledge tonight?

THIRD SOLDIER: No, sir, tomorrow mornin' . . . I'll feel like it then.

(*He goes hastily through door center.*)

SECOND SOLDIER: (*Still singing about his mother*)

> "You'll hold a spot down deep in my heart
> Till the stars no longer shine . . ."

(*From inside the house raucous singing of "Runnin' Wild . . . Lost control . . ." breaks in on him. He hesitates, then, abruptly:*)

See you later, boys!

(*He exits center, joining in the chorus of "Running Wild" as he goes, and his voice is heard backstage still singing.*)

BILL: (*Querulously*) They must a' cooked up a big party in there.

MACCARTHY: Sure . . . there's a whole crowd in there, I should kiss a cross-eyed canary if there ain't.

(*Enter* PHILLPOTS *right.*)

PHILLPOTS: Good evening, where's the fight?

MACCARTHY: What fight? Booze fightin's about all you'll see aroun' here.

(*Chorus off stage singing, "Runnin' Wild . . . Lost control . . . Runnin' Wild . . .*)

PHILLPOTS: What's that noise?

MACCARTHY: They got a woman in there.

PHILLPOTS: They have, have they?

MACCARTHY: Can you imagine some girl, jus' a spring chicken, tender an' soft, with come-over-here in her eyes, an' kiss-me written on her lips—can you picture it?

PHILLPOTS: Oh, yes, that's what I think about.

MACCARTHY: Well, there's no such animal, not here there ain't, so me for a drink!

(*He exits center.*)

BILL: They're all alike exceptin' me! I had experience, I gotta weak stomach.

PHILLPOTS: Quite a philosopher, aren't you?

BILL: Aw, bunk!

PHILLPOTS: I expected a big fight and I find you all boozing together.

BILL: A man only knows one thing: his mother's a good woman an' ever other girl is a bum!

PHILLPOTS: But maybe somebody's mother is in there.

BILL: Bunk! Strike, bunk! Army, bunk! Wimmin, bunk!

PHILLPOTS: Oh, I'm an artist at bunk myself, but sometimes it gets me!

BILL: Is that so?

PHILLPOTS: I'm a serious thinker, I am . . . sometimes I get to thinking, what's it mean?

BILL: Hear them drunks an' that woman singin'!

PHILLPOTS: We don't know who it is, without eyes, without a face, to us she's just a voice, a kind of a song that's behind change and politics . . . hear it! (*The raucous woman's singing goes on, above the low hum of men's voices.*) The jazz melody of a bad woman in a small town, nobody's listened to that or told it.

BILL: Everythin' means somethin' if you can only figger it out.

PHILLPOTS: Soldiers pass and a woman dances for them, laughs for them—

BILL: Gets their wads off 'em.

PHILLPOTS: It's history, that is—

BILL: Aw, don't kid me.

PHILLPOTS: Men have made religions out of woman and this is how they treat her, a mother image—

BILL: What?

PHILLPOTS: A dream . . . it might be a temple in Greece, they come to her to worship, it might be where the Chinese carved fairy-tales in stone—

BILL: Are you cuckoo?

PHILLPOTS: Thinking, that's all, something I can't explain—it might be some old Hindoo twilight, where men crowd around the perfumed body of a woman, without eyes, without a face—oh, it makes me sick!

BILL: You got wimmin on your mind, ain't you?

PHILLPOTS: Guess I'll be getting down to the telegraph office. Good night.

BILL: Hey, buddy! (PHILLPOTS *turns.*) About wimmin . . . don't let it get you, boy, like it got me—they ain't worth it.

(PHILLPOTS *exits left.* BILL *disappears right.* JIM *rises from coffin.*)

JIM: (*Stretching*) A woman, huh! God, I could use her . . . hot dawg! But it looks like this gimme my chance for a getaway . . . Been lyin' in jail thinkin' about flesh an' bones till it drives you crazy . . . drives you . . . mebbe it ain't flesh an' bones, mebbe some kind a' meanin' in it . . . (*Clenching his hands*) Gawd, send me a woman!

(*Enter* SADIE *left. She comes center.*)

SADIE: Stick with me, Moon, help me find my way, 'cause I'm scared! (*She looks up and sees* JIM; *backing away from him.*) Oo . . . (JIM *seizes her roughly.*) Leggo me, leggo—

JIM: I heard your voice like callin'!

SADIE: I'll kick you, I'll slap your face.

JIM: Go on, I like it.

SADIE: I'll bite—oo, ain't you strong?

JIM: Bust your bones I'm so stron—

(*Enter* BILL *right.*)

BILL: Who are you? Are you the guy? . . . Yep, that's who you'd be, Dynamite, huh?

JIM: Mebbe so, mebbe not.

BILL: (*Points gun at* JIM) Well, we'll see about that. I got you now, hands up.

JIM: (*Releasing* SADIE) All right, baby, excuse me, kid, run home.

SADIE: (*Approaching* BILL) Don't hurt him, please, don't—

JIM: (*Between his teeth*) I'll fix him! (BILL *is trembling a little.* JIM *approaches him calmly.*) You're one hell of a soldier.

BILL: Don't you come no nearer; I'll shoot.

JIM: Scared, ain't you?

BILL: Well, you know how a feller feels.

JIM: You guys is no good, ain't fit for an army.

BILL: I don' wanna be in no army.

JIM: Throw away your gun, then, an' fight like a man, huh?

BILL: I can't, I gotta kill you an' I don' want to!

JIM: One a' us has got to kill the other.

BILL: Hands up or I knock you down—

JIM: (*Shouting*) Come on then!

(JIM *lunges unexpectedly. They struggle.* SADIE *crouches at side.* JIM *wrenches the soldier's gun from his hands and* BILL *falls to ground. As he starts to rise viciously,* JIM, *gun in hand, jabs the bayonet down on the fallen body and wrenches it out. The soldier quivers and lies still.* SADIE *has watched intently. Now she faces* JIM.)

SADIE: I seen it go through him! (*A sob shakes her whole body. Beating against* JIM *with her fists.*) Oh, I hate you, you beast! I wanna kill you . . .

(JIM *stands stolidly paying no attention to her. She runs off, crying hysterically.*)

JIM: (*Bends over soldier*) He's getting' cold . . . went through him . . . must feel funny to be stuck through . . . they'll hang me now; s'all right to talk but I never kilt a guy before . . . (*From rear comes a sound of drunken laughter.*) That's for me, they're comin' for me . . . "hands up or I knock you down" was the last words he said. What curse makes a feller do them things? Getting' cold, his soul's gone up in the sky, his soul's a-sittin' in the moon; he had a mother too. . . . I want my mammy's arms 'cause I done a black thing, oh, mammy, help me now!

(JIM *bends over the dead body muttering and praying. Again drunken laughter.*)

CURTAIN

ACT 3

The Next Day

Scene 1. Mother and Son

A dilapidated barn which has been made roughly into a place in which to live. A wide opening in rear without a door through which sunlight streams in. Sunlight also filters through cracks in the dilapidated walls. Straw is stuffed in the cracks. One broken table center and two broken chairs. A lamp with red cloth shade on the table. One or two boxes scattered about. Right of door a tin washstand with pitcher and basin. Also a rusty stove. Pair of rickety wooden stairs without a banister goes up the right hand wall with a landing and a door at the top. Rusty farm machinery in shadowy corners. Left front, an iron bed, and right front a torn mattress lies on the floor. Both of these are occupied, figures huddled under bedclothes. OLD MAGGIE *occupies the bed and* MRS. FLIMMINS *sleeps on mattress on floor. But only the outlines of the human forms are visible, their heads being under the covers.*

Enter JIM *and* PSINSKI, *their clothes torn, evidently sleeping.* JIM *carries gun. They anxiously watch the sunlit door through which they have come.*

JIM: (*Muttering*) Home sweet home!

PSINSKI: We ain't safe here.

JIM: (*Looking at the beds, shouts suddenly*) For Gawd's sweet sake, wake up!

OLD MAGGIE: I had a dream an' it turned to steel against my belly!

JIM: Home to mommer an' all the folks is under the blankets sleepin' . . . (*He shouts again, hoarsely.*) Wake up!

(MRS. FLIMMINS *has risen from the mattress on the floor, gaunt in her frowsy nightgown.*)

MRS. FLIMMINS: It's the boy, it's Jim! (JIM *laughs, she comes to him.*) You ain't hurt, are you?

JIM: I ain't exactly hurt.

PSINSKI: They're after us, that's all.

MRS. FLIMMINS: Who's this?

PSINSKI: I'm an organizer here; the Sheriff's got my number.

JIM: Meet my pal . . . Jake, meet my mother that made me.

PSINSKI: They want to string us up.

OLD MAGGIE: (*Crying softly*) God deserts us an' the walls fall around our heads.

MRS. FLIMMINS: (*Standing by the old woman*) It's Jim, Ma, open your eyes an' look.

PSINSKI: We fun in the dark, we hide, yet it is a beginning, we start something that make a noise an' a smell everywheres—

MRS. FLIMMINS: Mostly smell—

JIM: (*Scratching himself, uncomfortably*) Cut out that ghost talk, it's mornin', li'l birds is singin' in the trees.

(*Off stage a distant regular tread of feet is heard, monotonous, frightening.*)

PSINSKI: Hear them feet!

MRS. FLIMMINS: Sounds like a train a-shufflin' along.

PSINSKI: More soldiers comin' off a train, comin' from the station, comin' to clean the town—

JIM: That's for me, they're comin' for me, comin' to take me from my mammy's arms.

PSINSKI: What's a' matter, it's only shoe leather.

MRS. FLIMMINS: It's a bad dream.

JIM: I know that feelin', sometimes I feel 'em in my sleep, guys bearin' down on me more'n you could count, with their bloody feet swingin' wide . . .

PSINSKI: Left, right . . . left right . . .

JIM: Some day it'll come.

MRS. FLIMMINS: What?

JIM: All them feet come to the door marchin' heavy, left, right, an' our ears'll bust . . .

(*He sits down on bed, his head in his hands. The sound of marching feet dies down gradually.*)

MRS. FLIMMINS: (*Her hand on his shoulder*) Ain't no dreams no more. We gotta save your skin alive now!

PSINSKI: He'll be strung up if they get him.

JIM: I stuck a feller through.

MRS. FLIMMINS: You what?

JIM: (*Vaguely, after a moment's hesitation*) Killed . . . had to . . .

MRS. FLIMMINS: Nobuddy's a-gonna touch him with me here.

PSINSKI: Ain't they?

MRS. FLIMMINS: (*Quietly*) No, I'm his Ma . . . ain't cryin', are you, Jimmie?

JIM: Dunno, you burn the strength right out a' me.

MRS. FLIMMINS: Never no harm in Jimmie. Didn't I fix up this barn real sweet? I had a nice bedroom ready for you up them stairs, Jim, where the hay loft was.

JIM: Six feet a' ground'll do me now.

PSINSKI: What'll we do? (MRS. FLIMMINS *pulls open a trap door center in floor.*) What's this?

MRS. FLIMMINS: A kind a' hole where nobuddy knows. Quick, both a' you go down.

JIM: It's dark there.

PSINSKI: We can talk. (*At door rear, excitedly*) There's someone pickin' their way across the field here, looks like a silk hat.

JIM: Go down first.

(PSINSKI *nods and starts down.*)

MRS. FLIMMINS: I'll bring you a candle, you stay there mebbe a week, mebbe . . .

PSINSKI: (*As he goes*) Good! In this place I will explain the worker's place in history, the Proletariat . . .

(*He disappears still talking.*)

JIM: Gimme the gun.

(*His mother hands it to him. He brandishes gun and disappears below.* MRS. FLIMMINS *shuts trap and rises, goes to door rear, then turns to the old woman.*)

MRS. FLIMMINS: We must act like nuthin' was happenin'. Come on, take your clothes, we'll dress upstairs.

(*They take bundles of clothes and start up rickety stairs.*)

OLD MAGGIE: What is it, are they comin' to take him away?

MRS. FLIMMINS: They won't touch him.

OLD MAGGIE: Why did he bust loose? Didn't he know you can't break the law?

MRS. FLIMMINS: He's heard too much a' this fool talk about the Proletariat.

OLD MAGGIE: It makes a buzzin' in your ears, what is it? Proletariat! It burns in your mouth.

(*They sit at top of stairs.* PHILLPOTS *and* MAN IN SILK HAT *appear rear and walk up and down in sunlit doorway without entering.* PHILLPOTS *is dapper and amused as usual.* SILK HAT MAN *carries a newspaper.*)

MAN IN SILK HAT: Law and Order, that's the slogan today.

PHILLPOTS: You sure this is the place?

MAN IN SILK HAT: Alleged to be headquarters of these gangsters.

PHILLPOTS: I don't see anything.

MAN IN SILK HAT: Exactly, that's what makes it dangerous.

PHILLPOTS: I'll tell the world—

MAN IN SILK HAT: That's just what you're here for. (*Tapping newspaper*) But emphasize the law and order side, don't send out these sensational reports.

PHILLPOTS: Sensational? I haven't begun yet.

MAN IN SILK HAT: The stock market will have a bad flurry this morning.

PHILLPOTS: Guess I understand news values . . . (*He opens papers, reads thoughtfully.*) "Plague Decimates China" . . . "Names Ape as Co-respondent in Sensational Divorce" . . . "Ireland" . . . there's a green place . . . "Man Stung on Head by Wasp Dies Immediately" . . . "Italian Woman Has Six Children at Once" . . . and they grow up to be stung on the head . . . that's news for you and this is the center of it where coal is made, because coal is power and power drives—

MAN IN SILK HAT: Remember the stock market!

PHILLPOTS: I should worry!

MAN IN SILK HAT: Stocks and bonds should be the main concern of a newspaper writer.

PHILLPOTS: Look out for me then, I'm going to make a panic before I finish.

MAN IN SILK HAT: What do you mean? (PHILLPOTS *hands him a telegram which he reads.*) "Keep the wires hot . . . signed . . . William Randolph Hearst"! Well?

PHILLPOTS: My job depends on getting a political sensation out of this.

MAN IN SILK HAT: There's no politics here.

PHILLPOTS: Don't make laugh, the threads of this strike go all over the country and you're the man that holds some of the strings. I'll stick to you like Mesopotamia feyer.

MAN IN SILK HAT: Is this a threat?

(*Enter the* SHERIFF.)

SHERIFF: I'm right sartain some of 'em is hid here.

PHILLPOTS: Well, what are you going to do about it?

SHERIFF: (*Pointing at* PHILLPOTS) I don' trust him, sir, he's laughin' in his sleeve.

PHILLPOTS: Just among gentlemen, there's no use deceiving ourselves, this strike is a comic opera. Look at the Sheriff you've got!

SHERIFF: (*With dignity*) Are you kiddin' me?

PHILLPOTS: You bet your sweet life I'm here to kid everybody. I'm the guy with the typewriter and I know what I know; it's to laugh!

MAN IN SILK HAT: Is this the place, Sheriff?

SHERIFF: Yes, sir, an' I got the soldiers waitin' near.

MAN IN SILK HAT: Good, where?

SHERIFF: Over this way.

MAN IN SILK HAT: I don't like the atmosphere of this place. I'd feel safer with the soldiers.

SHERIFF: This way, sir.

(*The three men disappear from doorway.* MRS. FLIMMINS, *dressed, comes downstairs, looks around, takes a candle from shelf, goes to trap door, taps once and speaks in a whisper.*)

MRS. FLIMMINS: Jimmie, darlin' . . .

(SADIE COHEN, *dressed in a crude red, dashes in rear breathless.*)

SADIE: Ma'am . . .

MRS. FLIMMINS: (*Rises hastily*) What is it?

SADIE: They're after him, they got the soldiers waitin' there.

MRS. FLIMMINS: What do you care?

SADIE: Your son, they're comin' to get him.

MRS. FLIMMINS: I dunno what you mean.

SADIE: (*Desperately*) Yes, you do, you gotta listen to me. It's about your son an' I want him—

MRS. FLIMMINS: (*Pursuing her threateningly*) What you want with him, little snip of a girl, don't you know nuthin'? Was you born yesterday, are you a week old, has you been washed yet after bein' born?

SADIE: Ma'am, ma'am—

(*But* MRS. FLIMMINS *goes on inscrutably.*)

MRS. FLIMMINS: Has they sung to you in the cradle, has they whipped your backside?

(*She stops for breath.*)

SADIE: I seen him las' night, lemme tell you—

MRS. FLIMMINS: Is it important?

SADIE: Yes'm, it's a message.

MRS. FLIMMINS: Quiet, stand back there, hold your tongue.

(SADIE *stand in shadow by stairs as* SHERIFF *appears in doorway.*)

SHERIFF: Mornin', ma'am.

MRS. FLIMMINS: Mornin'. (MAN IN SILK HAT *and* PHILLPOTS *appear behind* SHERIFF. *Two soldiers lounge by the open doorway.*) What you men want in my house?

PHILLPOTS: Do you live here?

MRS. FLIMMINS: We had a nice home till the company threw us out. The furniture got lost in a coupla' big rains. (*Turning calmly to* SILK HAT MAN) Nice mornin', ain't it? Have a seat, Sheriff.

SHERIFF: The men we want ain't far from here an' we'll get 'em if we have to burn the house down.

MAN IN SILK HAT: Tell her the facts, Sheriff.

MRS. FLIMMINS: Have you time to take a cup a' tea?

SHERIFF: You got a son, ain't you? (*She nods gravely.*) Well, he's a leader a' these bums . . . James Baldwin Flimmins.

MRS. FLIMMINS: He ain't never had the brain to lead nuthin' excep' a bottle to his mouth before this.

SHERIFF: (*Produces spectacles and pile of legal papers, reading*) "Conspirin' against the peace an' dignity a' the United States, ambush, lyin' in wait, assaultin', beatin', bruisin', an' killin' an officer a' the law—"

(SHERIFF's *chair falls to pieces and he goes heavily to the ground.*)

PHILLPOTS: Oh, Sheriff!

MRS. FLIMMINS: Oh, I'm so sorry, I knew that chair weren't strong, did it hurt you?

(PHILLPOTS *laughs,* SILK HAT MAN *looks very grave,* PHILLPOTS *helps the* SHERIFF *up.*)

SHERIFF: (*Approaching* MRS. FLIMMINS *angrily*) You done that a' purpose. Wait till we lay hands on your son!

MRS. FLIMMINS: They all come home to their mothers sooner or later, don't they? Wanna see him? (*She produces a little locket around her neck and snaps it open in* SHERIFF's *face.*) Two year old, with gold curls.

SHERIFF: Aw, hell.

MRS. FLIMMINS: Now he's walked with a gun an' taken life. Funny how they grow up! an' me always dreamin'—then he was old enough to work an' there was a war an' away with the flags flyin'—talk about a dream that turns to steel against your belly!

PHILLPOTS: Lived long in these parts?

SHERIFF: Descended from original settlers.

MRS. FLIMMINS: That's the Baldwins an' the Flimmins.

PHILLPOTS: American Protestants?

MRS. FLIMMINS: Church people, we been in these mountains a hundred years.

PHILLPOTS: You fight the soil a hundred years and this is the end in a shack tumbling around your ears.

MAN IN SILK HAT: American shack, but there's must be something rotten in it—

MRS. FLIMMINS: (*Flaring up*) Rotten yourself! Who made this strike? You did! Beatin' down the men till all the manhood in 'em was jus' liquor an' anger. You own the roads, you own the houses, you own the sky overhead—look at yourself in the glass.

PHILLPOTS: A man, monkey glands and all.

MRS. FLIMMINS: I only wish it was you he'd kilt.

SHERIFF: (*Looking at* MRS. FLIMMINS *admiringly*) She's got that red fire in the eye herself.

MRS. FLIMMINS: We're against outsiders here, we're a free people an' we're against soldiers—

SHERIFF: That's the mountain way.

MRS. FLIMMINS: Anyway, you're my kind, Sheriff, lemme speak to you alone, p'raps it would help—

(*They are interrupted by* BOOB, *who runs in closely pursued by* COHEN, *who is puffing like a seal. They erupt into scene wildly.* BOOB *breaks through the group center, then circles the stage, then runs down steps front to center aisle.*)

COHEN: (*Exhaustedly*) Stop thief.

SHERIFF: (*Producing both guns*) Come here, kid.

(BOOB *slowly comes up steps to* SHERIFF, *who collars him.*)

PHILLPOTS: What's the boy done?

COHEN: A thief, a thief, there's twenty dollars in his mouth.

MRS. FLIMMINS: That's a great deal a' money.

COHEN: He sneaked into my store, he picked a twenty out a' the cash register, but I heard the bell. I seen him put it in his mouth.

PHILLPOTS: Well, turn him up and shake him.

(BOOB *keeps his jaw tight closed.*)

SHERIFF: Open your mouth or I'll knock your jaw out.

(BOOB *opens his mouth wide.*)

PHILLPOTS: He swallowed it.

COHEN: (*Plunges hand in* BOOB's *mouth*) Ouch, he bit my hand.

SHERIFF: Well, the money's inside him.

COHEN: Have you got a hammer?

MRS. FLIMMINS: Good for him, anybuddy fools the law I'm right with 'em!

MAN IN SILK HAT: (*Fuming*) This is really of no consequence.

(SADIE *comes forward from stairs.*)

COHEN: What you doin' here, Sadie?

SADIE: Never mind.

PHILLPOTS: Good morning, Miss Cohen.

(SADIE *giggles.*)

COHEN: (*Pointing at* BOOB) A thief. I always knew it, and we caught him now.

BOOB: You got nuthin' on me. Who says I tuk it? Where is it? I'm too slick for you, see! Wait an' see who's United States Senator ten years from now, that's where a guy goes that can swaller coin!

MRS. FLIMMINS: (*Laughing heartily*) G'wan, kid, talk up.

SADIE: Ain't that swell, to be a reg'lar crook!

MRS. FLIMMINS: (*To* SHERIFF) There you are, take the kid to jail an' don't bother me no more, you see for yourself there's nuthin' you want in my home.

SHERIFF: I ain't so sure.

COHEN: How do we know what else he stole? Better search him.

MAN IN SILK HAT: A very reasonable idea.

SHERIFF: All right. (*To* COHEN) You hold him. (SHERIFF *puts hand in one of* BOOB'*s pockets.*) Marbles. (*Music plays off stage while the* SHERIFF *continues to produce articles from* BOOB'*s pockets.*) Hold him tighter, will you? Jack knife . . . cigarette butt.

COHEN: What's that?

SHERIFF: It's a cent.

COHEN: Put it back; he may need it.

SHERIFF: Chewing gum.

COHEN: Ugh, it's been used.

(SHERIFF *produces from* BOOB'*s inside breast pocket a girl's fancy garter with big pink flower on it.*)

PHILLPOTS: The woman in the case.

COHEN: Did I tell you he was a ripper, or didn't I?

BOOB: I guess I know about wimmin.

(*One of* SADIE'*s stocking is down almost to her ankles. She starts to sneak toward the door.*)

MAN IN SILK HAT: Look.

(*Everybody stares at* SADIE, *who giggles, embarrassed.*)

COHEN: (*Gazing tragically at bare leg*) Do I see what I see or am I blind already?

(SADIE *clutches desperately at stocking.*)

SHERIFF: Pull up your skirts. (*She hesitates.*) Up higher.

PHILLPOTS: Oh, Sheriff!

(*They see garter on other leg, it is unmistakably the same.*)

BOOB: Sure, it's her garter. Why wouldn't she give me her garter, she's my girl, ain't she?

(SADIE *giggles.*)

COHEN: My daughter ain't friends with no crook.

BOOB: He an' me is gonna go dance on Broadway together.

SADIE: (*Nods*) We been practicin' them fancy steps; wanna see, Pop?

COHEN: (*Pulling her away from* BOOB) No, I seen too much already: take the boy to jail, Sheriff, I make the complaint on him.

SHERIFF: (*Nods and calls to the soldiers lounging by the door*) Boys!

SADIE: Don't you touch him!

PHILLPOTS: Now really, Miss Cohen—

SADIE: Don't nobuddy touch me, neither, 'cause I got my own idea.

COHEN: (*Persuasively*) Lemme hear an idea out a' my child's face before I bust it!

(SADIE *and* BOOB *dance side by side like a vaudeville team, and off stage music grows louder.*)

BOOB: Her an' me will go to New York an' Philadelphia.

MAN IN SILK HAT: (*Muttering*) Disgraceful . . . disgraceful . . .

COHEN: (*Gives* SADIE *a resounding thwack*) I'll fix you—

(SADIE *hides from* COHEN *behind* MRS. FLIMMINS.)

SADIE: Don't let him spank me no more, it hurts too much.

MRS. FLIMMINS: (*To* COHEN) If I was you I'd go easy on this.

(*Off stage music stops.*)

MAN IN SILK HAT: None of this is of the slightest interest to me. My advice would be to send children of this type to the house of correction, but there are more serious matters in hand . . . h'm . . . the immediate capture of this criminal, that's your duty, Sheriff, you know where to reach me if you need me. Law and order, Sheriff!

(*He exits rear,* PHILLPOTS *follows him.*)

PHILLPOTS: I'm going to stick right with you till you tell me all I want to know.

(*Exit* PHILLPOTS.)

SHERIFF: I wouldn't arrest the kid if I was you.

COHEN: I make the complaint on him. Take him before I lay a hand on him myself.

SHERIFF: Oh, all right. (*Calls to soldiers, who have again retired to doorway*) Hey, one of youse guys come here.

(*As the soldier comes forward, he comes face to face with* MRS. FLIMMINS. *He surveys her in evident surprise.*)

SHERIFF: What's a' matter?

MRS. FLIMMINS: You don't know me.

SOLDIER: No, but you look like a dame that gimme a good time las' night!

SHERIFF: Is that so?

SOLDIER: I was drunk when I seen her before.

MRS. FLIMMINS: Bums.

SOLDIER: Who's a bum?

SHERIFF: The lady's right, there's no argument.

SOLDIER: Well, I ain't startin' no argument.

(SHERIFF, *holding* BOOB *firmly by arm, passes him to* SOLDIER.)

SHERIFF: Here's a package for you, take him to the coop, shove him in anywhere there's room.

SOLDIER: Pretty crowded now, but I guess he might fit in that closet under the stairs. (*The* SOLDIER *picks up* BOOB *by back of trousers and carries him off kicking.* SOLDIER *sings as he goes.*)

"When them lovin' arms is waitin'
When them lovin' lips is hot."

SHERIFF: (*To* COHEN) Now, take your daughter home an' there's an end a' it.

COHEN: (*To* SADIE) Now for you.

SADIE: (*Hysterically*) No, no, don't touch me.

MRS. FLIMMINS: You better go with your father.

SADIE: Never goin' home, never! I'm goin' away, gonna find a lotta men to gimme kisses an' diamonds!

(*She dances wildly center.*)

MRS. FLIMMINS: (*Comes to* COHEN *quietly*) If I was you I'd leave her alone, I know them kind, lemme talk to her.

SADIE: I won't go home.

MRS. FLIMMINS: (*To* COHEN) Go away, what she needs is common sense.

COHEN: You promise to send her home later!

MRS. FLIMMINS: Sure, she'll come by herself, don't you worry.

COHEN: I don't understand it all.

(SADIE *laughs and continues to dance.*)

MRS. FLIMMINS: None of us can understand, it's like walkin' in a mist with shoutin' an' strange words.

COHEN: Sadie . . . (MRS. FLIMMINS *motions to him.*) I'll go, then . . . (*Wiping a tear from each eye*) Didn't I raise her good, didn't I, with sugar candy an' a good lickin' on Saturdays?

(*He exits, head bent.* SHERIFF *looks on thoughtfully sitting on bed.*)

SADIE: (*Suddenly serious, comes to* MRS. FLIMMINS) Y'see, I don't really mean all that, I ain't so bad, but he wants to lick me all the time, I can't stand it.

MRS. FLIMMINS: You don't know what you mean; you're a shallow little dancin' fool.

SADIE: I am not, you wait an' see.

MRS. FLIMMINS: Keep still, I'm not thinkin' a' you at all. (*She goes to* SHERIFF.) Why don't you go?

SHERIFF: I'm gonna set right here till I get your son.

MRS. FLIMMINS: What then?

SHERIFF: Then I reckon he'll hang on Lone Mountain, danglin' till he turns green with big birds peckin' at him all the time.

MRS. FLIMMINS: (*Turns from him, then turns back with determination*) Gimme a minute to explain, lemme talk to you.

SHERIFF: Always ready to listen to a lady.

(MRS. FLIMMINS *picks up empty pail near door.*)

MRS. FLIMMINS: (*To* SADIE) Wait here an' don't you stir till I come back.

SADIE: Yes'm.

MRS. FLIMMINS: Walk with me to the well, Sheriff, I'll tell you what I think can help.

(*They go out together rear,* MRS. FLIMMINS *talking earnestly.* SADIE *goes to trap door and taps three times. She jumps back as trap door opens and* JIM *stand waist-high in opening carrying his gun.*)

JIM: I thought you was my mother.

SADIE: (*Scared*) Stay back, stay back, I didn't think you was really there. (JIM *laughs and rises.*) Don't, don't, one'll see you, there's soldiers roun', Sheriff 's jus' outside—

JIM: Is he alone?

SADIE: With your mother.

JIM: I got a mind to kill that Sheriff—one more or less, what's it matter?

SADIE: You must go back down.

JIM: No, gotta breathe, that feller talks his head off, mebbe I could make a run for it!

SADIE: Soldiers is right in sight: your Ma's tryin' to fix it. She thinks I'm a dumb-bell, but I ain't, I gotta message. The men are waitin' down a mine, mebbe they come out an' help you, anyways they gimme this paper for you.

(*She takes ragged slip of paper from dress.* JIM *scans it carefully.*)

JIM: Ahuh.

SADIE: What's it say?

JIM: I can't read.

SADIE: (*Takes it and reads*) "Hail the chief, will strike when the iron is hot."

JIM: What's it mean?

SADIE: They heard you busted loose, they heard about stickin' the soldier, you're a hero they says—

JIM: (*Spitting thoughtfully*) I ain't so much.

SADIE: Mebbe they help you, they got pitchforks an' knives an' flags—

JIM: (*In a whisper*) That dress is like a flag!

SADIE: Don't shout at me, they'll hear!

JIM: I ain't shoutin'.

SADIE: Yes, you are, inside you're beatin' like a drum, a drum that says, "Come here, come here!"

JIM: Go 'way then.

SADIE: Why?

JIM: (*Shaking her*) 'Cause I don' wanna hurt you an' I feel like layin' my hands on somethin'—

(*He pushes her away from him.*)

SADIE: You're like you was las' night when you kilt him.

(*She runs out rear scared.* JIM *hides under stairs as* POP PRATT *enters rear hobbling energetically.*)

POP PRATT: (*Calling loudly*) Hallo . . . hallo . . . (*He pounds stick on floor.*) Anybuddy here?

(OLD MAGGIE *comes out on landing above.*)

OLD MAGGIE: What you want?

POP PRATT: Figgered I'd drop in keep you comp'ny for awhile. Heard there was a peek a' trouble up this way.

OLD MAGGIE: What you heard don't matter, don't hand roun', we don't need you.

POP PRATT: Eh? (MAGGIE *motions angrily toward door.* PRATT *at foot of stairs turns and looks out.*) Yep, li'l breeze blowin', looks like fixin' for one a' them thunder showers, but I don't mind the thunder so much now I can't hear nuthin'.

OLD MAGGIE: You must go 'way, don't you hear?

POP PRATT: (*Nodding head*) All right, let's set awhile an' keep comp'ny bein' as us is the old folks that knows the meanin' a' things . . . what's a' matter, Maggie? You gotta funny look in the eyes.

OLD MAGGIE: Look at me then.

POP PRATT: A face full a' jimjam mem'ries: remember, Maggie, the day Abraham Lincoln stood on the hill yonder with his arms wavin' an' his voice like a taste a' bitter almonds in the wind!

OLD MAGGIE: It's all diff'rent now.

POP PRATT: You an' me walked on that hill when your hair was yaller an' the moon was bright on your hair—

OLD MAGGIE: Don't talk like that, you old scarecrow!

POP PRATT: Eh? What's a' matter with you, Maggie? Your jaws move but nuthin' comes out.

OLD MAGGIE: I'm thinkin' have I brung men into the world, am I a mother a' drunken bums? That's the Proletariat!

POP PRATT: What's that, one a' them new-fangled things for the bowels?

OLD MAGGIE: Fools . . . fools . . .

(*She exits above,* MRS. FLIMMINS *and* SHERIFF *return rear.* SHERIFF *is carrying pail full of water.*)

MRS. FLIMMINS: I tell you, I could raise the money.

SHERIFF: (*Indicating* POP PRATT) Easy now, look who's here.

MRS. FLIMMINS: He can't hear nuthin'.

SHERIFF: He sees a lot.

MRS. FLIMMINS: (*To* POP PRATT) Get out.

POP PRATT: I jus' stepped in for a minute . . . (*As she pushes him toward door*) But yep . . . mebbe I'll jus' be goin'.

(POP PRATT *exits rear.*)

MRS. FLIMMINS: (*Turns eagerly to* SHERIFF) I'll give you money.

SHERIFF: I thought you was dead busted boilin' up roots to eat.

MRS. FLIMMINS: But wimmin always got ways a' raisin' money.

SHERIFF: (*Looking her over critically*) Huh! Where'll I set this pail?

MRS. FLIMMINS: You'll help Jim? I'll have the money in cash by tonight.

SHERIFF: I'll say you got a way with you, ma'am.

MRS. FLIMMINS: I'll do anythin' for my son.

SHERIFF: An' supposin' I says, "No, let 'im hang!"?

MRS. FLIMMINS: (*Flaring up angrily*) You won't get him, my son's stronger'n you, mebbe he take you by the neck, throttle you, shake you—

SHERIFF: Don't you fret, ma'am, I know this game.

MRS. FLIMMINS: Man-huntin'. (*Suddenly becoming gracious, smiles blandly*) Try woman-huntin', it's better.

SHERIFF: I figgered you was one a' them prayin' kind, hot for God.

MRS. FLIMMINS: I am, I'm prayin' God right this minute.

SHERIFF: You sure look handsome shinin' like that.

MRS. FLIMMINS: Soften your heart, Sheriff, let a little love-light in your heart. I'd do anythin' for a big man like you.

SHERIFF: Would you now?

MRS. FLIMMINS: Help a lone woman that's so weak with nuthin' but prayer to guide her.

SHERIFF: I'll drop in tonight. P'raps you an' me could take a li'l walk when the moon's out.

MRS. FLIMMINS: Guide me with your hand, Sheriff. I got lovin' ways when I—

(*Enter* MACCARTHY *rear.*)

MACCARTHY: (*Angry and excited*) Look a' here, Sheriff, I'm in on this, have you caught the guy yet?

SHERIFF: What guy?

MACCARTHY: He's done in my buddy, I want 'im, that's all, want to wring his dirty neck personally.

SHERIFF: Don't get excited.

MACCARTHY: I'm all broke up 'cause he done in my buddy.

SHERIFF: We gotta go at this very quietly.

MACCARTHY: (*Looking fixedly at* MRS. FLIMMINS) Who's she? I seen you before somewhere.

MRS. FLIMMINS: Why not? I got more right in coal town 'n you have.

MACCARTHY: (*Scratching head*) Then you sure are diff'rent from las' night.

SHERIFF: What you mean?

MACCARTHY: Aw, she's just sweaty now, but supposin' . . . just supposin' at night with flower water on her hair an' her voice like music playin' . . . can you picture it?

MRS. FLIMMINS: Is this house a street like you all come in to look me over? You want me to lay down for the army to walk all over my body?

MACCARTHY: You ain't the same, an' yet . . . (*Turning to* SHERIFF) She ain't so young but she got somethin' in her makes a ringin' in your ears.

SHERIFF: Then you mean . . . ? (SHERIFF *and* MACCARTHY *whisper together.* MACCARTHY *laughs.*) She was up with all them soldiers?

MACCARTHY: In that marble house.

SHERIFF: Drinkin' with 'em?

MACCARTHY: Gettin' their wads off 'em.

MRS. FLIMMINS: (*Interrupting tensely*) No . . . no . . .

SHERIFF: Mebbe you're right.

MACCARTHY: Oh, boy, I know it.

SHERIFF: She told me she had lovin' ways . . . an' it's my idea she got her son hid here. Well, if she's that kind . . .

MACCARTHY: If the guy that stuck my buddy is hid here I'm gonna lay my hands on him and then . . . then . . . (MRS. FLIMMINS *instinctively goes and stands over trap door center.* MACCARTHY *listens for a few moments thoughtfully.*) Sheriff, I hear a kind a' scratchin' like a rat somewheres. Let's have a look at this floor.

MRS. FLIMMINS: (*Screaming*) No, there's nuthin' there!

MACCARTHY: (*Over the trap*) Looks like a kind a' trap. (MRS. FLIMMINS *tries fiercely to keep them away from the trap.*) Pull her away.

(SHERIFF *pulls her roughly off.*)

MRS. FLIMMINS: Listen . . . listen, it's true, I'll give you anythin', it was me with them soldiers, I got money hid away, I done it for my son, I'm a bad woman!

MACCARTHY: What'd I tell you?

MRS. FLIMMINS: Go away, only go away, I'll give you money . . . anythin' . . .

(MACCARTHY *has opened the trap.*)

MACCARTHY: Guess we can bring home the bacon.

SHERIFF: Come out, I got my gun on you. This ain't the one we want, but step out, you're under arrest.

(PSINSKI *comes out.* SHERIFF *peers down.*)

PSINSKI: The jail-house is better'n that hole.

SHERIFF: Nuthin' else down there, but we got one Bolchevik rat.

MACCARTHY: What we do with him?

SHERIFF: Hand him over to some people that treat him good! You know!

(*He shuts trap door.*)

MACCARTHY: The other one must be somewheres, an' we'll find him.

PSINSKI: I protest—you can't arrest me without a warrant.

MACCARTHY: My Gawd, did you hear that, Sheriff? (*He sticks* PSINSKI *violently with gun.*) Tar an' feathers is what this bird needs.

SHERIFF: Bring him along.

PSINSKI: I don't care what you do to me, but the workers'll lick you yet.

SHERIFF: Treat him rough, we been too easy with these guys.

MACCARTHY: That's right, they don't appreciate kindness.

(*Exit* SHERIFF *and* MACCARTHY, *the latter pulling* PSINSKI *along.*)

MRS. FLIMMINS: (*Alone still on floor*) Jimmie, where are you?

(JIM *comes forward, stands beside her white with anger, gun in hand.*)

MRS. FLIMMINS: Jimmie, go down there an' don't come up no more.

JIM: (*Blankly*) What?

MRS. FLIMMINS: Down, quick.

JIM: I can't, Ma, till I get my strength back.

MRS. FLIMMINS: You mean?

JIM: You know what I mean!

MRS. FLIMMINS: What's it matter? It's safe for you now, they won't never look down there again.

JIM: They called my mammy a bad name. Suppose I gotta kill ev'ry guy calls you that.

MRS. FLIMMINS: But what if it's true? Ain't you proud of it? It's for you, it's the money, we ain't been eatin' so much here, but I put away my little pile, watched it grow.

JIM: A guy's sweet mother!

MRS. FLIMMINS: Waitin' for you till we could go away, to New York, where people live, where we'd go to church—

JIM: What do I care now?

MRS. FLIMMINS: (*Passionately*) You're my son, mine . . . this ain't goin' on, I'm gonna learn you, an' make you a man—

JIM: I'm learnin' what ain't in the Bible.

MRS. FLIMMINS: Oh, you don't know what I'm feelin' inside me.

JIM: It's rot, it's decay, there's worms in us.

MRS. FLIMMINS: No, Jim, we're all right.

JIM: Ev'ry guy's had my mammy's arms!

MRS. FLIMMINS: We're up against somethin' we don't understan', somethin' black, takes a man's muscle an' a woman's flesh.

JIM: All right, I'm gonna find out what that is!

MRS. FLIMMINS: If we could get away from here, New York, a big city.

(OLD MAGGIE *comes out at top of stairs above, stands on landing unnoticed by the two intent figures.*)

JIM: So's you can get more men, huh? So's you can walk on a big main street givin' the glad eye to ev'ry stranger?

MRS. FLIMMINS: Don't, Jim.

JIM: Dirty sin, rottin' inside us.

MRS. FLIMMINS: If I search my heart, mebbe somewhere in me there was the flesh cryin'.

JIM: It's in our blood.

MRS. FLIMMINS: We're good blood, Jim, proud, pioneers.

JIM: Well, them pioneers was sons a' bitches.

MRS. FLIMMINS: They dug in the ground.

JIM: They got the sinful dirt a' the earth in 'em. All right, let the earth have its way then, my blood's ready to spread on the ground!

MRS. FLIMMINS: (*Clinging to him*) Jim, your father was a decent man.

JIM: Every guy's my father now, I shake ev'ry guy by the hand.

MRS. FLIMMINS: We're all right, there's somethin' inside us, somethin' stirrin'—

JIM: Hell stirrin'.

MRS. FLIMMINS: No, no, somethin' good, like when you pray till it burns.

JIM: I got a feelin' that burns my stomach.

MRS. FLIMMINS: Las' night you kilt a man.

JIM: That's nuthin', but somethin' soft come into me, somethin' I hadn't known, what can a guy do when he's got that thing in his stomach stronger'n liquor?

MRS. FLIMMINS: Go down there, Jim, an' wait.

JIM: Nuthin' to do but die.

MRS. FLIMMINS: You needn't die, now I've known how to save you.

JIM: Yes, an' you're proud about it, ain't you?

MRS. FLIMMINS: (*Trying desperately to calm him and explain*) Las' night I was proud, 'cause my body's strong enough to drive men even when I'm old like walkin' in a mist.

JIM: What do I care now?

MRS. FLIMMINS: Gimme that gun.

JIM: Get away from me, don't touch me! If you touch me, I'll curse you to hell!

MRS. FLIMMINS: All right, sometimes mothers an' sons is a cursin' matter.

JIM: I'm goin' out an' fight, ain't kilt enough yet.

MRS. FLIMMINS: If there's more fightin' to do, I'll do it. Gimme that gun.

JIM: (*Fiercely*) Stand back!

(OLD MAGGIE *suddenly doubles up as if with a cramp, and rolls straight from top of stairs to bottom, where she lies in a heap.*)

MRS. FLIMMINS: (*Screaming*) Your granny, Jim, she heard the truth an' fell like a stone. (*Bending over* OLD MAGGIE) She ain't hurt.

JIM: What do I care? I'm ready now, to the ashpile with all of you!

MRS. FLIMMINS: (*Clinging to him*) Jim, I'm your Ma. Whatever I done, I done for you, you gotta stay with me now.

JIM: (*Waving gun*) I'm through, I'm free now, Goddamn this house, I'll fight alone! (*Holds up his gun and shouts in sunlit doorway*) Let hell loose!

(Darkness covers the stage.)

Scene 2. What Happened to Sadie

Evening of the Same Day

A mine entrance. Drop curtain represents a criss-cross of bars and derricks against a dirty yellow background. The black opening of the mine right. Fading gray light.

A noise of shooting and shouting off stage. There is rhythmic frightened music at intervals throughout this scene. A single shot rings out. Enter PHILLPOTS *right.*

PHILLPOTS: Just missed me! Say, I didn't bargain for this, it's a real fight now . . . who goes there?

(COHEN *enters left, dishevelled and worried.*)

COHEN: What's a' matter?

PHILLPOTS: The matter? You may well ask! The miners came out from where they were hiding and they're sniping from behind every tree.

(*A shot off stage*)

COHEN: Ouch!

PHILLPOTS: (*Supporting him*) Are you hurt?

COHEN: I ain't had time to look.

PHILLPOTS: The soldiers are driving the strikers into the mountains, they'll soon capture the man they want—hear that?

COHEN: Oi, oi . . .

PHILLPOTS: You'd better go back home and put your head in a pillow.

COHEN: (*Pitifully*) Where is she, what's happened to her?

PHILLPOTS: Who?

COHEN: My daughter Sadie, who else is there?

PHILLPOTS: You mean she's gone?

COHEN: I can't find her nowheres, all day she is gone.

PHILLPOTS: (*Preoccupied, looking off stage*) From what she said, maybe she's gone to New York.

COHEN: Fightin' everywheres, how do I know somebuddy won't hurt my little girl.

PHILLPOTS: Well, she's nowhere around here, that's sure, and you'd better look out for yourself.

COHEN: What do I care for myself? I will give her yet a weddin' dress with bells on it, I will find her if I have to walk to New York lookin' for her—

PHILLPOTS: A wandering Jew!

COHEN: A Jew yes, an' all of a sudden the curse a' the race rises up an' slaps you in the face . . . but wait, in the end we'll beat you all, a people cursed but with wisdom in the heart, a lawful people living' in the law ever since Moses; we win in the end!

PHILLPOTS: You don't all do so badly right now.

COHEN: Say what you like, but your children's children will be shoutin' oi, oi, because we conquer . . . Sadie . . . Sadie . . .

(COHEN *goes away muttering.*)

PHILLPOTS: (*Alone*) No more shots . . . guess it's almost over, guess the miners are licked, guess they caught the one they wanted. (*A shot off stage.* PHILLPOTS *turns.*) It's a girl, somebody shot at a girl!

(SADIE *stumbles in, her clothes torn, spatted with mud, her hair loose.*)

SADIE: (*Forlornly*) Mister . . .

PHILLPOTS: Sadie Cohen . . . (*Holding her arm*) This way, keep out of sight.

SADIE: Have they kilt him yet? Jim Flimmins, the man they're huntin' for?

PHILLPOTS: I am informed that they'll have him any minute now. He started things going, he ran through Main Street shooting off a gun, but they'll get him now.

SADIE: Sweet God . . . Mister, where you goin' to, Mister?

PHILLPOTS: I'm going to get out of this before somebody shoots me by mistake, I've got the biggest story of my life, now I'm called back to New York and the quicker I get there the better.

SADIE: What's that light there?

PHILLPOTS: A burning cross, can you beat that? The Ku Klux Klan has got into the fight now. They must have come up by train loads from Charleston.

SADIE: I'm so tired.

PHILLPOTS: Where have you been? Why are your clothes torn?

SADIE: I tuk to the open country, I climbed a mountain an' I got all tore, but I was scared alone with the moon an' the stars, I thought I'd go roun' the world but it looked kind a' big.

PHILLPOTS: Better go back to home sweet home.

SADIE: (*With passion in her childish voice*) Never no more!

(*An exchange of shots nearby*)

PHILLPOTS: Hear that, aren't you scared?

SADIE: (*With a little giggle*) Not so much, it tickles my spine.

PHILLPOTS: I must take you home, take you to a safe place.

SADIE: Never goin' home!

PHILLPOTS: What do you expect me to do then?

SADIE: You take me to New York with you.

PHILLPOTS: What?

SADIE: (*Fiercely, coming close to him*) Take me away anywheres.

PHILLPOTS: (*Shakes his head and speaks very gently*) Little girl, haven't you learned your lesson yet?

SADIE: I ain't done nuthin' yet.

PHILLPOTS: Don't you see the impossibility of running wild? I'm sorry for you, but—

SADIE: Then take me to New York.

PHILLPOTS: I'd look pretty bringing you to New York.

SADIE: You gotta take me with you.

PHILLPOTS: What?

SADIE: 'Cause I had a dream an' God come to me in a dream an' said, "Go to New York an' get a job in the movies—"

PHILLPOTS: (*Shocked*) God said that?

SADIE: I think it was God.

PHILLPOTS: You were mistaken.

SADIE: I gotta get away from this dirty valley, gotta see pleasures an' palaces.

PHILLPOTS: Look at me. I've gone round and round looking for the news that's blown on the four wings.

SADIE: (*In a pitiful little singsong voice*) Take me away from here anywheres wherever the winds blow.

PHILLPOTS: No, I'm a careful man.

SADIE: You liked me yesterday.

PHILLPOTS: Kidding, that's all. I'm just a poor fish who tries to make his way by kidding people.

SADIE: Were you kiddin'?

PHILLPOTS: Yes.

SADIE: Well, even if you were . . . somewhere there's sweet flowers an' violins playin' them waltzes . . . that's love music . . . an' champagne . . .

PHILLPOTS: (*Doubtfully*) Perhaps.

SADIE: An' barrels full a' real diamonds.

PHILLPOTS: Is that all you want?

SADIE: I want all the love in the world an' then some, an' then I wanna dance on my toes!

PHILLPOTS: (*Softly*) Desdemona, flower of the smoke, you'll get what's coming to you, I can't help it.

SADIE: I'd call you my sugar-popper.

PHILLPOTS: My heart's breaking and you can't mend it.

SADIE: Go 'way from me then. I thought you was straight goods an' you're a fake.

PHILLPOTS: Be a good little girl.

SADIE: I ain't a good li'l girl, I won't be, I ain't.

PHILLPOTS: Listen, Sadie—

SADIE: Lemme alone then, can't you, I need a man, not a dummy.

PHILLPOTS: Sorry.

SADIE: Beat it then, what you so sad about?

PHILLPOTS: Being a good middle-class man, I'm sorry for everybody, but I never know what to do about it. (*He laughs again.*) Shooting is all round us now. Look here, I've got to get you out of this.

SADIE: You don't care if I get kilt.

PHILLPOTS: We've got to get across that field there and back into town. I'll see if there's a safe way. You stick right here where they can't see you, understand. I'll be right back. I'll see if there's a safe way.

(*Exit* PHILLPOTS *right.* SADIE, *alone, calls after him.*)

SADIE: Mebbe I won't be here when you get back. . . . (*Pause. She is frightened, uncertain. Shouts and shooting off stage. She kneels down pounding her little clenched fists against the ground.*) Oh, God, what'll I do? Sweet God, where'll I go? Lemme go roun' the world, lemme ride in an aeroplane, lemme put smelly stuff on my hair—

(JIM *appears, shouting as he comes.*)

JIM: You ain't got me yet, not yet you ain't!

(*He almost stumbles over* SADIE, *stops short abruptly.*)

SADIE: I thought you was kilt!

JIM: Not yet, but soon.

SADIE: They're lookin' for you everywheres.

JIM: I give 'em the slip. They want me; if they knew I was here they'd be closin' in on me—catch me like a rat.

SADIE: What you gonna do?

JIM: Die like a good guy.

SADIE: All them soldiers with guns—

JIM: All right . . . I'll get one good laugh on 'em! (SADIE *makes a wild dash to run away from him; he catches her.*) Nobuddy can get away from here now.

SADIE: (*Struggling with him*) Lemme go—

JIM: (*Still holding her*) I'm the guy stands alone against everybuddy . . . me, myself, understan'!

SADIE: That's awful!

JIM: Afraid a' me? You seen me kill a man.

SADIE: I don't care.

JIM: I kilt others since then, I hid in the ground an' then I went out with a gun, I walk like a ghost, you smell the cold groun'?

(*Shouting and shots off stage*)

SADIE: What you gonna do?

JIM: A black thing.

SADIE: I don't know what you mean.

JIM: You an' me, huh?

SADIE: What you mean?

JIM: You'll find out quick.

SADIE: No, I'm goin' away somewheres.

JIM: I can't go with you, gotta date pretty soon.

SADIE: Who with?

JIM: Coupla' hundred soldiers an' the gents a' the Ku Klux Klan—ain't you proud be with a guy got frien's like that? (*Noise and confused shouting come closer.*) Them soldiers is lookin' for me everywheres.

SADIE: I don't like this.

JIM: What you want, huh?

SADIE: Lemme go—

JIM: Tell me what you want?

SADIE: Oh, diamonds an' silks an' a job in the movies . . . I got a hunch—

JIM: (*Squeezing her arms, lifts her off the ground*) Me, too, I got a drivin' hunch!

SADIE: You're so strong!

JIM: You know what you want, huh? I can fix you so you won't want nuthin' . . . afraid now? I curse the mommer that made me! Wimmin is all bums, you squeeze 'em, you bust 'em an' you got nuthin'. I used to be scared a' wimmin but not now—(*A terrible determination in his voice*) Not since today!

SADIE: I'll be your sweet mommer!

JIM: Then I curse you too!

SADIE: Me, why you could lift me in your arms . . . if you want to.

JIM: Mebbe I want to. (*He lifts her up.*) I can lift you higher'n that.

SADIE: Go on . . . hold me higher . . .

(*He lifts her high in his arms; she giggles wildly.*)

JIM: I raise you high to the moon, I steal a barrel full a' diamonds for you, reach up an' pick a bunch a' stars.

SADIE: You're kiddin'.

JIM: I ain't kiddin' . . . (*Still holding her in his arms*) Listen, feet . . . comin' closer, ghost feet . . .

SADIE: I see shadows movin' everywheres.

JIM: Comin' closer but not so quick, they think there's a crowd here with guns, soldiers behind every tree, they got me here like a rat in a hole, no chance to get away.

SADIE: You must hide.

JIM: They'll find me quick enough. Let them soldiers come. They'll get me in a minute, but you're comin' with me.

SADIE: Where?

JIM: (*Indicating the mine entrance*) Down there.

SADIE: Bluffin', that's all you are, ev'rybuddy kids me!

JIM: I don' bluff, not me, I'll fix you, I will . . .

SADIE: No, no, I don' wanna, lemme go—

JIM: Let them soldiers come, I'll have my way first.

(*He carries her down into the mine. Absolute darkness.*)

Scene 3. The Man Hunt

(*Voices of soldiers shout in blackness from either side of stage.*)

FIRST VOICE: Have they got him yet?

SECOND VOICE: No, he got away.

FIRST VOICE: While we was waitin' for him at the front a' the mine he sneaked out like a mole through a hole at the back.

SECOND VOICE: He done wrong to a girl.

FIRST VOICE: There he goes across the fields there.

SECOND VOICE: Get him.

FIRST VOICE: Get him.

(*Shouting grows in volume, with drum beats and rapid rhythm of music. Then gradually revealed an open space suffused with ghostly light, across which stands a railing of heavy iron bars nine feet high, grim and foreboding against a wan sky.* JIM *crosses from left to right, his arms gesticulating wildly. Then* MACCARTHY *and other menacing figures, some with guns, others with torches, cross, following him. Soldiers come down through audience shouting as they come and join in the pursuit.* MAN IN SILK HAT *appears in an upper box with a megaphone through which he shouts like an announcer at a race.*)

MAN IN SILK HAT: Jim Flimmins has escaped! This man is an enemy of society, a beast. He killed men, he attacked a woman, sinner, moral leper, society must be justified! They're off the Man Hunt! Round and round men are unchained against him! (JIM, *alone this time, his arms gesticulating wildly, crosses from right to left.*) Stop him . . . he's in the field . . . hunted he runs . . . Halt! . . . Shoot! . . . The Man Hunt! (JIM *climbs grotesquely up the iron railing.*) He climbs the big fence . . . Stop him! Over the fence he's safe, he's up to the top, over the fence he's free in the woods! (JIM *has reached the top of the fence.* MAN IN SILK HAT *shouts louder.*) No . . . No . . . (*In trying to get over,* JIM *has got caught by the back of his trousers on the point of one of the iron bars, where he hands in mid-air, hanging downward, arms and legs sprawling.*) Caught by the pants, caught on the fence, he hangs like a rag on a railing, he hangs like a flag, a human flag, with arms and legs that wave in the wind, the flag of defeat, torn by the East wind, the North wind . . . They've got him now!

(*A flashlight is turned on* JIM *where he hangs sprawling in the air, a figure of grotesque defeat. Points of guns bristle in a circle round him on the edge of the light. Blare of music.*)

CURTAIN

ACT 4

Six months later
The Jazz Wedding

A hilltop above the town. It is just before dawn. Trees and bushes are outlined blackly against the sky.

Enter MRS. FLIMMINS *and* SADIE.

MRS. FLIMMINS: Come on, child, no use cryin'.

SADIE: Ain't cryin', I'm laughin'.

MRS. FLIMMINS: Sounds the same.

SADIE: Jus' thinkin', where do we go from here? (MRS. FLIMMINS *is silent.*) Look . . . look, you can see it plain.

MRS. FLIMMINS: They've driven us out, it's burnin' up an' that's an end a' it. We was real cosy in that barn.

SADIE: Yes, ma'am.

MRS. FLIMMINS: Burn up mem'ries.

SADIE: It's an end a' us.

MRS. FLIMMINS: Not yet it ain't . . . but I dunno where to burn . . . The Sheriff's one a' the Klan himself. If we go into town he'll catch us an' hand us over to 'em.

SADIE: We *got* to go somewheres.

MRS. FLIMMINS: How'd you know we have? Mebbe they save us the trouble—I tell you they hate us all.

SADIE: Why should they hurt us?

MRS. FLIMMINS: They burned the shack, ain't they?

SADIE: But why . . . I don't see why . . .

MRS. FLIMMINS: Don't keep askin' why like your brain was full a' soap bubbles.

SADIE: Yes, ma'am—

MRS. FLIMMINS: Don't "yes" me like that, if you hadn't said yes when you shouldn't you wouldn't be in this pickle now.

SADIE: I didn't say nuthin', it jus' happened.

MRS. FLIMMINS: (*With a harsh laugh*) I know my son, I know his way.

SADIE: I don't care.

MRS. FLIMMINS: Carryin' a baby inside you without a name.

SADIE: (*Laughing softly*) I don't care.

MRS. FLIMMINS: You'll care when the Klan get you an' punish you for bein' bad.

SADIE: They're after you too, they call you bad names, kids throw stones at you!

MRS. FLIMMINS: I'm diff'rent. I *know* what I do, I ain't a little sap-head fool like you.

SADIE: If I was somewheres else where people didn't know.

MRS. FLIMMINS: Mebbe they'll put you on a train after they get through with you.

SADIE: The men in sheets?

MRS. FLIMMINS: We got no money to get away, all the men that might help us has left the country.

SADIE: There's my Pop.

MRS. FLIMMINS: He threw you out.

SADIE: He might help us now.

MRS. FLIMMINS: He can't, what they won't do to him! A Jew storekeeper is what these people eat for breakfast, wait an' see!

SADIE: They mustn't touch me till it's born; they must let me alone till it's born. (MRS. FLIMMINS *laughs harshly.*) I want it, I want it.

MRS. FLIMMINS: What makes wimmin do it?

SADIE: (*Crooning half to herself*) Kind a' feelin' stealin' over you.

MRS. FLIMMINS: Aw, shut up, don't sing to youself like that. I'm sick a' hearin' you sing an' say you don't care. I'm sorry I tuk you in.

SADIE: You've treated me white, all right.

MRS. FLIMMINS: Well, it ain't for you, don't think that; it's for Jim an' what he done to you.

SADIE: A guy as strong as an ox, a guy that burned like liquor!

MRS. FLIMMINS: He wouldn't accept things, wanted to fight all the time, so they strung him to a sour apple tree—

SADIE: Don't talk about it, don't—

MRS. FLIMMINS: I ain't done hopin'.

SADIE: He's mine as well as yours, now.

MRS. FLIMMINS: Don't you say that: you think he'd care if he come back now walkin' free? He'd call you a fool an' laugh it off.

SADIE: He won't come back.

MRS. FLIMMINS: They never found the body . . . strung to that tree it was, an' it jus' disappeared.

SADIE: He's gone six months now.

MRS. FLIMMINS: I got a feelin' perhaps he'll come back . . . Pray hard, pray with all you got in you, an' mebbe he'll come. (*Funereal music off stage*) I hear those Kluxers.

SADIE: They're after us, they want us.

MRS. FLIMMINS: Come this way.

(*As they move right an enormously tall man appears rear, in Ku Klux regalia, looking eight feet high. He smokes a large cigar from which come colored sparks when he puffs it. The* KING KLEAGLE *is, of course, another incarnation of the* MAN IN THE SILK HAT. MRS. FLIMMINS *and* SADIE *hide in shadows right. Funereal music grows louder, and a strange double procession comes down the aisles of the theatre. These are the* KLAN *members, in robes, masks and full regalia, the man at the head of one line carrying a cross, at the head of the other line an American flag. They assemble about the commanding figure of the* KING KLEAGLE *center. He motions right, two members of the* KLAN *hurry off, and reappear dragging* SADIE *and* MRS. FLIMMINS, *whom they throw roughly to the ground at front of stage.*)

MRS. FLIMMINS: Leggo me, leggo . . .

KING KLEAGLE: You will await judgment in your turn.

(*The* KLANSMEN *point accusing fingers at the two women.*)

MRS. FLIMMINS: Judgment! You cowards! You're a bunch a' old wimmin yourselves! (SADIE *screams.*) Let that little girl alone, she done nuthin' to you—

(*The* KING KLEAGLE *motions to have* MRS. FLIMMINS *removed. She is dragged away right, and* SADIE *remains on her knees front center.*)

KING KLEAGLE: (*In a deep false voice sounding as if it came from heaven*) Kleagles, wizards, goblins gathered in this Kloncilium!

(*They all face the* KING KLEAGLE *with arms outstretched and the whole group chants in answer.*)

RESPONSIVE CHANT: Glory . . . glory . . . Halleluiah . . .

KING KLEAGLE: We gather this night to protect mortals. (*The group grumble and grunt ominously.*) Native-born Americans, Patriotic Protestants, regular citizens.

RESPONSIVE CHANT: Glory . . . glory . . .

KING KLEAGLE: Have you taken the oath to exterminate foreigners?

RESPONSIVE CHANT: God's will be done!

KING KLEAGLE: Are the tar and feathers ready?

RESPONSIVE CHANT: God's will be done!

KING KLEAGLE: Are the guns and knives on hand?

RESPONSIVE CHANT: (*Very loud*) God's will be done!

KING KLEAGLE: Clean up the dirty foreigners, make 'em kiss the flag! Skin the Jews, lynch the niggers, make 'em kiss the flag!

RESPONSIVE CHANT: (*Quite breathless and with a good deal of grunting*) Halleluiah . . . Halleluiah . . .

KING KLEAGLE: Order. (*Silence*) I wish to announce, the entire Congress of the United States joined the Ku Klux Klan last night.

RESPONSIVE CHANT: (*The whole crowd point finger directly at audience and shout.*) Halleluiah!

KING KLEAGLE: We gather in holy judgment, moral judgment . . . First case! Name?

(*White figures in circle sway and chorus answers.*)

RESPONSIVE CHANT: Sadie Cohen . . . Sadie Cohen . . .

(SADIE, *seeing them sway, sways too, standing on one leg and then on the other.*)

KING KLEAGLE: For six months she has embarrassed the community by her appearance and manners.

FIRST GOBLIN: (*Stepping forward*) Look at her dance, look at her sway.

SADIE: I can't help it.

(*They all begin to sway more emphatically.*)

SECOND GOBLIN: (*Stepping out*) She's a Jazz kid.

FIRST GOBLIN: Got a Jazz bug.

KING KLEAGLE: It's outrageous!

FIRST GOBLIN: It's contagious!

LOW CHANTING: Glory . . . glory . . .

KING KLEAGLE: Look at her condition! It's unfortunate.

FIRST GOBLIN: It's contortionate!

KING KLEAGLE: It's disreputable.

SADIE: (*Waving arms*) Ghosts . . . ghosts, go away . . .

(*And she tries to find a way out of the circle, but they surround her swaying.* KING KLEAGLE *looms above her importantly.*)

KING KLEAGLE: Outraged womanhood!

A VOICE: Halleluiah . . .

(*Hushed by his companions*)

KING KLEAGLE: We'll teach her to be outraged, we'll lash the devil out of her.

SADIE: I'm a-walkin' in the dark, I ain't goin' home no more, my father cried an' swore . . . (*Half sings in crooning voice*) He sighed an' he cried an' he pretty near died . . .

(*She weaves in and out among the masked figures.*)

RESPONSIVE CHANT: (*Picking up the refrain of a well-known song*) "For the loss of her honor and her pride!" (*They all suddenly point at* SADIE *and shout.*) Shame!

SADIE: I ain't ashamed, I'm glad. (*Sudden silence. All members of the* KLAN *stop stock still.*) I'm the glad girl, I don't care.

(KING KLEAGLE *stretches out his arms, touching flag and cross on either side of him. Both light up, the cross on either side of him. Both light up, the cross outlined in electricity, and a red, white and blue cluster on flag pole.* SADIE, *scared, sinks down on knees center.*)

KING KLEAGLE: She's walking the dark, the cross and the flag will save her, we must give her Christian punishment.

(*They all kneel.*)

RESPONSIVE CHANT: (*In a whisper*) "'Cause she's walkin' in the dark!"

(PHILLPOTS *enters right, pushes the kneeling men out of his path so that they all fall on top of one another and stands protectingly by* SADIE.)

PHILLPOTS: You will, will you? A lot of men picking on one little girl! Take a fellow your own size. (*Looking up at* KING KLEAGLE, *who towers above him*) Come on, who's going to fight me?

(*But the figures only go on chanting around him.*)

RESPONSIVE CHANT:

"There's a black time comin' . . .
A-walkin' in the dark . . ."

KING KLEAGLE: Back, back! You don't know what you're doing.

PHILLPOTS: I know, all right, King Klux, I don't care if there's a thousand of you cowards! You attack a woman because it's easier—

KING KLEAGLE: We protect morals.

(*Cheers from the* KLANSMEN)

PHILLPOTS: This little girl—

SADIE: I'm all right, Mister; they can't hurt me no worse.

PHILLPOTS: I'm here to help you, little girl. I'm right with you.

(*He takes hold of* KING KLEAGLE, *who towers above him, and they circle round as if dancing.* SADIE *grabs* PHILLPOTS *to protect him and a little goblin grabs* SADIE *to pull her away. In this way the four circle, swaying. One by one the other masked figures take hold of the turning group while chanting goes on.*)

RESPONSIVE CHANT:

"'Cause she's walkin' in the dark,
There's a black time comin' . . ."

KING KLEAGLE: (*Raising both arms*) Stop! (*Silence*) We will give her the proper punishment, following which we will ride her out of town.

RESPONSIVE CHANT: Halleluiah . . .

PHILLPOTS: Now, look here—

KING KLEAGLE: (*Roaring at him*) Back! Back! And you may be glad that we don't skin you alive! March on, Klansmen! The Cross and the Flag and the world's eyes on us!

(*The* KLANSMEN *are now grouped in a compact crowd at edge of stage,* SADIE *amongst them. They withdraw, chanting softly.*)

RESPONSIVE CHANT: (*As they go*)

"There's a black time comin' . . .
A-walkin' in the dark . . ."

PHILLPOTS: (*Trying to hold them back.*) Look here, don't take her with you, don't—(*The* KLANSMEN *disappear.* PHILLPOTS *alone*) I must get help . . . why, one of them's coming back! (*One of the* KLANSMEN *reappears right, dragging* SADIE *roughly.* PHILLPOTS *confronts him.*) Let go of her, leave her alone!

(*The figure tears off its mask. It is* COHEN.)

COHEN: (*Gesticulating in his most Jewish manner*) She was give into my care an' I got charge of her, ain't it?

SADIE: Popper!

COHEN: Look at her, my little daughter, a girl that don't know nuthin'!

SADIE: Look at yourself, you ain't so much in that nightgown.

COHEN: That's why I done myself up in fancy dress, to save my girl, the first one a' them devils touched her, he'd got a butcher knife in the head.

(*He shows a knife under his robe.*)

SADIE: Nobuddy can hurt me now. Nobuddy can touch me now.

COHEN: Listen Sadie, for the last time I argue with you.

SADIE: (*Disregarding her father, turns eagerly to* PHILLPOTS) Have you been a long ways off, Mister?

PHILLPOTS: I went all around, to Tokio and Rome . . . but I was haunted—

SADIE: What?

PHILLPOTS: Haunted, Sadie Cohen, by a dream of a little girl.

SADIE: (*Smiling*) What did she want?

PHILLPOTS: Love and champagne and a barrel of real diamonds.

SADIE: Ain't that the cat's earmuffs, though! What did she get?

PHILLPOTS: She got tears in her eyes and a weight on her heart: what are you going to do?

SADIE: Don't worry about me, I ain't really alone.

COHEN: Look at her only, there it is for a girl I relied on, a girl I made a dream for.

PHILLPOTS: Perhaps she made her own dream.

SADIE: When he's born, I'm gonna go to New York an' be a bad woman.

COHEN: There it is for a father's tears. She used to have her hair in a braid. She's a nightmare with her hair wild.

PHILLPOTS: (*To* SADIE) Better listen to reason.

SADIE: Ain't no reason in things, jus' a feelin' stealin' over you that tells you what to do, jus' a kind a' jazz—

COHEN: Ouch, jazz! Ain't I acted right, what have I done, where have I failed?

SADIE: (*Laughing and singing*) I'm gonna raise my kid . . . sing to him . . . show him the moon . . .

COHEN: She's got a jazz itch. No use speakin' to you, Sadie, while you got such an itch.

SADIE: I don' wanna talk to you, I know what I must do! I'm a-gonna raise my kid . . .

(*She runs away from* COHEN, *who tries to catch her. She exits.*)

COHEN: (*Following her*) Listen, only listen . . .

PHILLPOTS: Really, Miss Cohen, my advice would be . . .

(PHILLPOTS *and* COHEN *follow* SADIE *off. Enter right a member of the* KLAN *running.* PSINSKI *appears left, carrying a gun with a ragged red flag tied to the muzzle.*)

PSINSKI: (*Shouting as he comes*) Come on, men, we ain't afraid a' them white devils! (PSINSKI *sees the* KLANSMEN.) Stop or I shoot! (*The* GOBLIN *trembles visibly under his robe.* PSINSKI *seizes him, throws him on ground center.*) One a' you I got anyways. Show me the face, Ku Klux, before I finish you!

(*Slowly figure on ground lifts hood and mask, revealing the black face of* RASTUS *scared so that eyes pop out of his head.*)

RASTUS: (*Chants tragically*)

"I ain't done nuthin' to nobuddy no time,
I ain't here to stay, I'm just a-goin' away
With them doggone Bow Wow Blues . . ."

PHILLPOTS: You can't belong to the Klan.

RASTUS: How come? Anybuddy owns a sheet can belong. I reckoned it was safer—

(PSINSKI'*s men appear in a compact mass behind him rear. Confused shouting.*)

PSINSKI: You ain't fit to associate with class-conscious workmen.

RASTUS: I'se willin' to withdraw.

(RASTUS *picks up skirts and runs left.*)

PSINSKI: (*Shouts*) I'm with you, men! Come on!

(*He raises gun above head and leads men across through shadows rear. They carry flags, pitchforks, knives. Shouting grows to a crescendo. Then sudden silence. The scene begins to frighten. Enter* JIM *in tattered clothes, feeling his way with a cane. He is evidently blind.*)

JIM: Can't find nuthin' . . . help . . . who's there? (*Noise of shouting off stage*) Where am I? (*Swinging around with cane*) Help, I say. Goddamn, why do they leave me alone like this? Who's there?

(SADIE *runs in, gives a little gasp. Pause*)

SADIE: (*Breathless*) He's come.

JIM: Who's that, what voice is that?

SADIE: Your ma told me I should pray hard.

JIM: My ma?

SADIE: She must be right, 'cause I prayed like a steam engine an' you're here.

JIM: Damned if I know what you mean.

SADIE: Come over here an' then you'll know.

JIM: (*Waving cane in front of him*) Can't . . . Can't find nuthin' . . .

SADIE: You can't see?

JIM: When the Klan strung me to that tree, they stuck things in my eyes, things to burn, won't never see no more.

SADIE: Oh . . . but you come . . . even like this, don't matter, you come.

(*Noise of shouting and fighting off stage*)

JIM: What's that?

SADIE: The men, they're fightin' down there.

JIM: Where's that crazy Pole gone to?

SADIE: He's down there with the men.

JIM: I come with a bunch a' fellers, but I lost 'em all.

SADIE: (*Coming nearer to him*) Don't matter. I'll lead you.

JIM: Why in hell should you?

SADIE: I knew you'd come.

JIM: (*Sullenly*) Then take me to my mother. That's what I come for, get my mother out a' coal town, don't give a blue damn for anythin' else, I says, excep' my mother's waitin'! (*Shouts*) Where is she?

SADIE: (*Frightened*) Hush . . . quiet.

JIM: We went to the shack, me an' the bunch that come with me—

SADIE: Jus' too late, they burnt it down tonight.

JIM: I smelt the smoke.

SADIE: The Klan got everythin' their own way now.

JIM: I need my mammy's arms.

SADIE: They got her, now.

JIM: Where? Let me at 'em.

SADIE: Hush, be quiet.

JIM: Gotta find her, get her out a' this.

SADIE: We'll fool them men in sheets. We'll get away. (*She laughs excitedly.*) Some men have gone to help your ma, we better wait here—don't you know me?

JIM: (*Shaking head*) Got a voice like a bell ringin'. I dunno no one with a voice like that.

SADIE: Who'd you think I am?

JIM: Some tall dame with hair all gold laughin' in the sun.

SADIE: (*Softly*) I'm here for you.

JIM: (*Reaching out his arms*) Hell then, lemme touch you—

SADIE: (*Backing away*) No, no . . . who am I?

JIM: Voice of a li'l bell . . .

SADIE: Go on . . . go on . . .

JIM: Wearin' clothes all silk an' hair that smells a' pink roses.

SADIE: I'm here for you.

JIM: Where are you?

SADIE: (*Comes close to him. Whispers, trembling*) Here.

(JIM *takes hold of her, fingers her shoulders brutally, her arms, her face, her hair.*)

JIM: I got you now, I got you—(*Abruptly, as he recognizes her*) Li'l girl with them funny eyes, li'l Sadie Cohen.

SADIE: Don't call me that; call me your daisy, call me Desdemona, call me funny names.

JIM: But your voice ain't the same, what's happened? (*She laughs.*) Bells . . . I hear somethin' stirrin' in your voice.

SADIE: Somethin' stirrin' in me I come to meet you—

JIM: What you bring me so early in the mornin'?

SADIE: Hush . . . somethin' to sing to, somethin' to be born.

(*Enter* MRS. FLIMMINS *left.*)

MRS. FLIMMINS: Jim . . . Jim . . . (*He starts wildly toward the voice. She clings to him.*) Can't you see me?

JIM: No.

MRS. FLIMMINS: Jim . . .

JIM: I come to take you away from here.

MRS. FLIMMINS: Your eyes, Jim, your eyes . . .

SADIE: They stuck things in his eyes.

MRS. FLIMMINS: It's me must take you away, lead you . . .

SADIE: How can we get away from the Klan?

MRS. FLIMMINS: A li'l crowd a' them Klan men had me in a circle askin' me questions, then a bunch a' other fellers come an' one man told me to run.

JIM: Jake Psinski done that. That's my pal Jake.

SADIE: Where are they now?

JIM: The Klan?

MRS. FLIMMINS: We're on the hill and they're all around us, but the men are fightin' 'em.

JIM: Smells like mornin'.

MRS. FLIMMINS: How'd you get here, Jim? You ain't broke the law again?

JIM: No, I know about the law now.

MRS. FLIMMINS: It's law what you do you can't undo no ways.

JIM: I've been thinkin' 'bout that six months now, thinkin' how us folks got blood boilin' inside us, an' someways we can walk through hell in an asbestos skin.

SADIE: Me too, I know that now.

JIM: Are you laughin' or cryin'?

SADIE: It's nuthin', I jus' keep singin' to myself.

MRS. FLIMMINS: (*Bitterly*) She's one a' us kind now.

(*Enter* PHILLPOTS *left.*)

PHILLPOTS: (*Seeing* JIM) So you're here again!

MRS. FLIMMINS: What are them Kluxers doin'?

PHILLPOTS: Guess it's turned into something of a fight, but the Klan's too strong for them. They're all around us—see the lights.

JIM: (*Mutters between his teeth*) If I had my sight—

PHILLPOTS: They told me you were done for six months ago, strung to a tree—

JIM: Farmer come an' cut me down, put me in a bed, hid me till I could walk, then I walked to Charleston feelin' my way with a stick. They set me in the jail down in Charleston, then the Judge says, there's no what you call evidence, he says. I jus' kep' my jaw shut tight an' they threw me out on my ear; they says can't do no harm no more, a guy without eyes is nuthin', the curse ain't on him no more . . . (JIM *shouts triumphantly.*) The curse is lifted, let 'im walk!

MRS. FLIMMINS: (*Tensely*) A woman has tuk the curse off you, that's what.

JIM: You mean you?

MRS. FLIMMINS: (*Indicating* SADIE) I mean her, she carries the curse you give her.

SADIE: (*Singing softly*)

"I'm a-gonna raise my kid,
I'm a-gonna sing to him soft . . ."

JIM: (*Roughly*) What you laugh for, what you sing for?

SADIE: It's all for you, Jim.

PHILLPOTS: Little Desdemona bearing a burden, little Desdemona from the black monster's hand!

JIM: I ain't so black.

PHILLPOTS: It's not you, the black monster upon her is coal, rising upon her in a pillar of smoke.

MRS. FLIMMINS: I tried to make her see reason but she wouldn't.

SADIE: They says to me, there's ways a' fixin' it, I dunno how . . . but not me, I'm a-gonna raise my kid, I'm wise now!

JIM: What's bein' wise?

SADIE: It's a sickness in the stomach.

JIM: Does it kick?

SADIE: Sometimes it kicks.

MRS. FLIMMINS: 'T'ain't worth it.

SADIE: It's my turn now, I'm ready—

MRS. FLIMMINS: To make men. You poor fools, you think, you fight, an' make trouble, but rebellion comes out a' our stomachs.

PHILLPOTS: As a member of the good old middle class, I consider this conversation very irregular and I would suggest marriage.

JIM: (*Thoughtfully*) I wouldn't care.

(*Pause*)

SADIE: I wouldn't care.

MRS. FLIMMINS: None of us would care.

PHILLPOTS: It will set you right with the community. They don't care about a killing or two, but this is a serious matter.

MRS. FLIMMINS: I guess it's what the law would ask.

SADIE: When can we get married?

JIM: Right away!

(*Enter* COHEN *with Ku Klux uniform wrapped in a bundle.*)

COHEN: I'm through, I resign from this lodge, it's no good.

(*He throws the bundle away.*)

PHILLPOTS: Come here, Mr. Cohen, you're just in time.

COHEN: (*To* JIM) There you are, loafer . . . crow . . . jail-bird!

JIM: What's eatin' him?

COHEN: My daughter—

MRS. FLIMMINS: (*Interrupting him harshly*) That's just a joke too. He's gonna marry her.

COHEN: Married, you say? Married, is it? That's another thing again.

MRS. FLIMMINS: Can't you laugh, old man? Back up an' laugh like me, mebbe you an' me get married too!

COHEN: (*Turning from her, sadly*) I don't understand it at all.

(*A sound of raucous music off stage*)

MRS. FLIMMINS: What's that?

JIM: It's my pals, it's them musical miners . . . (*Triumphantly*) They're comin', I say, they're comin'!

(*Everybody turns to left as* JAZZ BAND *enters playing violently, led by* PSINSKI, *still carrying his gun. They line up across stage. Only* RASTUS *is not among them. The music stops in straggling manner. Other miners appear still carrying guns and knives.*)

PHILLPOTS: Where are the night riders?

PSINSKI: They all went away 'cause it's mornin'. Night riders don't work in daylight.

(*He is swaying a little, speaks thickly. The stage has become brightly illuminated.*)

PHILLPOTS: Psinski, I believe you're drunk!

PSINSKI: (*Thickly*) What of it?

PHILLPOTS: (*Smiling*) You, the revolutionist, the idealist, turned to whisky at last.

PSINSKI: Go on, make a joke a' me, it's all hopeless.

PHILLPOTS: That's the Russian in you speaking.

PSINSKI: I ain't a Russian, I'm a Pole, an' it's all hopeless.

SMITH: You're in America now, boy.

PHILLPOTS: Land of optimists.

PSINSKI: (*Thickly*) I'll speak to these Americans.

SMITH: Speech . . . speech . . .

PSINSKI: (*Climbs uncertainly on to a soap box left, trying to find words*) Comrades . . . we been fightin' like in a fog . . . (*Pointing to* JIM) This guy lost his eyes . . . I speak in a god a' thoughts now . . . in ten years, in fifty years, mebbe it will be clear . . . we got ideals, the, them guys in sheets got ideals, I am drunk with ideals . . . here's a girl gotta baby will be a workman in twenty years. Ask her what it means . . . I am tired!

SADIE: I carry a gravestone inside me, but I don' care, I'm a-gonna raise my kid . . .

PSINSKI: (*Bitterly*) An' his name shall be called Wonderful!

RESPONSIVE CHANT: (*Of miners swaying in a row behind*) "Wonderful . . . wonderful . . ."

PSINSKI: Mebbe that child will stand on the last barricade wavin' a red flag in the face a' all time! An' behind him will come marchin' a lot a' ghosts, all the soldiers that died at Bunker Hill an' on the Marne marchin' to be free—

PHILLPOTS: (*Calmly*) Bunk!

PSINSKI: (*Flustered, steps down*) Sure, ev'rything's bunk, so I wanna die, why won't some fool shoot me? (*He throws down his gun. Stands forlornly center*) Any guy will shoot me, I'll shake his hand, call him brother!

(MAN IN SILK HAT *appears suddenly, pushing his way through the crowd importantly.*)

MAN IN SILK HAT: (*Shaking* PSINSKI *warmly by the hand*) Give me your hand, my friend, I greet you. My friends, I bring good tidings. I'm glad you men have come, I am instructed to meet you half way.

PSINSKI: Is this half way?

MAN IN SILK HAT: We want to open up the mines, make concessions, boom business, sign contracts, all that sort of thing!

(*The men cheer and waves arms in perfunctory manner.*)

PSINSKI: (*Dazed*) You mean, the strike is over an' you agree?

MAN IN SILK HAT: Yes, indeed, I may say a lasting agreement, everybody fully pardoned.

JIM: Pardoned?

MAN IN SILK HAT: (*A little flustered, but shaking him warmly by the hand*) My friend, this is indeed a pleasure . . .

PSINSKI: The Klan? Where is the Klan?

MAN IN SILK HAT: Disbanded! All around you, you see the shining faces of loyal workmen!

(*He makes a grandiose gesture.*)

PHILLPOTS: (*To* PSINSKI) The laugh is always on you.

MAN IN SILK HAT: If you'll just come with me and sign the documents, the motion picture machines are ready for the ceremony.

PSINSKI: Ceremony?

MAN IN SILK HAT: (*Muttering as head leads way to right*) Of course . . . by all means.

(*He meets* SHERIFF *at extreme right. He motions* PSINSKI *off right and turns to the* SHERIFF.)

SHERIFF: What's the meanin' a' this, sir?

MAN IN SILK HAT: (*In a low voice*) The moral effect . . . can't afford further trouble . . . publicity value . . . dollars and cents.

SHERIFF: What are your orders, sir?

MAN IN SILK HAT: Make a list of the marked men and we'll get them in their beds tonight! (*Turning suavely to group on stage*) My friends, we have each other's confidence.

(*Exit* MAN IN SILK HAT *right.*)

PHILLPOTS: Just a minute, Sheriff. (*Leading* SHERIFF *to* JIM) This gives you your chance for a wedding.

JIM: Howdy, Sheriff . . . Can you fix me up with a marriage license right off?

SHERIFF: (*Produces his enormous sheaf of legal papers and starts thumbing them over industriously*) Might be somethin' here that would do. (*He adjusts his glasses.*) If it ain't a weddin', it's a lynchin'—lemme see, war, insurrection an' riot—no that won't hardly do.

JIM: Never mind, marry us right away quick, Sheriff

SHERIFF: (*Finding another paper*) I'll have to fix you up with a dawg license. I'll revise it a little.

MAN IN SILK HAT: (*Appears suddenly in an upper box, with bright spotlight on him, and announces in best oratorical style*) Gentlemen, I wish to announce that this is Mother's Day! I have here a telegram from Calvin C. Coolidge stating that all men are brothers.

(*He holds up the telegram. Applause from men on stage.*)

PHILLPOTS: (*Picks up a megaphone at edge of stage right and announces through it as if addressing a huge crowd*) Gentlemen, Industrial Peace has come! (*Turning to* SADIE *and* JIM) Cemented in this marriage! A pact, a compact, an agreement, a document! The nation is rejoicing! There's going to be coal to keep 'em warm!

(*Enter* RASTUS *left. Standing at edge of stage he begins to sing, softly twanging banjo.*)

RASTUS:

"'Cause there's no land so grand as my land
From California to Manhattan Isle
North an' South, my sunny sky land,
I love every mile . . ."

(*All sway and sing.* PHILLPOTS *continues to announce.*)

PHILLPOTS: Kindly turn to the financial page, wait till the market opens, all for Wall Street!

(SHERIFF *goes around shaking hands with everybody.* PHILLPOTS *puts away his megaphone. The crowd gather around* RASTUS *and join in the singing, in the manner of a college glee club.*)

RASTUS and CHORUS: (*Loudly*)

"Yankee Doodle . . . that melody
Keep on ringin' in my ear,
Yankee Doodle . . . that melody
Makes me stand up right an' cheer,
I'm comin', U.S.A., I'll say,
I love you . . .
Make me lose those . . . Yankee Doodle Blues . . ."

(*The* SHERIFF *is preparing for the marriage ceremony.* JIM *raises his arms and shouts.*)

JIM: Come on aroun', fellers that dig in the earth, make a cloud aroun', a cloud a' men like coal dust, a whirlwind makin' music—

(*The men, chanting softly, crowd around the marriage group, and jazz music continues.*)

COHEN: She ain't my Yiddisher Rose no more.

PHILLPOTS: She's an American Beauty now.

COHEN: (*Wipes a tear from each eye*) Babies they will have an' babies . . .

PHILLPOTS: And their children's children will be shouting oi, oi!

COHEN: We should break a bottle over the bride's head!

(*Swaying and dancing to the music, the* SHERIFF *is performing the wedding ceremony with* MRS. FLIMMINS *and* COHEN *on either side of* SADIE *and* JIM.)

SHERIFF: An' I hereby pronounce you—

JIM: (*Interrupting him*) Sheriff, has it got a red seal on it?

SHERIFF: No, I didn't have no seal.

JIM: Put my blood on it, put a drop a' blood on it.

SHERIFF: Shut your mug till I finish.

JIM: Wait, got a knife? (SHERIFF, *annoyed, takes a knife from* COHEN *and hands it to* JIM. *In dead silence,* JIM *holds out his arm, pricks it and with awful ceremony lets a drop fall on the paper.*) There's blood, now go on. (*Singing and music start again with a blare of sound.* MRS. FLIMMINS, COHEN, SADIE, *and* JIM *embrace one another dancing. The whole crowd forms a compact, swaying group behind them.* OLD MAGGIE *and* POP PRATT *appear and hobble forward doing an old-fashioned jig. Again a silence breaks the rhythm, and* JIM *shouts:*) Shake a leg, Ma!

MRS. FLIMMINS: (*Harshly*) We can dance with our hearts breakin'.

JIM: Everybuddy shake a leg.

MRS. FLIMMINS: I can dance too, I can dance as well as any old fool.

(*She raises her skirts, revealing a bright red petticoat, and dances wildly. The violent rhythm grows in volume.*)

SMITH: (*Shouts with megaphone*) Join the Procession!

(*Down the aisle of theatre comes* BOOB *with newspapers.*)

BOOB: (*Shouting as he comes*) Extry! Extry! Big peace!

PHILLPOTS: (*At top of steps front*) Here kid, I'll buy those papers. (*He takes them and starts tearing them, throwing them around.*) Here, boys, here's confetti, there's where the news belongs!

(JIM *stands center, smiling blindly.* SADIE *at a little distance from him swaying wildly, while the whole crowd marches around them, the* JAZZ BAND *and all the other characters. Then the Procession marches down through the audience. With an increasing noise and rhythm, the Procession disappears at rear of theatre. Then there is silence.* JIM *and* SADIE *alone on stage.*)

SADIE: They're gone, we're alone.

JIM: (*Feeling his way toward her*) Where are you now?

SADIE: (*Swaying and singing softly*) I'm a-gonna raise my kid, sing to him soft . . .

CURTAIN

Singing Jailbirds

A Drama in Four Acts

UPTON SINCLAIR

Time: The Present
Place: The Harbor Jail in a California City.

All scenes outside the jail are dreams of the prisoner.

Act 1.
Scene 1: Office in the Jail.
Scene 2: A Tank in the Jail, the same evening

Act 2.
Scene 1: In the Hole, the same evening.
Scene 2: A Workingmen's Restaurant.
Scene 3: In the Hole.

Act 3.
Scene 1: In the Hole, two weeks later.
Scene 2: A Ranch-House
Scene 3: In the Hole.
Scene 4: A Road-house
Scene 5: In the Hole
Scene 6: The Hall of Hate

Act 4.
Scene 1: In the Hole, two months later.
Scene 2: The Jungles.
Scene 3: In the Hole.
Scene 4: In the Hole.

Characters

THE DISTRICT ATTORNEY
"RED" ADAMS, The Wobbly
PETE
JERRY
MATT
JOE GUNTHER
IKE
THE DOMINIE
THE CHIEF OF POLICE
JAKE APPERSON
ONE LUNG, THE CHINK
NELL, wife of "Red" Adams
A JAILER
MRS. SMITH, a Neighbor
MURIEL, the Stenographer
THE BAILIFF
THE TIGER
THE JACK-IN-THE-BOX
SECOND JAILER
STRIKE-PRISONERS, JAILERS, POLICE OFFICERS, a DOCTOR, a WAITER, a CLERK, and the two children of "Red" Adams

ACT 1

Scene 1: An Office in the Jail.

At the front of the stage, nearest to the audience, a small room, bare and severe. Entrance center; a flat-topped desk in middle of room, with swivel-chairs on two sides of it; a barred window at right.

At rise: The DISTRICT ATTORNEY *sits in chair at right of desk; a smooth-faced, keen-featured lawyer.* "RED" ADAMS *stands behind the desk, facing the audience; a lean, wiry, young workingman with pale, tense face, reddish tousled hair, a manner of defiance. He wears old trousers and shirt, no tie. He does not look at the* DISTRICT ATTORNEY, *but stares straight before him. Outside, through the window, right, a mob is parading before the jail, singing to the tune* "Hold the Fort for I Am Coming":

We're here from mine and mill and rail,
We're here from off the sea:
From coast to coast we make the boast
Of Solidarity.

From the rear, offstage, comes an answering chorus of several hundred STRIKE-PRISONERS *confined in the cells and "tanks" of the jail:*

In California's darkened dungeons
For the O.B.U.
Remember you're outside for us
While we're in here for you.

DISTRICT ATTORNEY: Well, this might be a strike we're running, and again it might be a grand opera. (*No answer from the prisoner*) So, you're Red Adams?

RED: They call me that.

DISTRICT ATTORNEY: Name Bert, I believe.

RED: Yes.

DISTRICT ATTORNEY: Belong to the I.W.W.?

RED: You've got my card at the desk.

DISTRICT ATTORNEY: Give me a straight answer.

RED: I belong to the I.W.W.

DISTRICT ATTORNEY: You understand that I'm the district attorney of this county, and that what you tell me may be used against you?

RED: (*Looks at* DISTRICT ATTORNEY *for the first time*) Mr. 'Cutor, did you ever know a Wobbly to crawl?

DISTRICT ATTORNEY: Out for martyrdom, eh? (*A silence*) You're the leader in this strike?

RED: We don't have leaders in our organization.

DISTRICT ATTORNEY: You've given a few orders, however.

RED: Let your stools tell you about that, Mr. 'Cutor.

DISTRICT ATTORNEY: You're feeling a little sore?

RED: In places. The Chief nearly twisted off my arm this evening.

DISTRICT ATTORNEY: Tried to get away from him?

RED: Hell! You know we never try to get away. You only have to tap us on the shoulder.

THE CROWD (*Singing, outside, at the right*)

> We make a pledge—no tyrant might
> Can make us bend the knee;
> Come on, you workers, organize,
> And fight for Liberty!

THE PRISONERS (*Singing in the rear*)

> In California's darkened dungeons
> For the O.B.U.
> Remember you're outside for us
> While we're in her for you.

DISTRICT ATTORNEY: Well, Red, you've been having things you own way for the past week.

RED: (*Laughs*) Ah, Mr. 'Cutor, you don't know what our way is! Some day we'll show you!

DISTRICT ATTORNEY: Dictatorship of the Proletariat, eh? I get you! But meantime, you've tied up the ships.

RED: With you loading a dozen a day?

DISTRICT ATTORNEY: Where d'you get that?

RED: I read it in this morning's "Times."

DISTRICT ATTORNEY: Well, we have to whistle to keep our courage up—the same as you fellows have to sing.

THE CROWD: (*Outside, singing, to the chorus of "John Brown's Body"*)

Solidarity forever!
Solidarity forever!
Solidarity forever!
And the Union makes us strong!

RED: Well, what's the point? You didn't bring me here to chat on the class struggle.

DISTRICT ATTORNEY: Have a seat, Red. (RED *sits stiffly in chair at left of desk; the* DISTRICT ATTORNEY *takes out cigars*) Have a smoke?

RED: No, thanks.

DISTRICT ATTORNEY: Don't smoke?

RED: Not with parasites.

DISTRICT ATTORNEY: No use to quarrel, Red. Our point of view differs. I think the public has some rights in this harbor.

RED: If you want to talk to me, Mr. 'Cutor, cut out the Sunday school stuff. The public isn't loading these ships—it's the Shipowners' Association. They've given you the orders—over the telephone. I've no doubt. (*A pause*) You see, I know the Dictatorship of the Capitalist class.

DISTRICT ATTORNEY: Well, my boy, there'll be this much dictatorship—we're going to load the ships.

RED: By arresting all the men who do the work? You must have pinched a thousand tonight.

DISTRICT ATTORNEY: We figure about six hundred.

RED: Well, you go down to the waterfront and take a broom and sweep the harbor dry, and then start to mop up the discontent of the workers.

DISTRICT ATTORNEY: We're going to mop up the agitators and troublemakers—

RED: Troublemakers! Hell, man—get these finks that run the employment business for the Shipowners! You knew how they were robbing the men—

you saw us herded there in the slavemarket, showing our muscles to the dealers, trampling each other to get a job! The troublemakers! But shucks—you don't want any preaching from me. You know all the facts. What am I here for? Come to the point!

DISTRICT ATTORNEY: Suppose I just wanted to make the acquaintance of a worthy foe?

RED: Idle curiosity? No, there's something else—and it's something for you, not for me. I wasn't weaned yesterday, Mr. 'Cutor.

DISTRICT ATTORNEY: You were nursed on vinegar, it would seem Red.

RED: My mother was a working woman—a miner's wife. I guess she got her share of vinegar—the kind your class feeds to my class.

THE CROWD: (*Shouting outside*)

Solidarity forever!
Solidarity forever!
Solidarity forever!
And the Union makes us strong!

RED: What is it? Come across, man!

DISTRICT ATTORNEY: You know we've got your whole executive committee?

RED: I saw a few of them in my tank.

DISTRICT ATTORNEY: We've got the rest.

RED: Well, there'll be a new committee.

DISTRICT ATTORNEY: They can't give orders without finding them.

RED: Oh, sure! You'll crush this strike. This is only practice.

DISTRICT ATTORNEY: Don't forget, it's practice for the police also.

RED: (*Fixes him with an intent look*) Good God, are you figuring to win me over? Make a deal with me—like I was some old line labor leader?

DISTRICT ATTORNEY: (*In a business-like tone*) You know Jake Apperson, don't you?

RED: Sure; old pale of mine.

DISTRICT ATTORNEY: You went through the Oakland strike with him?

RED: I sure did.

DISTRICT ATTORNEY: You know he's out of jail again?

RED: I heard it.

DISTRICT ATTORNEY: Expecting him down here?

RED: Ask your spies, Mr. 'Cutor. You'll get nothing like that out of me.

DISTRICT ATTORNEY: Jake Apperson! One of your barn-burning gang!

RED: (*Starts*) Barn burning? Cut it out! You aren't such a fool!

DISTRICT ATTORNEY: Oh, you're a choir of lily-white angels, you Wobblies! That's why you sing all the time! Well, you know what you stand to get, Red: criminal syndication.

RED: Twenty-eight years—yep.

DISTRICT ATTORNEY: You won't live through that.

RED: Nope.

DISTRICT ATTORNEY: (*Studying him curiously*) I don't see what you figure to gain.

RED: You don't see, and I couldn't make you see. (*With a laugh*) However, it's more comfortable here than in the tank, so if you're looking for a lecture, you can have it. I've been what you call a leader of the Wobblies for three years. I've traveled from Vancouver to San Diego; I've visited every lumber camp and every harbor on the Pacific Coast. I've talked to the men on the job—there must be ten thousand that know me, and they know I'm not in the business for my pocket. Tonight the word goes out—they've got Red Adams in jail. Pretty soon it'll be: They're trying him in their dirty courts. It'll be: Their bulls and their lousy stools are lying about him. The 'cutor of the Shipowners' Association is accusing him of burning barns. Then it'll be: They've sent up Red Adams for twenty-eight years! They've got him coughing out his lungs in the jute mill! They've got him in the hole—he's hunger striking, because he wouldn't stand for the beating of some fellow-worker. Then some day it'll be: Red Adams is dead! Red Adams died for us! Do you think they're all skunks and cowards, Mr. 'Cutor? Why, man, when you get through there'll be a thousand on the job in my place!

THE CROWD: (*Outside singing*)

> Long-haired preachers come out every night,
> Try to tell you what's wrong and what's right,
> But when asked how 'bout something to eat,
> They will answer with voices so sweet.

THE PRISONERS: (*At rear, offstage*)

> You will eat,
> By and bye,
> In that glorious land above the sky.
> Work and pray,
> Live on hay,
> You'll get pie in the sky when you die!

DISTRICT ATTORNEY: A little comic relief!

RED: You might learn something from that song. Ever hear of Joe Hill? He wrote it. And out in Utah, the master-class stood him up against a wall and shot him with a firing-squad. They called him a burglar—just such a frame-up as you'd delight in. But now Joe Hill's songs are all over the land. We sing 'em in Dago and Mex, in Hunkie and Wop, we even sing 'em in Jap and Chink! We're teaching 'em to five or ten thousand tonight—you hear the lessons! In California's darkened dungeons, for the O.B.U. They say: What's the O.B.U? We answered The One Big Union! They say: What's the One Big Union? We answered The I.W.W.! Solidarity for the workers! The hammer that will smash the doors of all the jails!

THE CROWD (*Outside singing*)

In California's darkened dungeons
For the O.B.U.
Remember you're inside for us
While we're out here for you!

RED: Don't you see how you're doing our work, Mr. 'Cutor?

DISTRICT ATTORNEY: And you're sure you don't want to work for me, Red?

RED: Hey?

DISTRICT ATTORNEY: You know, we could make it easy for you. We could find some trick to let you get away—

RED: Oh! So that's it, after all!

DISTRICT ATTORNEY: We could find you a very good sum of money.

RED: Judas Iscariot, Benedict Arnold, and Red Adams! California for climate, hell for company!

DISTRICT ATTORNEY: A lot of your fellows are getting theirs, you understand. We carry three of your executive committee on our payroll.

RED: That may be true, and again, it may be a shrewd lie to take the heart out of us. We soon spot the ones you get.

DISTRICT ATTORNEY: They become tame and conservative, eh?

RED: Quite the contrary! They become real, sure enough red revolutionists—regular fire-eaters. Want to get something done—maybe burning a barn or two! (*With a smile*) You see, Mr. 'Cutor, we fellows who are nursed on vinegar and go to work at the age of ten—we grow just as sharp wits as you fellows who go to college and live on bootleg whiskey.

DISTRICT ATTORNEY: So, Red, you're bound to fight us!

RED: We nail the I.W.W. preamble to the wall: "We are forming the new society within the shell of the old."

DISTRICT ATTORNEY: (*Earnestly*) You're an intelligent man, Red—one of the keenest. Take it from me—this lousy gang isn't worth what you'll suffer for them.

RED: They're just average stiffs, of course; some of them are scum. But they're learning the great lesson, Solidarity; and somebody has to teach it.

DISTRICT ATTORNEY: You weren't always an agitator, I take it.

RED: No, I was an honest workingman. I read the advertisements of your boosters, and came to sunny California, and put my little savings into a ranch. You know what happened when the war was over and prices went down!

DISTRICT ATTORNEY: Married man?

RED: I was then.

DISTRICT ATTORNEY: Where's your wife?

RED: Where you want to put me.

DISTRICT ATTORNEY: In jail?

RED: No—in her grave.

DISTRICT ATTORNEY: I understand you had some children.

RED: Yes, a boy and a girl.

DISTRICT ATTORNEY: Where are they?

RED: They're being taken care of.

DISTRICT ATTORNEY: By you?

RED: No, by others.

DISTRICT ATTORNEY: You support them?

RED: They don't need it.

DISTRICT ATTORNEY: In other words, you deserted them?

RED: Who told you that yarn?

DISTRICT ATTORNEY: You left them to other people so you could go off with some other woman?

RED: (*Starts*) You dirty cur—Is that what I'm here for—to have you spit on my grief?

DISTRICT ATTORNEY: (*Sneering*) Looks like I've found a sore spot, eh?

RED: If you weren't a coward, you'd say that outside where I could knock your block off! You whore-master, with your little stenographer! (*The other clenches his fist as if to strike him.*) Ohio! You think we didn't hear about the lady that you had in the private room at the roadhouse and the suit she threatened and the dough she got out of you! And you dare to throw at my life's tragedy in my face!

DISTRICT ATTORNEY: (*Coldly*) Well, Red, I guess we won't prolong this discussion.

RED: No—since you're not having it all your own way.

DISTRICT ATTORNEY: You'll find the law will have its way, my man!

RED: To hell with you and your law! Bring on your perjurers and your torturers! Send me up for criminal syndicalism—or choke the life out of me, if you want to! I wipe my feet on you—lackeys and lickspittles of the capitalist class! You and the whole crooked game that you call your law—bribers and bribe-takers—

DISTRICT ATTORNEY: Rave on—we'll stop your foul mouth. (*He presses a button on his desk.*)

RED: Yes, you may stop mine—but there are others you'll not stop! (*He rushes to the window and waves his arms through the bars, shouting.*) Solidarity for the workers!

THE CROWD: Hooray! It's Red! Red Adams! Red! Red! Three cheers for Red! Hooray for Red! Red! Red!

(RED *starts singing to the crowd outside, which takes it up.*)

We speak to you from jail today,
Six hundred union men;
We're here because the bosses' laws
Bring slavery again.

(*Two police officers enter; the* DISTRICT ATTORNEY *indicates* RED *with a jerk of the thumb, and they collar him and drag him from the room. He sings, in unison with the crowd outside and with the prisoners inside the jail.*)

In California's darkened dungeons
For the O.B.U.
Remember you're outside for us
While we're in here for you.

(*The curtain falls; the singing continues until the rise on Scene 2. The audience is invited to join the singing.*)

We're here from mine and mill and rail,
We're here from off the sea;
From coast to coast we make the boast
Of Solidarity.

(*CHORUS*)

We laugh and sing, we have no fear,
Our hearts are always light'
We know that every Wobbly true
Will carry on the fight.

(*CHORUS*)

We make a pledge—no tyrant might
Can make us bend the knee;
Come on, you workers, organize,
And fight for Liberty.

(*CHORUS*)

Long-haired preachers come out every night,
Try to tell you what's wrong and what's right;
But when asked how 'bout something to eat
They will answer with voices so sweet:

(*CHORUS*)

You will eat, bye and bye
In that glorious land above the sky;
Work and pray, live on hay,
You'll get pie in the sky when you die.
And the starvation army they play,
And they sing and the clap and they pray,
Till they get all your coin on the drum,
Then they tell you when you're on the bottom:

(*CHORUS*)

Holy Rollers and Jumpers come out,
And they holler, they jump and they shout;
"Give your money to Jesus," they say,
"He will cure all diseases today."

(*CHORUS*)

If you fight hard for children and wife—
Try to get something good in this life—
You're a sinner and bad man, they tell,
When you die you will sure go to hell.

(*CHORUS*)

Scene 2: A "Tank" in the Jail

The scene occupies the rear two-thirds of the stage, away from the audience. At the right are two "tanks," in a row, the corridor leading to them being at the left, running towards the audience. At the end of the corridor farthest from the audience is a solid iron door, guarded by a keeper with a shot-gun. Along the left-hand side of the corridor a row of barred windows, looking to the street outside, the windows are open, and through them can be heard from time to time the shouting and singing of the crowds of strikers. The audience looks into the nearest of the two tanks through a row of steel bars. A steel-barred door, facing left, opens into the corridor. The other two walls of the tank are solid.

The tank is packed with men, so tightly that not all can sit down; some are half standing, half hanging to the bars. Most of them are ordinary sailors and longshoremen on strike, having been swept up off the streets for attempting to parade, or for jeering at the police.

At rise: All are singing lustily.

Workingmen of all countries, unite.
Side by side we for freedom will fight;
When the world and its wealth we shall gain,
To the grafters we'll sing this refrain:
You will eat, bye and bye,
When you've learned how to cook and to fry;
Chop some wood,
'Twill do you good,
And you'll eat in the sweet bye and bye!

PETE: (*A frail, consumptive fellow in the back part of cell*) Christ, fellers, can't you make a little room for us?

MATT: (*A big longshoreman in shirt sleeves, near the door*) What the hell we gonna make it outta?

PETE: We're just suffocatin'!

JERRY: (*A young Wobbly*) Give us a turn near the door—that's fair.

PETE: Stick your legs through them bars; that'll give room for the rest of us.

MATT: The hell you say! An' the bulls come crack our shins?

JOE GUNTHER: (*A Wobbly leader, young, energetic, a machinist*) If we make any room they'll only jam some more in.

JERRY: Don't let 'em jam no more in. Crowd up there, pack the entrance.

MATT: Sure, an' have 'em jab their sticks in yer guts!

PETE: Well, let me get out there! I'd rather have a stick in my guts than be suffocated.

IKE: (*A spy of hang-dog appearance*) Cut out the shovin'!

JERRY: Git off my feet!

IKE: Gimme some room there!

MATT: Where 'm I goin'? Through the wall?

JOE GUNTHER: Forget it, fellers! Don't get to scrappin'! Solidarity!

PETE: We're solid, all right, in this crate!

JOE GUNTHER: Give us a song!

MATT: How the hell can we sing when we got no air?

JOE GUNTHER: Sing, you jailbirds! Sing!

(*He begins, and they take it up, but rather feebly.*)

Solidarity forever!
Solidarity forever!
Solidarity forever
And the Union makes us strong!

(*Three figures appear up the corridor; a chorus of yells as they pass the entrance to the other tank*) Here come some more! Don't let nobody else in here! Crowd up to the door! This this is a sardine cannery? Give us some air in these tanks! D'ye want to kill us? (*Chorus of cat calls, hisses and curses*) You goddam bunch o'murderers! Let us out o' this hole! We'll all be dead in this tank before long! We gotta stay in here all night? Give us some air! Give us some air!

PETE: Don't let 'em in!

JERRY: Jam up the door there!

MATT: Spit in their eyes! (*The newcomers are discovered to be* "RED" ADAMS, *escorted by a jailor and a police officer.*)

JOE GUNTHER: It's Red!

JERRY: Red Adams!

PETE: 'Ray for Red!

MATT: Good old Red!

JOE GUNTHER: Three cheers for Red Adams!

ALL: Hooray! Hooray! Hooray!

JOE GUNTHER: What'd they do to you, Red?

MATT: Good old scout!

JOE GUNTHER: Come on in, Red!

JERRY: Git back there, make room fer Red!

PETE: Where we gonna git to?

JOE GUNTHER: We want Red if we have to hold him on our shoulders

JERRY: Move up.

IKE: Take him on your lap. (*They crowd back and make room; the* POLICE OFFICER *stands with club in hand while the* JAILER *opens the cell door and shoves* RED *inside, then shuts the door again.*)

JERRY: Hello, fellow-worker!

JOE GUNTHER: Welcome to our city! (*All who can reach him grasp his hand.*)

MATT: What did they do to ye?

RED: They tried to buy me out!

JOE GUNTHER: The dirty skunks!

RED: The 'Cutor offered me money.

JOE GUNTHER: I'll bet he got a good ran-a-tanging!

RED: I told him we nailed the I.W.W. preamble to the wall: "We are forming the new society within the shell of the old!"

JERRY: Hooray fer Red!

RED: And then he talked about my dead wife—accused me of deserting my children.

MATT: Oh, the lousy bastard!

VOICES: (*From the other cells*) Talk up, Red, so us fellers can hear!

ALL: Speech! Speech!

RED: (*Stands facing entrance and shouts*) Fellow-workers! Fellow-workers!

ALL: Hooray for Red!

RED: The 'Cutor tried to put me on his payroll. He threatened me with twenty-eight years—and he'll give it to me, too, for I bawled him out!

ALL: To hell with him!

RED: Fellow-workers! They won't send you all up! They'll let most of you out —and when you go, take this story to the rest of the bunch.

ALL: We will! We will!

RED: Tell them how they're suffocating us here! Tell them how they beat Jim Kearney's face to a mash!

ALL: We will! We will!

RED: Tell them how they're suffocating us here! Tell them how they beat Jim Kearney's face to a mash!

ALL: We will! We will!

RED: They'll try to send your committee to the pen! But you'll raise up new ones, you'll study and think, you'll never forget this night!

JOE GUNTHER: You bet your life!

JERRY: We'll stand by you!

RED: Remember—this may be the last word I'll get to say.

MATT: We'll stick! We'll stick!

JERRY: Yes, and we'll bring ye out o' the pen, too!

IKE: Hooray fer the strike!

ALL: Solidarity forever!

THE CROWD: (*Singing outside, left*)

In California's darkened dungeons
For the O.B.U.
Remember you're inside for us
While we're out here for you.

THE PRISONERS: (*Taking up the chorus*)

In California's darkened dungeons
For the O.B.U.
Remember you're inside for us
While we're out here for you.

RED: (*Whispering to* JOE GUNTHER) Joe!

JOE: Hey?

RED: You heard anything about Jake Apperson coming here?

JOE: No, who told you?

RED: The 'Cutor. That's one of the things he was trying to get out of me.

JOE: Maybe he was just fishin'.

RED: I know that.

JOE: Be careful, Red. They're bound to put a stool in here with us.

RED: I know that, too.

JOE: (*Turns suddenly upon* IKE *who is next to him*) What yer crowdin' on me for?

IKE: How can I help crowdin'?

JOE: You tryin' to hear what we're sayin'?

IKE: Why not?

JOE: Who are you?

IKE: I'm Ike.

JOE: You a Wobbly?

IKE: Sure, I'm a Wobbly.

JOE: Got a card?

IKE: Not in here I ain't.

JOE: Did they get one off you?

IKE: Sure they did.

JOE: When did you come to town?

IKE: A week ago.

JOE: Well, nobody ever saw you at headquarters. Git back there by the wall, and don't do so much rubberin'. (*Shouts*) Remember, fellow-workers, they got this place full o' stool-pigeons, and be careful what you talk.

PETE: (*From back of cell*) Fer Christ's sake, you stiffs by the door there, give us a chance fer some air.

JERRY: Where we gotta go to?

PETE: Change places with us.

RED: That's fair—we got to take our turn, boys. Move round and let the ones in back get the air. Let me get back there.

JERRY: We don't want to kill off our good men.

RED: There'll be plenty more of us—don't worry. (*He crowds his way to back part of cell; four figures appear at entrance to the corridor and the prisoners start to yell.*) More coming! To hell with you! We're packed tight enough! There's no room in here! Put 'em on the roof! Give us some air! You want to murder us? Ya! Ya! Ya! (*A chorus of shrieks and curses; men pound on the doors, or shake their fists through the bars.*)

PETE: Let me out o' this crate! We're dyin back here!

JERRY: Crowd up, boys!

MATT: Don't let no more git in here!

JERRY: We got our share.

JOE GUNTHER: Fight 'em back!

PETE: We might as well die in a hurry! (*The newcomers are the* JAILER *and the* CHIEF OF POLICE *escorting the* DOMINIE *under arrest. They come down the corridor and stop outside the barred door of the front tank. The* CHIEF *is a broad-shouldered, stern-featured man in civilian clothing.* The DOMINIE *is an Episcopal clergyman, fifty years of age, in full regimentals, stoutish, florid in face, prosperous in appearance, the very picture of an English bishop, except for the gaiters; a man of the world, urbane and sophisticated, he takes this adventure with zest, which not all his indignation can mar.*)

MATT: Hell! It's a sky pilot!

JERRY: Holy mackerel! They've pinched a Bible-shark!

DOMINIE: (*A magnificent pulpit voice which rolls through the corridor*) Fellow-workers, I greet you in the name of the Crucified.

RED: (*Shouting from back of tank*) It's the Dominie!

PETE: What the devil's a Dominie?

RED: (*Shoving*) He was coming to preach to us! He's on our side!

JOE GUNTHER: Gangway! Coming through here! (*They make room so that* RED *can get up to the door of the tank.*)

RED: (*Elbowing his way to the door*) Hello, Dominie!

DOMINIE: Welcome, my lad!

RED: By God! They pinched you?

DOMINIE: By Satan, you should say!

RED: Welcome to our midst! Boys, this is the Dominie. Squeeze up and make room for him.

PETE: Where the devil we gonna squeeze to?

JOE GUNTHER: I'll hold him on my lap, if I must!

RED: He was coming to make us a speech tonight!

DOMINIE: (*To the* CHIEF OF POLICE) Chief, I call your attention to this outrageous condition of crowding.

THE CHIEF: You'll love to be close to them.

DOMINIE: I protest against this devilish inhumanity! I denounce this indignity to a wearer of the cloth! (*The* CHIEF *makes no reply, but stands while the* JAILER *opens the door and shoves the* DOMINIE *by main force into the tank.*) Once more I warn you—every man who participates in this outrage is incurring a suit for damages and prosecution for false arrest.

THE CHIEF: All right, Dominie, go to it! (*They lock him in and depart.*)

RED: (*Grabs* DOMINIE *by hand*) Well, well! So they knocked you off!

DOMINIE: They have done me that honor!

RED: What did you do?

DOMINIE: I walked down your main street, having in mind the criminal intention to commit the criminal act of preaching to the strikers when I got to where they were. But the telepathic department of your city detective service discovered the aforesaid criminal intention, and laid hands upon me.

RED: Three cheers for the Dominie!

ALL: Hooray! Hooray! Hooray!

DOMINIE: Being a citizen of the United States, as well as a minister of the Lord Jesus Christ, I rejoice in having accumulated a most gorgeous series of damage suits against the public authorities of your city.

JOE GUNTHER: Go for them, Dominie!

DOMINIE: With all my heart and soul I shall do that!

RED: Preach to us, Dominie!

JOE GUNTHER: Sure thing! We'll never need it more!

DOMINIE: I could ask no better pulpit.

RED: (*Shouts through bars to the men in the other tank*) Fellow-workers! Fellow-workers! The Dominie, who got in jail for us, is going to preach us a sermon.

VOICES: (*From the other tank*) The hell you say! Go to it, old timer! 'Ray fer the Bible-shark! Up with the sky-pilot!

DOMINIE: (*Stands facing the door of tank and orates in best pulpit style, with gestures through the bars*) Fellow-workers! There has befallen me this night the proudest honor that can come to a minister of the Son of Man on earth. Standing a prisoner before the bar of World Capitalism, I have been dowered with my celestial title—my crown of thorns—my halo of glory. Him, mocking, they called the King of the Jews; me, mocking, they call the Dominie of the Wobblies, the Parson to the I.W.W. Fellow-workers in the cause of social justice, I put the question to you: Will you ratify that appointment? May I wear the badge of honor before the Throne of Grace?

ALL: (*Tumultuously*) Hurray! You bet! Go to it, old scout! You're our parson! 'Ray for the Dominie!

DOMINIE: Fellow-workers, the bond is sealed, the everlasting glory is mine. I hear the thrilling words of my Lord and Master "For I was hungry, and ye gave me to eat; I was thirsty, and ye gave me drink: I was a stranger, and ye took me in; naked, and ye clothed me; I was sick, and ye visited me; I was in prison, and ye came unto me!"

ALL: Hooray! Three cheers for the Dominie!

THE CROWD: (*Outside, through the windows*) Hooray! Hooray! Hooray!

DOMINIE: They hear me outside on the street! I can preach my night's sermon after all! (*Raising his voice to a mighty bellow*) Friends and fellow-workers! Fellow-strikers against the rule of greed! You hear me out there?

CROWD: (*Outside*) We hear! Hooray!

DOMINIE: I proclaim unto you Christ and Him crucified! Not the stained glass window saint of the fashionable churches, but the working-class revolutionist, the rebel carpenter, the First Wobbly of the World!

CROWD: (*Pandemonium both inside the tanks and outside on the street*) Hooray! Hooray! Hooray!

DOMINIE: Glory hallelujah, and deliverance unto all the oppressed! In the name of Jesus Christ the Redeemer I prophesy and ordain the downfall of World Capitalism, and the Second Coming of the Saviour in the Social Revolution!

CROWD: Hooray! Hooray! Hooray!

DOMINIE: I preach to you Fellow-worker Jesus! Forget Him not in this your time of trial, for He is here tonight among you. All that you have borne, He bore' all that you hate, He hated—He scourged it with whips from His holy temple! All that you have borne, He bore; all that you hate, He hated—He scourged it with whips from His holy temple! All that you love, He loved—He was the brother of the humble and the lowly! Like you, fellow-Wobblies, He faced the cruel power of the money-masters! Like you, He was scourged by the hired soldiery of a predatory class! Like you, He was thrown into prison! Like the best of your glorious martyrs,

He died in anguish, that mankind might be free from the enslavement of Mammon!

ALL: Hooray! Hooray! (*While the crowd yells, the* DOMINIE *fishes out with some difficulty from under his long clerical coat a snowy linen handkerchief and mops the perspiration from his brow.*)

VOICES: (*From the rear tank*) You'll lose your job if you talk like that!

DOMINIE: I've lost it already!

RED: Come join the Wobblies!

JOE GUNTHER: We'll pay you a living wage.

DOMINIE: (*With a touch of melancholy*) Ah, boys, I have no delusions on that score. I have lived in the world, and learned its temptations. I like my muffins toasted just right. I like my beefsteak properly turned. I like clean linen and polished silver. But more than all these things I like the salvation of my soul!

THE CROWD: Hooray! Hooray!

DOMINIE: (*Raises his voice again, to reach the crowd outside; he speaks with the gestures of a trained pulpit orator, and in tones of especial solemnity.*) Once more a new religion is born into the world—a new church is founded—a new covenant is sealed with the blood of holy martyrs! Stand firm, Industrial Workers of the World! Stand firm for the rights of the toilers, and against the might of the exploiters! Know that every tear you shed is sacred, that every drop of blood from your veins is caught in a heavenly chalice, and serves to fructify the future of the human race!

THE CROWD: Hooray! Hooray! Hooray! (*As the tumult mounts, the* CHIEF OF POLICE *enters hurriedly at the end of the corridor, followed by the police officer and the jailer.*)

DOMINIE: (*Paying no attention to the* CHIEF) Fellow-workers in the Vineyard of the Lord, the time of the promised harvest draws nigh! The cries of the afflicted have mounted up to the ears of the Lord God of Sabbath—

CHIEF: Well, well, Dominie—you're getting in your spiel after all!

DOMINIE: (*Still paying no attention to him*) The salvation of the workers is promised! The people's hour draws nigh—

THE PRISONERS: Hooray! Hooray! Hooray!

CHIEF: (*To* JAILER) Open HER up! (*To* DOMINIE) We'll have to move you away from the windows, Dominie—

DOMINIE: (*Louder than ever*) Stand firm for the workers! Bow not to the servants of Satan!

THE PRISONERS: (*Shaking their fists at the police*) We'll stand! We'll stand! (JAILER *opens door, while policeman stands with club, as before.*)

CHIEF: Come on out! (*They pull* DOMINIE *from the tank, then close door with a clang; the officer leads him down the corridor, while he continues to orate at the top of his voice.*) In the name of God the Father, I denounce this torture of His children! In the name of the God the Son, I denounce this unchristian brutality! In the name of God the Holy Ghost—

THE PRISONERS: Shame! Shame! Hooray for the Dominie! Down with the cops! Spit on them! Hooray! Hooray! (*The* DOMINIE *is escorted off by the officer; the prisoners sing.*)

> Solidarity forever!
> Solidarity forever!
> Solidarity forever!
> And the Union makes us strong!

THE CHIEF: (*Stands waiting until they finish*) Now, boys, I have something to say to you!

PRISONERS: Go to hell! Shut your dirty mouth! Get out, you fat prostitute! Brig us our supper! Ya! Ya! Ya!

CHIEF: (*Shouting*) We're going to have order in this jail!

PRISONERS: To hell with your order! Come make it if you can! Give us some air in here! Give us your grub! Shut your mouth, you bloody bastard! (*A storm of yells, hisses and curses*)

THE CHIEF: (*With sudden decision*) All right, if you will have it. (*To* JAILER) Shut the windows; every damn one. (*The* JAILER *proceeds to slam down windows along the corridor, left.*)

PRISONERS: What's that? Jesus Christ, they're goin' to shut out the air! The murderers! They're goin' to suffocate us! The dirty hounds! The sons o'guns! Damn your soul! Ya! Ya! Ya!

CHIEF: Will you listen to me now? (*A partial silence*) We are going to have order in this jail. Make up your minds quick, for it won't take you more than three minutes to use up the air in this place. When you're ready to behave, you can have the windows open; but you'll have no more air to sing with, and no more to curse with.

PRISONERS: To hell with you! We'll sing! We'll sing all we please! We'll die before we'll quit! Take your lousy face out of here! Crook! Scab! Gashound!

THE CHIEF: All right, if you want to fight it out!

RED: (*Shaking fist at* CHIEF) Fellow-workers! Fellow-workers! Here is our chance to win the strike! They mean to break our spirit. We'll take up the challenge. We'll nail the I.W.W. preamble to the wall!

ALL: We will! We will!

RED: We'll die singing for Solidarity! It will be another Black Hole of

Calcutta! It will mean the end of the boss-class in California! It will make the One Big Union! It will win the strike! Will we stick?

ALL: We'll stick! We'll stick!

RED: Sing, you jailbirds! Sing while there's life in us! (*He sings*)

We speak to you from jail today,
Six hundred union men—

ALL: (*Taking up the song*)

We're here because the bosses' laws
Bring slavery again.
In California's darkened dungeons
For the O.B.U.
Remember you're outside for us
While we're in here for you.

(*While this is going on the* CHIEF OF POLICE *signs to the* JAILER, *who opens the door of the tank again. The* CHIEF *pulls* RED ADAMS *out. The* JAILER *locks door again.*)

CHIEF: We'll give you a few days in the hole, my lad.

RED: (*Shouts*) Three cheers for the One Big Union! (*The* CHIEF *strikes* RED *and knocks him down. A shriek of fury from the cells.*)

ALL: Ah, you brute! You dirty dog! Shame! Hit a helpless man! Thug! Bully! Coward! Ya! Ya! Ya! (*As* RED *staggers to his fee, the* CHIEF *seizes him, twists his arm behind his back, and pushes him down the corridor, followed by* JAILER) Hit a fellow your size! Stick it out, Red! He'll pay for it! We'll stand by you!

JOE GUNTER: (*As the* CHIEF, *the* JAILER, *and* RED *go off*) Sing, you jailbirds! Sing! (*He begins*)

We come from mine and mill and rail—

ALL: (*Taking up the song*)

We come from off the sea,
From coast to coast we make the boast
Of Solidarity.
In California's darkened dungeons
For the O.B.U.
Remember you're outside for us
While we're in here for you!

(*Voices begin to falter at the end.*)

JOE GUNTER: Keep it up! Keep it up!

PETE: How can we sing without air!

JERRY: We gotta sing!

MATT: Jesus feller, I'm dyin' in here!

JOE: We all got to die—what the hell?

PETE: (*Begins to shove*) Lemme git near them bars!

JERRY: Stay where you are! What's the diff?

JOE: Lay down there!

PETE: How can I lay when there ain't no room!

MATT: Oh! My God!

JOE: Sing, you jailbirds Sing! (*He begins*)

In the prison cell we sit,
And we broken-hearted—nit!
We're as happy and as cheerful as can be.

(*Others take up the song, but feebly; the men are seen to be wilting, hanging on to the bars.*)

For we know that every wob
Will be busy on the job,
Till they swing the prison doors and set us free.

(*While some are singing, others are trying to force their way to the door; there is a general pushing and milling about.*)

JERRY: Stay still, fellers, fer God's sake!

PETE: Jesus, I'm drippin' wet!

JOE: Don't let them beat us! Stand by your guns! Sing! (*He sings*)

Are you busy, fellow-workers?
Are your shoulders to the wheel?

(*The tune is kept up, feebly and quaveringly, by the few nearest to the bars.*)

Get together for the cause
And some day you'll make the laws;
It's the only way to make the masters squeal!
Though the living is not grand,
Mostly mush and "coffee and,"
It's as good as we expected when we came,
It's the way they treat the slave
In this free land of the brave,
There is no one but the working class to blame.

(*Gradually the men sink into heaps; the last words are sung in a faint whisper by half a dozen men clinging to the bars and gazing through with tortured faces.*)

CHORUS
Are you busy, fellow-workers,
Are your shoulders to the wheel?
Get together for the cause
And some day you'll make the laws;
It's the only way to make the masters squeal.

CURTAIN

The audience sings:

I'm as mild manner'd man as can be,
And I've never done them harm that I can see.
Still on me they put a band and they threw me in the can'
They go wild, simply wild, over me.
They accuse me of ras—cal—I—ty,
But I can't see why they always pick on me.
I'm as gentle as a lamb, but they take me for a ram;
They go wild, simply wild over me.
Oh! The "bull" he went wild over me,
And he held his gun where everyone could see;
He was breathing rather hard when he saw my union card—
He went wild, simply wild, over me.
Then the judge he went wild over me,
And I plainly saw we never would agree.
So I let the man obey what his conscience had to say;
He went wild, simply wild over me.
Oh! The jailer went wild over me,
And he locked me up and threw away the key—
It seems to be the rage so they keep me in a cage;
They go wild, simply wild, over me.
They go wild, simply wild, over me.
(I'm referring to the bed-bug and the flea.)
They disturb my slumber deep and I murmur in my sleep;
They go wild, simply wild, over me.
Even God, he went wild over me;
This I found out when I knelt upon my knee.
Did he hear my humble yell? No, he told me, "Go to hell";
He went wild, simply wild, over me.

Will the roses grow wild over me
When I'm gone to the land that is to be?
When my soul and body part in the stillness of my heart—
Will the roses grow wild over me?

Act 2

Scene 1: In the Hole.

A solitary cell, deep in the basement of the jail. The cell stands at the front of stage, center; it is eight feet wide and the balance of the stage is covered by curtains. One wall of the cell is missing, and through the missing wall the audience looks into the cell. The two side-walls of the cell open fan-wise towards the audience, so that all may see into the cell; also the roof of the cell slopes upward, so that those in the gallery may see in. The far wall of the cell, opposite to the audience, contains a sheet-steel door with two holes, one near the bottom of the door and the other near the top, each about two inches in diameter. There is a sliding device at the bottom of the door, which can be opened to admit of objects being shoved into the cell. When the door is opened, we see a narrow corridor, by which the jailer comes to the cell, his coming being heralded by the clang of a distant corridor door. There is a dim electric light with switch-button in the corridor, and the jailer switches this on and we see the light through the two round holes. When the jailer leaves the corridor, he switches out this light, leaving the cell in total darkness. The scene is then played in darkness until RED ADAMS *in his imaginings and dreams, leaves the cell, and we follow him to the outside world. As preliminary to this, the side curtains, the walls, door and roof of cell go up out of sight, so that when the light begins to appear there is no trace of the cell, but instead we are in the world of* RED*'s memories and visions.*

There is frequent return from these imaginary scenes to the reality of the solitary cell. When that change takes place, the light fades, and the side curtains and cell return to place, with RED *inside. It should be noted that the cell and the corridor occupy but a small portion of the stage, in front. The dream-scenes are set in the back portions of the stage, so that quick changes from one to the other are possible.*

At rise: The cell and corridor are empty; the cell door is open, and the light in the corridor is on. After a pause the clang of a corridor door is heard, then footsteps, and the JAILER *appears at the door of the cell, escorting* RED, *battered and bloody. The* JAILER, *without speaking, shoves him into the cell, closes door, locks it, and closes slide at bottom of door. The footsteps of the* JAILER *are heard down the corridor, the light is switched off, and the clang of the corridor door is heard. Then darkness and a long silence.*

RED: By God, I'm in for it! It's my turn! (*Slowly, in frightened voice*) All the times I spent imagining it—and here I am! Yes—he said he was going to break me. So I got it to do; I got to stick it out! You think it's some other guy! But you never thought it would be you—Red Adams! Like when you think about dying; others die, but you have the luck! Yes, old sport, don't fool yourself—they're not going to let you out of here in a hurry. This is the real thing! This is *it*!

(*With frequent pauses*)

In the hole! Dark as hell, not a sound, bread and water once a day, and nobody speaks to you! Not a damn thing to do, not a damn thing to think about! But you'll stick it, all right! What else can you do? You're here! They do it to you, and you got to stand it!

(*Silence*)

Gee, but my nose hurts! That old son of a monster must have broke it! And now it'll heal crooked. But what's it matter? If a man's going to die, why bother about his nose? The worms make all noses the same. A busted bone in a skull, buried in the ground, somewhere nobody knows! God, but life is queer! I could duck this trouble in a few minutes by biting an artery in my wrist. Where'd I be then? Maybe I'd have more troubles! Maybe the Shipowners' Association is running the next world, too! But I don't want to kill myself. No, I shan't give them that satisfaction. Christ A'mighty—men have done it, why can't I? Show 'em my nerve is better than theirs! Stick, till the boys outside make noise enough, and they have to give me a chance. Sure, that's what I'll do! I'll beat them! Sing, you jailbird, sing!

(*Sings in a feeble voice*)

In California's darkened dungeons
For the O.B.U.
Remember you're outside for us
While we're in here for you.

Gee, it's lonesome, singing by yourself. But that's one of the ways to keep my mind busy; sing all the songs I can remember, and maybe make up some new ones. I wonder if I could write a song! That would be a joke on them—write something that would get the boys going, give the movement a boost! The poet is born, not made. Sure, but who knows when he's born, or how? We've had some prison poets, real ones—like Joe Hill. And now Red Adams! Gee, I'm beginning to get nutty already! Sing, you jailbird, and cheer yourself up!

(*Sings*)

Solidarity forever!
Solidarity—

(*He stops abruptly.*)

Say, that sounds too funny. I'll have to put it off a bit. But I'm sticking pretty good, so far. Jesus, I wonder what the boys are doing. I wonder if they've opened those windows. The dirty skunks, would they dare let a whole crowd suffocate to death? No, that would make too much fuss. But they get things their own way more and more-they'll do anything pretty soon. God knows, it's raw enough to bury a man alive like this. It seems enough, if you're the man!

(*A pause*)

Well, here I am. Let's see what I got. Something to pass a couple of minutes, anyhow! Stone walls—

(*He pounds with his fist.*)

Good and solid! Three walls, and a steel door.

(*Shakes the door*)

Stay here, all right. And what do they give you for air? A hole near the top —two inches square. Another near the bottom—scientific ventilation! And some kind of a slide here, where they shove in the grub, I guess. Don't have to open the door at all! Seems tight. I suppose it's bolted outside. Well, I won't spend my time planning to escape. I can't bite stone and mortar— nor butt it with my busted nose. I got to beat them with my mind! Yep, that's the job, old sport; and you can set about it whenever you get ready. Plenty of time—no particular hurry! Tomorrow will do—only you won't know when tomorrow is. (*A pause*) Nothing to do but think! I wonder if a fellow could think everything—or if there's always something else. I'll find out a bit about the human mind; this psychology bunk they sell to poor suckers. I might get interested if this nose would stop hurting—and my head, and my arm that the old son of a monster nearly twisted off. Well—

(*The corridor door is heard to clang.*)

Somebody coming? Do I get out so quick?

(*The light is switched on, and the slide in bottom of the door is unbolted and pushed back. It is the jailer, who shoves in an empty slop-pail and then closes and bolts slide and goes off, switching out light and relocking door of corridor. Silence.*)

A present, hey? Slop-pail, by the stink. Say, that's swell! All modern conveniences! Hotel Biltmore! But I'd rather had a pail of water. That ought to come first. Well, I suppose I drink tomorrow. They'll come once a day and I'll count the days—if I can manage to remember them. That'll be something to work at. I remember the guy in the dungeon that made friends with a spider. Maybe there's one here, but I won't know it unless he bites me. They're rougher than in the old days—they don't give us light enough for spiders! I suppose that jailer isn't going to speak to me.

Well, I'll play the game—by God, he'll never get a moan out of me. Not unless I go crazy—and I'll try not to do that. I got to stick, for the sake of the boys. Yes, fellow-workers, they never broke Red Adams—he never squealed, he stood the gaff! When they had him in the hole, he sang—

(*Feebly*)

Solidarity forever!
Solidarity forever!
Solidarity forever!
And the Union makes us strong!

(*A silence*)

I got to figure out the way to live. Bread and water—they'll tend to that part. And sleep—I'll do lots of sleeping. But no blankets, and a stone floor —I suppose that means rheumatism. Exercise—let's see; this hole will be about eight feet long and five feet wide. Seven feet high, I guess.

(*He paces back and forth.*)

Three steps one way and three back—one, two, three—one, two, three—one, two, three. Not much exercise in that. Four steps from corner to corner—that's better—one, two, three, four—one, two, three, four—one, two, three, four. Who was that fellow wrote a poem about a man walking up and down in a cell? Dome Dago name, I remember. I can make it five steps by bringing up my other foot each time; that makes it seem like more—one, two, three, four, five. Jesus, that would drive me crazy if I did it very much! I remember that old tiger in the zoo! I'll have to find something that wild beasts don't do!

(*A pause*)

Seven feet high; I can't swing my arms up, but I can exercise them with the elbows crooked—up, down—up, down—up, down. I can work out body exercises—that part'll be all right. Only the air; there isn't going to be air enough in here for exercise. I must breathe in at the bottom hole, and breathe out at the top—that's scientific.

(*Breathing and stooping slowly*)

Up-down! Up-down! Up-down! That's the stunt! Only—what sort of air have they got out in the corridor? I heard the jailer lock that door—maybe it's tight. But no—that couldn't be, nobody could live that way. They've been fellows in here, lots of times before. That's something to think about—all the poor guys that have suffered here. Christ, they've done just what I'm doing—walking up and down counting their steps, thinking they were tigers; worrying about the air, feeling the cold floor, getting the rheumatism, kicking the damned slop-pail.

(*Gives the pail a kick*)

Poor fellow-worker slop-pail! A real manly, satisfying form of self-expression!

(*A pause*)

Yes, they're bound to have been in here—Wobblies, too! Maybe there's more cells, with some of the boys in now. They might be near!

(*Shouts*)

Boys! Boys!

(*Waits, then louder*)

Hello! Fellow-workers!

(*Silence*)

Nix on the society stuff. I remember reading about the dungeons of the tsar. They used to make tapping noises on the water pipes, and they worked out a telegraph code, and could talk all day. But I got no pipes here. I wonder if I could knock on the walls. The slop-pail! A fancy telegraph key!

(*He knocks three times with the pail, then listens, then knocks again.*)

Nobody home in Western Union! Maybe they're asleep. I haven't been in here long enough for it to be a day. I'll try that tapping off and on. When you're in solitary, you don't mind doing the same things over and over, thinking the same thoughts over and over.

(*A sudden hysterical outburst*)

Oh, my God! Let me out of here! I can't stand it—I'll go crazy, sure as fate! Jesus, you got no right to shut a fellow up like he was a beast! Let me go, I tell you! Take me where the others are!

(*He sobs.*)

I'll quit! I'll be good! Whatever you want—only I can't stay alone in the dark! Oh, it's too much! It's hell!

(*Frantic sobbing; then silence*)

Ah, you dirty cur! So that's all you amount to! Half an hour—maybe not that long, and you show the white feather. Yes, you'll lick their boots; you'll crawl on your knees to them! Maybe they got a spy watching—maybe he's gone now to tell the 'Cutor!

(*Imitates voice of* DISTRICT ATTORNEY)

So, Red, you've had enough! I thought you'd listen to reason after a bit!

(*Shouts*)

No, no! Damn your dirty souls—not while I live! Not while I've got the breath to curse you! I nail the I.W.W. preamble to the wall!

(*Laughing*)

No, Mr. 'Cutor, have another guess! Just a little joke that time! Thought I'd come out for a few minutes, to see if my nose was on straight! Yes, sure, I like it fine in my new lodgings—quiet neighborhood, and the rent's cheap!

(*A pause*)

Gee, I'm getting off my nut! That's always the trouble with me—too doggone much imagination. Mind works too fast. Why do I always have to be stewing inside—reading books, thinking things, arguing at the scissor-bills, making speeches, organizing? Why couldn't I be a regular bindle-stiff—carry my blanket, do my ten hours, hold my damned tongue, never mind the bugs in the beds and the weevils in the flour? Yes, Mr. 'Cutor, it's true. I've been one. I've argued and sassed the boss—raised Cain when the pay envelope was wrong. I'm made that way; I got a mind—yes, and I got it right here in the cell with me—the only thing I have got! By God, that's the problem—to save my mind, learn how to use it. What's that poet say:

> Stone walls do not a prison make,
> Nor iron bars a cage.
> They got my body here, but they haven't got my soul.

(*With excitement*)

Yes, get hold of that! Get it straight! That's the key to the problem—that's the way out! They can do what they please to my body, but they haven't got the real me—they can't touch that! They've no control of what I think, what I really am! I'm free—I've got the whole world for company! And I don't have to be afraid of them! I don't have to sit here, moaning in a hole, going crazy! I'm the master—nobody else! I wave my hand and the walls are gone. I go laughing, singing! I travel on wings of thought, I'm free—I'm free!

(*The cell, curtains and corridor go up in the darkness.*)

No, Mr. 'Cutor—I'm not your slave; you can't hold me in solitary! I've got friends that love me, and won't desert me. Yes—Jake Apperson, if you ask me! Jake's out of jail—Jake's on the job, for me and the whole Wobbly bunch, like he always was! Jake! Jake! Where are you?

(*Light begins to appear*)

Scene 2: A Restaurant for Workingmen

In the back part of the stage, to the left, is a lunch counter, with stools for four customers. To the right of this is an oil-cloth covered, table, with chairs for six customers. Entrance at the left.

As the light appears, three men are eating at the counter, their backs to the audience. ONE LUNG, *the Chinese proprietor, in soiled white apron, stands behind the counter, facing the audience. He and the customers are in shadow; the light brings out the center of the stage, where* JAKE APPERSON *stands—a six-foot lumberman, fair-haired, florid, jovial, a fellow to lean on; he wears a startled look, hearing the call of* RED ADAMS, *who is on the same spot where he lay when in the cell.*

RED: Jake! Jake!

JAKE: Who calls! Who's that? Red Adams, by God! (*Starts to him; they clasp one another.*)

RED: You old fuzzy-tail! (*Holds him at arm's length, stares at him in rapture, then hugs him again*)

JAKE: You old ding-bat!

RED: You old jungle-buzzard!

JAKE: You old scissor-bill!

RED: You old ho-atzin!

JAKE: Ho-atzin! What the hell?

RED: I read about 'em in a book—they're a bird!

JAKE: You're a bird—you red-head woodpecker!

RED: A woodpecker with a busted nose! Jake! Jake! I'm sure glad to see you! You're out again?

JAKE: Sure, they can't ever hold me!

RED: It hasn't hurt you either!

JAKE: I get fat on it! The workingman's rest-cure!

RED: Jake! They thought they had me in the hole! But I got away, too!

JAKE: They can't dig the holes deep enough for us Wobblies!

RED: (*His voice breaking suddenly*) Jake, hang on to me—I don't want to go back! Hold me tight, old pal! (*Clasps him again*)

JAKE: By heck, we're the original Siamese twins! One Lung, bring me a hammer, I'll nail his hoofs to the floor! (*Full light on the whole scene.* ONE LUNG, *behind his counter, grinning with pleasure*)

RED: One Lung! Say, old Chink! You remember me?

ONE LUNG: Su', lemember. Led Adam.

RED: (*Grabbing his hand*) You Celestial hash-slinger!

ONE LUNG: Good boy, Led Adam.

RED: (*To Jake*) Where's the gang?

JAKE: They're coming. We'll have an old-time feed this night! You got some grub, One Lung?

ONE LUNG: Plenty glub! All kind glub! Ham an' egg, hamblugg steak, fly fish, macaloni—hot allee samee hell. (*The door opens and* JOE GUNTHER, PETE, JERRY *and* MATT *enter.*)

JAKE: Here's the gang!

RED: Fellow-workers!

ALL: Red! It's Red Adams! (*They fall upon him, slap him, pound him, with laughter and shouts of greeting.*) Hurrah! Old red-head! Welcome to Chinatown! When did you blow in? What's the good word? (*They clasp hands and dance a fantastic caper, singing to the tune of "Steamboat Bill".*)

Scissor Bill, he is a little dippy;
Scissor Bill, he has a funny face;
Scissor Bill should drown in Mississippi.
He is the missing link that Darwin tried to trace.

(*They grab* ONE LUNG *and the three customers from the lunch counter, all dance and sing.*)

Hallelujah! I'm a bum!
Hallelujah, bum again!
Hallelujah, give us a handout
To revive us again!
Now why don't you work like other men do?
How the hell can I work when there's no work to do?
Hallelujah! I'm a bum!
Hallelujah, bum again!
Hallelujah, give us a handout
To revive us again!

JAKE: Fellow-workers, I'm just one big hole inside!

JOE: We'll have chow.

JERRY: We'll clean the old Chink out! (*A general rush for the table*)

JAKE: (*Parodying song*) We'll have pie—not bye and bye!

JOE: We'll have pie—if the Chink don't lie!

ONE LUNG: Chink no lie! Chink come along! (*He rushes to get food; they pound on the table with knives and forks.*)

JAKE: Fly fish for me!

JOE: Hamblugg steak, that's mine!

MATT: Macaloni! You got macaloni?

JERRY: Hot allee samee hell!

ONE LUNG: One Lung quick! (*He comes running with tray containing bread, butter and glasses of water.*)

JAKE: One Lung, I'm busted. You trust me?

ONE LUNG: Su', plenty tlust!

JAKE: Why you trust me?

ONE LUNG: You wobble-wobble!

JAKE: How you say I.W.W.?

ONE LUNG: I-Wobble-Wobble. (*They all laugh.*)

JAKE: Try again: W

ONE LUNG: Wobble. (*They laugh.* ONE LUNG *hurries back to get more food.*)

JAKE: Say, boys, you know that old Chink made a new word in the language. He made the name "Wobblies."

MATT: Come off!

JAKE: Sure thing! You hear him—he can't say the letter W.

MATT: But was that what began it?

JAKE: Sure as I'm here! Us boys took up the Chink's word; we got to calling ourselves Wobblies when we came here to a meal. In the big strike I telegraphed to Chicago—send a bunch of Wobblies that can be trusted. When the bulls raided us and went through our files they got that telegram, and me and the 'Cutor had a session on the subject of secret codes! A deadly mystery—was a Wobbly a dynamiter, or was he a gunman? Did he cause bank-safes to wobble, or did he cause the government to wobble? Holy Christ, he spent an hour trying to get it out of me—and next day the newspapers spread the mystery to the whole world, and Wobblies we've been ever since! (ONE LUNG *comes with more food.*)

JOE: You trust me?

ONE LUNG: (*Grins*) Su'! Tlust you.

JERRY: You trust me?

ONE LUNG: Tlust all I-Wobble-Wobble. (*They laugh.*)

JAKE: You belong I-Wobble-Wobble?

ONE LUNG: Me belong cook.

JAKE: You cook for I-Wobble-Wobble?

ONE LUNG: Su' cook! Good glub quick! (*He hurries to get more food.*)

JOE: (*Pounds on the table*) Hurrah for the Wobblies!

JERRY: We'll wobble on the job!

JAKE: (*Noticing* RED *who has sunk into silence*) Red, what's the matter with you? You haven't ordered anything.

RED: (*Looking dazed*) Boys, I hate to spoil the sport—but I—I don't think I can eat.

JAKE: Why not?

RED: I'm not really here, you know. I'm just dreaming all this. The truth is, they've got me in the hole on bread and water. (*He rises and begins to walk back to forth.*) One, two, three, four. One, two, three, four. One, two, three, four.

JOE: (*Looks at him anxiously*) Aw, fergit it! You're dippy, Red!

JAKE: Cheer up, boy! (*As* ONE LUNG *comes with tray of food and begins to set it before them*) Have some macaloni!

JOE: Hot allee samee hell! (*Brings him a steaming plate*)

RED: (*Earnestly*) Fellow-workers, you don't understand. I'm not here, I tell you—I'm just fooling myself. And you can pretend all right with songs and jokes and things like that, but when it comes to food—by God, its got to be real food!

JOE: The hell you say!

JAKE: Of course you're here!

RED: I'm in the hole! I can't eat any real food—I only get bread and water. I'm near crazy with pain—my nose is broke and my arm is twisted.

JAKE: (*Puts arm about him*) Poor old kid. They've got his nerve!

JOE: Cheer him up boys! He needs a good rebel song!

ALL: (*Shouting*)

You'll have pie
When you die,
In that glorious land above the sky!
Work and pray,
Live on hay,
You'll have pie in the sky when you die!

RED: (*His heart-broken tones*) Fellow-workers, they've got me! I'm done for this time for sure!

JAKE: Listen, old pal! Look what I've been through—and I always come out cheerful!

RED: I know, Jake; but in my case—

JAKE: Look inside your soul! Look at the movement! It's growing! Think of the rebel workers. They love you and need you! (*Leads him away from the table towards the audience; the light gradually fades from the table and the lunch-counter)* See here, Red, there's something wrong with you. I mean—not just this business about your being in the hole. I've watched you for a long time. You're melancholy, kid. You've got something on your conscience. Let's you and me have it out. You know, we've talked about it before. (*Puts his arm about* RED) Look here pal—it's a mistake to waste yourself. It's not fair to the movement—the others need your strength.

RED: Yes, Jake; but what can I do?

JAKE: Is it something you're afraid will be found out?

RED: No, it can't be found out—never in this world.

JAKE: Hell! Is it the next world you're worrying about? The sky-pilot's been scaring you?

RED: Nothing so silly.

JAKE: Well, boy, why worry? The man don't live that hasn't done things he's ashamed of. You can't undo them; put your old forgetter to work!

RED: Jake, you can't understand about this—

JAKE: Why can't I? Because you won't tell me.

RED: (*Withdrawing*) I just couldn't talk about it!

JAKE: (*Holding on to him*) Come on, old pal—have it out, and you'll feel like you've coughed up an alligator.

RED: I can't tell it!

JAKE: Red, you know I'm your friend!

RED: No man ever had a better.

JAKE: Is it some guy you bumped off? Christ, old man, in this world we're in don't they bump us off whenever they feel like it?

RED: No, Jake, not that.

JAKE: Well, what then?

RED: Jake, I had a wife. And I loved her—oh God, we were so happy. And then—she died—

JAKE: I know that. A long time ago, wasn't it?

RED: Four years. But it seems like it was yesterday. And it was my fault! You see—(*Starts away*) Jake, I can't talk about it! It almost kills me to remember! No, I don't belong, I can't stay with a happy bunch, with fellows who have no dead love. I got to go back to the hole—on bread and water! That damn black hole where there's nothing but the past to think of. (JAKE *steps backwards, with hands outstretched, fading into the darkness. The light dies on the scene.*) I can't stand it, on account of the pain. I'm going mad—I've got too many dreadful things in my head, things I can't face, I can't think about! Christ, what a life the world gives the poor devils who do its dirty work! And the wives of workingmen—that bear too many children and are poor and ignorant! (*The cell and curtains return to place;* RED *lies on the floor, moaning faintly.*) They begin as young girls, happy and innocent. Beautiful things, gentle, tender, quivering with life—how can they know what's coming to them—the horrors piled on horrors? Oh, Nell, Nell, you ought never have married any workingman! (*In a louder voice*) No woman should marry a workingman! No woman should bear a child in poverty! (*His voice drops low.*) Nell, why didn't you marry a rich guy? Why didn't you climb up and live on us poor stiffs—drink our blood and get fat—take our sweat and tears, and make pearls and diamonds of them, and wear them round your neck and in your ears! (*A pause*) I'm getting loony. I believe! I ought to go to sleep instead of lying here torturing my mind—trying to pretend I'm outside, having supper at One Lung's! How little you appreciate things while they're here! And how you do miss 'em when they're gone! A meal at that old Chink's! I-Wobble-Wobble! (*A pause*) God, my nose is swelled as big as my face. I wonder if it's going bad—gangrene, or something like that. I suppose I had a bit of fever—thought I was outside, sure enough! Only I couldn't pretend it was real grub; and I couldn't talk to Jake about Nell! (*He calls loudly.*) Nell, Nell! (*A pause*) What's happened to you since you died? I couldn't believe you were really gone. That you could fade away, body and soul—everything that used to be so real—your mind, your voice, your face—just go to pieces, disappear! If there's anything left of you, where is it? Do you know what's happening to me? You couldn't stand it if you did—surely you'd find some way to come to me, to talk to me, help me out! I could always stand things, so long as I had you! Oh, Nell, I'm so miserable! I daren't admit it to myself—but I'd tell you, my love, my blessed one! Nell, Nell! (*A faint light appears.*)

Scene 3: In the Hole.

(NELL *stands near the door, looking down at* RED; *a young woman with pale, gentle face, slender figure, wearing a faded calico dress.* RED *manifests no surprise, but takes her presence for granted.*)

RED: Ah, Nell, you knew how I loved you! But I think of all the chances I had, the times when I might have told you more! Then I think—no, I loved you too much! That was the trouble—love isn't for working people! We're too cheap, we have too many troubles, we can't afford fancy feelings! Sweetheart, where have you been hiding? (*She kneels beside him and takes his hand.*) Ah, if you'd only stay with me, Nell!

NELL: I've come to stay, Red.

RED: Here? In this cell?

NELL: Yes, here! We can always be together here—nothing can tear us apart.

RED: Kiss me, Nell!

NELL: (*Bending over him*) Dearest, truest heart!

RED: I try to be true, Nell, but I find I'm a coward. A wretched one—you've no idea!

NELL: No one else will ever have an idea, Red!

RED: Imagine, calling on you for help!

NELL: Who else should help you? Didn't I always try to?

RED: Ah, Nell, if I could only forget what happened!

NELL: I tell you to forget it, Red. It wasn't your fault! You did nothing but what I made you do. I loved you—I craved your love! You've no right to blame yourself. Don't you know, when things happen like that, it's the woman's fault as much as the man's?

RED: Ah, yes, I try to make excuses for myself—

NELL: Tell yourself that everything's different now. We belong to each other, there are no longer any penalties of love. Here in jail we can be happy—even poor working people, that can't afford to have children—that can't pay the doctor's bills, or buy food in the real world. (*With rising intensity*) Oh, Red, I never thought it would be so nice in jail. This is the one free place—the wage-slave's heaven! Dreams are free—joy and peace! You can have me, Red, without fear! I'll stay with you, day and night—just us two, with everybody else locked out! The world is in jail, Red—in a dungeon of greed and hate; the world is mad, while you and I are free and happy! You and I have love!

RED: (*Raises himself and clasps her in her arms*) Oh, my beautiful one! My darling!

NELL: Tell me that you want me to stay!

RED: I love you! I love you with all my heart and soul—dear, brave, blessed one—my sweet, good wife!

NELL: Press me to your heart! Tell me again! No woman ever hears it enough!

RED: I love you! I love you!

NELL: Kiss me! Kiss me, dear heart! (*Gradually the light fades*) My love! My love! My precious man! (*Their voices die away; faint violin strains, the Barcarolle from the "Tales of Hoffman."*)

CURTAIN

NELL's *voice sings to the above melody, the tribute by* Gerald Lively *to* FRANK LITTLE, *the* I.W.W. *martyr:*

> You've fought your fight, a long good night
> Is all that we can say.
> Sleep on, sleep on, your work is done,
> Brave fighter for the Day.
> Kind Mother Earth, who gave you birth,
> Receives you to her breast.
> For us the fight, for you the night,
> The night of well-earned rest;
> No more you'll feel the cling of steel,
> You've burst the prison bars,
> You gave your life in this our strife,
> Brave conqueror of stars.
> Sleep on, sleep on, your work is done,
> Sleep on, sleep on, sleep on.

Act 3

Scene 1: In the Hole.

At rise: RED *is in darkness, taking exercise.*

RED: (*Slowly*) Up—down! Up—down! Up—down! Up—down! Up—down! Up—down! Up—down! Up—down!

(*A pause*)

Well, am I tired yet? I never know if I'm tired, or only bored. A man wants sure enough will-power to keep at work for nothing. I can't ever decide if the air I get through that hole is better than what's in here. It don't smell any better, that's sure. But when I stoop down and rise up, I exercise my stomach muscles, and that helps to keep your bowels active, so they say. But hell, what can you expect, when you get nothing to eat but white bread? You expect just what I've got—a headache like my skull was split. All right, Nell, old girl, I promised I'd stick; I'm taking care of myself, the best I know. Now for the chest muscles. Arms front—arms back! One—two, one—two, one—two, one—two—

(*He exercises vigorously, so that his breath comes hard.*)

But maybe I oughtn't to do that! If I use up the air in here, I'm only the worse off. No, there's just one thing—stoop and breathe in at the lower hole—stand up and breathe out at the upper hole. All right, Nell, I'll keep at it! I'll sweat twice every day! Up—down! Up—down! Up—down! Up—

(*The* JAILER *is heard opening door of corridor.*)

My jailer!

(*The light is switched on and the slide is unfastened and pushed back.*)

JAILER: (*Speaking from behind the door in a mechanical tone*) Shove out your slop-pail. (*As* RED *obeys, he shoves in a full pitcher of water and hunk of bread; then the slide is closed and fastened, the light is switched off, and the sound of locking corridor door is heard.*)

RED: Beginning of the fifteenth day. Two weeks! And nothing but bread to eat! One Lung, if you ever put a slice of bread in front of me—I'll make you eat it. Fourteen days! Nell, did I tell you my scheme to make sure of the count? First I made a little pellet from each loaf of bread, and I laid them in a row against the wall. I'd count them whenever I was in doubt. I count them over, every one, apart, my rosary, my rosary! (*In sing-song tone*) Each hour a pearl, each pearl a prayer—

(*His voice breaks*)

No, Nell—I'm not going to go crazy! But you know how it is when I think about the songs you used to sing to me! Well, the reason the bread pellets didn't do for a calendar was because of the rats. The rats ate up my rosary! Now I've another scheme—I ravel out a thread from my shirt; I have a little sheaf of them that I count. I keep wondering—will the rats want them for a nest? Listen, Nell, I can't figure what I'm going to do about this white bread. I don't want to play the baby, but once in the library I read all about it—there's no minerals in white flour, so your teeth rot, your hair drops out, your bones go to pieces. It's scurvy—regular scurvy like the seamen get, that's what this headache means. Oh, what's the use, Nell? Mightn't I just as well die quick and have it over? Then I'd see you—at least so the preachers say. (*Pause*) I could go on a hunger strike—they say you can live a couple of months without anything but water. Wouldn't it be just as good for the cause? I've got to decide, for I'm near crazy as it is. Good God, it sounds so nice and simple—a bread and water diet!

(*In sudden excitement*)

I've got to stop brooding! Yes, that's the dope! Bring on the psychology bunk! I'm giving myself bad suggestions—that's what they call it. It's all right to deal in economics when you're outside, where they count; but when you're in the hole—by God, you're in, and psychology's all you got! So let psychology have a chance! Yes, Nell, you're right. I don't see why those religious guys and Christian Science bunk-shooters should get any favors that I can't get. I'm as worthy as they are. I'm sacrificing life for a cause. I suppose I ought to give that old French guy Coué a chance at me. All right, we'll try that! He says to be monotonous, and by heck, that's made to order for Wobblies in solitary! Come on, Mounseer Coué—here's for a monotonous nap!

(*The cell and curtains go up in the darkness;* RED *begins in a droning voice.*)

I am happy—I am happy—I am happy—I am happy—I am happy—I am happy—I am happy—I am happy! I'm with Nell—I'm with Nell—I'm with Nell—I'm with Nell—I'm with Nell—I'm with Nell—I'm with Nell—I'm with Nell—I'm with Nell! Nell is singing—Nell is singing—Nell is singing—

(*His voice gradually dies away to a murmur; Nell's voice is heard singing, and at the same time light begins to dawn.*)

Scene 2: A California Ranch-house.

The view is of the rear shed; the house itself being painted on the read curtain. A door at the center leads into the house; the shed walls project down stage, the shed being open towards the audience. There are washtubs at one side, a wood-pile at the other, with axe, shovel, hay-rake, buckets and general farm-litter. NELL *is seated in a chair by a tub in the front of the shed bathing a baby; a year old child sleeps in a clothes basket near by.* NELL *wears the same calico dress as in the previous scene, but fresh and bright. It is noon of a summer's day and* RED *is lying asleep on the ground in the sunshine, at the spot formerly occupied by the cell. He is young looking clean and attractive.*

At rise: NELL, *singing:*

The hours I spent with thee, dear heart.
Are as a string of pearls to me.
I count them over every one apart,
My rosary! My rosary!
Each hour a pearl, each pearl a prayer—

RED: (*Opens his eyes and sits up*) I've been asleep!

NELL: And I've been singing you love-songs!

RED: Sleeping like a pig, while you work!

NELL: I don't know who earns a Sunday rest if it isn't you.

RED: There are no Sundays at this ranching game. (*Bitterly*) Go West, young man! Get a stake in Sunny California!

NELL: No grouching, Red! This is God's country!

RED: Yes! The Great Absentee Owner! I was reading in the paper; it said: "Stick something in the ground and watch it grow." Oh, the stuff they feed to us come-ons from the East! Stick to something in the ground, and hold a hose over it the rest of your life!

NELL: We're going to win, Red! We're not going to *think* of quitting!

RED: Yes, dear; but what about the mortgage that falls due in three months?

NELL: We'll find a way! Keep your courage up.

RED: Yes, sweetheart, I know—the psychology bunk. Plenty of that in the paper too. Hold the success thought! But we can't feed these two kids on anybody's thoughts, and if the price of our lettuce and oranges goes on dropping, we'll lose our place at Mother Nature's breast.

NELL: And live in a slum again, Red!

RED: (*Gets up and moves restlessly about*) At least we'll have a bit of cash every Saturday night. Gee, it's a wonder how they get us poor ranchers fixed, Nell. Eggs go to forty cents a dozen—and you can't squeeze one out of your hens. Then, when the price drops to ten cents, the hens take to laying, just to be nasty.

NELL: Well, you can't blame California for that, Red. All hens behave that way.

RED: I know. The small farmer gets it in every part of the country.

NELL: Yes, and it's a good thing to know his side. The farmers and the workingmen have got to get together—

RED: Oh, sure! It's education, all right. Only I'm thinking it's time we got our diploma in poverty. The College of California Agriculture.

NELL: Cheer up, sweetheart. We're poor, but we have each other. Nothin' can take our love from us!

RED: Are you sure, Nell?

NELL: How can you ask?

RED: I find myself wondering—isn't that some more of the bunk they feed us? Can you keep love while you're in terror of starvation? While you're hounded by misery and debt?

NELL: (*Has put dress on the child and lays it in its basket. She leans back in her chair and holds out her hand to* RED, *who comes to her and kneels at her side.*) Dearest, I can't answer for you, but get my side of it clear—nothing the world can do to us is going to make any difference in my love for you.

RED: Oh, it's hell for a woman—to have a man that can't earn a living!

NELL: It's not one bit worse on the woman than it is on the man. Don't you think I read the strain in your face?

RED: Ah, Nell, you're too good for this devil's world!

NELL: I love you, dear.

RED: I ought not to have to be told it; but I see the way it's wearing on you, and it seems too much. I imagine you're growing cold—you keep away from me—

NELL: (*In sudden pain*) Sweetheart! Don't say such words! Surely you know—we can't afford another child!

RED: Yes, I know; but then—

NELL: Ah, my beloved! That's the real agony of my life—that I have to repress and hide my love. It becomes a terror—a flame that threatens to destroy us! I can stand everything else but that! Red, we simply dare not take any chances—if I were to have another baby while we're so near to starving, it would knock us flat—every hope, every chance. So what can I do? I love you—I see how you're tormented! But we must not, *must* not run any risks!

RED: Then it isn't coldness, Nell?

NELL: Sweetheart, how can you ask? There are times when I want to throw caution to the winds. Then I remember these babies that we already have, and what we owe to them! Oh, this curse of poverty! Our little ones must not be forced to endure any more of it. (*Suddenly sobbing*) The world is too cruel, Red!

RED: It isn't the world. It's the damned fools that live in it. We don't need to suffer like this—if only we weren't ignorant. There are ways—

NELL: I've asked every one I know—but they're all guessing, and I daren't trust their guesses.

RED: I talked with the doctor again; begged him to tell me. It was all I could do to keep from cursing him!

NELL: Oh, Red! We may need him again. Please don't quarrel with him.

RED: I ask him how you can keep from having another baby, and he shuts up like a steel trap. He says it's defying the will of the Lord. Be fruitful and multiply! (*Laughs sneeringly*) Sounds like a California booster's club. I said to him: For Christ's sake, man, what does the Lord expect the ranchers to feed the children on? Is it the will of the Lord that lettuce shall drop to forty cents a crate? Is it the will of the Lord to have the orange crop rot under the trees?

NELL: Let's not talk about it! I don't want to hate life entirely. (*She throws herself into his arms, weeping.*) Ah, dearest! Dearest! Life is too terrible!

RED: (*Comforting her*) Kiss me, sweetheart! Kiss me!

NELL: Ah! So long as you love me!

RED: I do love you; I love you more than anything else in the world. (*The light begins to fade; she responds to his embraces, but then, in terror, seeks to withdraw.*)

NELL: No, no! We must be careful! Ah, we must! (*She breaks away and runs from him; the light grows more dim, and she backs away through the door into the house.*)

RED: (*Stands in semi-darkness, alone*) Where am I? Am I dreaming? Was that Nell I had in my arms? I thought I was in the hole! I thought they had me on bread and water! I get things mixed up. I was talking to Nell, and it was day; but now it's night! I thought it was summer-time; but now it's cold! (JAKE APPERSON *enters from right and stands in silence.*) Who's that? Jake! Jake Apperson! I'm dreaming sure! Of course! Or I'm crazy! Why, I never met Jake till after Nell was dead—till I went on the road and turned into a Wobbly! Jake, is that your ghost? No, I'm in the hole. (*Stares hard at ranch-house*) I'm just plain nutty! Well, anyhow, old pal, I'm glad you came. You'll have a chance to meet Nell. My wife, you know. Listen! She's singing!

NELL: (*Heard singing offstage in the rear*)

> The hours I spent with thee, dear heart,
> Are as a string of pearls to me;
> I count them over, everyone apart,
> My rosary, my rosary.

RED: She comes and sings that to me in the hole, Jake. I hear her all the time. I lay on the ground here, listening while she sang it—and it was summer, the sun was shining, and she said she loved me-we forgot our fears, Jake we were happy in our love. Just once, Jake—you know how it is when you're in love. That was last summer, and we thought we were going to get the mortgage renewed on the ranch. Stick something in the ground and watch it grow! That's in my diploma that I got from the College of California Agriculture! (*Laughing wildly*) Nell, Jake, the mortgage on the ranch fell due—three months later; and the mortgage on our love fell due at the same time! First a notice from the bank—we were going to be turned out—we were going back to the slums to live! And then came Nell to me-it was one cold night in the fall— (*His voice rises in a tone of agony.*) Oh, my God, my God, I can see her now as she looked when she ran out here to me—white and terrified—

NELL: (*Calling offstage, in the* rear; *a voice of keen distress*) Red! Red!

RED: (*Turns to the sound anxiously*) Sweetheart! What is it? (*He starts towards the door of house; as he does so,* JAKE *withdraws into the shadows, where he stands watching the scene pitying, but helpless.*)

NELL: (*Appears in doorway of ranch-house, deathly pale and with a look of fear*) Red! Red!

RED: (*Rushes to her*) What's the matter?

NELL: Something horrible—

RED: What do you mean?

NELL: Red, it's happened!

RED: What?

NELL: The thing we said must never happen! Oh, how I hate that doctor! He could have told me!

RED: (*Starts back, whispering*) Oh, my God!

NELL: It's true!

RED: You're sure? Maybe you're wrong on the time.

NELL: I suspected it a month back, but I waited—I didn't want to frighten you. But it's true! (*He moans.*) Listen, Red! There's only one thing to do! I must get rid of it!

RED: No! No! You can't do that!

NELL: I've got to!

RED: It's too dangerous!

NELL: It's no more dangerous than for me to have another baby, and for all of us to starve! (*Hysterically*) Oh, I just can't have another baby! I can't! I can't! And I won't! I'll die first!

RED: Nell! Nell! For God's sake, wait! Give me a moment to think! (*He leans against the side of the shed.*)

NELL: All right! Think! (*She draws back, unnoticed by, him, and darts into the house.*)

RED: (*Alone*) Oh, Christ, have mercy all the poor! We're ruined—we're done for! What can we do now? Another baby! And what's to become of the two we've got? (*A piercing scream from* NELL, *inside the house*) What's that?

NELL: (*Appears in doorway, staggering, half falling*) Help!

RED: (*Leaps to her*) Sweetheart!

NELL: (*Wildly*) I've done it! (*He catches her in his arms.*) Run for help! Call Mrs. Smith! Call the doctor!

RED: What have you done?

NELL: Run! Run! I may die! I had to do it! There was no other way!

RED: Darling—

NELL: I tell you, be quick! Run! (RED *dashes off left; she clutches the wall of the shed for support and sinks gradually to the ground.*) Oh God! God! Such pain! I didn't know it could be! (*She sobs.*)

MRS. SMITH: (*An old country woman, rushes on left*) Child, what's the matter? (*She stoops over* NELL.)

NELL: (*Gasping*) I'm in agony! Oh! Oh! Call the doctor!

MRS. SMITH: He's coming! He was at my house.

NELL: God save me!

MRS. SMITH: Let me help you into the house.

NELL: I can't walk!

MRS. SMITH: I'll carry you. (*She lifts* NELL *to her feet and half carries her into the house; the* DOCTOR *comes running, carrying instrument case; he goes into the house.*)

RED: (*Rushes on the scene distracted; he is about to enter the house. but hearing* NELL'S *screams, he stops, and runs to* JAKE, *distracted*) Jake! Jake! Can't you help her?

MRS. SMITH: (*Appearing at door*) Some water! Water!

RED: (*Rushes to hand her a bucket of water*) Here! Tell me! What's the matter?

MRS. SMITH: Don't ask! Oh, the poor child, she was out of her mind! She's not to blame for it! (*He starts to follow, but she stops him.*) No, stay out! There's nothing you can do! This is woman's trouble. (*She enters house.*)

RED: Woman's trouble! Woman's trouble! (*He stands bewildered, moaning.*) Oh, my darling! My precious Nell! (*He enters through the door;* JAKE *moves to follow him, drawn by irresistible sympathy. But* RED *rushes out again, staggering and cursing.*) Blood! Oh, horrible blood! (*The light upon the scene turns to red. There is a crashing of thunder;* RED *plunges dizzily, and falls. Darkness. The curtains and cell return into position, with* RED *and* JAKE *inside the cell. Silence, then sobbing.*) Oh, Nell, Nell! Where have you gone? Oh, God, such a dream! It was just as real as if I'd been there. It comes like that all the time. I can never forget it. Never, never, never—no matter how I try! You see, Jake, why I couldn't talk about it. You couldn't ask a man to talk about a thing like that, could you, Jake? (*A faint light.*)

Scene 3: In the Hole.

(JAKE APPERSON, *standing in the cell, silent, with a look of pity.* RED, *lying on floor, lifts his gaze to him.*)

RED: Think of it, old man—that night of horror! When a man has seen his wife go like that, can anyone blame him for turning rebel—for hating capitalism, and the world of grafters? Nell wanted her husband—she wanted her child—she wanted life; and she got the most horrible death! That's what poverty is! And I say, God damn a world that stands for poverty! God damn the whole filthy system, masters and henchmen—stool-pigeons spying on wage-slaves, 'cutors throwing men into jail. (*He leaps up wildly; the light fades, and the cell and curtains disappear.* JAKE *goes off.*) I say, God damn that District Attorney! He dared to sneer at my tragedy! He dared to put his filthy hands on my grief—him with his little stenographer and his private room in the road-house, and the woman suing him for damages! (*Faint strains of a jazz orchestra;* RED *raises his voice so as to be heard above it.*) Imagine such as him having the power to put me in the hole! Because I dared to lead a strike and demand a decent life for the working-class! Because I wouldn't sell out to him, and betray my fellow-workers! That's what they call justice in their capitalist world! My Nell dies of an abortion, and my jailer dines in a road-house with his mistress! (*The strains of the orchestra become loud; light appears.*)

Scene 4: A Private Room in a Road-house.

A place of luxury and elegance; a couch against the wall, also a window, at right; an entrance door left; a serving-table against the rear wall. In the center of the room, a table set for two, with hand embroidered linen, silver wine-glasses, orchids, etc. Jazz orchestra heard through the open door.

At rise: The DISTRICT ATTORNEY *and* MURIEL *the stenographer, seated at dinner. She is the blue-eyed, doll-baby "vamp," in extreme décolleté. He is in evening dress, and flushed with wine; a bucket of ice with bottle on the floor by his side. The waiter enters, and with obsequious gestures serves steaming dishes of food.* RED ADAMS, *with tousled hair, torn clothing, battered face and distracted aspect, crouches in the far corner, near the door, watching the scene with eyes of fury. No one pays any attention to him. Elaborate business of serving and enjoying the repast. The scene begins in the spirit of melodrama, it being* RED'*s imagining of the life of the ruling-classes. It becomes more real as it progresses, as if* RED'*s hatred were making a reality of its own.*

MURIEL: (*A gushy voice*) Squabs en casserole! Oh, I adore squabs! Don't you?

DISTRICT ATTORNEY: (*Chewing and beaming at her*) I adore my honey-baby!

MURIEL: (*Pouting*) You old masher! This is a dinner party. Be dignified, now!

DISTRICT ATTORNEY: I'm dignified all day—that's what I'm paid for. Now I want to cuddle with my honey-baby! (*Ogling her.*)

MURIEL: How many people did you convict today?

DISTRICT ATTORNEY: Only a dozen or two. It's our off season.

MURIEL: Oh, you man-eating shark!

DISTRICT ATTORNEY: Oh, you squab-eating doll baby! (*Reaches over and pinches her*)

MURIEL: (*Slaps his hand*) Quit! You'll shock Pierre.

DISTRICT ATTORNEY: Pierre is shock-proof—eh, garcon? (*The waiter beams indulgently.*) She's still trying to play the lady! Get her a bigger glass, Pierre —she needs a real dose of fizz. Go on—I mean it. (*The waiter scurries off, and the* DISTRICT ATTORNEY *takes* MURIEL *in his arms and kisses her lips.*)

RED: (*Springing forward*) So this is where our money goes! (*They start and stare.*)

DISTRICT ATTORNEY: Red Adams!

RED: (*Seizes a knife from the table*) Here's the end of your debauchery! Pay for your crimes against the workers! (*He starts forward;* MURIEL *screams; he lifts the knife.*) A sharp, clean blade through your foul heart!

DISTRICT ATTORNEY: (*Recognizing his self-possession*) Forget it kid! (*To* MURIEL, *who seeks to drag him back*) Don't worry, ducky. He won't hurt us.

MURIEL: He's mad!

DISTRICT ATTORNEY: Yes, but he can't do anything.

MURIEL: Why not?

DISTRICT ATTORNEY: Because, he's in the hole! He's one of those Wobblies I've put away! Look at him.

RED: (*Lets the knife drop and moans*) Oh, God!

DISTRICT ATTORNEY: Aha! You see? He can only rave! I'll break him like a rotten stick! Back with you! (RED *recoils and wilts.*) See that?

MURIEL: Oh, marvelous man!

DISTRICT ATTORNEY: I mash these vermin under my thumb! I stamp them down! I teach them to respect our government!

MURIEL: My hero!

DISTRICT ATTORNEY: One of those "I-won't-works," that want to live on the fat of the land! You see the sort of ruffian we have to protect you from—we guardians of the public welfare.

MURIEL: (*Cuddles in his arms*) Oo won't let him hurt oo itty Muriel!

DISTRICT ATTORNEY: (*Moved to eloquence by her admiration*) Your people is a great beast, said Alexander Hamilton. A blind beast—I have taken a sharp scalpel and cut out its eyes! A deaf beast—I have pierced its ear-drums! A dull beast—I have snipped out its brains! Its leaders arise—and one by one I lop them off! I stow them in dark dungeons to rot and perish. Ahem! Well, you see, I shut up this fellow Red, and all of his ilk, in dungeons. I put him on bread and water-white bread, that has no minerals in it. His teeth rot, his hair drops out, his very bones go to pieces. There won't be much of him left to prey on society!

MURIEL: (*Snuggling to him*) You deserve a lot from society!

DISTRICT ATTORNEY: Well, I get it! Squabs en casserole, with mushrooms! Champagne fizz—the real stuff, from our private bootlegger! We put the workers on prohibition, but we get ours—you bet your bottom dollar!

MURIEL: Look at him, how he winces! (*She goes towards red, timid but curious, inspecting him as if he were some strange animal.*)

DISTRICT ATTORNEY: His hands shake, his teeth chatter with fury; but don't be afraid, I've got him safe. Three stone walls, and a sheet steel door! Eight feet long, five feet wide, seven feet high! Black as night, silent as the grave, and no fresh air in the corridor! A stone floor and no blankets—that means rheumatism! We've broken his nose, and left it to heal crooked! He hates us—he flames with hate—but he's powerless to move a finger!

MURIEL: The common workingman! Te, he, he!

DISTRICT ATTORNEY: (*Leaning back in his chair, studying her through half-closed eyes*) The common workingman! Your blood-brother—hey, my pet?

MURIEL: (*Turns upon him, startled*) What?

DISTRICT ATTORNEY: Just so! You climbed above them—got out on your pretty face!

MURIEL: Oh, wretch!

DISTRICT ATTORNEY: So much for Solidarity! Ha, ha, ha!

MURIEL: (*Furiously*) You'll pay for this some day!

DISTRICT ATTORNEY: Take it easy, kitten; don't spoil your make-up. You won't keep that pose—you know your master. You'll come when you're called! (*He crooks his finger and she comes to him, slowly and reluctantly, but helpless before his power.*) We, the owners of the world—We know how to stand together all right! We make our will into a law, and you of the working-class obey it. You toil and sweat, and we enjoy the fruits. You show your muscles in the slave-markets—or your pretty faces in the road-houses—and we buy you. We're the masters! We're on top, and we stay! (*Reaches and pinches her on the cheek*) But don't worry, cutie—your face is your fortune! We feed you on squab, and deck you with jewels, made from the sweat and tears of your brothers! Pearls and diamonds to hang round your pretty neck and in your cunning ears! (*Fingering her jewels*) See, here's a brooch! Each diamond a year he spent sweating pm the docks! A pearl necklace—the hours he spent in the dungeon! I count them over everyone apart— (*Sings, in mock sentimental tone*)

> My rosary, my rosary!
> Each hour a pearl, each pearl a prayer—

Ha, ha, ha! (*He catches her to him and kisses her, laughing at her efforts to remain indignant.*) His wife used to sing that song. She died—because she didn't know how to keep from having babies! A little secret that we keep for ourselves—eh, pretty one? He comes here to see how we do it! Ha, ha, ha! (*To* RED, *with commanding gesture*) Back to your hole, to your dreams of vengeance! Back to your psychology bunk! And when you get tired of that, sing a few songs of Solidarity!

RED: (*Shouts in sudden frenzy*) Sing, you jailbirds, sing! (*He starts to sing.*)

> Solidarity forever!
> Solidarity forever!
> Solidarity forever!
> And the Union makes us strong!

(*Voices offstage through the open window take up the song with power.*)

All the world that's owned by idle drones is ours and ours alone;
We have laid the wide foundations, built it skyward, stone by stone;
It is ours, not to slave in, but to master and to own,
While the Union makes us strong.
Solidarity forever!
Solidarity forever!
Solidarity forever!
And the Union makes us strong!

MURIEL: (*Shuddering and clinging to* DISTRICT ATTORNEY) Ugh! That frightens me!

DISTRICT ATTORNEY: (*Laughing*) See! You need your master to protect you! Well, we have a way to drown their songs. (*Strikes a bell on the table; the waiter comes running.*) Open the doors! We want music! Our kind! Leisure-class music! (*The waiter runs off, and the strains of the jazz orchestra rise loud* MURIEL *leaps into activity, enacting the music, pressing herself into the* DISTRICT ATTORNEY'S *arms, kissing him, cajoling him; they abandon themselves to a sensual orgy.*)

MURIEL: (*Sings*)

Oh, you're my bunny-hugger, you're my grizzly, you're my duck!
You're my tricky turkey-trotter all the day!
You're my chicken in the night-time, come a-running when I cluck!
You're my piggy, in the clover-patch at play!

VOICES: (*The revelers in the road-house heard through the open door;* MURIEL *and the* DISTRICT ATTORNEY *dance.*)

Quack, quack, ducky-duck!
I'm your chick, cluck, duck!
I'm your tricky turkey-trotter all the day!
I'm your rooster in the night,
I'm your grizzly, hug me tight,
I'm your piggy, in the clover-patch at play!

(*As the music ends,* MURIEL *and the* DISTRICT ATTORNEY *confront* RED *with roistering laughter.*)

DISTRICT ATTORNEY: Here we are! This is our music! Join the chorus-or we put you in the hole!

RED: (*With clenched fists, staring ahead, confronting the future*) Stand firm! Fight for the One Big Union! Solidarity, fellow-workers!

DISTRICT ATTORNEY: Solidarity! The boob thinks he's got somebody behind him! And we buy them like fish in the market!

RED: It's a lie!

DISTRICT ATTORNEY: I'll show you! (*He rings bell, and the waiter comes running.*) Serve the stool-pigeons! (*Waiter bows and runs off.*) Stool-pigeons en casserole! How's that for wit?

MURIEL: Oh, comical kid! (*Gives him a resounding kiss upon the lips.*)

DISTRICT ATTORNEY: A change of diet, Red! Pigeons instead of bread and water! (IKE *enters, escorted by the waiter; he has his coat-collar turned up, his cap pulled over his eyes, keeps his face averted from* RED, *and acts as slinky as possible.*) Stool-pigeons en casserole, piping hot! Here's the first one (*He hands a roll of money to* IKE, *who slips it into his pocket and slides off to the back part of the room.*) You get that Red?

RED: Sure, I know him. That's Ike. We spotted him for a stool in the crate.

DISTRICT ATTORNEY: Well, there are some you haven't spotted yet. Serve 'em up, garcon—quick! Get a move on! (PIERRE *brings in* PETE, *also acting slinky.* DISTRICT ATTORNEY *repeats business of handing him money.*) How's that?

RED: Who is he?

DISTRICT ATTORNEY: Show him your face, spy. (PETE *gives* RED *a glimpse of his face.*)

RED: Pete! My God!

DISTRICT ATTORNEY: The next one! Quick! (PIERRE *brings in* MATT, *who goes through the same procedure.*) You know him?

RED: No. (MATT *shows his face.*) Matt! It's a lie! I don't believe you!

DISTRICT ATTORNEY: Seeing's believing! Ha, ha ha! The next! Speed 'em up! (JERRY *enters and takes money.*) Show him your face! (JERRY *obeys.*)

RED: Jerry! It's a dirty frame-up!

DISTRICT ATTORNEY: More! Hustle 'em along! We'll convince him! (JOE GUNTHER *enters and takes money.*) Your whole executive committee, you see!

RED: Good God! Who is that?

DISTRICT ATTORNEY: Show him! (JOE *shows face.*)

RED: Joe Gunther! Ah, what you trying to tell me? A trick to break my nerve!

DISTRICT ATTORNEY: They've got my money in their pockets—the whole precious crew. I can buy anyone in your crowd!

RED: You lie! You lie! There's one you can't buy, and I know it. Jake Apperson never took your money.

DISTRICT ATTORNEY: Ha, ha, ha! That's a good one! Get a move on, garcon! Stool-pigeons for a whole banquet of the Shipowners' Association! Here's a big fellow! (JAKE APPERSON *enters, with especial precautions of secrecy, and takes money.*)

RED: (*Screams*) Christ A'mighty!

DISTRICT ATTORNEY: Look at him! Take off your cap and let him see.

RED: (*Getting a glimpse of* JAKE's *face; then laughing wildly*) You're playing me for a sucker! You crowd of cheats and grafters! Away with you—I'll waste no more time on you! I nail the I.W.W. preamble to the wall! (*He draws from under his coat a hammer and a rolled-up scroll, headed "I.W.W. Preamble," and containing one sentence. He nails it to the wall at rear, and stands shouting its message.*) "We are forming the new society within the shell of the old." That's our answer to your grafting and villainy—by that we destroy you—we wipe you from the earth! (*He seizes the table and hurls it over, scattering contents. A clatter and banging, peals of thunder, quick changes of colored light on the scene, juggled about in kaleidoscopic effect. Then darkness; the curtains and cell come down* RED *and* JAKE *inside the cell.*) My God, what things I see! And the devil of it is I'm never sure if they're dreams. That's what makes insanity. Yes, I'm cracking, sure enough! Stool-pigeons en casserole—by heck, that's a good one! Of course, they buy some of us—there's always crooks in every movement. But most of it is lies, to scare us, to spread doubt and distrust! Imagine Jake Apperson selling out! Jake! Good old Jake! (*Faint light appears.*)

Scene 5: In the Hole.

Jake stands gazing down upon RED, *as he lies on the floor.*

RED: Hello, old pal!

JAKE: Stick it out, Red! Stand fast!

RED: I'm doing it, Jake!

JAKE: You're going fine, boy! They'll never break you!

RED: What do you think? They tried to tell me you had taken their dirty money!

JAKE: Some sell out, Red—but the movement goes on! Remember, no one can buy the movement! The working-class of the world awakening to life and hope!

RED: I'm doing my part!

JAKE: We'll not forget you, Red!

RED: Are they really not forgetting me? It's been two weeks now, and my head aches like it was bursting—I'm near crazy with it!

JAKE: We're fighting for you, Red!

RED: I ought to have some kind of a trial, Jake! They can't keep me buried here forever—without a hearing in court!

JAKE: They do pretty much what they please, you know. But we're agitating —we're doing all we can! They've got so many in jail—we can't get lawyers enough, we haven't the money. The judge has assigned a lawyer to defend us, and of course he's no good; he plays the game their way.

RED: Yes, I know him—that fellow who defended the last bunch. A regular little jack-in-the-box!

JAKE: But stick it out, Red! Don't lose your nerve!

RED: I'm sticking, Jake—that's all I can say! (*The light fades; darkness again.*) A trial! Hell! Where do you get that stuff? That 'Cutor said it—they make their will into a law! It's their game—they've stacked all the cards, they've loaded the dice. I sat in that court-room and watched them railroading our lads to the pen. They had the skids greased all right! The boys named it the Hall of Hate! (*The curtains and cell disappear.*) Some day I'll have my turn. They'll put me up in the dock and snarl at me—tigers they are, and wolves! They'll bring in their spies and provocateurs—the hissing snakes! And that little jack-in-the-box of a lawyer pretending to defend me! The whole farcical show—my day in court! Oyez, oyez, oyez! (*His voice rises to a tone of proclamation.*) Be it known to all men that the master-class hereby calls the social rebels to judgment; the Hall of Hate is declared in session! The honorable supremacy of the master-class is present! Hats off before the honorable supremacy of the master-class! Take notice, all wage-slaves are hereby inspired with terror. Be it duly and legally made known that the grand jurors have been chosen, selected and sworn, in the name and by the authority of the Shipowners' Association of the State of California. (RED *speaks faster and faster, and the voice of the* BAILIFF *mingles with his; gradually* RED'*s voice dies away, and we hear the* BAILIFF. *Light appears.*)

Scene 6: The Hall of Hate.

A high raised platform, in the back part of the stage, away from the audience. Over this platform peers an enormous tiger's head, with snarling teeth. When the mouth opens, it reveals the face of a wizened, bald-headed old man in spectacles, who delivers judgments in a voice of senile vindictiveness. To the left of his seat, and slightly lower, is the witness-box—an arm-chair, upon which sits coiled a huge serpent, having a mouth which opens, revealing the face of IKE *the spy. In front of the bench runs a rail, to which* RED *is presently summoned. At the left is a stand, over the top of which appears a wolf's head, which opens, revealing the face of the* DISTRICT ATTORNEY. *At the right is a stand, the top of which pops open, revealing a living jack-in-the-box, the attorney for the defense. Farther to the right is desk of the clerk, who has the head of a rat, and occasionally runs about, displaying a long grey tail. The* BAILIFF *stands before the bar, having the head of a bear. Across the front part of the state, in a row, facing the tiger's head, and with their backs to the audience, are the spectators, including* MATT, JERRY, PETE, JOE GUNTHER, JAKE APPERSON *and others who were in the tanks in act 1. Behind them sits a row of policemen in blue uniforms, having the heads of bulls' each is armed with a club.*

At rise: The BAILIFF *stands before the rail, facing the audience, and declaiming with great rapidity. The whole scene is played fast and wildly, it being not a natural scene, but a delirium.*

BAILIFF: And be it furthermore made known that the said honorable grand jurors of the master-class of the State of California, within and for the body of the aforesaid master-class of the State of California, being duly empanelled, sworn and charged to inquire of charges and crimes committed against the interests of the aforesaid master-class of the hereinbeforementioned state of California, do on their oaths taken as by statute required, and in the name of the aforesaid master-class of the hereinbeforementioned State of California, furthermore find and solemnly present that the aforementioned organization, to-wit, the Industrial Workers of the World, have unlawfully, feloniously, criminally and maliciously conspired, combined, confederated and agreed to weaken, degrade, humiliate and threaten the prestige, power, rule and sovereignty of the aforesaid master-class of the hereinbeforementioned State of California: therefore the honorable authority of the aforesaid master-class hereby orders, decrees, ordains and enjoins that the said Industrial Workers of the World shall be willfully, feloniously and of malice aforethought, intimidated, assaulted, beaten, bruised, kicked, robbed, shot, hanged, mutilated, castrated and otherwise discouraged by all persons whatsoever belonging to the aforesaid master-class of the hereinbeforementioned State of California; and that all members of the said Industrial Workers of the World who shall be found, detected, discovered or otherwise ascertained to be within the boundaries or confines of the hereinbeforementioned State of California, shall be immediately apprehended, seized, possessed and incapacitated, and summoned and brought before the honorable presiding authority of the Hall of Hate. In accordance with which decree aforesaid, the honorable grand jurors hereby indict, present, and bind over the body of the defendant Bert Adams, who because of notorious radical affiliations and the habit of burning down barns is popularly known, designated, and referred to as Red. (*A sudden burst of red light all over the scene.*) And the honorable authority hereby commands that the body and person of the aforesaid Bert Adams, alias, Red, shall be and hereby is presented, brought forward, summoned and made available for inquiry, examination, torment, intimidation, mutilation, starvation, and harassment. Is the defendant Bert Adams present?

RED: (*Defiantly*) Here he is.

BAILIFF: Prisoner to the bar! (*A police officer grabs* RED *and jerks him before the rail.*)

THE TIGER: Guilty or not guilty?

RED: Of what?

TIGER: Silence!

RED: But you asked me a question.

THE TIGER: Hold your tongue! (*The policeman twists* RED's *arm.*)

RED: Ouch!

BAILIFF: Order!

THE SPECTATORS: (*Rising in their seats*) Shame!

THE BULLS: Sit down! (*They rise and smite the spectators over the heads with their clubs. The spectators collapse.*)

THE TIGER: What is the defendant's plea?

THE JACK-IN-THE-BOX: (*Popping open and declaiming rapidly*) Your supremacy, the defendant demurs to the indictment, and according to the form of the statute made and provided in such cases, hereby states and shows to the honorable authority that the aforesaid charges and the matters therein contained are not sufficient in law for the plaintiff to hold and maintain his aforesaid action thereon against the hereinbeforementioned defendant, and that he, the said defendant, is not bound at this time and under these circumstances to make answer or response thereto. And furthermore we cite to the honorable authority the decision of the Propaganda Department of the Commercial Hierarchy, section four hundred and seventy-three of the revised pronouncements, volume sixty-three hundred and forty-two, page ten thousand three hundred and eighteen, paragraph seven ninety-eight, that the charges and allegations presented in the said indictment are not applicable under the present jurisdiction—

THE DISTRICT ATTORNEY: I object, your supremacy!

THE TIGER: Objection sustained.

JACK-IN-THE-BOX: But may it please—

TIGER: Demurrer overruled. What is your plea?

JACK-IN-THE-BOX: Not guilty.

RED: Hold on there!

TIGER: Silence!

RED: But I demand to know—

TIGER: Hold your tongue!

RED: (*As the policeman twists his arm*) Ouch!

BAILIFF: Order!

THE SPECTATORS: (*Rising*) For shame!

THE BULLS: (*Hitting them over the heads*) Sit down!

TIGER: We will hear the evidence.

DISTRICT ATTORNEY: May it please the honorable authority, our first witness is an expensive and habitual prevaricator for the master-class, by whose testimony we propose to show that the defendant did feloniously, unlawfully, maliciously, and of deliberate intent conspire, confederate, and agree to think disrespectfully of the Shipowners' Association of the hereinbeforementioned State of California—

JACK-IN-THE-BOX: I object!

TIGER: What is the ground of your objection?

JACK-IN-THE-BOX: Exception, your supremacy.

TIGER: Exception noted. Proceed.

DISTRICT ATTORNEY: What is your name?

IKE: Ike Snake.

DISTRICT ATTORNEY: You know the defendant, Red Adams?

IKE: Sure, I know him.

DISTRICT ATTORNEY: You have heard him speak disrespectfully of the master-class?

IKE: Sure.

DISTRICT ATTORNEY: What have you heard him say?

IKE: I have heard him say that the District Attorney took his stenographer to a road-house.

THE SPECTATORS: (*In uproar*) Hurrah!

BAILIFF: Silence in the Hall of Hate! (*The bulls club the spectators.*)

JACK-IN-THE-BOX: Your supremacy, I object to this testimony as irrelevant, obscene, humiliating, and irrefutable. I ask that the testimony be stricken from the record.

TIGER: Objection sustained. It is so ordered. Proceed with the interrogation.

DISTRICT ATTORNEY: What else have you heard him say?

IKE: I've heard him say that the workers should stick together.

JACK-IN-THE-BOX: I object, your authority.

TIGER: Upon what ground?

JACK-IN-THE-BOX: May it please this honorable supremacy, according to the decision of the Unimpeachable Infallibility, recorded in the Transcript of Technicalities, volume three forty-seven, page nine eighty-two, it appears that the definition of colloquial terms is subject to various interpretations, of which many remain still in controversy, and accordingly—

DISTRICT ATTORNEY: Your supremacy, I refer to page six forty-seven, according to which the aforesaid devisers of technicalities declare that, all and singular the premises being submitted, and the said pleadings being fully understood and duly considered, and mature deliberation being had thereupon, it is decreed that the decision, order and adjudication aforesaid be hereby reversed, annulled and altogether held for naught. And furthermore—

JACK-IN-THE-BOX: (*Becoming excited*) May it please your authority, it is plain that this decision was only intended to be applicable in cases where the defendant had entered a declaration of assumpsit, or an averment upon final judgment for default in ejectment—

DISTRICT ATTORNEY: (*Enraged*) Not at all, your supremacy! May it please the honorable infallibility, I cite the exact words of the decision—the aforesaid defendant may not prosecute or maintain the said writ of error, because after the judgment aforesaid in the form aforesaid, and before the day of suing out of the said writ of error, to-wit—

JACK-IN-THE-BOX: The argument is not rogatory, your authority, because in the replication by way of estoppel to the plea of abatement—(*The* DISTRICT ATTORNEY *breaks in, and they both talk and gesticulate with furious excitement at the same time*)

DISTRICT ATTORNEY: In the record and proceedings aforesaid, and the giving of the judgment aforesaid, there is a manifest error, to-wit-that the declaration aforesaid, and the matters therein contained, are not sufficient in law for the said defendant to have or maintain the aforesaid replication; and we therefore desire and hereby formally demand permission to enter a plea of release to assignment of error—

JACK-IN-THE-BOX: We maintain that before the committing of the grievance by the said defendant hereinafter next mentioned, the said plaintiff, at the special instance and request of said defendant, did severally and each for himself assert that he denied responsibility for the said error in implication, and he now asks of the honorable supremacy a mandatory injunction requiring the continuance of the plea in respondeat—

TIGER: (*Pounds on the desk*) Order! The indispensable authority, having duly considered the respective arguments of the learned counsel, will take this matter under advisement. Proceed.

DISTRICT ATTORNEY: What else have you heard the defendant Adams say?

IKE: I've heard him say that the Hall of Hate is a necessary part of the master-class system.

THE SPECTATORS: So it is!

THE BAILIFF: Silence! (*The bulls club them.*)

DISTRICT ATTORNEY: Your authority, I submit to this honorable body that the above testimony is sufficient to render any member of the working-class liable to any penalty the master-class can inflict. Accordingly I move your honorable supremacy that the defendant be declared guilty. It costs a lot of money to run this show.

THE TIGER: Any one second the motion?

JACK-IN-THE-BOX: It's damn poor pay I'm getting. I second the motion.

TIGER: It is moved and seconded that the defendant be declared guilty. All employees of the Shipowners' Association will say aye.

CHORUS OF THE ANIMALS: Aye!

TIGER: It is so ordered

THE WOBBLIES: (*Springing up*) No!

TIGER: (*Furiously*) Silence!

BAILIFF: Order in the Hall of Hate! (*The bulls club them.*)

DISTRICT ATTORNEY: Your supremacy, we point out the monstrous nature of the offense of which this defendant has been adjudged guilty. We ask the severest penalties, the limit of master-class implacability. We ask that he have his nose smashed and healed crooked. We ask that he be shut in the hole for as long as I see fit, and fed upon a diet without minerals, so that his teeth will rot, his hair will drip out, and his bones will go to pieces. We ask that he have a stone floor and no blankets, which will mean rheumatism. We ask that he be permitted no fresh air, and no thoughts except nightmares and psychology bunk. We ask that the rats shall eat his rosary. We ask that once a day the jailer shall bring him a pail full of stool-pigeons—

TIGER: The application is granted. Let the sentence be executed—and if anything has already been done, let it be done again for good measure. The proceedings will now be ratified by all hundred per cent Americans singing in chorus.

THE ANIMALS: (*Rise, face the audience, and sing with religious fervor.*)

My country, 'tis of thee,
Sweet land of liberty.
Of thee I sing.
Long may our land be bright,
With freedom's holy light;
Protect us by Thy might,
Great God, our King.

RED: (*Turning to the spectators*) Sing, you jailbirds, sing!

THE SPECTATORS: (*Rise, face the audience, and sing to the same tune. The bulls step around behind them and begin to club them, the clubs falling at each italicized word. The singers wince at each blow, and gradually collapse to the floor, but go on nevertheless. red sings with especial fervor.*)

My job *is* no more,
My boss has *slammed* the door;
What shall I do?
Seems like my *end* is near,
My guts feel *aw*ful queer—
Where do we *go* from here?
This is *up to you!*
No, I've not *lost* a leg.
Why must I *starve* and beg?
What shall I do?
Where can the *an*swer lurk?
Why am I *out* of work,
*Gaz*ing on *all* this murk?
This is *up to you.*

CURTAIN.

The audience sings:

You may ramble 'round the country anywhere you will,
You'll always run across the same old Scissor Bill.
He's found upon the desert, he is on the hill,
He's found in every mining camp and lumber mill.
He looks just like a human, he can eat and walk,
But you will find he isn't when he starts to talk.
He'll say: "This is my country," with an honest face,
While all the cops they chase him out of every place.

CHORUS
Scissor Bill, he is a little dippy.
Scissor Bill, he has a funny face.
Scissor Bill should drown in Mississippi;
He is the missing link that Darwin tried to trace.
Don't try to talk your union dope to Scissor Bill,
He says he never organized and never will.
He always will be satisfied until he's dead,
With coffee and a doughnut and a lousy old bed.
And Bill, he says, he'll get rewarded thousand fold,
When he gets up to heaven on the streets of gold.

CHORUS
But I don't care who knows it, and right here I'll tell.
If Scissor Bill is goin' to heaven, I'll go to hell.

Scissor Bill, he says, "Not me, by heck!"
Scissor Bill gets his reward in heaven,
Oh! Sure. He'll get it, but he'll get it in the neck.

Act 4

Scene 1: In the Hole.

RED: (*Whispers in the darkness*) Nell! Nell! Where are you?

NELL: (*Whispers*) I am here.

RED: Take my hand! I must know you are here.

NELL: Yes, dear.

RED: I can hardly move my hand; but I feel yours, the same as ever.

NELL: I won't leave you, beloved. (*Faint light;* RED *lies on his back;* NELL *sits by his side, holding his hand.*)

RED: Nell, I'm happy!

NELL: Yes, Red; and I'm glad!

RED: I've won! They can never hurt me now!

NELL: Never! Never!

RED: I fought and suffered and hated—but now I'm free. I've conquered, not only my enemies, but myself. I am rid of fear.

NELL: Yes, beloved.

RED: Even fear of the rats, Nell! That was my last trouble. You know, when I began my hunger-strike, and my pain left me, I was so peaceful, and I thought that was the victory. But then came the horrible idea—I'm getting weaker and weaker, and some day the rats will eat me! Eat me alive! I feel them running over me—they come for the bread, you know. They learned to get in through the hole in the door, and I can't close it without suffocating. So I have to let them run over me; and now—any time—they'll discover I'm too weak to fight them.

NELL: The work you've done will live, Red, long after you are gone.

RED: I'm going soon—the way doesn't matter. I shall leave this old body—whether to the rats or to the worms.

NELL: You've fought the good fight.

RED: And I'm almost at the end. I think it's sixty days since I've eaten. I try to keep count, though I can't handle my threads any more. Fasting is a fine way to die.

NELL: Yes, dear.

RED: It's a marvel, how active my mind stays. I've roamed the whole universe

—I've seen the most wonderful things—more than words can tell. Mankind is only at the beginning of its life, Nell. You and I have suffered its birth-pangs, and those who come after us will have an easier time.

NELL: They will bless you for it, Red.

RED: They may never know what I've done. But my little bit will never be missed.

NELL: You've accomplished more than you know, Red.

RED: One thing I still can't feel sure about—the children. I want to believe I did right.

NELL: It was the only thing possible, Red.

RED: How could I, a workingman, with no home and no job, raise two babies?

NELL: You couldn't.

RED: At least they're getting good care, Nell. They won't starve—and they might have, with me. They'll grow up to ride on the backs of the workers; but then—so many do it! The workers' backs are broad! The thing that worries me is this—they'll be taught to despise us—the people who gave them life.

NELL: They won't know anything about us, Red.

RED: They'll despise what we are. (*A pause*) That lawyer made it good and clear to me. He didn't make any bones about it, or spare a father's feelings. I must surrender all rights; I must go away and never see the children. These rich people would raise them, and the children would never have the humiliation of knowing their origin. That's the way to put us in our place, us working-stiffs!

NELL: Peace, beloved! Peace!

RED: I wrestled over it a week, Nell. Oh, how I loved those babies! Not because they were mine—but because they were yours! They were the seal of our love, they were all I had left of you! But I had to choose, and give my life to two babies, or else give it to the working-class.

NELL: Dear heart!

RED: I tried to forget. But I was like a murderer returning to the scene of his crime. I found out where the people lived, and I used to watch the children come out into the park. There was a governess, who didn't know me; she was polite when I spoke to her and the little ones. Oh, such a strange sensation, Nell! I used to go off crying. But then I saw she was getting to be afraid of me; she'd draw the children away from me, with some pretext or other. So I knew I'd be found out, and I went away.

NELL: (*Crying softly*) You had a greater work to do than raising two children, Red. You had to help educate a whole world.

RED: I've educated some. The migratory workers—the poor devils that have no homes, and wander about, hunting the job. I've taught them—their rights, and how to get them. Oh, Nell, such fine fellows! Loyal hearted fellows—I've wished you could have met them. Dear old Jake Apperson—he's built like a big oak tree, and by God, he's good to lean on! And Joe Gunther—they had him in the crate with me, God knows if they suffocated him, or what. And the Dominie—say, did I tell you about the Dominie? That old boy used to be the Bible-shark in a swell church in Philadelphia—regular gilt-edge stuff. But he kicked over the traces—went to the bat for the reds, and they fired him. Poor old boy! But he stuck by his guns. Wherever there was a big strike, and they began to can the workers, he'd come preach to us. I'd sure like to see that old gent again.

NELL: He'd like to see you, I've no doubt.

RED: Yes; I've had a sort of conversion—I realize it more and more, what I'm talking is the regulation sky-pilot dope. By heck, it's true, when you're in a place like this, you've got your own soul, and God, or whatever it is—and that's all. You get no help from the world. You stretch out your thoughts to your friends—to your fellow-workers—but the thoughts don't reach. Fellow-workers! Where are you? (*The light fades; the cell and curtains disappear;* NELL *exits.*) Where are my wandering boys tonight? Out in the jungles somewhere—frying hot dogs, making flapjacks, singing songs—and wondering what's become of poor old Red Adams in the hole! Sing, you jailbirds, sing! (*He begins feebly to sing.*)

Where is my wandering boy tonight,
The boy of his mother's pride?
He's counting the ties with his bed on his back,
Or else he is bumming a ride.
Oh, where is my boy tonight?
Oh, where is my boy tonight?
He's on the head end of an overland train—
That's where your boy is tonight.

(*Gradually the song is taken up by other voices; light begins to dawn.*)

Scene 2: The Jungles

A forest with tall trees, at night; in the center of the stage a small camp-fire.

At rise: JAKE APPERSON, JOE GUNTHER, MATT, PETE, JERRY *and other workers sprawled on the ground, or sitting on their big rolls of blankets. Some are toasting frankfurter sausages on sticks, one mixing flapjacks in a tin can, and cooking them on a piece of tin beaten flat. Red is standing at the left, watching the scene unnoticed. The Wobblies are singing:*

I was looking for work, oh, judge, he said.
Says the judge, I have heard that before.
So to the chain-gang, far off he goes,
To hammer the rocks some more.
Oh, where is my boy tonight?
Oh, where is my boy tonight?
To strike many blows for his country he goes,
That's where your boy is tonight.

JERRY: Is that a Joe Hill song?

JOE: The little red book don't say.

JERRY: That feller sure could write pomes!

JAKE: Yes; and while you're singing them, don't forget that he was stood up against a wall and shot a firing squad.

JOE: Because he was a wob!

JAKE: That reason, and no other; he threatened the master-class!

JERRY: He won't be the last, neither.

JAKE: Not by many thousands.

MATT: Well, the hot dogs is ready.

PETE: No more ready than my stummick.

MATT: Move up, 'boes!

JERRY: This open-air life sure gives a feller the appetite.

PETE: I got something here to help it along. (*He pulls a quart flask from his pocket.*) The real stuff, too!

JAKE: Let me see it.

PETE: Keep it circulatin'.

JAKE: (*Takes bottle, uncorks and smells it, then starts to pour it on ground*) Let Mother Nature drink it.

PETE: Hey! Fer Christ's sake!

JAKE: (*Holding him back with his other hand*) Stand back, fellow-worker!

PETE: The hell you say!

JAKE: If there's anybody in this crowd don't know the difference between a scissor-bill and a Wobbly, here's where he learns it. One pours this stuff into his gizzard, the other pours it into the sewer. You get me?

PETE: (*Furiously*) Damn you! Who learned you that Billy Sunday spiel?

JAKE: Hard knocks learned it to me. We got a social revolution to make, and if you think it can be made by drunkards, you got a bum steer. You boys that have been through the real fights will back me up—wasn't it so at Portland, and at Seattle—every time we get power the first thing we got to do is to raid the booze dens and smash the kegs and pour the stuff into the gutters? Ain't that so, Joe?

JOE: Yep, that's straight.

PETE: A fat chance we'd have to get drunk on a pint o' gin!

JAKE: Well, a rule's a rule, no booze in the jungles. You can't fight booze and fight capital! Wobs have got to study and think, not drink and loaf. When we sing our songs, we want to mean every word, and be ready to act them.

JOE: (*A trifle sadly*) I gave up my share of the booze.

JAKE: (*To* PETE) Hell, man! Stop and think a moment! To spend good money for bad liquor, when you know there's hundreds of our boys suffering torments in jail, and no one but us to get 'em out!

PETE: What can we do about it?

JAKE: What can we do! And he calls himself a wob! You can spend your money for literature, and your time getting the scissor-bills to read it.

PETE: They don't want to read. They dunno how.

JAKE: Well, go into town and make a speech on a street-corner! Chain yourself to a lamp-post, so the cops can't drag you off till you've finished what you got to say!

RED: (*Steps forward*) Yes, fellow-workers, that's the talk!

ALL: (*Chorus of cries*) By God, it's Red! Red Adams! Hurrah! When did you blow in? How'd you get loose?

RED: Fellow-workers, I beg you never forget the man in jail. It means so much to him to know that those outside remember him; that the crowd is working to keep the fight alive! Don't forget us, fellow-workers!

VOICES: We won't! We'll stick, Red!

RED: Keep at it till the last class-war prisoner is out! Till the last wage-slave is free—no matter where he is, in what part of the earth! Nail the I.W.W. preamble to the wall: "We are building the new society within the shell of the old."

VOICES: You're right! That's the talk! Hurrah!

RED: They'll punish you—they'll torture you. But the soul of the working-class is unbreakable; there are no chains, no prison-walls, that can bind the will of the masses.

ALL: You're right, Red! Count on us! Hurrah!

RED: Brotherhood. Solidarity! That's our goal. The worker is nothing alone —but in the mass he is the world! Learn to forget self—learn to think, not as one person, but as part of the movement, as one cell in a great body. Put down greed and jealousy and fear. Cease to care what happens to yourselves. Live for the working-class! Live *in* the working-class, so that its life is yours, its joys, its hopes, its mission—to do away with capitalism.

ALL: Hurrah! Hurrah!

JAKE: Solidarity forever!

ALL: (*Rise and sing with solemn fervor*)

Solidarity forever!
Solidarity forever!
Solidarity forever!
And the Union makes us strong!

NELL: (*Offstage, at the left, sings in a soft, melancholy voice; all turn and listen wondering*)

The hours I spent with thee, dear heart,
Are as a string of pearls to me;
I count them over, every one apart;
My rosary, my rosary!
Each hour a pearl, each pearl a prayer—

(*Her voice dies*)

RED: (*Calls with tender longing*) Nell!

NELL: Sweetheart!

RED: Come to me!

NELL: (*Enters; radiant, charming, as in the days of her shining youth, all trace of care gone from her*) Dearest one! (*She takes* RED's *hand—they are as two spirits in perfect understanding; the other men show no surprise, but gaze enraptured at this pleasing vision.*)

RED: (*Turns to the crowd*) Fellow-workers, meet my wife. I've longed so to have you meet her! Nell, these are my friends! The heroes of the class-struggle!

NELL: (*Stretches out her hands to them*) Fellow-workers!

JAKE: (*With crude but ardent courtesy*) Hats off to the ladies!

JOE: (*Bowing low*) Pleased to meet you, ma'am!

JERRY: (*Inspired*) The rebel girl!

ALL: (*Sing with ardor*)

That's the rebel girl!
That's the rebel girl!
To the working class she's a precious pearl!
She brings courage, pride and joy
To the fighting rebel boy!
We've had girls before,
But we need some more
In the Industrial Workers of the World!
For it's great to fight for freedom

With a rebel girl!

(*During the singing* JAKE APPERSON *moves over to* RED *and* NELL; *the light becomes centered upon them.*)

RED: (*With concentrated earnestness*) Jake, there's a favor I want to ask.

JAKE: Yes, old man?

RED: You know my two children?

JAKE: Yes.

RED: The thought of them is my one trouble. I want you to find them, Jake —find some way to get next to them. Make them understand their father and his life. I don't want them to despise the workers.

JAKE: I understand, Red.

RED: Just because they're raised by rich people needn't mean they have no hearts. There are lots of young people that have understanding—boys and girls in the colleges. You know what I mean, Jake.

JAKE: Sure thing. I'll do my best.

RED: That's all I need to set me free. Nell and I are happy, Jake—oh, so happy, and at peace! (*He takes the hand of* JAKE.)

DOMINIE: (*Calling, off right*) Hail, fellow-workers!

JERRY: Who's that?

JOE: Watch out, boys! It may be a trap!

PETE: The bulls are watchin' us!

JAKE: Who are you?

DOMINIE: (*Off*) The Dominie of the Wobblies!

ALL: The Dominie! By God, the Bible-shark! Hurrah! Hurrah! Welcome to our jungles!

JAKE: (*Hastens to welcome the* DOMINIE; *at the same time* RED *and* NELL *step back into the shadows at left.*) We're glad to see you, Dominie.

DOMINIE: (*Enters right*) Glad to find you, fellow-workers!

JOE: Welcome to supper!

JAKE: Greetings in the name of the Workers' Commonwealth!

ALL: Hurrah! Hurrah!

DOMINIE: I bring you sad news, my friends. I fear it will spoil your feast. Red Adams—

JAKE: What about him?

DOMINIE: He's dead.

JAKE: Dead!

DOMINIE: I've had word from the jail.

JOE: But man, he was here!

DOMINIE: What do you mean?

JOE: He was here just a minute ago!

JERRY: As big as life!

DOMINIE: That's impossible!

JOE: But we all saw him!

MATT: And heard him!

JERRY: He made us a speech!

DOMINIE: But—are you sure?

JOE: Why, of course! Don't we all know Red?

JERRY: And his wife!

JOE: Come to think of it, his wife is dead!

JERRY: Been dead for years!

MATT: Four years, he told me! (*They stare at one another.*)

JOE: By Christ, it was his ghost!

JERRY: They were dead—the two of them!

JOE: It was a miracle!

MATT: He brought a message to us!

JERRY: His dying words!

PETE: Look! He's there still!

MATT: Both of them!

JERRY: Look!

JOE: For God's sake! (*A faint light on* RED *and* NELL; *the rest stare amazed.*)

DOMINIE: (*Raises his hands*) In the name of the Father, of the Son, and of the Holy Ghost!

JAKE: (*Imploring*) Speak to us, Red!

JOE: Just a word, old pal!

JERRY: We'll never forget it!

RED: (*In a gentle, deeply moved tone*) Fellow-workers! This is what I have learned from my suffering: in love and fellowship is deliverance for the workers. Man has been a beast, wandering alone, devouring his own kind, making torment for himself, but now comes the great day of solidarity. The purpose of your long agony is that the toilers shall become one being, one body with one mind, one soul. Be of good cheer, friends and fellow-workers, for when you suffer most, then is the time of great achievement, then are hearts brought together. It is only in white heat that steel can be smelted; it is only in persecution that solidarity can be forged. Rejoice, therefore, when men do revile you and torment you for the sake of the One Big Union, for then you fulfill your destiny, you become the sharp tool that shall cut the chains from the workers' limbs. This message I give unto you; write it in your hearts, take it with you into the blackest dungeon—that even there is unity, even there, in the midst of affliction and despair, brotherhood works its miracles of life and resurrection. Remember my words.

JAKE: We'll remember!

RED: Stand firm, Industrial Workers of the World!

ALL: We stand!

RED: I bequeath to you my love and my vision. I cannot stay now—my time is come, my light fades. But fear not, I shall be with you in the spirit of the One Big Union, which is the hope of all mankind. (*The light begins to fade.*)

JAKE: You are going?

RED: My word is spoken.

JAKE: You will come back?

RED: I live in your solidarity.

JOE: Speak once more! A last word, old man!

RED: I have one fight more before my deliverance. One more agony—(*With rising excitement*) It's the rats! The rats are eating my eye-balls! (*A crashing of thunder, and sudden darkness; the cell and curtains come into place. A long silence. The* JAILER *is heard opening the door of the corridor; the light is turned on, and the slide is unbolted and shoved open.*)

Scene 3: In the Hole.

Red lies in a crumpled heap on the floor.

JAILER: (*Speaking from behind the cell door*) Shove out your slop-pail. (*Silence*) You hear me? Shove out your pail. (*Silence*) What's the matter in there? (*Silence*) Hell! What's up now? (*Raising his voice*) Hey, you, get me straight! If you put me to the trouble of getting' the key to this cell, by God, I'll hammer the top of your nut off! (*Silence*) Last warning, now! Hand out your slop-pail, and no funny stuff! (*Silence*) All right, I'll go for the key. If you ain't dead, by Jesus Christ, you'll wish you were! (*He stands listening; faint voices are heard singing from upper part of jail.*)

We're here from mine and mill and rail,
We're here from off the sea;
From coast to coast we make the boast
Of Solidarity.

(*The* JAILER *is heard going away; the light is switched off, and the corridor door is heard to shut. The cell and curtains disappear, and light dawns. The singing swells to a loud chorus.*)

Scene 4: In the Forest

The same spot as in scene 2, but ten years in the future. The same trees and forest background, but in the center of the stage, in place of the campfire, is a monument, with Red Adams standing upon it as a statue. There is a crowd about the base. The pedestal consists of two broad steps, upon the first of which stand JAKE, JOE, PETE, JERRY *and* MATT, *with red sashes and badges. On the higher step is the* DOMINIE, *in priestly vestments, a youth and a girl on either side of him, in festive attire and holding a wreath of flowers. All are singing:*

In California's darkened dungeons
For the O.B.U.
Remember you're outside for us
While we're in here for you.
We laugh and sing, we have no fear,
Our hearts are always light.
We know that every Wobbly true
Will carry on the fight.
In California's darkened dungeons
For the O.B.U.
Remember you're outside for us
While we're in here for you.

THE DOMINIE: (*Beginning a speech*) Fellow-workers! In the name of the Industrial Commonwealth! We are here upon an errand of love, to revere the memory of One who gave His life for the freedom we now enjoy. Upon this hallowed spot, where first His spirit appeared to His disciples, and where His message of brotherhood was handed down to posterity—here we assemble with prayer and hymns, to pledge our loyalty to the new dispensation. What more fitting touch than that these tribute wreaths should be laid at His feet by His own children, whom He so dearly loved, to whom His thoughts turned even in His last agony? They were torn from Him by the cruel class system; but in spite of mental barriers, they fought their way out to His faith in solidarity and social justice, they stand here today as living testimony to the power of Truth, which overthrows all the schemes of its enemies, which smashes the doors of all cells and razes the walls of all dungeons. Fellow-workers, the Man whose statue shadows us today was one of the fathers of the Industrial Commonwealth; He lives as one of the heroes of the Great Deliverance. In love and gratitude we bare our heads, and join together in singing.

ALL: (*Sing*)

Solidarity forever!
Solidarity forever!
Solidarity forever!
And the Union makes us strong!

(*The light fades to darkness, and the cell, curtains and corridor come into place. The chorus dies to a murmur, heard from the upper parts of the jail.*)

Scene 5: In the Hole.

RED *lies as before. The sound of the corridor door is heard, the light is switched on, and then the door of the cell is opened. The* JAILER *enters, followed by a second jailer. They turn over the body of* RED.

FIRST JAILER: Christ A'mighty! He's a goner!

SECOND JAILER: Sure enough!

FIRST JAILER: Look at that! The rats have eaten his eyes!

SECOND JAILER: Holy Christopher, the Chief will be wild about that!

FIRST JAILER: Yes, and I'll be the one he'll land on!

SECOND JAILER: Didn't you guess anything wrong?

FIRST JAILER: Hell no! He shoved out his slop-pail every day.

SECOND JAILER: He's a skeleton! He starved himself to death!

FIRST JAILER: He took in the bread all right.

SECOND JAILER: The rats must have eat it!

FIRST JAILER: A quick funeral he'll have, I make my guess.

SECOND JAILER: Yes! The soreheads outside would raise a sweet stink if they ever got this story!

PRISONERS: (*Singing, offstage*)

Solidarity forever!
Solidarity forever!
Solidarity forever!
And the Union makes us strong!

(*The singing continues faintly through the following dialogue.*)

FIRST JAILER: Hell! That everlasting singing gets on my nerves!

SECOND JAILER: That new bunch they brought in!

FIRST JAILER: The devil himself can't stop them. I heard the Chief say he'd turn the reserves loose and club the heads off 'em.

SECOND JAILER: (*Shakes his head*) What do you suppose those birds have got that makes 'em take punishment like that?

FIRST JAILER: Search me—I can't figure it out. But it's got my goat, I can't stand bein' round here! (*Music grows louder; he shouts above it.*) Singin', singin' all the time! (*Shaking his clenched fist*) Stop your damn singin'! Stop it, I say!

SECOND JAILER: (*In a frenzy*) To hell with your singin'!

(*They turn towards the right, whence comes a man's voice, singing.*)

It is we who plowed the prairies; built the cities where they trade;
Dug the mines and built the workshops; endless miles of railroad laid.
Now we stand, outcast and starving, 'mid the wonders we have made;
But the Union makes us strong.

(*They turn left, frightened, as if seeing ghosts; another voice sings.*)

All the world that's owned by idle drones is ours and ours alone.
We have laid the wide foundations, built it skywards, stone by stone.
It is not ours, not to slave in, but to master and to own,
While the Union makes us strong.

(*The chorus swells to a loud roar.*)

Solidarity forever!
Solidarity forever!
Solidarity forever!
And the Union makes us strong!

(*The two men put their fingers into their ears and run out of the cell in a kind of panic, slamming the door. The singing continues.*)

They have taken untold millions that they never toiled to earn,
But without our brain and muscle not a single wheel can turn;
We can break their haughty power, gain our freedom
When we learn
That the Union makes us strong.

CURTAIN

The audience sings:

Solidarity forever!
Solidarity forever!
Solidarity forever!
And the Union makes us strong!

The Miners and *Mill Shadows*

Labor College Productions

Labor colleges are a fascinating phenomenon that began in the early 1920s with Brookwood Labor College in Katonah, New York; the Work People's College, an Industrial Workers of the World school in Minnesota; and Commonwealth College in Arkansas. The founders and supporters of the labor colleges believed that the education of workers in a full-time residential setting, with a curriculum dominated by the social sciences, best prepared them for service in the labor movement. Their goal was to train a cadre of activists, propagandists, and leaders who could organize workers and sharpen their awareness for a potentially worker-controlled society. To accomplish this, working-class radicals created and supported their own educational institutions (Altenbaugh 8).

The curriculum of labor colleges offered one- and two-year programs geared not only toward male and female industrial workers with some trade union experience but also toward workers from unorganized industries and centers who may have had little or no trade union experience (Altenbaugh 94). The goal of the curriculum was to equip potential union leaders with the skills necessary to organize and perpetuate a union. The reasoning behind the existence of labor colleges is evident in the statement delivered at the opening of Brookwood, arguably the most influential of the schools. Brookwood was the result of a conference of idealistic labor leaders and intellectuals who believed that the workers' cause and the goal of a new society could best be advanced through education. They decided to create a school for adult workers and received the backing of the labor movement. In their 1921 statement, the founders of Brookwood listed their reasons for the creation of the institution:

> First—That a new social order is needed and is coming—in fact, that [it] is already on the way.
>
> Second—That education will not only hasten its coming, but will reduce to a minimum and perhaps do away entirely with a resort to violent methods.
>
> Third—That the workers are the ones who will usher in the new social order.
>
> Fourth—That there is immediate need for a workers' college with a broad curriculum, located amid healthy country surroundings, where the students can completely apply themselves to the task at hand. (Muste 92)

In other words, workers within the college formed a community, and they were empowered with the ability to spread that communal philosophy to other workers.

Drama played a strong part in the curriculum of labor colleges and educational programs. In an article praising workers' education as more focused than a diffuse university curriculum, Eleanor Coit, a teacher at the Affiliated Schools, claimed that the arts had a function for the schools. "The most conspicuous example," she wrote, "is in the field of labor drama. Dramatic productions are encouraged not only as an enrichment of the workers' lives but as concrete examples of the advantage of cooperative effort toward a single end" (175). According to *Fortnightly,* the newspaper of Commonwealth College, modern drama became a formal part of the curriculum in 1927–28. Students focused on contemporary dramatists who considered social themes, such as Eugene O'Neill, George Bernard Shaw, and Henrik Ibsen.

Labor college playwrights produced radical plays that "assumed social reform themes, extolling liberty, encouraging rebellion, denouncing social injustice" (Altenbaugh 103). This was especially the case at Brookwood. Like Commonwealth, Brookwood saw a "role for drama as part of the learning experience" and integrated labor drama into the curriculum. Workers' plays gave worker-students some practical background in aspects of theatre, a background they could then take back to their unions so that these might perform plays at meetings and recruiting functions (105). A. J. Muste, a founder and president of Brookwood, said of labor drama:

> It may be a means of self-expression, making the Labor Movement more vital to the workers themselves; it may interpret the Labor Movement for the public in more sympathetic and appealing terms than abstract reasoning can do; it may be a means of entertainment, particularly in isolated regions where the pool room and [speakeasy] are the only means of diversion. (19)

According to Brookwood student Jesse Slaughter, "the true working-class spirit" of drama created by workers "is of tremendous significance and value to Labor, in that it can be easily, effectively, and successfully done by students in all various phases of labor dramatics" (3). Labor drama was, then, "an educational tool" that dealt "*truthfully* with the lives and problems of the masses of the people, directly or suggestively, in a way that workers can understand and appreciate" (Ransdell, untitled 2).

The drama produced by labor colleges reveals the deeply held desire of the worker-students to create a connection with workers outside the school. However, if this became impossible, then the creation of unity within their own ranks would suffice. According to Slaughter in the December 1927/January 1928 *Brookwood Review* newspaper:

> With complete unanimity our worker audiences agreed that a labor movement which moves must have its drama and its marching songs. It must appeal to the heart as well as the head[,] to the emotions as well as the intellect. . . . Our plays held the mirror of social struggle in the United States . . . up to the workers; they recognized themselves and took new heart for the struggle. (3)

Through labor colleges, labor drama spread and became more directly concerned with its effect on the audience. The worker-performers strove to represent a community on stage that the audience might, in turn, embody. In order to achieve this embodiment, these stage communities needed to cast women in more prominent roles than they had been allowed in earlier labor dramas.

Labor colleges sequestered workers in order to instill the idea that communal goals took primacy over the ambitions of individuals. As a result, labor college dramas were developed, to an unprecedented extent, out of the workers' experiences. According to Muste, "There is material for drama in the experiences and thoughts and emotions of workingmen and women that other people do not know and the workers themselves do not really appreciate because they are too close to it" (19). The students in the labor drama course developed these incidents and life experiences into plays to which they and other workers could relate sympathetically.

At the same time, in labor college dramas, commitment to the union takes precedence over love and family. In the dramas of Brookwood, the plays represent a kind of genderless community created in order to empower the workers as a whole, and they present a view of the woman worker that invests her with a power not heretofore seen in labor drama.

In the plays of Bonchi or Beckie Friedman, the woman worker is absolutely necessary to the success of the labor community. Friedman, a Russian immigrant and member of New York Local 248 of the Amalgamated Clothing Workers, wrote her first play, *The Miners,* in 1926. Imitative of the plays of Maxim Gorky and Ernst Toller, this work attempts to combine the chants of Soviet and German expressionistic drama, allegory, and melodrama. The play opens with a call and response chant between Man and the Masses, with Man imploring the Masses to follow him to victory. The second scene draws on an allegory familiar to workers' theatre: An old Capitalist, fat and drunk, sides with two Pinkerton detectives during a strike, while the Mayor, Judge, Priest, head of the Klan, and wholesale Businessman pay homage to the Capitalist. Eager to get rid of Martha Noble, a local labor organizer who is inspiring the striking workers, the group agrees to kidnap, rape, and kill her.

Friedman then plunges the audience into the middle of a violent coal miners' strike in West Virginia. Martha's children and father fret over her safety because Martha and the strikers are in constant battle with the scabs —strikebreakers—the company attempts to hire. Peter, Martha's husband, is also on the front line. In this battle, Martha has apparently been the most threatening presence to the mine owners because of her ability to rally the workers. In the heat of the strike, we learn that miners in other towns are going on sympathy strikes without union approval.

In the moving final section, Martha has been killed on a picket line, and her family and the community are attempting to come to grips with her martyrdom. A black woman fears reprisals from the Klan if the strike breaks down. She and a Polish woman pay off Martha's debt to the grocer. Joe, a miner, tells of Martha's heroic death; it took ten bullets to stop her. The play ends with Peter channeling his grief into nonviolent resistance. Peter leads the gathered workers in a chant and returns to the picket line to fight on.

The Miners is a powerful play in many ways, perhaps because it creates for its audience an image of the woman worker unlike any we have seen before. Martha does not await approval or instruction. She is equally fiercely a mother and a union organizer. In *The Miners,* a woman becomes the kind of romantic hero of the caged male plays of the 1920s, but she is perhaps a purer kind of hero because her motives are never suspect. Friedman's foregrounding of Martha presents new threats to the capitalist class: the opening scene of the play, with the capitalist and his cronies plotting to destroy the union leader, is typical of labor drama, but here they speak a more violent language when discussing Martha.

The emphasis on rape as a tactic of the capitalist class is reinforced in the union office scene of Act 2, when a young girl runs into the union office, her clothes torn because detectives have tried to rape her. This revelation is something new to labor drama: a woman union leader threatens the male capitalists on the levels of class and gender, and must, then, be dealt with on those levels and more severely than the male organizers. This centering of the woman in the labor community creates new opportunities for violence, but Martha nevertheless refuses to relinquish that center. To yield to the impending violence would mean that Martha would subjugate herself, an act that would, in turn, mean defeat not only for union women but for the union itself. Martha's acquiescence would upset the balance that has created the community for the workers; therefore, she will face whatever violence comes in order to lead the community to victory in the strike.

The Miners was first presented at Brookwood's National Workers' Education Conference in 1926. In *Labor Age,* Helen Norton confirmed the play's effectiveness in addressing the labor movement from the workers' perspective:

> There was the real stuff of life in that play—the loyalty of workers to their union; the sacrifice not only of self but what is infinitely harder, of one's family; resentfulness of workers who have no alternative [but] violence against the schemes of the capitalist boss; mob action that is well intentioned but dangerous unless held steady by clear-sighted leaders—these things were as the author of the play had seen them. (18)

This critique is surprising since Friedman specifies the particular threats to women and points out how the female radical worker could be attacked for sacrificing patriarchally prescribed female roles for the movement. Norton denies certain aspects of the play and wishfully confirms what some in the labor college community hoped to achieve: a genderless, firmly bound group of workers.

The propagandistic thrust of the plays of labor colleges and education departments tapped into the growing role that women took on within the labor movement. Martha Noble's roles as union strike leader and mother are shown reinforcing each other; each role was integral to the other. According to Margaret Dreier Robins, the founder of the Women's Trade Union League, "The glory and strength of motherhood" was being sapped by commercial values and industrial exploitation (Payne 117). An organizing poster of the period showed women sewing in a sweatshop, trying to keep their jobs with one hand and comfort their crying infants with the other. Clearly, the poster suggested, true industrial peace could not be possible without the recognition of motherhood's circumstances as part of a complete agenda for the working class. Fannia Cohn, head of the Educational Department of the International Ladies Garment Workers Union, felt motherhood endowed women with instincts that gave them the legitimizing authority to organize and control crucial dimensions of sociopolitical life (Payne 124).

Motherhood as a subject came to labor culture as so many other subjects did, through union and labor songs. For instance, one song, "The Mill Mother's Lament," written by Katie Barnet in 1928, was sung over the casket of Ella May Wiggins, a union organizer killed in fighting during a Gastonia, North Carolina, strike in 1929:

We leave our homes in the morning,
We kiss our children good-bye,
While we slave for the bosses,
Our children scream and cry.

And when we draw our money,
Our grocery bills to pay,
Not a cent to spend for clothing,
Not a cent to lay away.

And on that very evening
Our little son will say,
"I need some shoes, dear mother,
And so does sister May."

How it grieves the heart of the mother,
You, everyone, must know,
But we cannot buy for our children,
Our wages are too low.

Now listen to me, workers,
Both you women and you men,
Let us win for them a victory,
I'm sure it will be no sin.

For union members, the workers argued, industrial America could pervert the idea of motherhood as inimical to workers who could barely support themselves.

That argument was at work in the creation of another dramatic piece. According to a YWCA labor drama pamphlet:

> An interesting dramatic project was worked out at the Southern Summer School in 1929. A group of students from the Marion, North Carolina, strike area related the conditions leading up to the strike and of the strike itself to a tutor who had considerable technique in playwriting. The scenes, the dialect, actual characters and strike songs were reproduced and the strike students acted it before the rest of the school. (*Use* 9–10)

The instructor was Brookwood economics teacher Tom Tippett, who had previously written a drama about the dangers of mining titled *What Price Coal?* Tippett was described as having "as much real experience with workers' groups as anyone in the country" (*Use* 9), and he believed drama should be propagandistic without forgetting the entertainment: "About half the time the workers like a whimsical play. They wish to be gay ladies and gorgeous men and forget that they are coal miners and cotton weavers" (*Use* 9).

In *Mill Shadows,* Tippett ties together motherhood, physical place, and labor, locating these at the center of a town whose citizens attempt to transform the town into a union community. All the activities of the town revolve around the union, and no worker is against the union. The town metamorphoses from a simple industrial village into a place of rebellion. Town and labor community become so completely intertwined that the distinction between the two becomes nonexistent. In other words, the town at first is based on the mill work, so that leisure, family, and other aspects of life are controlled by the mill. In its transformation the town has allowed the union to take the place of the mill as the center of town activities. This change is, for the workers, necessarily an improvement because the union is a center created by the workers; the union may dictate their lives but only because, in the end, it is dictated by the workers. If the union succeeds, then an equilibrium will be created between the mill and the union, which will inevitably mean an improvement in the lives of the workers. The effort to create a labor community out of an industrial community represents a movement away from alienation and toward engagement and, in that engagement, toward a true balance of work and nonwork life.

Called "the major play produced at Brookwood" by Lanza (212), Tippett's *Mill Shadows* reveals division not only between urban and rural activities but within the rural community itself. The play, first performed at Brookwood Labor College, dramatizes the 1929 textile strike in Marion, North Carolina. In his foreword, Tippett declares, "For the most part I was on the scene of the real drama and saw and heard much of what now appears in the form of a play. All the characters are real; they lived and died as the play characters do" (see page 185 in this volume).

The play was performed twice in New York City by the Brookwood Labor Players: on February 28, 1932, at the New School Theatre and on March 19 at the Labor Temple. Brooks Atkinson in the *New York Times* gave the players more credit for the effort than the play itself (28), but Stark Young in the *New Republic* was enthusiastic about the performance, calling it "a step toward the new theatre of labor" and repeating the program's label of *Mill Shadows* as "probably the most authentic American labor play." According to Young, "the play is successful in that it holds the interest of the audience, rouses them to sympathy, impels them to make generous gifts." Although Young was also confused about the audience for the play: "Tippett has tried to write for trained apostles of labor at Brookwood, kindly liberals at the New School, or workers themselves" (98). The play's message also concerned Young; by the end, he felt uncomfortably sure that Tippett was advocating violence in order to effect a tangible gain for the workers.

Of all the plays performed by the Brookwood Players, a group of traveling actors, this seems to have been the most successful. The actors toured the South and East, playing in union halls and classrooms or wherever space was available. From 1932 to 1936, *Mill Shadows* played to over 30,000 people around the country (Lanza 219).

The Miners

A Play in a Prologue and Three Acts

Bonchi Friedman

Student at Brookwood Labor College, Katonah, NY. Member of Local 248 Amalgamated Clothing Workers of America.

Dedicated to Those Who Will Act Like Martha and Peter.

Persons of the Play (in order of their appearance)

AN ALL DEVOURING CAPITALIST
THREE DETECTIVES
A CITY MAYOR
A JUDGE
A PRIEST
A KLEAGLE
A WHOLESALE BUSINESS MAN
AN OLD MAN—Martha's Father
MARTHA'S CHILDREN
JOHNNY
FLORA
MARTHA—Temporary Union Organizer
SKINNER—A Wholesale Business Man
FATHER BLUFF—A Priest
PETER NOBLE— Martha's Husband—Organizer Dist. #13 UMW of A
RAY—An Office Girl.
COOL-TEMPER—General President of the Miner's Union
A WOMAN — Whose Husband is in the County Jail Hospital
AN OLD WOMAN—Whose Son Was Killed
JOE BUCK—A Miner
ALEXIS—An Organizer
A YOUNG WOMAN
A POLISH WOMAN—Martha's Neighbor

A NEGRESS—Martha's Neighbor
A LOCAL GROCERY MAN
THE MASSES

Presented by:
The Brookwood Players at Brookwood Labor College
Katonah, New York on February 20, 1926.

The Scene of the Play is a West Virginia Mine Community of Today

Prologue, Scene 1 "The Workers"

THE WORKERS	Stanley Quest, Morris Lewitt, Ala Rosenfelt, Anna Sasnofsky, Polly Solomons, Sarah Greenberg, Charles Maute, Donald Calhoun, Constance Muste.
THEIR SPOKESMAN	Bonchi Friedman

Prologue, Scene 2. "The Explorers"

AN ALL-DEVOURING CAPITALIST	Frederick Hoffman
DETECTIVES	George Flick, Eddie Codemo
A CITY MAYOR	Glen Atkinson
A JUDGE	A.E. Matlack
A PREACHER	William Daech
A KLEAGLE	Tom Moriarty
A WHOLESALE BUSINESS MAN	Horst Berenz

Act 1. The Home of Martha and Peter

MARTHA'S FATHER	Morris Lewitt
JOHNNY	Donald Calhoun
FLORA	Constance Musto
MARTHA NOBLE, Temporary Union Organizer	Anna Sasnofsky
SKINNER, A Wholesale Business Man	A.M. Corazza
PREACHER BLUFF	William Deach

Act 2. The Union Office.

PETER NOBLE, Martha's Husband, Organizer Dist. 13 UMW	Bonchi Friedman
RAY, An Office Girl	Polly Solomons
COOL-TEMPER, General President, The Miner's Union	James Pick

A YOUNG WOMAN, Wife of a striker	Nattie Silverbrook
AN OLD WOMAN, Mother of a striker	Sarah Rozner
JOE BUCK, a miner	Charles V. Maute
ALEXIS, an organizer	William Shainack
A YOUNG GIRL, sister of a striker	Sarah Greenberg

Act 3. The home of Martha and Peter

A POLISH WOMAN, Martha's Neighbor	Ada Rosenfelt
AN OLD COLORED MAN, Martha's Neighbor	Thomas Dabney
A LOCAL GROCERY MAN	Stanley Gurst
RAY	Polly Solomons
JOHNNY	Donald Calhoun
FLORA	Constance Musto
ALEXIS	William Shainack
PREACHER BLUFF	William Deach
JOE BUCK	Charles V. Maute
BIG TOM, Leader of the Masses	Horst Berenz
THE MASSES	Sarah Greenberg, Geo. Flick, Ed. Codero, Wm. Rollover, T. Moriarty, G. Atkinson, S. Rozner, F. Hoffman, N. Silverbrook, A.R. Matlack

Staff

DIRECTOR	Hazel MacKaye
MART(sic), Carpenter	Sam Arntzen
ASST. CARPENTERS	E. Codero, Adolph Gersh
MASTER OF PROPERTIES	Rudolph Harju
ASSISTANTS	A. Ainsworth, E. Guest
MASTER ELECTRICIAN	A.M. Corszza

PROLOGUE

Scene 1: As the curtains part, voices are heard and the scene discloses the silhouetted figures of men, women, and children against a dark, ruddy glow. In the shadowy foreground a single, tall figure of a workingman is vaguely perceived.

THE MAN: You who always slave!

THE MASSES: We always slave.

THE MAN: I am one of your ranks.

THE MASSES: You are one of our ranks.

THE MAN: Hear the voice of one of your ranks!

THE MASSES: We hear the voice of one of our ranks.

THE MAN: Leave those dark graves.

THE MASSES: We will leave the dark graves.

THE MAN: We will strike for the right to work!

THE MASSES: We will strike for the right to work!

THE MAN: We will die fighting for the right to live!

THE MASSES: We will die fighting for the right to live!

THE MAN: We want bread for our starved children!

THE MASSES: We want bread for our stared children!

THE MAN: We make rich the world!

THE MASSES: We make rich the world!

THE MAN: We are ragged, hungry, and homeless! We want sunshine!

THE MASSES: We are ragged, hungry, and homeless! We want sunshine!

THE MAN: Are you coming out of the graves?

THE MASSES: We are coming out of the graves!

(*A heavy noise is heard, of picks, shovels and the sound of many heavy boot; there is talking. Curtain.*)

Scene 2: Before the curtains part for this scene, there is the sound of talking and triumphant laughter. As the curtains part, three voices are heard crying: "Hurrah for the 18th Amendment!" When the lights come on slowly, revealing the scene little by little, a sinister figure is discovered seated at a narrow, long table with wine bottles and glasses before him. He is exceptionally fleshy, bald-headed, old, devouring, and half-drunk: the CAPITALIST. *Three detectives are seated before him at the table. One of the detectives, about 35, has a face covered with pimples and has a red nose. The other two are abominably ugly. The* CAPITALIST *is trying to rise from his seat, with a glass in hand, talking as though his mouth were full of tongue.*

OLD CAPITALIST: For the 18th Amendment! For the 18th Amendment! (*He drinks.*)

(*Five people enter, dressed as follows:* A CITY MAYOR, *in official costume; a Judge, in official costume, cap and gown; a* PRIEST, *in gown with a silver cross on his chest, carrying a Bible, wearing the proper hat, etc.; the* KLEAGLE *of the Klan, with a wooden cross in hand, dressed in full regalia, white robe and mask; a* WHOLESALE BUSINESSMAN, *looking preposterous. They enter individually, but all have dancing, springy steps.*)

DETECTIVE and CAPITALIST: (*As* MAYOR *enters*) Welcome, welcome, City Mayor! Man of Law and Order.

MAYOR: I keep Law and Order, Brothers! I keep Law and Order.

(JUDGE *enters while* MAYOR *speaks, carrying an injunction in one hand.*)

GROUP: Aha! Welcome, Judge!

JUDGE: Yah, Yah, I am Judge! I give orders to keep order at the mines. (*He stretches forth the hand hold the injunction paper to the* CAPITALIST; *his other hand is outstretched at the same time, for money.*)

CAPITALIST: I give hundreds, thousands, for injunctions, and for Law and Order.

(PRIEST *enters.*)

GROUP: Welcome, welcome, Father! Drink with us for God and Church, for the 18th Amendment.

PRIEST: (*Extending bible toward the* CAPITALIST.) I feed them with this food, this wine, it puts them to sleep. Ha, ha! (*Extending left hand also, to* CAPITALIST.) How much?

CAPITALIST: I give tens, fifties, hundreds. Put them all to sleep, like sheep! A hundred dollars!

(KLEAGLE *enters. The others become silent.*)

CAPITALIST: Who are you?

KLEAGLE: (*In a hoarse voice.*) I am the Kleagle of the Klan, a Protestant, and therefore hundred percent American. I am anti-catholic, anti-Jew, anti-Negro, and against foreigners.

CAPITALIST: You're against Negroes, Japanese, and Italians? You are against foreigners coming to this country?

KLEAGLE: America for Americans only.

CAPITALIST: If you are against foreigners, then you are a union leader!

ALL (*Except* KLEAGLE.): Ha, ha! A Union leader!

CAPITALIST: (*Commanding.*) Take off his robe!

KLEAGLE: (*Begins to shiver, holding his robe tightly.*) I killed a union leader with my own hands.

CAPITALIST: (*Murmurs.*) Time's short. (*Speaks louder*) Can you break strikes?

KLEAGLE: No, but we break the strikers' heads and then the strike is broken.

(*The* KLEAGLE *grabs a bottle and attempts to drink. The* DETECTIVE *notices him and snatches the bottle from him.*)

DETECTIVE: Son of a bitch!

(*The* DETECTIVE *drinks from the bottle himself. The* KLEAGLE *enviously goes through the same motions of drinking, but without the bottle.*)

CAPITALIST: Hey, Kleagle, how many strike-breakers have you got?

KLEAGLE: Every member of my Klan.

(*The* KLEAGLE *stretches his hand out for money and the* CAPITALIST gives. *The Wholesale Businessman enters as the Capitalist is giving the* KLEAGLE *money.*)

GROUP: Here comes the Wholesale Businessman. Welcome! Welcome!

WHOLESALE BUSINESSMAN: We starve them all. No bread for them. No bread for rascals.

DETECTIVES: We kill them all! We'll bring you Martha here alive. (*To* CAPITALIST.) But before we kill her, you'll seduce her first. (*Pointing to the whole crowd.*) We next. When all of us will have enough, we'll kill her. (*To* CAPITALIST.) How much?

CAPITALIST: Fifty, a hundred, for the whole night. (*He pays, commanding.*) All of you on your knees. Lick my boots. Who will do it?

THE GROUP: All of us will do it!

CAPITALIST: Father, you will be the first! (*The* PRIEST *grovels at his feet.*) City Mayor, you next. (*The* MAYOR *also grovels.*) My other shoe! (*To the* JUDGE *and* KLEAGLE *as they fawn upon him.*) Hey, you Father, put them all to sleep! Mayor, you will keep Law and Order! Judge, give orders to keep order! And you, Kleagle, break their heads! (*Pointing to the* BUSINESSMAN.) No bread to scoundrels! Starve them all! I paid you all! You Detectives, kill them all! I paid enough.

DETECTIVES: We will kill them all.

(CAPITALIST *throws several coins on the floor. They all fall down and scramble for the coins.* CAPITALIST *dances out of the room.*)

CAPITALIST: (*Triumphantly*) Hah! They will kill them all.

CURTAIN

ACT 1

In MARTHA'S *house, a miner's house, very poor but clean. A door on the right, leading to another room. A shelf made out of old boards, unpainted, with several books and magazines on it. On the wall near the entrance to the room, hangs a large picture of* MARTHA. *Nearby hangs John Brown's picture, next Mother Jones', Kate O'Hare's, and Fanny Zelling's. On the right hand an* OLD MAN, MARTHA'S *father, about 70, is seated in a chair, suffering with minder's asthma; both hands leaning on a cane. Two children, a boy about ten,* JOHNNY, *and a girl of about six,* FLORA; *poor clothed and pale; both sitting on the floor. There is a box near the* OLD MAN, *serving as a chair. There is a table and a chair on the right.*

JOHNNY: (*He bites a piece of tobacco from a plug, spits into the corner.*) Flora, let's play strike. You'll do the same that Mamma does at meetings.

FLORA: Mamma doesn't like us.

JOHNNY: Who told you that?

FLORA: She goes away every day and leaves me here alone.

JOHNNY: Mamma has to go; she's on the strike.

FLORA: What's a strike?

JOHNNY: (*Embarrassed*) A strike? A strike? People fight.

FLORA: (*Insulted*) It's a lie! Mamma never fights.

JOHNNY: No, it's not a fight like Andrew does when he's drunk. Mamma fights scabs.

FLORA: What's a scab?

JOHNNY: A scab is if I want more money for my work in the mine and the foreman says no, then Freddy comes and takes my place. Then he's a scab.

FLORA: So Mamma goes every day to beat Freddy because he took your place?

JOHNNY: Aw, you're too small! When you'll be big like me and work in the mine you'll know. Ma never beats anybody. She says to the scabs: "Don't work."

FLORA: And they listen to Ma?

JOHNNY: They love Pa and Ma because we are as poor as them.

FLORA: Johnny, why don't you buy bread?

JOHNNY: Because the baker won't sell it.

FLORA: Why?

JOHNNY: You're too small. (*He spits again into the corner.*) See, when you're big like me and work in the mine, you'll understand. But let's read the paper.

FLORA: I can't read.

JOHNNY: I'll read to you. (*He gets up and takes the paper from the table; puts it on the floor beside* FLORA *and sits down to read.*)

JOHNNY: (*Reading*) "Miners' children, be happy." (*Reading very slowly*) "If miners' children don't cry for bread when their fathers are on strike, they help win the strike." Grandpa, there was a big fight today near Mine No. 7, but the pickets wanted to speak to them, then a fight started.

OLD MAN: Was Mamma there?

JOHNNY: Mamma? No, I didn't see her, but Pa was there.

OLD MAN: (*Shaking his head; looking at children*) Did you tell Papa to go home?

JOHNNY: No, Papa has to fight the scabs.

(*As the boy speaks,* MARTHA, *hurried and tired, appears at the door, noticing the boy, and the paper on the floor; she draws back, remaining on the threshold, stretching her arms toward the children. She makes the door squeak, in order not to scare the children by her sudden appearance. When both children notice her, they run to-*

wards her. She bends down, embraces them and kisses them. They embrace her. The children go back and look at the paper.)

JOHNNY: (*Looking at "The Miner"*) Mamma, we are not hungry.

(MARTHA *glances at the paper and notices the caption. With a fiery glance, she embraces them again.*)

JOHNNY: Ma, there was a lot of fightin' today near Mine No. 7. Papa was there too.

MARTHA: What was Papa doing there? (*Picks paper up and puts it on table*)

JOHNNY: All fighting the scabs. Three trucks of scabs.

OLD MAN: (*Whispering*) Poor orphans.

MARTHA: (*Overhearing his words, turns toward him questioningly*) What did you say, Pa? (*The* OLD MAN *remains silent. Walking over to the* OLD MAN, MARTHA *puts her hands on his gray hair and tenderly touches it, speaking.*) Why should you worry so much? You are old and weak and these worries will make you sick. This isn't the first time I've ever been in a strike and nothing has happened so far.

OLD MAN: (*Speaking brokenly*) Martha, Martha, you're the only one I have. You and Peter. When your brother Fritz was killed in the mine I suffered enough but I had you left, my only daughter, and now . . .

MARTHA: (*Softly*) But, Father, I'm alive and not working in the mine.

OLD MAN: It's worse, Martha. You know this present strike is more dangerous than all the strikes we've had before. The powerful Universal Coal Company!

MARTHA: Yes, Father, I know the Universal—the bloody Coal Company.

(SKINNER *enters, with a hypocritical smile, looking at the walls, then at the miner's paper, which is on the table.*)

SKINNER: Hm! A very busy woman you are, very busy.

(MARTHA *looks at him, surprised.*)

SKINNER: It's true I'm a wholesale food dealer but I didn't come to sell nothin' to you now. Never mind, you wouldn't guess what I did come here for, and you'd never expect me to be the one who would bring happiness into your house. Ha, Ha!

MARTHA: Happiness! The strike is not settled.

SKINNER: It's about time you left the strike alone.

MARTHA: Leave the strike!

SKINNER: Don't get excited, my dear woman. I knew you fifteen years ago when your skirt didn't reach your knees.

MARTHA: Anything important?

SKINNER: Important? It's more than that. (*He takes a seat at the table.* MARTHA *sits down also.*) It's about time the coal strike . . .

MARTHA: Are you representing the operators? I can speak for the miners only.

SKINNER: That's just it. I came to you because you are representin' 'em.

(MARTHA *gets impatient.*)

SKINNER: Are the miners concerned about you as much as you are about them?

MARTHA: If this is what you came for, well—it's our private affair, between the miners and myself.

SKINNER: There's where you're mistaken. This strike is damn serious for the business men. We can't have the miners starvin' and dressin' in old rags that the workers send from other cities.

MARTHA: Did you also think of those things when you, as president of the Business Men's Committee, urged them not to give the strikers any credit? Was it because you didn't want to see our miners starved that your bakers decided not to sell us bread?

(SKINNER *embarrassed; looks out toward the audience, wiping the sweat off his face.*)

SKINNER: (*To himself*) How she knows everything! (*To* MARTHA) But we had to do that because the bank and the coal company ordered us to do it and we are business men, Martha. We got to protect our business as well as you got to protect your union business.

MARTHA: Business!

SKINNER: Yes, business. If the miners are out on a long strike, we'll be ruined, and we thought we could prevent the strike, or make it short.

MARTHA: At the expense of the miners?

SKINNER: To save our business.

MARTHA: And what did you come to see me for?

SKINNER: To see whether you learned anythin' since the strike.

MARTHA: Whether I have learned? I've learned that every brutal scheme that was ever invented is used against the strikers, to compel them to go back to work without a union.

SKINNER: No, not exactly that. I mean, don't you see, I mean . . . I mean that you are an honest and a capable one too. It's about time you considered your own life and also your children's. You've got to be more practical and there ain't much use in givin' all of your days to the miners. They wouldn't give even a moment of their time to help you, if you should be unable to give those wonderful talks to them. We business men ain't no enemies of the miners, but it's business you know. I, myself, was even a socialist and voted for Bryan, but I decided it's no use.

MARTHA: (*Rises from her chair, folds her arms, looking at him with an openly expressed hatred*) And what do you expect me to do . . . (*emphatically*) when I get wise?

SKINNER: Do nothin', just do nothin'. The universe is ready to forgive Pete, your husbin' for all the fightin' he done durin' the strike and he can get a good job now. He's a smart feller and . . . here's a thousand dollars. (*Speaking hurriedly*) You have children . . .

MARTHA: (*Enraged*) There is no one in this world I want to see worrying about my children and not only my children but not even the thousands of miners' children shall I feed with the food bought with this kind of money, even when death is looming over their bodies. The only time we shall use your money or food is when we will have taken it away from you by force.

(MARTHA *opens the door and points the way out for him.* FATHER BLUFF *enters. He is about forty, self-satisfied, a fleshy face with small eyes, and a soft voice.*)

FATHER BLUFF: I never thought you were such a harsh woman. (*Pointing with a finger toward God*) He is against it.

MARTHA: (*Not noticing him pointing his finger*) Who is against it, the coal trust?

FATHER BLUFF: Martha, you are blaspheming God! He has nothing to do with things here. He has nothing to do with coal.

MARTHA: So God doesn't like to hear words against men that take bread from starving children and has nothing to do with coal!

(FATHER BLUFF *wipes his face with a handkerchief, confused.* SKINNER *starts to go out but looks at the priest as the only savior in the situation, stretches a hand toward the priest, and indicates by the expression on his face that* MARTHA *is a terrible woman.*)

FATHER BLUFF: (*Taking a seat on the box near the* OLD MAN) Hard times.

OLD MAN: It's a sin to let old men and children starve of hunger and die of cold.

FATHER BLUFF: We dare not question His doings. The world is full of sin.

(*The* OLD MAN *tries to rise from his chair, supporting his body on the cane; gets angry; his eyes sparkle.*)

OLD MAN: Catherine is full of sin.

(MARTHA *turns from tidying* FLORA'S *tumbled hair, and looks at the* PRIEST *and the* OLD MAN.)

FATHER BLUFF: (*Displays ignorance*) Catherine, who is that? What happened to her?

MARTHA: (*Sarcastically to her father*) Oh, Pa, why should you embarrass Father Bluff with such sad stories? Father Bluff is only the mail carrier between

(*Pointing up*) Him and us, and to tell us whether he likes our cry for bread or no

FATHER BLUFF: (*Insulted*) Martha, you are insulting the holy . . .

MARTHA: (*Interrupting*) Yes, I am insulting His representatives, who refused to bury little Catherine, who was killed by the company thugs when they ransacked her father's house because he was chairman of the picket committee in this town.

FATHER BLUFF: I didn't refuse. I asked for the money before the ceremony.

MARTHA: When you knew he didn't have a cent!

FATHER BLUFF: (*Gets red in the face, wipes the perspiration off; embarrassed, digs into his bosom pocket as if hunting for something*) Hard times. The world is full of sin. (*Notices that* MARTHA *is getting ready to leave*) I came to propose peace to you and not to quarrel with you.

MARTHA: (*With controlled coolness*) Peace with whom?

FATHER BLUFF: Peace with the operators.

MARTHA: (*Suspiciously looking toward* FATHER BLUFF) Peace with the operators is not my private affair. The suggestion has to come to the union.

FATHER BLUFF: For the last twenty-give years I have been the miners' priest. I know all their leaders well and not one of them is as stubborn, as violent as you; not one is as inconsiderate.

MARTHA: Inconsiderate! Towards whom?

FATHER BLUFF: Towards the rights of the operators and the losses to the miners.

(MARTHA *is angered but calm. The* OLD MAN *infuriated, tries to rise from his chair.*)

FATHER BLUFF: You could not expect the operators to have mercy for the miners after you forced the pump men out of the mines which flooded the mines, and it is not only the operators, but the country's public opinion is against your action. You have the right to strike but to destroy what (*pointing upward*) He gave to the operators is a sin against Him.

MARTHA: (*Bitterly*) A Sin! And Public Opinion is against it! If we should permit the strike to drag along for twenty-five weeks and give the company a chance to sell well rock instead of coal, charging four times as much for the rock as for good coal, then (*emphatically*) "*public opinion*" would not be against us!

FATHER BLUFF: (*Dumbfounded*) What a woman! (S*howing despair because he can do nothing with her. Clasping his hands, he tries one more trick.*) Fear God, Martha. I am the miners' friend. You have children.

MARTHA: (*Determinedly*) The lives of my children and all miners' children are worthless as long as we remain at the mercy of the coal operators.

FATHER BLUFF: God is against women doing men's work. You are the only woman among so many men. (*He tries to speak in an artificially merciful voice.*) And the Devil, my daughter is always awake.

MARTHA: (*Vehemently and indignant, but challenging*) You dare not insult our mines and you better chase the devil out of Mr. Thompson, the brutal director of the Universal Coal Company, who donated four thousand dollars to your church and may you know that neither the business men whom the company sent to bribe us nor the holy men, (*pointing upward*) His representative, whom the company sends to scare us with the Devil, will help them. We are striking for a union and we are a good and disciplined army.

(*A rumbling noise is heard, of men, women and children in the distance.*)

MARTHA: (*Hurrying*) There is fighting again around the mine.

(*She grabs a short coat and hurries out of the room.*)

CURTAIN

ACT 2

Scene opens in the Union office. A Union charter covered with black crepe hangs on the rear wall. A picture of Abraham Lincoln hangs from the wall on one side of the room, and on the other above the desk hangs a union label calendar. PETER *is sitting near the table, writing with pencil. Not far away at the desk,* RAY *is at the telephone.*

PETER: (*To* RAY) It's no use waiting at the telephone. It will not ring.

COOL-TEMPER: (*Enters*) Why won't it ring? You should have been prompter in paying your bills for the telephone service.

RAY: We have always been prompt in that.

COOL-TEMPER: Is it out of order?

PETER: It is not out *of* order. It is out *by* order.

COOL-TEMPER: By order of whom?

PETER: Of the Universal Coal Company.

COOL-TEMPER: It's against the anti-trust law, Pete.

PETER: (*Ironically*) Then the District President of the Coal Miners Union may sue the telephone company for damages.

COOL-TEMPER: You can't remain without a telephone in the office during a strike. I will speak to the president of the city board.

PETER: You can speak, if you want to, Cool-Temper, but not to the president of the city board.

COOL-TEMPER: Why?

PETER: He's dead. The Universal Colliery invited him to supper and poisoned him.

COOL-TEMPER: Why?

RAY: No one knows, but it was soon after he gave the miners permission to hold a meeting in the city hall.

COOL-TEMPER: Who is acting president of the Board now?

PETER: The Universal Coal Company. (COOL-TEMPER *silenced takes up a newspaper.* PETER *walks toward* RAY, *with a paper in hand, dictates.*) "Brother Ernest, District 12, Bloodville, Ill. The spirit of Solidarity which you have shown us, by your courageous action, in calling out the men of the whole district, has greatly encouraged our men. This is a death blow to the Company that thought it could break our strike by evicting our men from the houses and getting injunctions against them; prohibiting strikers from picketing the mines and the union from using its own money. As for our own district, we are picketing the mines and have succeeded in forcing the maintenance men out in spite of the injunction, which threatens destruction of the mines all along the lines with the exception of Beastville and Redtown, where the company has paralyzed our wire connections. But there also we will ignore the injunction and carry on our strike activity."

COOL-TEMPER: (*Interrupts*) Stop for a moment. Defy injunctions issued by an Official of the government? It's a dangerous road you have picked.

(RAY *listens attentively.*)

PETER: (*Looking at* COOL-TEMPER *and shaking his head*) And you know me as one who is giving way to a desperate mood in such a serious situation, ha, ha, ha . . . Men, I am sending this message to District 6 where the miners are out on a sympathy strike unless it is authorized by the general board and its president.

RAY: The president of the district writes in his message that the miners themselves decided to strike and that he approved it after the men went out.

PETER: And it's about time you knew (*speaking slowly and emphatically*) that I also am not giving way to emotion and feeling. In the many towns of this district we have a hundred-thousand men out on strike and *they* are deciding the poll of the strike.

COOL-TEMPER: With your approval.

PETER: Yes, with my approval; I am *also* a miner.

COOL-TEMPER: You are antagonizing the Coal Company and the State Officials with your irresponsible action.

PETER: (*Looking at him and pausing*) Antagonizing the Coal Company!

RAY: But this is the only thing we can do. We can't wait to fight the government but when the government granted the injunction against picketing and everything, we were forced to violate it. The company will strike with us for ten years unless we picket and keep the scabs out of the mines.

COOL-TEMPER: (*Angrily*) Who's asking you, Ray?

RAY: I'm just informing you.

COOL-TEMPER: (*To* PETER) And is this enough cause to violate an injunction issued by the government? If you hadn't hurried in declaring the strike, you wouldn't have had to violate the injunction.

PETER: Wait with the strike? This is the worst non-union district of all the coal fields in this country. The Company announced another slash in wages of fifty percent. It would have ruined entirely the unions in organized fields.

COOL-TEMPER: Why didn't you notify me about it?

PETER: (*Looking at him, speaking emphatically*) We did try to inform you but nobody could locate you.

COOL-TEMPER: I wanted to postpone the strike.

PETER: You knew about it?

COOL-TEMPER: Yes, I knew; you could wait a little longer.

PETER: Wait! Until it would be too late?

COOL-TEMPER: I wanted to learn the attitude of the government toward your strike.

PETER: And you found out that the government's attitude is against the strike?

COOL-TEMPER: Yes.

PETER: Then let the government go down in the mines and work.

COOL-TEMPER: You are violating the law.

PETER: Yes, we are. We are violating the injunction, and we are going to force the pump men out of each mine possible.

COOL-TEMPER: You'll ruin the mines!

PETER: We'll win the strike!

COOL-TEMPER: You can't win a strike with public opinion against you.

PETER: To hell with public opinion! We have always lost out strikes because we had Public Opinion *with* us. The only public opinion I know of is the strikers' wives who suffer heroically in every great battle, who bury their children that die in the tents, without showing a symptom of sorrow in order not to discourage their men. And the rest of the Public Opinion wants a cheap coal even at the expense of the miner's lives.

(*A woman enters; she looks ragged and old, but has the voice of a young woman.*)

THE YOUNG RAGGED WOMAN: (*To* PETER) Brother, my husband is in the county jail hospital since last week.

PETER: (*Noticing her clothes*) Where are you from, sister?

THE YOUNG RAGGED WOMAN: From Rockville.

PETER: Was your husband on the picket lines when the sheriff fired on the strikers?

THE YOUNG RAGGED WOMAN: Yes, he was. Only four weeks ago his face was terribly burned when the accident occurred in the Rockville mine, but husband said he just got on the picket line.

COOL-TEMPER: Have you seen your husband since?

THE YOUNG RAGGED WOMAN: No, he's in the prison hospital and I don't know whether he's alive. They won't let me see him.

(*An* OLD WOMAN *whose son was killed enters. She is poor and ragged, bent over, walks slowly, speaks in a low voice.*)

OLD WOMAN: (*To* PETER) Brother, my son was killed. We are in a tent in this cold weather, and his three children are sick, they are starving. We can't get a doctor and there's no place to get warm water for the children. Help save the orphans! My son was always a good union man and was killed on the picket line.

PETER: (*His face showing suffering, runs his hands through his hair; looks at the first woman, then at the second woman; then to* COOL-TEMPER.) We are desperate! Look at them! Killed on the picket line. Shot on the picket line. Children sick; children are dying. (*He grabs a registry and reads.*) "Five hundred families living in tents in Beastville. Pneumonia epidemic. Ten children died in the second week of the strike. Women are sick and men on the picket line, in prison and hospitals; ten men were shot to death by company thugs." What do you suggest, Brother Cool-Temper?

COOL-TEMPER: I know all that I'm an old timer.

(*Enter* JOE BUCK, *a miner; dressed; he is tall.*)

JOE: Yes, I know you're an old-timer, and we are new timers. (*He is clenching his fists, looking at* COOL-TEMPER, *the old-timer, with painful sarcasm.*) You see that wound? I was wounded in a strike. (*He takes a piece of paper and a pencil and hands it to* COOL-TEMPER, *saying*) Figure out. I got this wound from a Pinkerton detective in Ludlow, Colorado, during our strike. (*Pointing to the number on his chest*) It's 1913. I made it myself, to remember it, and this is 1925.

(*The* YOUNG WOMAN *looks at him.*)

YOUNG WOMAN: How old are you?

JOE: Thirty-two, sister.

OLD WOMAN: When did you start in the mines?

JOE: I was eight years old, mother. (*To* COOL-TEMPER) It's not what you done before, it's what you do now that counts. (*He walks over so close to* COOL-TEMPER *that the latter draws his face away.*) No son of a bitch, whoever he is, is going to fool the strikers this time. We will win or die. (*To* RAY) Here's a message for Martha from Beastville.

COOL-TEMPER: (*To* PETER) You taught them all to be desperate. Your methods will ruin the union.

PETER: We had a union in name. We are building a real union now in this strike with the blood of the Rockville men.

(COOL-TEMPER *walks out.* ALEXIS *enters. He is above middle-size; terribly weary; about 35; wears loggings, a summer coat on top of his shirt; he drops in a chair, looking in front; frowning, then hides his face and head in both hands.* RAY, PETER *and the* WOMAN *look at him.* RAY *wants to call* ALEXIS, *but* PETER *motions to her to leave him alone. Finally* ALEXIS *wakes up.* RAY *speaks to him*).

RAY: Poor Alexis, you must have a hard time picketing Stonyville. Are the men out?

ALEXIS: The unions are out, but Martha is still trying to get the pump men. Any message for me?

RAY: Yes. (*She hands him a paper and he reads it.*)

ALEXIS: They want me to go to Beastville, I've got to go.

PETER: Can't you rest a minute?

ALEXIS: No, I must go.

(*He is extending his hand to* PETER, *but before parting, a girl of 17 rushes in screaming, her bobbed-hair disheveled and her waist torn in several places, so that parts of her arms and back show.*)

YOUNG GIRL: No, no! I'd rather die! I'll kill myself. (*The group is aghast. The* GIRL *runs to* RAY, *as if trying to hide herself. Speaks first to* RAY *and then to* ALEXIS.) I was alone. My brother Tom is on the picket line. Two company thugs attacked me. I struggled with them until I broke away. I'll kill myself. Please save me! (RAY *rushes over to her.*)

RAY: Come, come with me, poor girl. Don't be so scared, you will be safe here. Nobody will harm you. (RAY *leads the girl off into another room. The group in the office is shocked by this last occurrence.* PETER *displaying terrific suffering says, "Oh God!"*)

(JOHNNY *and* FLORA *appear.* JOHNNY *wears a big man's coat and a big cap. They both look terribly neglected; the little girl coughs. She begins to cry; "I'm hungry." Both run to* PETER.)

FLORA: (*When both children appear in the office and notice* PETER, FLORA *exclaims*) Johnny, here's Pa.

PETER: How are you my son? (*Then to* FLORA) Did Johnny play with you?

JOHNNY: Pa, she is askin' too many things. (PETER *lifts up* FLORA *and carries her to the table,* JOHNNY *following him.*)

FLORA: When will Ma come home? (*The group looks at the children sympathetically*).

PETER: Mamma is in Stonyville; she'll soon come home.

JOHNNY: Papa, I was near Mine No. 7 yesterday when you were there fighting; I saw the sheriff hitting big Tim. I threw a stone at the sheriff and he fell.

FLORA: (*To* PETER) Will Mamma come home tonight? We are afraid to sleep.

(MARTHA *appears wearing a short coat; she looks worn out. The Children, noticing her, run to her immediately. She embraces them and they beg her not to leave them again.*)

MARTHA: (*To* JOHNNY.) But you, my big boy, understand that if Mamma goes away, she has to go. It's a big strike.

JOHNNY: Yes, Ma, I went to Mine No. 7. There was a big fight and I threw a stone at the sheriff.

(MARTHA *looks at* PETER; *they look at each other with admiration, showing no sign of relation outside of strike affairs. The group proudly looks at her.*)

PETER: Well, Martha, what news?

MARTHA: News? Who can tell so much? There is blood, starvation, misery and terror everywhere. Injunctions prohibiting everything. I prepared the pumpmen at Stonyville to quit tomorrow but the engineers and pumpmen in the most important mines are still working. We must stop them. The Beastville and Redtown Mines must be completely paralyzed. That's the only weapon left in our hands.

PETER: And . . .

MARTHA: Yes, the injunction!

RAY: (*Who has returned, handing her a paper*) Here's a message from Beastville. Joe Buck brought it.

MARTHA: (*Reading aloud*) "The town is surrounded. The injunction prohibits everything and permits the shooting of strikers in case of intimidation of scabs." I am going there, and will get the engineers and pumpmen off the job.

ALEXIS: That's what they told me, too, in my message. *You* will *get* them off, if they'll go.

MARTHA: We will make them go!

PETER: If mines are surrounded by armed guards.

MARTHA: We will surround them by armed miners.

ALEXIS: You're a desperate woman, Martha.

MARTHA: (*Looking at* ALEXIS) Are these your words? If I am desperate, it is because you are driven to despair, but does taking engineers off the job in the face of such injunctions mean despair? No! Remember, this is the fifth strike and yet we haven't succeeded in organizing a union. It is either this strike that we win or we shall have no Union.

PETER: No, Martha, not this. The men have to leave the pumps, but it's the danger and we want you to celebrate with all of us our victory, Martha.

MARTHA: And therefore . . .

ALEXIS: Be careful, Martha.

MARTHA: My dear Alex, hundreds of men already have been wounded. Women and children die in tents in alarming numbers every day. Why is my life worth more? I have children? Of course. But all miners have children. (*She turns to* PETER.) Do you remember, Peter, your words before the strike? You said, "Now is not the time to think about ourselves and our children. We are the thousands of miners, their wives and their children, and as real union people we have to give all that we have and all we can, even our lives to win a strong union for the coal industry." With this belief we plunged into the strike and this gives us courage to fight. With these words in my heart, I shall start out for Beastville and from there to Redtown to keep the scabs from going into the mines. One gives her life on the picket line, another woman encourages her husband to go on the picket line, and a third woman buries her children, not showing tears in her eyes because she knows her husband has yet to fight. And I am only one of these women, doing my share for the strike (*Then with a smile and a light gesture pointing toward* PETER, ALEXIS *and* JOHNNY) and as for victory, (*She closes her eyes for a moment.*) it will be a great victory to have the dictator of the Universal Coal Company, Mr. Thompson, who offered five thousand dollars for my head, sign an agreement with the miners' union.

PETER: (*Worriedly, seriously*) Yes, Thompson. He is planning a surprise for us.

MARTHA: (*Stretching both hands out, one to* PETER, *the other to* ALEXIS) Well, it's time to go. Beastville is calling.

PETER: (*Looking into her eyes*) Martha!

MARTHA: (*Looking at him; with a forced smile*) Yes, and celebrate this victory without me, if this is our fate. (*She turns swiftly and says to* ALEXIS *and* JOE.) Well, boys, let's go, they are waiting for us. (*Pointing her finger into the distance*)

(ALEXIS *and* JOE *follow her out.* PETER *and* RAY *are proudly looking after her.*)

CURTAIN

Act 3

In MARTHA'S *house. At the left is a door leading to another room. Sounds are heard of two or three voices whispering outside the house and this grows louder. Then many threatening voices are heard crying: "Death!" Then murmuring again. Then again loudly: "Death!" Then constant noise, groaning and threateningly, louder, is heard for about half a minute. Then distinctly a man's voice cries: "Revenge!"* A POLISH WOMAN *enters the house, clad in a ragged skirt and a short man's overcoat. Her head is thrust forward, with a piece of old gray parcels around her head and tied at the neck; her hands folded into the coat sleeves. As she walks in she stops hesitatingly for a little while. Then she draws one hand out and wipes her eyes with the sleeve of her coat. She walks around the room, returning back to the door she entered by. Then looking at the pictures, without much attention but shaking her head, until she notices Martha's picture; she looks at it, then towards the ceiling, shaking her head, whispering to herself and crying silently. A razor strop and razor hand near the window.*

POLISH WOMAN: (*Softly sobbing*) M—mar-tha! (*She looks towards the ceiling again, again at Martha's picture; crosses herself. Shaking her head, speaks in a crying voice, with a pronounced Polish accent.*) You such a good lady. All Polish ladies like you. Droga Martha! Dear Martha! (*Crosses herself*) Kohanna Martha! Beloved Martha!

(*A loud noise is heard in the distance. Individual voices are heard in question and answer, but two words are indistinguishable to the audience.* A NEGRESS *of about 30 enters, poorly dressed, disturbed and desperate.*)

NEGRESS: Now we are lost! All colored people are lost! All colored people are lost!

POLISH WOMAN: All Polish people are lost! All miners lost!

NEGRESS: Lady Sobeski, the Klan is going to kill all the colored people.

(*Enter* MARTHA'S *father, slowly, bent over his cane, his whole body shaking. The* POLISH WOMAN *looks at* MARTHA'S *picture again.*)

POLISH WOMAN: (*Crying*) Lady Martha.

(*The* OLD MAN *rests a considerable time after each step; trembles. At the outer door appears the grocery man, with dirty notebook in hand; his voice is harsh.*)

GROCERY MAN: (*Pointing at his notebook*) She's gone! My five dollars! She owes me five dollars for groceries. Now she's dead. Who told her to go there?

POLISH WOMAN: (*Clinching her fingers, puts her fist to her mouth, speaks in Polish*) Meetz! Shut up! You no talk like dat for Martha. (*Pointing towards Martha's picture*) He good lady! He golden lady! (*Shaking her head*) Kohanna tzurka. Beloved daughter, kohanna lady!

GROCERY MAN: But my five dollars. (*He again points at the credit notebook.*)

POLISH WOMAN: (*Angrily*) Martha Boska! God's Mother! (*She takes out of her bosom a small bag, made of an old sock and gives it to the grocery man hastily.*) Idzz! Go!

GROCERY MAN: (*With a slight smile, grabs the bag and begins to count*) Only four and a quarter!

NEGRESS: (*Angry*) Here's seventy-five cents, and five cents I'm leaving for myself. Go!

GROCERY MAN: Thank you. (*He tries to sigh.*) A good woman she was, a very honest woman. (*He walks out of the house.*)

(MARTHA'S *father finally succeeds in walking over to his chair. When near to it, he labors trying to sit down, his body shaking terribly. He is trying to turn around, in order to sit down. A noise is heard, far away, a wave of sound as of turbulent voices.* RAY *enters, weeping, her hair smoothly brushed from her forehead, she indicates crushing pain which she is not able to overcome; she speaks to herself in soft whisper; both hands are closed in horseshoe form clasped down in front of herself, below the waist.*)

RAY: (*Brokenly, walking back and forth*) M-a-r-t-h-a! Oh, dear Martha!

(*The* OLD MAN *sits in his chair, silently; he indicates a controlled silence showing readiness to burst out. He is trying to raise his cane with both hands but he can't. The upper part of his body is bent forward. He closes and opens his eyes nervously. Then he opens them very wide, in an attempt to see far off. Every few seconds he contracts the muscles of his face and tries and tries to stare far off, into the distance where he is trying to call up the picture of Martha's death. Then he begins to move his lips slowly, as if whispering, trying to elucidate to himself in his silent imagination.* JOHNNY *and* FLORA *appear; the boy wearing the dark overcoat, his face is terribly pale, and his eyes express a terrible hopelessness; as the children enter they look around at the group of people there; they walk to* RAY.)

JOHNNY: Ray? (RAY tries *to evade his question, but his persistent voice compels her to listen*). Ray? Did Henry the Kleagle say the truth? (*He gazes upward, right into* RAY'*s eyes. The* NEGRESS *and the* POLISH WOMAN *turn toward the children, fearfully listening to the question.*)

RAY: (*Choked with tears*) What did he say?

(*Before the boy answers, the* OLD MAN *shows interest, slowly turning his hand toward* RAY.)

JOHNNY: He laughed and told me that Ma . . . In Beastville . . . was killed by the gunmen!

FLORA: (*Crying*) Mam-ma!

(*The* POLISH WOMAN *looks at Martha's picture again and crosses herself. The* NEGRESS *tries to pacify* FLORA. RAY *again attempts to speak to* JOHNNY, *who keeps his mouth open, waiting for an answer.* FATHER BLUFF *enters. He looks at each person separately. The* OLD MAN, *noticing him, gives a jerk.* RAY *looks at the* PRIEST *as if he were an enemy.* FATHER BLUFF *walks heavily toward the box chair that is near the* OLD MAN.)

FATHER BLUFF: (*Making a sad face*) Sad news. Sad news. (*Takes a handkerchief out, takes off his hat and wipes his forehead*) I told her, in the name of our Almighty, I warned her! (*The* OLD MAN *is trying to gather strength to rise.* FATHER BLUFF, *looking toward the ceiling, speaks with very distinct meaning, slowly.*) Oh, God! Forgive her!

OLD MAN: (*The* OLD MAN is *still trying to rise from his chair. With much effort he manages to rise slightly, lifting his cane furiously speaks with a terribly weakened voice, pointing at the* PRIEST *with the cane; nervously closing and opening his eyes; in a screaming voice, softly.*) S-t-i-l-l

(*The group looks at the* OLD MAN.)

OLD MAN: (*Same voice*) Not a word about her. (*Pointing with stick toward ceiling.*) He-should-forgive-her? He-should-forgive-her, after he killed her?

FATHER BLUFF: Old Man! It's a sin to talk such words. There are children left.

JOHNNY: I know everything. God is good to the rich.

RAY: (*Looking at* FATHER BLUFF) Why doesn't He punish the Coal Company for throwing children out on the street in mid-winter?

FATHER BLUFF: (*Glancing at the ceiling, hypocritically*) Oh, God! Forgive them their audacity. Forgive that woman for teaching them blasphemy!

(*Crying voice of a young girl is heard in the momentary silence. The* YOUNG GIRL, *whose brother wanted to sell her to the Coal Company, runs in, in torn waist.*)

YOUNG GIRL: (*To* RAY) Are they going to bring her here?

(*Again is heard the wave of turbulent sound, many voices in the distances; strains of the Marsellaise and "The Star Spangled Banner" are heard far off also.* ALEXIS *appears in the doorway, one arm in a sling made of an old towel; there are scars on his face. He wears a frown. Walks toward* RAY, *asking her something quietly; not heard by the audience but noticed.*)

FATHER BLUFF: Good Day, Alex.

ALEXIS: (*Without paying attention to him*) Good-day. No, I was in Redtown. We parted on the way. She went to Beastville, advising me to go to Redtown, while she went with Joe Buck.

(*As he speaks* JOE enter *with a bundle of Martha's belongings. He throws a fiery glance at* FATHER BLUFF. *He puts the bundle on the table.* FLORA *goes to a corner and lies down on the floor to sleep.* JOHNNY *covers her with his coat, sitting down near her. The attention of the whole group is centered on* JOE.)

ALEXIS: (S*oftly to* JOE) Where were you at the time?

JOE: (*Trying to speak, puts his hand on his forehead, as if trying to recall where he was. He speaks tragically.*) I wish I was in Hell!

FATHER BLUFF: Don't be so harsh, brother. (*Points towards God*) It is his will.

JOE: (*Angrily pounds on the table with his fist*) His will to kill Martha! He is in one company with the coal operators and gunmen.

RAY: (*To* JOE) Did you see her before she was killed?

ALEXIS: Was it before they surrounded the pumpmen?

JOE: When she got there it was dark. (*As he speaks he sits down on a chair at the table. Lowering head.*) I and Big Jam was waitin' for her on the road that goes to Pit No. 3. Sheriff Donough and ten gunmen were there. She must have noticed them. She turned back and walked along for three miles and came through the south side into Beastville. We called the pumpmen and they agreed to quit but the pumpmen of the two mines, twelve and fourteen, wouldn't come. They are controlled by the Klan. Martha advised the committee to notify the sheriff that the pickets are demanding protection against the thugs and that Bastard answered that he would take off the thugs if we would take off the pickets. Then he ordered Martha to leave town. We had seven hundred men there. Sheriff Donough read the injunction. Then the Klan pumpmen were brought in a closed truck and the fight started. The men jumped toward the sky when they saw Martha coming to lead the strike. By, God! What a brave woman! She was knocked down by a horse, picked herself up and ordered us to retreat because the mounted men tried to surround us. Then with a group of about fifty miners she surrounded the Klan pumpmen and a few thugs. Then we crowded the pumpmen and thugs to one side, but dear Martha remained alone, rushing back to the place where the fight was still on, then . . . (*He clenches his fist and speaks fiercely.*) God! Pah! Pah! Pah! Pah!

(*While he speaks he covers his face with his hands. At one time, the* POLISH WOMAN, *the* NEGRESS *and* JOHNNY *speak. The* OLD MAN, *sitting in his chair, strains forward.*)

POLISH WOMAN: (*Crossing herself*) Kohanna Martha!

NEGRESS: Klan will now kill all colored people.

JOHNNY: Mamma!

JOE: (R*aising his face, concentrated expression*) Ten bullets were fired into dear Martha's body!

(*The* OLD MAN *tries to visualize the ten bullets being fired into* MARTHA'S *body.* PETER *appears in the doorway as* JOE *says the last words.* PETER *is worn-out, his eyes flash with anger. His leggings are covered with mud. He looks round at everyone quickly, throws a sharp glance at* FATHER BLUFF; *notices* FLORA *sleeping on the floor. Walks to the center of the room and stoops. Throws a sudden glance at Martha's picture.*)

PETER: (*Biting his lower lip, speaking in a low voice*) So, it is true. (*His whole body shrinking, he speaks softly and tragically.*) Martha! (*Then apathetically; meaning*

JOE *but not looking directly at him*) And what did the man do when the bullets ran into Martha's body?

(*The group suddenly shows eagerness; turn their attention to* JOE *as if they had just been awakened to something about which they hadn't thought before and which is now of great concern to them.*)

JOE: (*Looking downward, as if in shame for not having rescued Martha; speaks in a low voice*) What could we do? The men were fighting like devils; with picks, and everything else; but what could we do? There was an iron wall of mounted police and thugs and when our men saw Martha falling, all lost control. Many were thrown to the ground by the mounted police; many were wounded and the rest almost got crazy. All wanted to run, some pushing to the mines; wanted to destroy them, but mounted police and thugs . . . what could we do?

(*There is heard in the distance, again the sound of the turbulent mass of voices, very far off. The group in the room, except* PETER, *listens to the sound.* PETER *is frowning and has shrunken into himself; is trying to picture the scene* JOE has been describing.)

PETER: (*Sarcastically*) What could we do? (*Then bursting out*) Cowards!

(*Again the turbulence is heard, slightly louder, as though nearer.*)

PETER: The same that Mr. Thompson's thugs did to Martha! (*He paces the room nervously, waving both fists in the air; looking at both children, he indicates with his hands their height. Long-drawn, ending in a scream.*) A————ah——a————oh! Thompson, the great director of the Universal Coal Company, he must pay for Martha's blood. (PETER *trembles and laughs hysterically for a long time.*)

(*The turbulence comes much nearer and threats are heard outside. The Mass doesn't speak in unison, but each voice seems contradicting the other. Words cannot be understood, however. A part of the mass outside begins to sing the second stanza of the Marseillaise. The group in the room hears the noise.* PETER *stops for one second, listens, and speaks hysterically.*)

PETER: Thompson, the philanthropist! (*Noticing the razor near the window, he rushes to it and grabs it. The group is stunned. There is suspense.*) Five thousand dollars for the Catholic Church. Four thousand dollars for the Klan's church. A thousand for a prison reformatory. And five thousand for Martha's life! (*He again laughs and trembles, hysterically. Suddenly becomes serious, speaks distinctly.*) "And celebrate the victory without me if this is our fate," she said. (*He looks at the razor again.*) Revenge for Martha's blood!

(*The* CROWD *is heard rumbling outside.* PETER *fixes the razor as if ready to fight* THOMPSON, *whom he thinks he sees in front of him. Then he gives a last scream and suddenly looks at the picture of Fanny Zelling. He stops instantly, staring at it; forcing his eyes open, displaying nervousness and also awakening.*)

PETER: (*Reads*) "Fanny Zelling. Killed in the steel strike of 1919 by steel trust thugs." (*He then looks at John Brown's picture, with increasing soberness—reads*) "John Brown. Killed because he fought to free the slaves." (*The noise outside is now heard close to the house. Indistinguishable words are heard, but they sound threatening.* Peter *looking at the third picture, reads, tremblingly.*) "Martha Noble." Killed . . . (*With still greater soberness*) Killed by the thugs of the Thompson Univeral Coal Company."

(*Before he finishes, the* CROWD *has already burst in the house, shouting.*)

SOME OF THE CROWD: Universal Coal Company!

ONE OF THE CROWD: Martha!

SEVERAL OF THE CROWD: Shot by Thompson!

SEVERAL INTERRUPTING: Revenge! Revenge!

(*There is still a mass outside, part of which is still forcing its way into the house; leaving only a portion actually able to get in on the rest peering in from outside; most of them shaking their fists in the air, shouting.*)

CROWD ALL: We got to pay for Martha's death!

ONE OF THE CROWD: Thompson paid five thousand dollars for Martha!

PART OF THE CROWD: Death to Thompson!

PETER: (*Who had been standing by the picture, caught unexpectedly by the crowd, until now not uttering a word; trying to regain strength by raising and lowering his shoulders several times; he notices Martha's bundle on the table, grabs it and shows it to the* crowd, *who are now silenced by his gesture.*) Yes, our Martha is dead but we must go on with our strike!

ONE OF THE CROWD: Martha's death must be . . .

PETER: (*Controlling himself from breaking into tears*) Not now! Not now! Martha is not the *only* one killed in this strike.

SEVERAL OF THE OTHERS: He's afraid. (*Discontented*).

OTHERS: We'll go to . . .

STILL OTHERS: To Thompson.

ONE OF THE CROWD: Revenge, Brothers!

PETER: (*Stretching his hand toward them*) No, no, Martha died on the picket line and you've left it now. For Martha's sake, picket the mines!

JOE: (*Arises now from his chair*) Boys, we must not show the company now that we are weak.

CROWD: Who are you to talk?

PETER: He was with Martha on the picket line.

SEVERAL: Why didn't you save her? Why did you let the thugs kill Martha?

JOE: (*Apologetically*) Dear Martha said: "I ain't better than any of you men," and she went. Nobody could keep that woman back.

ONE: What did she say before she died?

ANOTHER: What was her last word?

ANOTHER: She said we should kill Thompson!

PART OF THE CROWD: To Thompson!

STILL OTHERS: Revenge!

SEVERAL: Picket!

SEVERAL: Martha! (*There is general noise.*)

CROWD: Martha gave her life for us!

CROWD AGAIN: She died for us!

PETER: She died on the picket line.

ONE: Thompson paid five thousand dollars for Martha's life.

PETER: Because she was on the picket line.

CROWD: Martha!

ONE: What can we do without Martha?

(PETER *raises his hand toward the crowd, appealingly, but the crowd continues making its noise. Grabs the bundle again in order to silence the crowd and lifts it. He jumps on a chair in an attempt to dominate the* CROWD. *This silences the* CROWD.)

CROWD: (*Gazing at the bundle; in unison speak*) Martha!

PETER: Yes, Martha! (*He is immediately interrupted by the* CROWD, *which murmurs.*)

CROWD: Martha! (*Murmingly*)

PETER: Martha lived for the miners!

OTHERS: Martha lived for us!

STILL OTHERS: She died for us!

PETER: Many of your wives and children also died. *We Must Win the strike!*

NEGRESS: Who will now protect the Negroes from the Klan?

CROWD: (*Groaning*) Martha!

PETER: Go back for Martha's sake!

PART OF THE CROWD: For Martha's sake we will go, we will go back!

OTHERS: No, to Thompson, the bloody beast!

OTHERS: (*Snarlingly*) Yah, the beast!

STILL OTHERS: (*Interrupting*) No, go back!

MOST OF THE CROWD: No, to Thompson! We will burn him alive! We will burn him, burn him! (*The whole* CROWD *begins to move out, ready to go to* THOMPSON.)

PETER: (*Screaming to the crowd with bundle*) Remember Martha died for the Union! (*Showing bundle*) Look! Look! Her things! She died for the Union!

CROWD: (*Hesitatingly*) The Union! But we can't win unions without Martha! (*A jumble of voices*)

PETER: But if you kill Thompson you wouldn't bring Martha back to life.

ONE OF THE CROWD: Wait! Listen! Wait!

(CROWD *turns.*)

PETER: Martha died fighting to win the strike, for all of us.

PART OF THE CROWD: For all of us! For all of us!

PART OF THE CROWD: We have no bread!

(*Voices from far away, outside. The crowd silent, listening. Voices of* WOMEN *are heard echo into the room.*)

WOMEN'S VOICES: Our babies are starving, and children. We want bread.

MEN AFAR: We are fighting for bread! We are fighting for Union!

CROWD INSIDE: How can we fight without Martha?

OTHERS INSIDE: Who will lead us?

STILL OTHERS: (*To* PETER) You will lead us in the strike!

PETER: Yes, I will lead you in the strike!

CROWD: For Union!

OTHERS: For bread!

STILL OTHERS: (*To* PETER) You will take Martha's place!

PETER: We will all take Martha's place! On to the picket line!

CROWD: On to the picket line!

PART OF THE CROWD: For Martha!

CROWD: For Martha!

SEVERAL: For bread!

ALL: For bread!

SEVERAL: For all of us!

ALL: For all of us!

SEVERAL: For Union!

(*They begin to move; the crowd starts to sing the Marseillaise. The* OLD MAN *remains seated, looking at the crowd.* RAY *holds the little girl on one side,* JOHNNY *on her other side, watch the crowd go out.* PETER *has gone off with the* CROWD.)

CURTAIN

Mill Shadows

A Drama of Social Forces in Four Acts

TOM TIPPETT

DEDICATED TO THE TEXTILE WORKERS OF MARION, N.C.,
AND THE LABOR MOVEMENT
THE WORKERS WILL ONE DAY BUILD.

Foreword

MILL SHADOWS is an attempt to dramatize certain episodes of the Marion, N.C., textile strike of 1929. In writing the play I have made no attempt to exaggerate the theme for dramatic or propagandistic reasons. For the most part, I was on the scene of the real drama and saw and heard much of what now appears in the form of a play. All the characters are real; they lived and died as the characters do. The Brookwood Players, who first gave the play, are themselves intimately acquainted with that struggle. In their own way they have brought the dead back to life to tell the story of Marion—and that is the object of the play.

Tom Tippett
Brookwood Labor College
Katonah, N.Y.

Characters in the Play
In the Order of Their Appearance

GRANNY—An old mountain woman who has recently come to live in the mill village.
EMMY HOWELL—Her nine year old granddaughter.
MRS. EMMALINE HOWELL—Granny's daughter, about 40 years old.
JAMES ROBERTS—A 17 year old mill worker.
ROY PRINCE—A mill worker. He is 27 years old.
JOHN HOWELL—The husband of Emmaline Howell, 45 years old.
OLD MAN JONAS—A crippled mill worker, 65 years old.
FRED—A farmer.

LAWRENCE HOGAN—A mill worker, 24 years old.
DAN ELLIS—A mill worker, 30 years old.
THE VILLAGE PREACHER—Employed by the mill.
MRS. ROBERTS—The mother of James, also a mill worker.
ED WATKINS—The village merchant, later the sheriff.
JOSHEPHINE
HELEN—Young girls who work at the mill.
JUDGE HERRING—A representative of the Governor.
DEPUTIES 1, 2, 3, 4,—With criminal records.
MILL SUPERINTENDENT—The overseer of the mill, a northerner.
CORNELIUS—The Governor's Negro servant.
THE GOVERNOR OF CAROLINA
CICERO QUEENS—A mountain preacher.
SONG LEADER—"FROM UP NORTH."
STRIKERS AND SINGERS

Time: During the year 1929.
Places: Carolina, U.S.A.

Act 1

The yard of the Howell-Roberts homes in a Carolina mill village on a Saturday night in late April.

Act 2

Scene 1. Union Headquarters, three months later
Scene 2. The same, August 31.
Scene 3. The same, October 1, late afternoon.

Act 3

Scene 1. The cotton mill, 8 o'clock the same night.
Scene 2. The same, midnight.
Scene 3. The same, 6 o' clock the next morning.
Scene 4. The Governor's mansion, two days later.

Act 4

Same as Act 1, December 22, late afternoon.

Mill Shadows

Act 1

The yard of the HOWELL *and* ROBERTS *homes in a Carolina mill village, on a Saturday evening early in April. The* HOWELL *home, on the left, has a small porch; the* ROBERTS *home, across the yard, does not boast one. A guitar leans against a box by the house. Separating the yard from the dusty road is a fence, beyond which can be seen in the distance the Carolina mountains. A stunted cedar tree by the gate and a few spindling flowers in cans on the* HOWELL *porch contrast sharply with the verdure of the mountains. A clotheslines stretches from the gatepost to the* HOWELL *house.* MRS. EMMALINE HOWELL *is doing the family washing and appears now and then to hang the wash on the line.*

GRANNY, *an old mountain woman, white haired but energetic, is seated in the yard in front of a wooden frame on which she is making a hooked rug. Her cane hangs on the chair back. Her grand-daughter,* EMMY, *a frail, under-sized nine-year-old, sits by her, holding the ball of carpet rags.*

GRANNY: You allers make it from the back, honey. Push the needle th'u, pull it tight, then back again. Allers pull tight, an' befo' you-all know hit, you git a pitcher done.

EMMY: But why do you-all make a ship, Granny? I never seen a ship. And what's all these things here?

GRANNY: They air waves. Ocean waves. An' this is the ship what brung the mountain people from Scotland.

EMMY: Did you come on the ship?

GRANNY: No, honey, no. I never did see a ship, or the ocean nuther. My maw learnt me to draw the pattern. She learnt it from her maw, an' her maw learnt it from her'n. When I wuz a young gal they used to tell us that they made the ships so as not to fergit the old country an' the long v'yage acrost the water.

EMMY: Tell me the story again, Granny.

GRANNY: Hit's too long, Emmy, you got to larn it as you grow up. Our folks come from Scotland an' England long, long ago. They warn't no place fer 'em over here but in them-thar mountains. They lived thar in their own cabins what they built out'n the trees. They wuz happy thar, too, honey. Gettin' 'long all right 'till they moved down here to this-here mill village an' took to workin' in that-air cotton mill over yander.

EMMY: Tell me 'bout the mountains, Granny. Hain't you goin' to take me thar? You said you would.

GRANNY: 'Course I am—some day. Hit air nice up thar, Emmy. Cabins, pine trees, wild roses, and rhodedendrons. We growed our own livin' an' worked when we wanted to.

EMMY: You make hit all in the rugs and quilts, don't you?

GRANNY: We shore do. We used to put 'em on our jugs and crocks what we made our se'ves out'n our own clay. You jest ort-a see them wild roses and rhodedendrons, honey. Go out any place an' thar they stand a-smilin' and a-noddin' at you. Everywhar, all smellin' sweet. Above you the pine trees 'way up to the sky—an' a soft carpet of pine needles to walk on.

EMMY: Why don't they grow here?

GRANNY: Nothin' grows here, honey, nothin' right. No trees, no flowers, nor children, nuther. Too much pizen in the air—an' in the people, too, I reckon. Come an' try to make this-here wave. You'll larn all 'bout everything as you grow up.

(MRS. HOWELL—GRANNY'*s daughter—finishes her wash and sits on the porch to rest.*)

GRANNY: Git hit all out, Emmaline?

MRS. HOWELL: All done, but that's the dishes waitin'. Hain't none of the men come yit? (*To* EMMY) Better put somethin' else round you, Emmy, hit's a-gittin' kinder chilly. (MRS. HOWELL *takes off her apron.*) Here, throw this 'round your shoulders. (EMMY *obeys.*)

GRANNY: What air the men folks up to? They been studyin' a heap lately.

MRS. HOWELL: More trouble at the mill.

GRANNY: Thar's nothin' but trouble at that-air mill. What air hit this time?

MRS. HOWELL: They put more work on to us. The men say they won't stand fer it no longer. 'Pears like mill folks is kickin' all over the South.

GRANNY: Serves 'em right fer leavin' the mountains whar thar warn't no mills.

(JAMES ROBERTS *comes out of his home and speaks across the yard to the* HOWELL *family.*)

JAMES: Howdy, folks. Nobody here yit? We're goin' to have a meetin'—thought everybody was here. (*Goes to fence, looks down the road outside*) Oh, here they come now.

GRANNY: What's hit about, James?

(MRS. HOWELL, JONAS—*an old man who walks with a crutch, and* ROY PRINCE—*a tall, lanky mountaineer type, but fairly young—enter.*)

JAMES: Ask them. We're goin' to have some fun in this-here village.

(JONAS *sits on a bench by the* ROBERTS' *house and begins whittling.* JAMES *talks with him.* ROY *stands by the gate, rolling a cigarette.*)

HOWELL: (*Going over to* EMMY) How air you tonight, Emmy? Feelin' better? (*To* MRS. HOWELL) Don't you think Emmy ort to be inside? Hit's a-gittin' damp.

MRS. HOWELL: Come along, honey. (*She and* EMMY *go into the house.* HOWELL *sits in the yard and reads a newspaper.*)

(GRANNY *leans her rug frame against the house and sits on the porch.* ROY *comes up to her.*)

ROY: Did Irene talk to you yit, Granny?

GRANNY: No, she didn't, Roy . . . Hit ain't that, air it?

ROY: Yes, hit's that.

GRANNY: (*In a worried manner*) I was afeared when I heard she was feelin' porely. When?

ROY: We don't know for sure, but in 'bout three months, I reckon.

GRANNY: Roy Prince, you ort-a be licked—gittin' that girl that way agin after the terrible time she had with the last 'un. Have you fergot what the doctor said? He told you both she couldn't never have another young 'un.

ROY: Yes, I know. But he didn't tell us how to keep from it. He said three kids wuz enough and that Irene warn't built to have many children. He wouldn't tell us nothin' more, though.

GRANNY: You men ort-a have the babies. Thar wouldn't be so many of 'em then.

ROY: Hit's no use, Granny, we did try. Irene took everything we ever heerd 'bout—quinine, hot lemonade, ever'thing, but nothin' worked. I've studied 'bout it lots. Irene knowed you'd be mad, that's why she didn't tell you, I reckon.

GRANNY: Pore child! I hain't mad, Roy, but you got to git the doctor. An' you ort-a git him now so's he can see how hit's comin' long. Hit wa'ar most too late last time. I thought she'd shore die on us. I'm too old to manage hard births any more.

ROY: We cain't git the Doctor, Gran. (*Speaking more slowly*) We hain't paid fer the last 'un yit. He won't come if'n we cain't pay him, and we cain't.

(MRS. HOWELL *comes out of the house sits on the porch and sews.* GRANNY *takes up an unfinished rug and begins clipping it.*)

MRS. HOWELL: (*Walking across yard to where* JONAS *and* JAMES *are*) Well, boys, what air we a-goin' to do 'bout that-thar mill over yander? The time's come when we've got to take some kind of action.

ROY: (*Walking over to where the men are talking*) Dan and Lawrence air tryin' to telephone to the organizer over at Elizabethton. They'll be here pretty soon. Maybe he'll he'p us.

HOWELL: Time someone was he'pin' us!

JONAS: (*Slowly*) 'Pears like to me as what we ort to do is to go on strike with t'other mill workers. Mill folks would be better off if'n they stuck together. They air out over at Elizabethton and Gaston. We ort-a go out here too.

ROY: The newspapers are full of the strikes. Everybody is talkin' 'bout it down at the mill. The bossman don't like it, nuther. He was cussin' out the workers in our section today. Said a lot of northern agitators wuz down here stirrin' up trouble.

JONAS: Well, fellers, that air just why I'm fer a strike. 'Pears like to me, if'n they's somethin' the boss is again, we orter be fer hit.

(FRED, *a farmer, enters the yard, carrying a basket of fresh vegetables.*)

FRED: Good evening, folks. How you-all? (*He shakes hands with* GRANNY *and* MRS. HOWELL.) Here's some garden truck the old woman sent you.

HOWELL: You're lucky, Fred. Stay on your farm. Here we are cookin' up a strike for a little more bread and butter, while you-all grow yourn in yore own ground.

FRED: Tain't so easy on the farm, nuther, boys. I 'lows you-all clear 'bout as much as I do. We git it in the neck too. Got a fine calf out thar in the wagon what I cain't git more'n nine dollars fer from the company store. I'm plagued if I'll sell her for that.

GRANNY: I wisht we could buy hit so we could raise her an' have the milk what Emmy needs to git well. The doctor said she's got to have fresh milk and green vegetables, and we hain't got nuther one.

MRS. HOWELL: We couldn't even give you nine dollars fer hit, Fred. We never sees no money. The bit we make is used up at the store long 'fore we earn hit.

FRED: Well—shucks, Emmaline, you take the heifer. You can git me stuff at the store on yore credit—an' I can git hit from you here.

GRANNY: I'll have enough money to pay you, Fred, when the storekeeper in Ashville what buys my rugs comes for his next lot. I've got three done and another on the frame.

FRED: All right, Gran, I'd ruther give her to you anyhow then let that store butcher her. Never did like to sell a heifer for meat no way. (*Walks to center of yard and speaks to men*) What's the trouble about, boys?

ROY: About the stretch-out, mostly.

FRED: About what?

ALL: The stretch-out.

MRS. HOWELL: (*Coming into the yard off the porch*) Fred, you don't know what that is. I'll show you. Take my own case. I'm tendin' my looms—and enough too. The bossman adds two more on this side. (*She illustrates by extending her right arm.*) I cain't reach that far. He says, "Stretch a little." I do. Next day he adds more on this side. (*Illustrating with her left arm*) Again I cain't reach. He says, "Stretch a little." Then he adds more and I stretch and stretch, an' stretch (*She illustrates with body, arms, and legs, by reaching as far as possible.*) 'til I'm all stretched out. They done hit all of us.

ALL MEN: An' we sho' air stretched out.

FRED: (*Laughs*)

MRS. HOWELL: It hain't funny, Fred. We do twic't as much work and we're all tired to death.

JAMES: Twic't as much? Some of us do six times as much—and we don't git no more pay, nuther.

FRED: And how long do you stay in that-thar factory?

JAMES: Twelve hours every day.

FRED: Well, that's worse'n us on the farm. We put in long hours in summer —but we take our time. In the winter we git rested up a bit. Well, I'll have to be goin'. I'll tie the heifer out back, Gran. (*Goes out*)

(DAN *and* LAWRENCE, *both energetic young fellows, enter—they meet* FRED *as he walks out. Both men speak to the farmer.*)

LAWRENCE: Well, boys, we got the organizer on the 'phone. Seems like a nice feller. Was glad we called him.

DAN: Have you seen the paper? Look! (*Produces a newspaper*) It's full of strike news. More'n 5,000 people are on strike in Elizabethton, and all of Gaston is out. The paper has it all here in pitchers. (JAMES *takes the paper.*)

LAWRENCE: The organizer says we oughter git together quiet-like at first. Says maybe we won't have to strike if'n we do.

DAN: And he wants us to come over and see him. Think of it—5,000 workers all walkin' out'n a mill at one time! That's power fer you.

JAMES: I think we oughter strike. We'd git a rest, and besides, we'd have some fun. Look here (*Exhibits paper*) see the people marching with banners? They air all laughin' an'—happy. Why, we'd put some life into this here village!

GRANNY: Life! They ain't no life in this-here village. I told you-all what you'd git if'n you listened to them real estate men what come up thar an' talked you-all into sellin' out and comin' to this-here fact'ry. We should-a stayed up yander in our hills where we wuz free.

JAMES: (*Teasingly*) Aw, now, Granny! The hills ain't so hot, nuther. I went up thar with Maw last smmer. That's nothin' up thar but trees and rattlesnakes.

GRANNY: Nothin's up thar but trees and rattlesnakes? You're right, son. They air trees up thar. Trees . . . trees . . . tall an' straight. Straight like men ort-a be. What I'm missin' most here is them pines. (*She turns and looks in the direction of the mountains and speaks half to herself.*) Jest to hear the wind a-blowin' th'u the trees again . . .

JAMES: An' to step on a rattlesnake.

GRANNY: An' the rattlesnakes! They give you ca chance't in the hills. But the kind you meet here don't. They jest sucks your life away without you knowin' hit. What's yo' Pa? Out thar in his grave years afore his time—killt slow in that-air cotton mill, shut up away from God's sunshine. He'd-a been livin', spry as ever, if'n he'd stayed up in them hills like'n I wanted him to. No rattlesnakes here, eh? Hain't a rattler in all the Carolina mountains would kill a man like that.

JAMES: Well, just the same, old woman, I ain't going back to no mountains. No siree! I'm goin' to stay right here'n git a hautomobile an' me some of the country.

GRANNY: Better git somethin' to eat, first. Besides, hautomobiles don't run on hot air, James. They cost money.

JAMES: Oh, don't git mad, Gran. I know you'll never fergit the mountains an' I don't blame you—but we're not like that. I never lived in the mountains and I ain't goin' to.

ROY: That's right, Granny. We cain't go back there even if we wanted to. We went up that way in the early spring. It's all changed now.

JONAS: Sho' is. Fences everywhar. Power company land now. Signs up tellin' you-all to keep off.

GRANNY: Our mountains with fences? They hain't nary a fence up thar! Them hills belongs to anybody who'll setlle in 'em.

ROY: We sold our rights up thar, Granny, and you may as well stop cussin' us out about hit. We're here now, caught like a rat in a trap an' cain't run back. We hain't got no homes now.

GRANNY: (*Fussing angrily*) Fools! Cowards! You-all air a'feared. Mountain folks knowed their enemies and knowed how to fight 'em. Here you don't know, you're all mixed up. You hain't mountain men no more. Why, our men in the mountains—

(GRANNY *has the attention of the men in her speech. Lawrence gets up and walks toward her.*)

LAWRENCE: You're right, Granny. We air all mixed up. But cain't you see somethin's happenin' here? We air goin' to fight, but not like our paps did —a different fight right in this-here village. Hit's comin'. Hit's come to other places. Cain't you feel it in your blood? Why, mine jest tingles all over.

(LAWRENCE'S *speech is full of emotion—it is cut off by the entrance of the mill village* PREACHER *who walks in the gate.*)

PREACHER: Howdy, folks. You-all havin' a friendly time, I see. I jest wanted to drap by an' tell you-all not to forgit our church meetin' tonight. Preacher Hawks up from Swanee way is a-goin' to preach to us, and I want to git out a big crowd.

ROY: (*Bored*) We're all comin' over, preacher.

(ED WATKINS, *a heavy-set man with a weak, good natured face, enters, and talks with the men from other side of fence.*)

JAMES: What do you-all want to have preachin' on Saddy night fer? Saddy night is a time fer fun.

PREACHER: Lawd, James, you-all air goin' to the devil and hell for sho'. The Lord is to be worshipped, boy, on Saddy night as well as every other night.

(MRS. ROBERTS *comes out of her door. She is thin and pale and coughs a great deal.*)

MRS. ROBERTS: Air you havin' a meetin', Roy?

ROY: (*Getting up*) Yes. Have my seat, Mrs. Roberts.

MRS. HOWELL: Mrs. Roberts, you come over here and set with us.

(MRS. ROBERTS *walks slowly across the yard. She coughs violently again is gasping for breath as she sits on the Howell step between* GRANNY *and* MRS. HOWELL. JAMES *looks kindly at his mother.*)

JAMES: Hello, Ma. Is the baby asleep at last? (*He goes over to his mother.*) Why, what's the matter, Ma? Hain't you feelin' good?

MRS. ROBERTS: I'm feelin' tolable, Jimmy. Jest tired out. The baby's so fretful. She's getting' sick again, I'm feared.

PREACHER: You come to our services tonight, Mrs. Roberts. Hawks is a powerful preacher. Hit'll do you good.

GRANNY: (*Filling her pipe*) Do her good, nothin'! You mill preachers don't know nothin' to preach 'bout 'cept'n hell fire. Never did hear nothin' but punishment fer sin in these-here churches. Our mountain preachers wa'n't like that. Old Cicero Queens never did preach 'bout hell. Allers talked 'bout love an' bein' kind to one-another. We allers felt kind-a better after he'd come 'round.

PREACHER: Now, Grandmother, you needn't rile up 'gin the church. This-here village is full of sin. There ain't no way to escape God's punishment. You got to git right with the Lawd.

GRANNY: That-air cotton mill is the only devil in this-here village, preacher. And you're a-feared of hit.

JAMES: Everything hain't wicked, preacher. Why last Saddy night me and another mill-boy went out to the lake where the town folks go. You just ought-a been with us, Gran. We sneaked up to whar they wuz dancin' an' stood hid behind some trees. The boys an' girls wuz dancin' over the floor —like shadows. You ought-a seen the girls' dresses. They wuz all colors— just like the lights.

PREACHER: (*Astonished*) James, boy, that wa'ar a devil's dance! That place is full of sin.

GRANNY: Sin, nothin'! Go on, Jimmy.

JAMES: (*Taking up his guitar*) Sometimes a man would sing th'u a big paper horn and the dancers joined in too. Onct all the lights went out 'cepten a big moon in the center of the roof and they sung a song like this: (JAMES *stands up, puts foot on box, facing center of stage. He plays and sings a chorus of "Carolina Moon." The music interrupts the rest of the stage business. All look at* JAMES . . . *At the end of the chorus,* HOWELL *interrupts* JAMES.)

HOWELL: Why didn't you-all go inside, Jimmy, and git you a gal?

JAMES: Go in! Why didn't I go in? You know damn well why I didn't go in. With *these* clothes? No, that hain't fer mill folks . . . we're different. (*Turns his back and looks into the mountains*)

PREACHER: (*Putting his arm around* JAMES) You better come to church tonight, James. What you-all need is God. (*Exit* PREACHER)

GRANNY: What he needs is some fun.

MRS. HOWELL: John, ain't it time you wuz a-goin' to work? Your lunch is packed in on the kitchen table.

HOWELL: Well, fellers, I shore hate work on Saddy night but I guess I'd better go 'long. (*He goes toward his house.*)

LAWRENCE: Say, John—be sure and tell the folks on the night shift to meet us tomorrow in the woods after the ball game. (HOWELL *nods his head and goes inside.*)

WARKINS: Then I can count on your support in the election?

LAWRENCE: Sure, you'll make a good sheeriff.

MRS. HOWELL: Air you goin' to run fer sheeriff, Ed?

WARKINS: Yes. My store is about bankrupt. The boys say you-all will help me and if you do, I'll be elected.

MRS. ROBERTS: We'd all take more at your store, Ed, if'n we had the money.

WATKINS: I know you would, Mrs. Roberts. It's the company store credit system that's got me licked.

ROY: Give me a cigarette, Ed.

WATKINS: Have a real smoke! (*Hands around cigars*)

GRANNY: I never did think I'd live to see the day that mountain folks would be after makin' a sheeriff.

LAWRENCE: But Watkins is all right, Gran. He's our friend.

GRANNY: When you-all 'lect him sheeriff he'll be the law, and the law hain't yer friend.

WATKINS: Why, of course. I'll always be your friend, Grandmother. The law is different down here. Here, have one of my campaign cards. (*Goes out*)

GRANNY: The law air is the law. Hit's agin the common people. (*She tears the card up and throws it in the yard.*)

(*In the distance a hymn can be heard from the church. It is: "When the Roll Is Called Up Yonder."*)

DAN: There goes the openin' song. Let's go over an' give Hawks a good turnout.

LAWRENCE: Then it's agreed that we go over to Elizabethton in the mornin'?

(MRS. ROBERTS *is asleep with her head against the porch.* MRS. HOWELL *comes out ready for church.*)

DAN: Air you comin', James?

JAMES: No, I'm stayin' in tonight with the children. Ma'll want to go, I reckon. (*He takes his guitar, walks over toward his own house, sit on a chair in the yard, begins to pick the strings of the guitar.*)

(*All the men go out.* MRS. HOWELL *attempts to awaken* MRS. ROBERTS.)

GRANNY: You go 'long, Emmaline. Let her stay. The sleep'll do her good. (MRS. HOWELL *goes out.*)

(GRANNY *places her rug over* MRS. ROBERTS, *hobbles to fence and looks up into the mountains as* JAMES *commences to play "Carolina Moon."* GRANNY *sits down—fills her pipe—listens to the music.* JAMES *plays the tune louder.* GRANNY *smiles.*)

GRANNY: James, boy, that air a devil's tune!

(JAMES *smiles broadly at* GRANNY *and plays louder.*)

CURTAIN

ACT 2

Scene 1

Union Headquarters, in late July. A shabby hall with doors right and left and two windows in the rear, behind which figures pass during the scene. A long table stands between the windows. There are smaller tables along the right and left walls, and two or three wooden benches and boxes. On the rear wall are crudely lettered placards—"Join Our Union," "Strike Call," "Relief Given Out Today," etc. A big pot of coffee is boiling on a stove.

JOSEPHINE *and* HELEN, *two girls in their teens, are working on union records when the curtain opens,* JOSEPHINE *at the big table, and* HELEN *at the small table, right.* OLD MAN JONAS *is stretched out at the front of the stage, left, asleep.* JOSEPHINE *goes to waken him.*

JOSEPHINE: Jonas . . . wake up! (*He awakens.*) Why don't you go home and get some sleep right? You stay on the picket line all night and you stay 'round here all day. You need some rest too. (JONAS *smiles and shakes his head.* JOSEPHINE *goes back to table; she speaks to* HELEN.) I can never get him to go home. He stays around here all the time.

HELEN: Hit's a pretty good place to stay, hain't it, Jonas? (JONAS *smiles and begins to whittle.*) Say, Josie, did you hear what that woman from Hammertown said at the meeting last night? (JOSEPHINE *shakes her head.*) You were there, Jonas! She said that in the spring when her little girl died she went to the boss-man and asked him for the boards to make her a coffin. What do you think the boss-man told her? He said, "This hain't no coffin factory," and he wouldn't give her the boards because she had joined the union.

JONAS: Hit hain't no coffin factory—but it shore gits bodies ready for 'em all right.

(*Singing can be heard out of doors as a group of strikers come toward the hall. The song is "Solidarity Forever."*)

JOSEPHINE: I hear them singing. The parade must be over. They are coming this way, too.

HELEN: Did you put the coffee in, Josie?

JOSEPHINE: Yes, but it'll need more water, I reckon. And you better make some more sandwiches too; the boys said they didn't have half enough last night. (JOSEPHINE *goes to stove, puts more water in coffee.* HELEN *takes food from paper sacks and makes sandwiches, puts them in large basket. Off stage singing continues louder and louder, as the singers approach the hall.*)

JAMES: (*Coming in carrying parade banner*) Oh boy! What a parade we had. Everybody in both villages was in line! (*Puts banner on table*)

(*Both doors open and crowd of strikers bursts in singing—all carry banners, all laugh and mill round the hall.* HELEN *runs to door and closes it on another group trying to get in. She keeps them out, and takes their banners in through the door.* MRS. HOWELL *has come in with group.*)

HELEN: (*Loudly*) Say, you-all come on, git out of here. We've got work to do. That girl from the North is here to learn you them new songs—go on outside to the singing. (*The group commences to go,* HELEN *addresses a group of men.*) And she'll need the men too—go on out; you-all can sing as well as the girls. (*Group begins to go out left and can later be seen passing windows outside.*)

JOSEPHINE: (*Coming to front*) If you ain't got your relief cards yit, get 'em fixed now. (*Several strikers form line and get relief cards from* HELEN; *they pass on to* JOSEPHINE, *who files their cards—as they pass out of hall.*)

MRS. HOWELL: (*To one of the women as they go out*) And you know they say we cain't be Christian people an' stick by this-here union. I figger I can. They put us out'n the church fer belongin' to the union. Well, all I can say is we air better off outside that kind of church than we air on the inside of hit. This cause has got into my blood and they cain't get hit out. (*They go out.*)

HELEN: How wonderful the strike is! We're learnin' everything. Hain't them northern boys nice? (*She begins to clean up table.*)

JOSEPHINE: They sho' air, everybody seems to be sendin' us relief. The people in this village never wuz so well fed—an' we've been out four weeks too.

JAMES: Is it four weeks, Josephine? Hit don't seem like hit.

JOSEPHINE: Yes, hit is. Four weeks ago yistiddy we walked out of that last mill, an' nary a worker has gone through the gate since.

(*Outside a young woman, the* SONG LEADER, *can be heard talking to the crowd of assembled workers.*)

SONG LEADER: (*In good English, with northern accent*) What shall we sing while the speakers are getting here?

WOMAN'S VOICE: (*From the outside assemblage*) Sing "Jacob's Ladder" with them-thar new words.

SONG LEADER: All right. But let's sing it with the old words first to get the tune. (*She then sings the first line of the Negro spiritual, "Jacob's Ladder."*)

"We are . . . climbing . . . Jacob's ladder

(*Other voices join in.*)

We are . . . climbing . . . Jacob's ladder
We are . . . climbing . . . Jacob's ladder
Soldiers . . . of the . . . cross."

SONG LEADER: The Negro slaves sang that song because they thought that was the only way to freedom, by dying and climbing up Jacob's ladder to Heaven. We know better than that now. We can't afford to wait until death for our freedom so we sing the song in a new way. The words are different but the idea is pretty much the same. Now try it after me.

(*The* SONG LEADER *then sings as before:*)

"We are . . . building . . . a strong union"

(*Other voices join in the next lines:*)

"We are . . . building . . . a strong union,
We are . . . building . . . a strong union,
Workers . . . in the . . . mill."

(*As the singing develops off stage* JAMES *walks to window, stands looking out at cotton mill.* JOSEPHINE *closes the door; the song is still heard, but in diminished volume.*)

JAMES: (*Looking at the cotton mill and speaking very earnestly*) We've got the cotton mill licked. Look how big and powerful hit is—always grindin' us—always rulin' us. But hit's helpless without us. Not a wheel can turn less'n we-uns go in and tend 'em with our own hands. (*Turning around to others*) Say, folks, hain't hit a wonderful feelin' to know we have got power of our own? Why—we air stronger than the cotton mill.

(*The singing continues but becomes less and less dominant.* ROY *enters from the right.*)

JOSEPHINE: How's Irene, Roy?

ROY: She's pretty sick, Josephine. Is Mrs. Howell around? Gran wants her to come over.

JOSEPHINE: She's out at the meetin'. I'll go tell her.

HELEN: An' how's Granny? Is she still scoldin' you?

ROY: Nope. She's so on fire with the strike that she fergits me. Takes all her temper out on the mill now. (*He faces the men.*) Do you know that that's a load o' raw cotton come to the mill?

JONAS: O' course we know hit. The sheeriff's bin after the pickets all afternoon. They want us to leave the yard gang unload hit.

JAMES: An' we hain't a-goin' to let 'em unload hit. They kin settle the strike. If'n we cain't all work, none of us'll work.

ROY: The sheeriff's comin' to talk to you-all into hit—if'n he kin.

JOSEPHINE: (*Coming in*) She had already gone, Roy. (ROY *goes out, left, leaving the door open.*)

LAWRENCE: (*From outside*) Listen, folks—let's all come to order. The committee has an important conference with the sheeriff, and we'll report later, but before we git to that, I want to tell you what I think of our strike. We got a powerful strike. (*Cheers*) Everybody's stickin' together. We have woke up at last. The 12-hour day has got to go. An' we hain't goin' to work no more for eleven dollars a week. (*Cheers*) Our strike has got this-here whole village united. We see a light a-comin' over the hilltop, a light that will make us free, us mill people, free men an' women.

(*There is applause and cheers from the outside meeting.* MRS. HOWELL *suddenly appears outside the window, right.*)

MRS. HOWELL: (*Frantically*) Josephine! Where's Roy? Irene's took awful bad. Granny wants him to come quick.

JOSEPHINE: (*Also excited*) He's at the meeting. (MRS. HOWELL *disappears.*) Helen, you run for the doctor. Say you done got the money; he'll come then, and when he gets here he'll have to he'p her. Granny says Irene'll die if'n she don't have a doctor and Gran knows. (HELEN *runs out.*)

(LAWRENCE, DAN, *and* MRS. HOWELL *enter with the former grocer* WATKINS *who is now the sheriff. The men form a committee meeting,* JONAS *assumes membership in the meeting.* JAMES *is not a part of the committee. He paces up and down watching the committee.*)

SHERIFF: (*Gruffly*) You men know what I'm here for. All he wants is permission to unload the raw cotton. He ain't goin' to start the mill.

JONAS: He sho' hain't sheeriff. Hit takes we-uns to start that-air mill, an we-uns hain't ready to start yit awhile.

LAWRENCE: Why don't he talk with us?

SHERIFF: He thinks that would be recognizing the organization and he only wants to unload the cotton. He don't want to start up.

DAN: He wants us to unload his cotton so he'll have hit ready to start with new hands. He's a-tryin' to bring outsiders in right now.

JONAS: Hit 'pears to me like you're kind-a anxious to he'p the ol' man out, sheeriff.

SHERIFF: I got to do my duty and I'll you-all somethin' more. I heard him say that unless you let him unload his cotton, he'll send for the soldiers.

DAN: But he cain't send for the sojers. The sheeriff has to do that, an' you're a friend of our'n. We elected you, you know.

SHERIFF: But the law is the law. Unless I do protect 'em, they'll go over my head. And anyway, he's got a right to have that cotton unloaded. There's a extra charge for every day the car stands there.

JAMES: (*Shouting across the room*) You're a damn rat, sheeriff! We know what you bin a-doin' ever since the strike begun. Why don't you tell him to unload his own cotton? We'll unload hit if'n he'll settle this-here strike an' he knows hit, an' so do you. This is a trick to get some of the workers back in the mill.

SHERIFF: Say, young feller! You're talkin' to the law. Do you know that?

LAWRENCE: You stay out of this, Jimmy. We'll handle hit.

JAMES: (*To the* SHERIFF) To hell with the law! To hell with all of you. We're somebody now. We got power too. *He* even knows that—sendin' his little errand boy, the sheeriff, 'round to git our permission to do somethin'; but just as allus, they air a trick in hit.

SHERIFF: You'll be sorry for them-thar words.

JAMES: The hell I will! The only thing I'm sorry fer is that the mill people wuz fools enough to elect you sheeriff. Ol' Granny wuz right. The law's crooked! (*Goes to window, looks out at cotton mill*)

DAN: Now, sheeriff, keep yore pants on. You go back an' tell him we'll send over some o' the men he turned out fer joinin' the union to unload the cotton. If'n he'll give them the job, all right. Otherwise, let the cotton stay whar hit is.

SHERIFF: Otherwise . . . he'll send fer the troops.

JAMES: Git to hell out'n here, you dirty skunk! You're he'pin' him beat us. You can't fool us no longer.

SHERIFF: (*To others*) You'll be making a mistake, boys.

JONAS: Accordin' to the boss-man, we-uns don't never do nothin' 'cept make mistakes, sheeriff. I reckon we better keep hit up fer a spell.

(*The* SHERIFF *goes out. There is a pause.* LAWRENCE *shrugs his shoulders.*)

DAN: Oh, to hell with the sheeriff. Let's go report to the meeting. (*All the men except* JONAS *and* JAMES *go out.*)

JOSEPHINE: James, you shouldn't-a sassed him like that. He kin arrest you.

JAMES: I don't give a damn if'n he does. He's agin us—Ever' body's agin us. Everybody but ourse'f. But we don't need the he'p o' the sheeriff. We kin win on our own.

JONAS: I'm only sorry Granny warn't here to a-heerd you, son. She'd sho' been proud.

(JAMES *opens door, right, looks out in distance.*)

LAWRENCE: (*From outside*) Listen, folks, hit's time to go to the picket line. Everybody down to the mill.

SONG LEADER: Let's all go singing!

(*The workers sing "On the Picket Line." The song dies down as workers go toward mill, but can be heard faintly until curtain.* LAWRENCE *and* DAN *come into the hall.*)

LAWRENCE: Is the coffee and sandwiches ready for the pickets?

JAMES: Here you are. (*Gives them coffee and basket*)

(GRANNY *enters, right. All stare at her.*)

JOSEPHINE: Granny, you here! How's Irene?

GRANNY: (*Slowly*) Irene—air—dead!

ALL: Dead?

JOSEPHINE: Oh, Granny! Didn't the doctor come? We sent fer him. Wouldn't he do nothin'?

GRANNY: It wa'ar too late. (*She walks across the stage to the window through which the cotton mill can be seen.*) She wa'ar kilt in that-thar cotton mill yander, a-standin' on her feet twelve hours a day, with a baby tryin' to grow inside her.

CURTAIN

Scene 2

Union Headquarters a month later. The hall is in disorder, with strike banners lying on the table and floor. On the back wall, the "Relief Today" sign has given way to a "Bulletin Board" with notices, clippings, and pictures on it. Boxes of clothing sent to the strikers are piled at the front of the stage, left and right.

As the scene opens, GRANNY *is sitting on a box, smoking.* MRS. HOWELL, JOSEPHINE, *and* HELEN *are sweeping and dusting the hall. They put things in order, then sit down to repair the damaged strike banners.*

JOSEPHINE: I cain't see why a place gits so dirty. After every meetin' we clean an' clean an' clean.

HELEN: I don't mind. I rather like it. Hit's part o' things an' hit's all fun. I didn't know a strike could be like this.

JOSEPHINE: Oh, I like hit too. Hit's been powerful nice—like a camp meetin'. I git the same feelin' when I go to our meetin's. The labor speakers air better'n the preachers, seems like, an' they's bin so many of 'em.

MRS. HOWELL: They air more real, seems like. Ever'thing they say is so clear. Hit's like fightin' the devil, though, hain't it? The cotton-mill devil.

GRANNY: Them boys is got real religion. I never seen hit clear afore, but I do now. Like that un what whar speakin' last night. "Poverty," he sez, "air the only real sin in the world." We-uns has allers bin pore, an' the mill preachers hain't after more money fer us. They're after sendin' us all ter hell less'n we toe the mark.

MRS. HOWELL: Well, Mother, you oughter be glad we were put out'n the church, if'n you air agin the preachers so hard.

HELEN: Gran wa'arn't put out'n no church. She wa'arn't never in hit, wa'ar you, Granny?

GRANNY: I never voted for the sheeriff, nuther. I wa'n't borned a plumb fool altogether. An' anyhow, they hain't no preachers here. Thar-is mill tongues. The preachers, the sheeriff, the town folks—all mill tongues.

JOSEPHINE: They sho' air, Gran. You'd think we wuz niggers.

HELEN: How'd you-all like what them northern speakers said t'other night 'bout the niggers?

JOSEPHINE: Seemed all right to me. They work in the mill, too, an' nary a one of 'em's gone back to work on us.

MRS. HOWELL: That speaker wa'ar over to our house t'other night, talkin' to the boys 'bout them colored people. He always says "Negro"; says we ortn't to call 'em niggers—cause they don't like hit no better'n we do when folks call us hill billies or white trash.

JOSEPHINE: Funny, hain't it, 'bout the Negroes? The first donation we got from a outside union was from the colored hod carriers an' they've sent regular ever since—an' none of the Negroes air in our union.

MRS. HOWELL: We hain't asked 'em to jine, nuther.

JOSEPHINE: But the boys takes 'em strike relief every week, an' they say the colored folks is with us.

MRS. HOWELL: He says some day all the pore folks 'ull be organized together, no matter what their color is.

JOSEPHINE: I heerd him. He made it sound like church, I thought.

MRS. HOWELL: The preacher didn't know whar to look when he asked him if'n he thought God wa'ar goin' to build a jim-crow heaven fer the colored Christians.

GRANNY: That thar preacher air a fool if'n thar ever wa'ar one. He don't know nothin' but sin an' hell. He ort to go to a jim-crow heaven hisse'f.

MRS. HOWELL: Well, Mother, you cain't talk! Didn't you fetch a baby fer that colored farmer woman last winter?

GRANNY: An' I'd fetch 'nother'n, too. The pain air jest the same. Hit wa'ar a right peart piccaninny, too. I see him often. He air my child like all t'other'ns I fetched. Folks air jest folks—'specially pore folks.

JOSEPHINE: How is Irene's baby, Gran?

GRANNY: Tol'able. She air's a good baby.

HELEN: What's Roy goin' to do with her, Granny?

GRANNY: Hit air my baby. Roy's got his hands full with t'other two.

HELEN: But you cain't raise her. How you goin' to?

GRANNY: Hain't the first child I've brung up. I kin make rugs—an' maybe I'll take her back to the hills. I don't like the way folks grow up in this-here village, noway. Hain't no cotton mill a-goin' to git that young-un.

JAMES: (*Coming in through door, left*) Well, Granny, we caught you. An' you're goin' to ketch hit.

MRS. HOWELL: Ketch hit fer what, James?

JAMES: (*Smiling*) Let her tell you. She knows what I mean.

MRS. HOWELL: What'uv you bin up to now, Mother?

GRANNY: Up to nothin'—'cept what these men-cowards wa'ar a-feared to do.

JOSEPHINE: Gran!—Did you do hit? I bet that's what you wuz this mornin'. I seen you goin' by.

JAMES: I'm glad you did, Gran. I wanted the men to do hit but the northern boys wa'ar agin hit—said hit would go agin us in the end.

HELEN: Say, young feller, this hain't no picnic. You better get busy and unpack them boxes.

JAMES: (*Going to boxes*) Oh, yeah?

JOSEPHINE: Gee, Jimmy's even talkin' like them northern boys now.

(LAWRENCE *and* DAN *enter.*)

LAWRENCE: Granny, wa'ar you in on hit? The sheeriff an' a judge from the governor's is here. Say they air goin' to arrest us for tearin' up proppity.

GRANNY: 'Course I was in on hit. Think I'm goin' to sit around, feared like you brave men folks sir?

MRS. HOWELL: (*Excitedly*) Mother, what have you bin ta'arin' up now? You wa'ar gone most of the mornin'?

GRANNY: I never tore up nothin'.

JAMES: I wuz over there just now, Gran. You done a good job.

MRS. HOWELL: Mother, what is hit? What you gone an' done?

GRANNY: (*Smiling*) I never done nothin', Emmaline.

LAWRENCE: Well, that hain't what the sheeriff says. He says you took a gang of women an' toted all that furniture out'n the company house.

GRANNY: That family wa'ar brought in here to take your jobs, wa'n't hit? An' you-all wa'ar feared to drive 'em out, wa'n't you? Well, thar air some folks left in this-here village what hain't feared—an' me and them t'other mountain women air some of 'em.

MRS. HOWELL: So you wint over that an' tore up things, did you?

GRANNY: No, we never. We-uns wint over thar an' toted all their belongin's out on the road an' we told 'em to load 'em up an' tote 'em back whar they come from. Them jobs in that-thar mill is yourn—an' if'n you-all air a-feared to stand up an' fight fer 'em, we has to do hit fer ye, an' that's what we done.

DAN: An' you slapped the sheeriff's face when he tried to hinder you. He tole me so hisse'f.

JAMES: Hurrah for Granny! (*Goes to* GRANNY, *embraces her*) You're all right, Grandmother.

GRANNY: (*Pushing him aside*) That-thar sheeriff oughter be glad I didn't shoot him. If'n he'd been in the mountains messin' into folkses business he'd a been kilt. We-uns knowed how to deal with the law up thar.

JAMES: The damn dirty polecat! (*Goes to a corner and sits with head on his knees*)

DAN: But hit'll git us into trouble.

GRANNY: (*Rising, angrily*) All you-uns kin think of is gittin' into trouble. Every last thing we-uns want to do you-uns get up an' say, "No, hit'll git us into trouble!" They hain't much in this-here village, son, 'cept trouble, mostly 'cause the mountain men has lost their nerve. You-all elected that law. "He's our friend," you said. Well, I tole you! I bet I'll have to shoot that sheeriff afore we're done.

DAN: You better clear out, folks. The sheeriff an' t'other law's comin' here afore the meetin' an' Granny'll jest git us into more hot water.

GRANNY: (*To her daughter*) Emmaline, you see that little-un gets her bottle when she wakes up. Emmy's watchin' her, an' Emmy gits a cup too. Hit air hangin' in the well. You-all go 'long, so's you kin git back fer the meetin'. (*Sits down as if for a long stay*)

DAN: You go 'long, too, Granny.

GRANNY: Did you-all say the sheeriff an' t'other law wa'ar a-comin' here afore the meetin', Dan?

DAN: They'll be here any minute, an' you better not let 'em ketch you here, nuther.

GRANNY: (*To women*) You-all go 'long. Me an' the Law's run into each other, an' I hain't a-feared—so I hain't runnin' away. I bin achin' to give that-thar sheeriff a piece o' my tongue, an' I low t'other'n kin git some of hit, too.

HELEN: Better come 'long, Granny—the men knows best.

MRS. HOWELL: Hit's no use, Helen. She's stubborn as a mule.

(*The women go out.*)

GRANNY: (*Goes to the door and calls out*) You tend that young-un, Emmaline, an' git ever'body back here to the meetin'. (*She reenters the room, and seeing that her pipe is out and that she has no more tobacco, goes up to* JAMES, *who is seated with his guitar.*) Got some terbaccer, son?

JAMES: (*Giving her some tobacco; she sits by him and lights her pipe.*) I wisht we wuz all like you, Gran. We'd win then.

GRANNY: (*Taking up his guitar, begins to play it and sings*)

"Snoopy is the stretch-out man,
Snoopy is the stretch-out man—
Lost 40,000 on the stretch-out plan.
Oh, Mr. Yaller Dog! Take him away, take him away.
The boss man bought a big '48
The boss man bought a big '48
The boss man bought a big '48—
But that didn't git 'im th'u the gate,
Oh, Mr. Yaller Dog! Take him away, take him away."

GRANNY: (*Smiles, smokes, and taps her foot in time to his singing*)

(*A knock is heard on door, left.*)

LAWRENCE: Hit's them. (*Goes to door*) Remember, we don't know nothin'!

(*Another knock. He opens the door and the* SHERIFF *enters with* JUDGE HERRING, *a suave, middle-aged man of the politician type.*)

SHERIFF: Howdy, boys. This is Judge Herring who the governor has sent.

(*The* JUDGE *shakes hands with the men, goes over and shakes hands with* JAMES, *offers his hand to* GRANNY.)

GRANNY: Air you the law?

JUDGE: Well, I guess you might call me that. I'm the personal representative of the governor, and in that capacity I suppose I do represent the law. I'm very glad to meet you, Grandmother. (*Extends his hand*)

GRANNY: (*Moving back*) I hain't used to shakin' hands with the law, an' I'm gittin' too fur 'long in years to start doin' hit now.

JUDGE: Well, just as you like, although I'm sorry we can't be friends.

GRANNY: Oh, you be a frien' of our'n too, be ye? Jest like the sheeriff over thar. He's our frien' too—least-wise he said he wuz afore he wa'ar elected. Now, he's servin' that-thar cotton mill over yander agin' we-uns. You've come to he'p him out, I reckon.

JUDGE: I'm awfully sorry if you look at it that way. I'm on neither side of this controversy. I'm merely here to see that you all obey the laws of our state. I want everybody to get justice.

GRANNY: I used to hear 'bout that jestice in the mountains when the law come 'round to tote our men folks off to jail fer makin' their own likker—an' sellin' hit. The law allus called hit jestice. Hit's the same kind o' jestice what you-all air talkin' 'bout here, hain't hit?

JUDGE: I suppose you would think so. (*He addresses the others.*) Well, men, shall we talk business?

LAWRENCE: Yes, sir—we're ready to listen.

(GRANNY *sits opposite others, and* JAMES *joins the men.*)

JUDGE: I may as well tell you that following the violence this morning, there was a call for troops. I am in charge. I have them stationed at the court house uptown. There is no need for them here in this village—if you men will be reasonable.

DAN: An' do what?

JUDGE: You must withdraw your pickets from the mill. You cannot interfere with those workers who want to go to work.

LAWRENCE: But they are all outsiders brung in here to defeat our strike. They air takin' our jobs. Them jobs belong to us.

JUDGE: No, they don't. You walked out—and left your jobs.

DAN: Not until 22 of us was turned out. Our strike is fer the reinstatement o' those first men.

JUDGE: We needn't go into that. It doesn't matter what the strike is about. The fact remains that you are picketing the mill, preventing people from going to work, and that must be stopped.

DAN: We have a right by law to picket peacefully.

JUDGE: You wouldn't call what you're doing here peaceful, would you?

DAN: O' course hit's peaceful. An' they hain't nobody wantin' to go to work. Even the new families hain't bin to the gate yit.

JUDGE: And you, therefore, go to their homes and destroy them. Is that your idea of peace?

LAWRENCE: Oh shucks! Judge, that was only a little bit o' fun. None of the furniture wuz busted.

JUDGE: That constitutes a riot in this state, and here are the warrants for you men who were mostly responsible. (*Exhibits warrants*)

JAMES: Men?

JUDGE: But that won't go so hard. We'll leave the names here, and not even arrest you. Just come up to the court house tomorrow, and we can arrange your bonds. You will come up for trial at the next term of court, and you'll get off pretty easy—especially if the strike is settled.

GRANNY: (*Poking the* JUDGE *with her cane*) You needn't go to no trouble 'bout that trial, Judge. I done toted that-thar furniture out'a that house myse'f, an' I hain't sorry I done hit, nuther.

JUDGE: Well, that's very generous of you, Grandmother—but I'm a little too much of a gentleman to permit an old woman like you to shoulder the blame—for these men.

JAMES: But the strike hain't goin' to be settled, less'n hit's settled, right. We hain't 'feared. You don't know 'bout this strike. The sheeriff's agin us—bin doin' ever'thing the mill boss tole him to. Now he's lied to you, too, 'bout that-thar furniture what was toted out-a that new family's house.

JUDGE: It's only natural that you should think that way, son. At the trial you can prove your innocence—if you are innocent. That's what the courts are for.

(*Outside in the distance an explosion is heard. Everybody runs to the window.*)

LAWRENCE: What in the world is that? Sounds like shot guns?

JUDGE: *More like dynamite!* (*He and the sheriff rush out.*)

JAMES: Let's go too. It sounds like hit come from whar the mill is. (*He rushes out.*)

DAN: Let's all go over.

GRANNY: (*Barring their way*) You're as bad as the sheeriff, jumpin' every time somebody shoots a chicken. Better stay an' unpack them-thar boxes. Do you want them gals to have to do hit in the mornin'?

LAWRENCE: That's right, let's get 'em out'n the way. (LAWRENCE *and* DAN *unpack the boxes of clothing.* GRANNY *grins at her trick and then watches the mill from the window.*)

DAN: Well, here's a box of clothes and books from—let's see. (*He examines the card.*) "The Carolina University students who wish you success."

LAWRENCE: These bundles are all from that church bunch, what that nice young feller from New york was with. They air some from the South too—Mississippi, Georgia, an' here's one from Tinnessee.

DAN: There's some good people everywhar. They don't know 'bout mill conditions less'n there's a strike.

GRANNY: Here comes Roy, walkin' quick.

LAWRENCE: Do you suppose there was somethin' to that shootin', Dan?

GRANNY: (*Opening the door for* ROY) What air hit, Roy?

ROY: (*Excitedly*) Somebody blowed up that ole shed-room in the mill yard whar the worn-out machinery's kept. That's a big crowd over thar.

DAN: Somebody's blowed it up? What fer?

ROY: The bossman is blamin' hit on us, an' the sheeriff says so too. The judge is all riled up 'bout hit.

GRANNY: Jest what I thought. They tried to git you when you-all talked that yard gang out'n unloadin' that raw cotton a month back. They tried to call that vilence. That didn't work, an' even the furniture what us women toted in the road this mornin' wa'n't sech a dangerous crime. Now they got somethin' real! That's how the law allus works.

LAWRENCE: (*Slowly*) My God, ole woman, do you think so? Say, do you think they would? Well, I'm damned.

GRANNY: (*At the window*) Here comes the sheeriff an' t'other law.

(JAMES *rushes in, followed by the* SHERIFF, *the* JUDGE, MRS. ROBERTS, *and a groups of men and women.*)

JAMES: They're liars—dirty liars! Hit's a trick!

JUDGE: (*Addressing the others in a loud voice*) Well, now, what do you say? You people are the biggest fools I have ever seen. You make it impossible to win your strikes. The very minute I'm talking peace to you, you blow up the mill.

(*Others, including* MRS. HOWELL *and* JONAS, *crowd in both doors.*)

JAMES: (*From his corner, breaking away from his mother*) That's a lie! (*The* JUDGE *turns quickly to him.*) We never done hit. That's an old shed—nothin' in hit worth a cent—(*His mother puts her hand over his mouth and forces him back in the corner.*)

LAWRENCE: See here, Judge! Even you cain't accuse us of that. We hain't dynamiters, an' we don't know nuthin' about that blow-up. You kin try us for the furniture. We wuz in the wrong there, but by God, that hain't blowin' up mills.

JONAS: (*Interrupting* LAWRENCE) Listen here, people! Hit air as plain as the nose on yore face. That-that mill over yander wants to git started, an' as long as we-uns stand by that gate thar hain't nary a one to go in. When they gits the sojers down thar, we cain't go down that no more. Then they'll ship in t'other ones to fill our places. Watch an' see!

JAMES: (*From the corner*) The dirty, lousy pole-cats. God damn 'em! God damn 'em! (*Again the women quiet him.*)

GRANNY: (*Pushing her way to the center of the stage*) So this air the jestice you wa'ar talkin' 'bout, air hit? (MRS. HOWELL *tries to quiet her but* GRANNY *shakes her off.*) I got somethin' to say an' nobody better stop me. Listen to me, all o' you-uns. The only vi'lence what's bin done on our side was done by me. I toted that furniture out'n that house this mornin' an' none o' these boys knowed a thing 'bout hit. But you got yore warrants out fer them, 'cause hit's them you want. We never done that blowin' up, an' you know hit as well as we do. But what good is hit fer us to argue with the law—

JUDGE: (*Interrupting sharply*) Come, come! I've had enough. The troops are at the court house. You know my terms. Stop your strike activity or I'll move them into the village . . . and protect anyone, imported or not, who wants to work. You had better take my advice and stop listening to northern agitators and all go back to work. You can settle your trouble afterwards, when the mill is in operation.

LAWRENCE: Like hell we will!

JAMES: An' lose our strike after fightin' all summer? We'd be a bunch o' cowards. We'll not do hit. We'll not do hit.

JUDGE: (*Going to the door, takes out his watch*) I'll give you exactly two minutes to decide. If you say no, I'll fetch the troops. (*Everybody stares at the* JUDGE.)

JAMES: (*From the rear*) You go to hell!

(*The* SHERIFF *starts toward* JAMES. GRANNY *picks up a chair and raises it above her head to strike the* SHERIFF. *The* SHERIFF *withdraws.* GRANNY *lowers the chair but still keeps her hands on it.*)

JUDGE: (*Lifting his finger in the air*) One half minute . . .

GRANNY: (*Defiantly, folding her arms on her breast*) Bring on yer sojers!

(*Everyone stands erect in defiance of the* JUDGE.)

CURTAIN

Scene 3

Union Headquarters on October 1 is eloquent of a defeated strike. The old placards are gone from the wall or hang dispiritedly by one corner. A "Strike Settlement" placard has displaced the "Bulletin Board." At one end of the big table, pulled out from the wall, ROY *and* LAWRENCE *are playing checkers.* DAN *is copying numbers into a ledger at the small table, right.* JONAS *sit on a bench against the left wall, silently smoking, watching the players. All seem nervous and tense.*

ROY: (*Pushing his chair back*) I cain't play no more.

LAWRENCE: Oh, come on, one more game. Hit kills time.

ROY: No, I'm th'u. (*He gets up from the table—goes over to the window and looks out.*)

LAWRENCE: Come on, Jonas, let's play another game, or are you sour too?

JONAS: (*Getting up slowly and taking his place at the checker table*) I sho' am sour, but not at the checkers.

ROY: (*From the window*) Hit's a hell of a settlement. Strike called off, an' none of us with a job.

LAWRENCE: (*Angrily*) Oh, fergit hit, cain't you? He agreed to the conference. Why in hell cain't you fergit it—'til tomorrow, anyway?

ROY: (*Coming to the table*) I cain't put much stock in the conference. I don't believe he'll come. (*Nobody answers. There is a pause.*)

LAWRENCE: Hit's your move, Jonas.

JONAS: (*Scratching his head*) I'm trying to figure hit out. You got me here, an' you got me there. I cain't move.

LAWRENCE: (*After waiting*) Well, move one way or t'other. I got you either way you make hit.

ROY: (*Angrily*) Say you! Listen to me. We're jest like these-here checkers—caught any way we move. (*He breaks up the game by folding the checker-board.*) We've got to talk this out.

LAWRENCE: (*Rising—angry*) Well, talk hit out. Where'n hell will it git you? Hain't we talked ourse'f out yit?

ROY: (*With more calm*) But maybe we can figger it out some way.

LAWRENCE: Roy, for Christ's sake! We know we've been tricked. We voted to settle the strike three weeks ago. We voted to settle if'n he would take us all back. He said he would take us all back but twelve. And then we voted to accept that proposition—to sacrifice our best men—an' I know as well as you do that that's whar we made our mistake.

ROY: But hell, he—

LAWRENCE: Let me finish. But—hell—I know. The super hain't only not took us back. He hain't took back more'n a hundred others. An' he hain't lived up to any point of the settlement. I know that—all of us know hit. So what do you want to keep a-rubbin' hit in all the time fer? Hain't it bad enough to know hit in your head without mouthin' it forever an' ever?

ROY: We oughter not settled.

LAWRENCE: I think so too, now, but we all voted fer it—or leastways we didn't vote agin hit.

DAN: Well, what else could we a-done? The sojers wa'ar guardin' every road to the mill. We couldn't even go to the postoffice fer our mail, an' every day, more families wa'ar brought in from outside. If'n we didn't settle when we did, by now nary a old family in this-here village would have jobs.

LAWRENCE: An' we know that too. The judge brought the sojers to break our strikem an' he done hit. Now sing hit, why don't you?

ROY: But damn it all! I hain't talkin' 'bout that. We agreed to a settlement that was bad enough—an' we agreed because the sojers broke up our strike. But they hain't carryin' out even that agreement. Hit hain't twelve of us left out, hit air more'n a hundred—and what air to come of 'em?

DAN: (*With much more calm*) That's the worst part o' hit. When I voted to settle, I figgered that maybe we could sneak away an' get jobs somewhere else, but where'll this whole crowd go to find work?

(JAMES *enters.*)

ROY: Hello, Jimmy. How air things in the mill?

JAMES: 'Bout the same. The boss-man is still sour on the union. I had a quarrel last night with him. He said I wa'n't supposed to talk union, an' I said the settlement give us a right to belong to the union.

ROY: (*Angrily*) You see! They don't intend to keep any part of the agreement.

JAMES: The mill folks is sore. Powerful put out. We feel like we oughtn't to work less'n the other folks git back too. They'll strike agin.

LAWRENCE: Well, let 'em wait awhile. Maybe they'll git a chance to strike!

JONAS: What about the conference? Hit's tomorrer, hain't hit?

(GRANNY, MRS. HOWELL, *and* MRS. ROBERTS *come in.*)

DAN: (*Angrily*) Well, what brings you-all here? There hain't no meetin' going on?

GRANNY: Well, that ort to be a meetin' goin' on, my son. (*Sits down*)

LAWRENCE: What's up now, Gran?

MRS. HOWELL: All the people that went ter places wa'ar told that no more union folks wa'ar goin' to git took back, an' they better look fer jobs some other place, 'cause the company wants their houses fer new families what air comin' in.

LAWRENCE: (*Slowly*) Then hit *air* so—that's what I feared!

ROY: What the hell can we do?

JAMES: We kin call another strike, that's what we kin do—an' stay out this time 'till ever'body's took back.

LAWRENCE: (*Slowly, speaking half to himself*) We're supposed to see the old man tomorrow. He's bin away since the settlement, an' he's agreed to meet us. He thinks the agreement is bein' carried out. He's comin' home in the mornin' an' we see him in the afternoon.

GRANNY: He's comin' home *tomorrer* mornin', did you say, Lawrence?

LAWRENCE: Yes, on the early train.

GRANNY: (*Lighting her pipe*) Maybe hit'll interest you-all to know he come home today, an' that him an' the law air bin talkin' together all afternoon.

LAWRENCE: What air you talkin' 'bout? He hain't comin' 'till tomorrow. We telephoned to his house not an hour ago.

GRANNY: He air home now, I tell ye. I seen the law and the super go by, an' I follered 'em. They're a-settin' in the ole man's front room right now makin' up some meanness.

LAWRENCE: I'll be God damned! I'll go telephone and see. (*He goes out.*)

GRANNY: Thar's trouble a-comin', folks. This-here fight has jest begun. Maybe you-all will larn how nice yer friends air—atter you turn 'em into sheeriffs.

ROY: If'n he won't meet with us tomorrer, what'll we do?

JAMES: We'll strike—that's what we'll do. All the people in the mill want to anyway. We come out three months ago to git 22 men back, an' after fighting all summer we go back with more'n a hundred added to the list. A hell of a strike settlement!

MRS. ROBERTS: You better run 'long home, sonny, an' eat yore supper. You air back at the mill, an' you got to work tonight, you know.

JAMES: Yes, an' I feel like a—like—a scab. (*Goes to door*)

GRANNY: (*As he passes, pats him*) You go 'long, son; this pot'll bile over agin soon, an' you-all have larned somethin'. You go 'long an' have a peep in at Emmy an' the little-un. Tell Emmy I'll be 'long too.

JAMES: (*Going out*) The bloody buggers!

GRANNY: (*To* MRS. ROBERTS) You air got a fine son thar, Miz Roberts. He's 'bout the only real mountaineer left in this-here village—the only one what hain't a-feared. He used to be, too. The strike's made a man out'n that lad.

MRS. ROBERTS: (*Standing by the window*) Jimmy air a nice son. Got a hot head—kinder bad temper, but he's allus kind to me an' the childern. Ever since his daddy's been dead, he's had to go 'long ahead fer all of we-uns.

He's tied back 'cause of we-uns too. If'n it warn't fer we-uns, he'd go fur—always wantin' somethin'—wantin' to go places. But he don't never spent a cent fer hisse'f—all goes to he'p us out.

MRS. HOWELL: Lucky you had him, Miz Roberts. He's sho' been a father to yore childern, an' he's only a child hisse'f.

GRANNY: James like chilern. He allers comes in an' plays with my young-uns.

ROY: (*Coming up to* GRANNY) How is the baby, Gran?

MRS. HOWELL: She's a good baby, Roy.

GRANNY: She's tol'able. I named her t'other day, Roy.

MRS. ROBERTS: You named her, and she hain't christened yit?

GRANNY: An' she hain't goin' to be christened, nuther; leastways not 'till I kin tote her up to them-thar mountains, an' have a real preacher like old Cicero Queens do hit.

ROY: What air you callin' her, Granny?

GRANNY: She air named Piney—Piney Strike. The first part air fer the pine trees what me an' her ma loved. An' the second part air fer the strike agin the cotton mill, the mill what kilt her ma.

ROY: (*Slowly*) Piney Strike. Why, that air a purty name, Grandmother. Irene'ud like hit.

GRANNY: 'Course she would, she knowed 'bout hit. I told her when she wa'ar a-tryin' to have the baby. I wanted her to fergit the pain, so I'd talk 'bout the good times we useter have up home—an' Irene allus talked 'bout the pine trees. I'd hum to her like it wa'ar the wind blowin' th'u the trees—an' she'd go to sleep fer a spell.

(ROY *turns his back to conceal his emotions.*)

MRS. ROBERTS: You cain't call a girl baby "Strike," kin you?

GRANNY: She air a strike baby, hain't she? All the clothes she air got to her back I made out'n that box o' things what had that card in hit, with them words what I liked.

JONAS: "Workers of the world unite. You-all hain't got nuthin' to lose but yore chains."

GRANNY: That air hit. An' hit comes all the way from Canady. Irene wanted to lose them-air chains, an' she air gone now. Her baby'll bear a name that'll mean somethin'.

LAWRENCE: (*Coming in*) They said he warn't home, not expected 'till tomorrow. Gran, are you sure?

GRANNY: I saw 'em with these two eyes. The law air there, an' that means they air cookin' up somethin' dirty.

ROY: By God, I'm goin' down to the mill as they go in on the night shift an' tell everybody to come to a meetin' tomorrow. If'n he don't meet us, we'll have another strike.

LAWRENCE: (*Thoughtfully*) Somethin' crooked back of this.

DAN: Everybody what wa'ar he'pin' us air gone. We don't know what to do.

GRANNY: (*Rising*) What the mountain people in this-here village needs more than anything else is to stand up on their own hind legs. Go on down to that-thar mill an' larn what to do!

ROY: Come on, fellers. (*The men go out.*)

GRANNY: (*Watches the mill from the window. The women get ready to go.*) I reckon we'd better unpack that box back ahind the door 'fore we go.

MRS. HOWELL: What's in hit?

GRANNY: Take hit out. It's somethin' we'll most likely need agin soon.

(*The two women unpack the old strike banners.* GRANNY *takes them one by one, dusts them off, and stands them against the wall as the curtain falls.*)

CURTAIN

ACT 3

Scene 1

Outside a cotton mill, at 8 o' clock the same evening. The red brick mill, two stories of which are indicated by windows, runs clear across the back stage with a door at the right. A gate in a 12-foot iron-barred fence gives entrance to the mill yard from the road. From the mill comes the noise of machinery. In the late evening light, the figures on the stage are only dimly seen.

Two DEPUTY SHERIFFS *are sitting on a long bench outside the fence; another sprawls on the ground, and a fourth walks back and forth at intervals. They are all obviously tough characters, armed with rifles and holstered revolvers. A whisker bottle is passed around at intervals.*

FIRST DEPUTY: (*After taking a drink of liquor*) This hain't bad likker. Whar did the old man git hit, I wonder? Out'n his private cellar, I reckon. (*Takes a drink*) Leastwise hit tastes like hit.

SECOND DEPUTY: You ort ter be 'shamed, breakin' the law. Hit air a sin and agin the government to drink likker. (*Takes a drink*)

FIRST DEPUTY: This air a good joke on you or the sheeriff, one. You just got out'n jail for sellin' likker, didn't you? And the same sheeriff what put you in fer tampering with moonshine is now furnishin' you real likker to drink yourse'f. The way to git 'round the law, I reckon, is ter git on the inside o' hit.

SECOND DEPUTY: Yeah, he put me in jail for toting corn-juice all right. But when my trial comes up hit will be all turned 'round. I'll git off . . . don't you-all fret 'bout me.

FIRST DEPUTY: Wouldn't be so shore if'n I wuz you. Old Judge Jones hits 'em plenty hard. He's straighter laced than a fence . . . 'especially on likker cases.

SECOND DEPUTY: This here cotton mill fixed hit up with the judge . . . he'll come 'round when he sees me in court. That's why I'm here a-doin' a favor fer the old man tonight.

FIRST DEPUTY: Still I wouldn't be so shore if'n I wuz you. Maybe you-all hain't going to get a chanct to do this here mill a favor. (*Turns and looks into the mill*) I don't reckon they're figgerin' on striking. Looks pretty quiet ter me. Hit's eight o' clock. They bin in two hours and nothin's happened yit.

SECOND DEPUTY: Well, boys, maybe they hain't a-comin' out on strike but if'n they do or if'n they don't, I'll git off in that-thar court. I've already done one purty good turn for this-here cotton mill. You-all hain't forgitting that old shed room what wa'ar blowed up, air ye?

(*The* SHERIFF *walks out of the mill yard onto the scene.*)

FIRST DEPUTY: Well, sheeriff, when does the show begin? What's that strike you wa'ar 'feared of?

SHERIFF: It don't look like they air comin' out. I tole the old man yesterday that he had the wrong dope. But he said they was a-comin' out on a "surprise" strike jest afore the night shift went on.

FIRST DEPUTY: Well, they didn't.

SECOND DEPUTY: Mebbe they got wind of what wa'ar a-comin' to 'em, if'n they did.

SHERIFF: No, I'm sure they didn't know. No one but us did, an' we wuz all hid when they went in.

SECOND DEPUTY: Do you reckon that meetin' stuff wa'ar real, what their committee wa'ar announcin' when they wint in?

SHERIFF: I think it was. The ole man promised them he'd meet 'em tomorrow. That was just to give 'em time to git set. He come home today. They think he won't be here 'till tomorrow mornin'.

FIRST DEPUTY: Well, have a drink, fellers. I reckon we better drink hit up. Mebbe the sheeriff hain't goin' to need us after all—an' he'll come 'round an' tote us off to jail fer takin' a little nip. (*The* DEPUTIES *drink; one offers bottle to* SHERIFF.)

SECOND DEPUTY: Have one, sheriff?

SHERIFF: What? No, I won't drink any. We might have to use our heads tonight. The super says he'll make 'em come out. He's bound on settlin' hit fer good tonight.

(*The* MILL SUPERINTENDENT *comes out of the mill, walks through the yard and joins the* DEPUTIES.)

SUPERINTENDENT: You fellers all set? Got your orders so as not to forget? (*The* DEPUTIES *nod.*) We got to settle this union business now or never. They're coming out, and when they do you see that they don't stay 'round the mill. We've enough others ready to break their nerve. They'll all be crawling back for their jobs before I'm done with them.

SECOND DEPUTY: Well, get 'em out here, Mister, an' we'll shoot some light into their thick heads.

SHERIFF: Now for Christ's sake, give your trigger finger a rest. You don't shoot nothin' into nobody—understand?

SECOND DEPUTY: Well, what in hell be we here fer? Hain't no camp meetin', is hit?

SUPERINTENDENT: Now, wait a minute, Sheriff! You might have to shoot. (*He goes up to* SHERIFF.) You're the Sheriff, you know. (*Jabs him in the ribs with his thumb*) Buck up!

SHERIFF: When the sojers was here the captain always advised against rough stuff. He said you could get just as far just by bluffin'.

SUPERINTENDENT: Which is precisely why you, and not the soldiers, are here now. We've got to teach these people a lesson that will go for all other mill workers as well. If you don't, they'll be demanding the whole mill. They aren't licked. We can't handle them like we could before the strike. Christ a-mighty! They walk out the minute the whistle blows. The other day a whole section refused to clean up just because it was a few minutes past quittin' time. How in hell are we going to run a mill like that?

FIRST DEPUTY: Well, git 'em out here, an' we'll larn 'em a lesson.

SHERIFF: The old man said they was armed, but they hain't. I wuz through the works, an' not one of 'em has a gun.

SUPERINTENDENT: They smelled a rat there, I think. I even left two guns in the wash room. They wouldn't pick 'em up—an' every foreman is wearing a gun in plain sight.

SHERIFF: They air waitin' fer the conference tomorrow. Whatever they do, they won't do hit 'till after that meetin'.

SUPERINTENDENT: There won't be a conference tomorrow. I'll get them out, if I have to throw them out! Do you know how to work that gas gun?

SHERIFF: (*Taking what looks like a small pistol out of his pocket*) Here it is. You operate it just like any gun, don't you?

SUPERINTENDENT: I never saw one before. The old man brought it home with him from up North. It is suppose to blind them for a few hours. Now, listen, if they won't leave the mill, that is, if they stay to make a demonstration, you give 'em the gas. That may teach them their lesson. We've got a crowd to come to work in the morning, and we want nobody here to interfere with them, understand? If you don't get the crowd away, the new families won't come in. They're already backing out.

SECOND DEPUTY: An' what air we-uns to do? Stand 'round to keep the women from slappin' the sheeriff?

SUPERINTENDENT: That's just about it. You're supposed to give him moral support—and the other kind too, if necessary. Say, isn't there a little drink around here to liven up the party.

FIRST DEPUTY: Here you are. (*Offers* SUPERINTENDENT *the bottle*) Hit's the best likker I've tasted in many a moon.

SUPERINTENDENT: (*Taking a long drink*) Not half bad. Just keep a swig of that under your belt; there's plenty of it. If we keep the factories down here, this labor trouble's got to stop, and it's got to be settled once and for all. If you understand that, just sit around awhile and we shall see what we shall see.

(*He walks through the mill gate into the yard and goes into the mill.*)

CURTAIN

(*Curtain remains down to indicate the passage of three hours time.*)

Scene 2

The same scene, three hours later. The DEPUTIES *are drowsing. Through one lighted window of the mill,* JIMMY ROBERTS *can be seen at work.*

FIRST DEPUTY: (*Rousing*) Well, hit air twelve o' clock an' nothin' in the air. As quiet as a grace. I don't think he kin git 'em out.

SECOND DEPUTY: Well, what air you whinin' 'bout? This air easy money. Keep your trap shut. Let's get some sleep. (*They settle down and sleep.*)

(*Inside the mill, the* SUPERINTENDENT *comes up to* JAMES' *machine.*)

SUPERINTENDENT: (*In a hostile manner*) Well, you're back, I see. This machine's been runnin' itself for the last hour. I thought you'd gone out on another strike.

JAMES: I bin at my place all night.

SUPERINTENDENT: Like hell you have! I've been by here a dozen times looking for you.

JAMES: I wuz in the wash-room, but I wa'aren't gone more'n five minutes.

SUPERINTENDENT: You're a damn liar. You've been cookin' up another walkout. But I'm here to tell you, young feller, that we're set for you lot this time.

JAMES: Is that why you-all air totin' your guns on the outside tonight? Your foreman's bin bullyin' us all ev'nin'. What you tryin' to do? Start a war?

SUPERINTENDENT: We beat you to it, didn't we? You thought you'd catch us like you did last time—and pull our help out agin. Why don't you try it? Go on—try to take our hands out.

JAMES: They're not yore hands. They're ourn. We're goin' to have a conference with the old man tomorrow an' we're goin' to tell him 'bout yore carryin' on tonight, too. What wa'ar the sheeriff doin' in the mill tonight? Thar hain't been no trouble here yit.

SUPERINTENDENT: That's none of your business, you damn little scoundrel! I suppose you'd like to have us ask your permission before we bring anybody in. Listen, boy, it's none of your Goddamned business how we run this mill. If you don't like it, get to hell out of here . . . understand?

JAMES: You bet I understand. That's the way it allus wuz. If'n we didn't like hit, we could git out—an' go into another mill what wa'ar jist as bad. We don't go out by ourse'f no more, we all go out together. That's what we air goin' to tell the old man at our conference tomorrow.

SUPERINTENDENT: So you did fall for that conference stuff, did you? The old man's been home since morning—you damn fool.

JAMES: I don't believe you. He said . . .

SUPERINTENDENT: (*Slapping* JAMES *in the face*) Don't you call me a liar, you half-baked hill billy. Get to hell out of here, too. Now show me how strong you are. Try and pull the others out if you dare!

JAMES: God damn you! . . . I'll show you! (*Reaches up and pulls off the power on his machine, then calls loudly*) Hey, people, stop! Strike! Follow me! Run through the mill! (*Disappears, calling very loudly*) Everybody out! (*The noise of machinery stops. Workers shout and cheer.* JAMES *appears running out of the mill door. He calls.*) You-all see that everybody comes out. I'll go tell the others. (*He runs through the mill yard, through the gate and down the street left—off stage. Workers start pouring out of the mill. The* DEPUTIES *awake, grab their guns.*)

CURTAIN

(*Curtain remains down to indicate the passage of six hours.*)

Scene 3

The workers are picketing the mill in the early dawn. They crowd the road at the left of the stage, carrying their strike banners. The SHERIFF *and his* DEPUTIES *face them, just outside the mill gate, with their rifles ready for action. The* SUPERINTENDENT *and two foremen are inside the fence. The machinery is not running.*

Before the curtain rises, the workers can be heard singing:

The union is the place for me,
The place for working men,
Who want some time to sing and play,
And money we can spend.

As the curtain opens, they continue:

On the line, on the line,
We'll win our fight,
Our fight for the right,
On the picket, picket line!

SHERIFF: (*In a frightened manner, interrupting the song*) Folks, you-all better go home and settle this at your meetin'.

LAWRENCE: Like hell we will! Them jobs air our'n an' we're goin' to stay an' picket that gate.

SHERIFF: You-all got to get out of here and let the other workers go in. You ain't got no right to stand out here.

LAWRENCE: This air a public highway an' we got as much right here as you have an' we're goin' to stay.

SUPERINTENDENT: (*Calling from inside the fence*) You better get away from that gate. The other workers are standing back there on the hill, afraid to come down. If you don't want to get into trouble you better go on home. (*Shouts of "Let 'em stay there!" etc.*)

JAMES: (*Pushing forward from the crowd, yells at* SUPERINTENDENT) No, we'll not go home. Thought we couldn't get 'em out, didn't you? Well, now you see. (*The strikers cheer.*)

GRANNY: (*Coming forward, calm and self-controlled*) Well, sheeriff, we-uns hain't so 'feared as you reckoned, air we? (*Strikers cheer.*)

SHERIFF: If you don't want to get mixed up in the court, old woman, you'd better go on home where you belong.

JAMES: To hell with the court! To hell with you! We hain't 'feared. You cain't fool us agin.

SUPERINTENDENT: I'll show you! (*Goes inside mill, starts machinery*)

GRANNY: (*Raising her voice above the sound of the machinery*) I 'low we-uns belong right here whar our jobs be. (*She turns to crowd.*) Don't nary one of you move an inch. This-here road is our'n—an' we're goin' to stay on hit.

JONAS: (*In his usual slow manner*) 'Pears to me, sheeriff, you-all better go 'long yourse'f an' git yer breakfast. We-uns hain't goin' to do nothin' 'cept tell them t'other folks what fools you-all be makin' out'n 'em.

(*The workers sing the chorus of "Solidarity Forever." Tune: "Battle Hymn of Republic."*)

"Solidarity forever!
Solidarity forever!
Solidarity forever!
For the union makes us strong."

(*As the strikers sing,* LAWRENCE *forms them into a parade; they march in a circle in the street in front of the mill.* JONAS *stands aside and directs them with his crutch. As the song closes the* SUPERINTENDENT *comes to the gate, calls the* SHERIFF.)

SUPERINTENDENT: Give the bastards the gas. That'll scatter 'em.

SHERIFF: (*To* DEPUTIES) I'll give 'em the gas. No rough-stuff—unless you have to.

STRIKERS: Speech—Jimmy! Lift him up!

JAMES: (*Lifted into the air by* LAWRENCE *and* DAN) Listen to me, people. The law air on the side o' the cotton mill. We got to show 'em we hain't a-feared. We wuz fooled into goin' back when we struck afore. This time we got to lick the cotton mill. All of us has . . .

(*While* JAMES *is speaking, the* SHERIFF *moves near workers, releases tear gas. The gas interrupts* JAMES' *speech.*)

JONAS: (*To* SHERIFF) Say—what air you doin' there, sheeriff? (*Grapples with* SHERIFF)

MRS. HOWELL: What air hit? Hit's burnin' my eyes out.

DAN: Hit's gas like what wa'ar in the war. The dirty devils!

OTHER VOICES: Oh, my God! Run! God he'p us!

(*From the moment the* SHERIFF *releases the tear gas, all is confusion.* JONAS *grapples with the* SHERIFF *who tries to hand-cuff him.* JONAS *fights back. A deputy comes to help the* SHERIFF; *he strikes* JONAS *on the head with a revolver.* JONAS *is hand-cuffed. The dialogue of "Other Voices," etc. is said quickly, almost simultaneously. The* SUPERINTENDENT *sees the* SHERIFF *scuffle with* JONAS *and comes out of the mill gate with drawn revolver. As he reaches the gate, the* THIRD DEPUTY *fires a shot. It strikes* JONAS *who sinks into the ground, dead, with hand-cuffs on his wrists. All the lights go out. Twelve shots are fired in rapid succession in the dark. A polic whistle is heard. Then the* SHERIFF'*s voice.*)

SHERIFF: My God, men, stop shooting. We've killed enough.

VOICE: (*In the dark as they run away*) They're killing us.

VOICE: I'm shot. Oh, my God!

(*Sounds of workers running in the dark. As quiet returns, heavy breathing and groans are heard—then complete stillness for a few seconds. The light begins to appear, breaking gradually on the scene.* JONAS, DAN, *and two other strikers lie dead in the road.* JAMES *and* GRANNY *are injured.* JAMES *lies in center of stage,* GRANNY *kneels over him, holding his body in her arms. He is bleeding.* GRANNY *takes off her head shawl and attempts to stop the blood. The dead lie in the background.*)

GRANNY: (*Tenderly*) Are you bad hurt, Jimmy?

JAMES: (*Feebly*) Oh, Granny! They got us. They got us.

GRANNY: Rest still, sonny . . . You air bleedin' . . . don't talk, son.

JAMES: Air you shot too, Gran?

GRANNY: Jest a little nip in the leg. (*Pats his face*) Rest still, Jimmy.

JAMES: Whar's my mother?

GRANNY: She air safe, son. Don't talk, Jimmy.

JAMES: (*Very feebly*) Granny . . . you tell her . . . I warn't 'feared.

GRANNY: (*Looking up. She speaks tenderly.*) I'll tell her, Jimmy. You warn't 'feared. Us mountain people's got to fight. You air brave, son.

JAMES: (*Slowly*) Gran . . . you got to lick 'em. You will, won't you, Granny?

GRANNY: We'll lick 'em, Jimmy! (*Lifts her right hand as if making a vow*)

(*The dawn has gradually been breaking while* GRANNY *and* JAMES *have been talking. Shadows of the mill fall across them.*)

JAMES: (*With great difficulty*) Granny . . . hit air gittin' dark. What air that?

GRANNY: That air shadows, Jimmy. (*She looks up over the mill into the mountains.*) Hit'll soon be warm. (*She turns her face to his, sees that he is dead.*) Jimmy! (*Whispers*) Jimmy!

(*Holding* JAMES *close she rocks back and forth, pounding the right with her tightly clenched right fist.*)

CURTAIN

Scene 4

In a drawing room in the GOVERNOR*'s mansion, two days later. There is a fireplace in the center of the stage, an easy chair and small table left, a similar chair right.*

There are two stacks of telegrams piled on the table. Only these details of the room can be seen. The rest of the stage is dark. JUDGE HERRING *is leaning against the mantle of the fireplace, looking into a fire burning in the grate.* CORNELIUS, *an aged negro servant enters, carrying several telegrams on a tray. He places the telegrams on the table with the others.*

JUDGE: More telegrams, eh? How many are there?

CORNELIUS: Too many to keep track of, sir . . . and still coming.

JUDGE: How long have the labor people been here?

CORNELIUS: 'Bout two hours, I reckon.

JUDGE: Did you tell the Governor I'd come?

CORNELIUS: Yes, sir. I told him. He knows you're here. (*Goes out*)

(*The* JUDGE *walks to table, picks up a handful of telegrams. He examines them, but does not open the envelopes, puts them back in order on the table, sits down, lights a cigar, looks into the fire and smokes. In a few seconds the* GOVERNOR OF CAROLINA *enters, carrying a folder of papers in his hand. He is a man in his early fifties, well groomed. He is a large man with a kind and intelligent face. His voice is soft and well modulated.*)

GOVERNOR: (*Putting the folder of papers on the table*) Sorry to have kept you waiting . . . I just got through.

JUDGE: What do you think of the labor skates?

GOVERNOR: It's a pretty mess. I can see no need for the shooting at all. The sheriff must be a fool of the first order, and the mill owner seems to be without faculties altogether. If this is the type of manufacturer the South is recruiting—I wonder where we shall end.

JUDGE: How many were there at the conference?

GOVERNOR: Quite a delegation. Eight or ten, our own state people, and some northern men and a woman. It was the northern people who did most of the talking, but the southern men stood solidly with them. They know as much about the industry as I do and much more about civil rights and that angle. They have a very good case against us. Who are they?

JUDGE: Some crazy intellectuals out to save the world.

GOVERNOR: Not crazy by a long shot.

JUDGE: So they won you over, did they? Instead of it being the other way around? I was afraid of that. Poor old John—still being just. What did they want specifically—the whole industry, of course, and what else?

GOVERNOR: They wanted to put us in a hole, and they've done it. Here's their proposition (*Hands* JUDGE *papers*) all written out so it could be handed to the newspapers. (*The* JUDGE *reads the papers.*)

JUDGE: Pretty clever, eh? You're going to do it, of course?

GOVERNOR: They knew I couldn't do it, but the press will carry their proposal to signify that they aren't afraid of a searchlight and that we are. And there are six dead men—killed in front of a cotton mill—to add interest to the story. The last thing they said was that they would carry the issue right to the public—both South and North—and let Carolina answer to the public conscience as best we can.

JUDGE: Carpet-baggers?

GOVERNOR: No, they aren't carpet-baggers. You don't right a wrong by calling up ghosts. And anyway, this particular mill is a northern concern, you know. In reality it is we who are defending the carpet-bagger. Are the bodies buried yet?

JUDGE: The funeral is this afternoon. (*Looking at his watch*) Being held now, I guess.

GOVERNOR: Where are the services? Is there a demonstration? What about an outbreak of violence over there? They are mountain people.

JUDGE: There will be no serious demonstration. I have the troops stationed there. The funeral service is being held in the field where they carried on all their strike activity.

GOVERNOR: What a ghastly spectacle it will be! Tomorrow everybody in the country will read the story.

JUDGE: John, it's getting late. We may as well come to the point. You and I have been good friends all our lives. I know you. I haven't forgotten our college days—your ideals, your championship of the right. But you are governor now. All your friends have enjoyed your rise in the state. They are proud of their governor. But you have enemies too—waiting patiently for a chance to ruin you politically and put one of their own kind into your office.

GOVERNOR: And now they have a chance—is that what you mean?

JUDGE: That depends on how you handle this situation.

GOVERNOR: But in this case, where human life is at stake—southern human life, I mean. And economically, we are mistaken too. The mill workers must be assimilated into larger communities. The mill village ought to go. And our wage policy is ruining rather than building up our section.

JUDGE: We are poor down here, and if we keep pace, or even attempt to catch up with the rest of the country, we must have wealth—wealth to correspond with our good manners. The factory system is the road to power for the South . . . and our factories are no worse than other factories have been and are now in many places.

GOVERNOR: But we don't have to make those same mistakes. We have an industrial history from which to learn.

JUDGE: But we don't learn from history. We muddle along and learn as we must. What we need now is capital, and it must be attracted here. Our cheap labor supply is what draws investments. Take that away and the money will go elsewhere.

GOVERNOR: That policy of yours will ruin the South, I tell you. It will actually kill the goose that lays the golden egg.

JUDGE: Not necessarily. Some improvement can be made now. In this particular village they must have a sewer, for instance. There is an epidemic of typhoid breaking out there now that will have to be checked.

(CORNELIUS *appears with a tray of telegrams. Crosses room, puts telegrams on table.*)

GOVERNOR: More telegrams. There have been hundreds from all over—the South, the North, and even from Europe. Listen to this one: (*Reads*) "It is with a feeling of shame that we in Pennsylvania have to hand the mantle of cruelty in labor disputes to Carolina. The brutal murder of six workers in front of a cotton mill moves your state one notch ahead of Pennsylvania's ghastly record. For shame, Carolina!" It is signed by thirty men from a university in Pennsylvania.

JUDGE: Pennsylvania has a right to talk.

GOVERNOR: If it were from that state alone—but the South too is divided. The southern people would not stand for this sort of thing either—if they knew all the facts. (*Indicates a separate pile of telegrams*) Read that batch of telegrams there all from below the Mason-Dixon line and just as critical as the rest. Our university men know. They aren't fools.

JUDGE: They can afford to know. But it is we who must build the South . . . so we can have universities. The professors have no responsibilities. A college professor can very easily point out the road to an ideal state—as they did even when we went to college. But who will travel it? What good is their philosophy? We don't need philosophy—we need factories. Factories to give these poor downtrodden mill workers, if you please, bread. And that's our job, John. It's different from the professors'.

GOVERNOR: And in your scheme there can be no justice. Is that your conclusion?

JUDGE: John, have you ever seen or heard of an industrial system, a political system, a religious institution, or any other kind of human mechanism that was just? I can't find it; now or in history. The world's like that, man.

GOVERNOR: And what do you advise?

JUDGE: There's only one course to follow. This revolt of the mill people must be suppressed. That shooting was unfortunate, I grant you. But since it happened, we must accept it. Perhaps because it did happen, a larger conflict will be obviated. There must be some gradual improvements, granted. You must make that plain to the owners. That will quiet the revolt. But there must be no investigation—no conviction of those deputies.

After all, they were deputized. No matter whether that was or unwise, they did represent law and order—they were officers of Carolina. You can't convict your own officers. One never knows what officers will be compelled to do. All of them must be protected.

(*During the* JUDGE'*s last speech, the last strains of "Nearer my God to Thee" become faintly audible, and as the song increases in volume the lights on the front of the stage go down and the backstage lights come up, revealing a scene of the funeral of dead strikers. This takes place back of a gauze curtain which forms the back wall of the* GOVERNOR'*s room and against which the* JUDGE *and* GOVERNOR, *in darkness, are silhouetted. The mourners are grouped around a rude platform in the open air, on which* LAWRENCE *and the choir stand. Rough caskets are visible as the crowd shifts.* MRS. ROBERTS *is being supported by* MRS. HOWELL *and* GRANNY. *In the distance are the mountains. The foliage of the trees among which the crowd stands are brilliant in the autumn sunshine. When the song finishes,* LAWRENCE *steps forward.*

LAWRENCE: Folks, we shore air sorry we hain't got no preacher to preach us a sermon. We done searched evertwhar, but none of 'em would come 'cause we air strikers. But as I look over this gatherin' I see our old mountain preacher, Cicero Queens, a-standin' out thar and I'm goin' to ask hin to come up here and say a prayer for our dead brothers. Cicero Queens, will you please come forward?

(CICERO QUEENS *makes his way through the crowd, and climbs onto the speakers' stand. He is an old man, tall and straight, with a flowing beard. He wears high leather boots and blue overalls, the legs of which are stuffed into the boots, and a long-tailed coat. He carries a wide brimmed hat in his hand. He faces the caskets, stretches long arms high in the air, kneels down slowly and prays. His words are full of emotion, his diction is clear and sharp.*)

CICERO QUEENS: O Lord Jesus Christ, here are six men in their coffins, blood of my blood, bone of my bone. I trust, O God, that these friends will go to a better place than this mill village or any other place in Carolina. O God, we know we are not high in society, but we know Jesus Christ loves us. The poor people have their rights too. For the work we do in this world, is this what we are to get if we demand our rights? Jesus Christ, your son, O God, was a workin' man. If he was to pass under these trees today, he would see these cold bodies lyin' here before us. O God, mend the broken hearts of these loved ones left behind. Dear God, do feed their children. Drive selfishness and cruelty out of your world. May these weeping wives and little children have a strong arm to lean on. Dear God—what would Jesus do, if he was to come to Carolina?

(*As* QUEENS *prays there is a sobbing heard from the funeral throng.* MRS. ROBERTS *can be heard to say* "JIMMY!" *At the close of his prayer, his listeners say "Amen."* QUEENS *goes off elevated platform into the crowd and* LAWRENCE *steps forward.*)

LAWRENCE: And now we want our song leader from the North to say a few words to us. (*A young woman steps forward to speak.*)

SONG LEADER: The time will come when these soldiers who have fallen in the battle of labor will be honored in this land beyond the boys who died in the great war. I hope the workers of Carolina will anticipate that time by building a monument presently to these martyrs whose bodies lies before us. But the only truly, adequate monument we can raise to them will be to carry to complete victory the cause for which they died. We must keep after it day after day, month after month, year after year, if necessary. We must try again and again until this monument is built. The cotton mill must be conquered. It is slowly killing all of you. One day we shall triumph. We shall keep the faith of our dead. They shall not die in vain. (*Bowed heads have been gradually lifted during this speech.*)

LAWRENCE: And now let us sing the song that they loved the best. (*To the* SONG LEADER) Will you lead us?

(*The* SONG LEADER *leads in singing "We Are Building a Strong Union." As the funeral throng sings, their mood changes from one of sorrow and despair to one of hope. They stand straight.* GRANNY *can be seen with body and head erect during the song. As the second verse of the song is sung the lights change and as the song is finished the* GOVERNOR'*s room is lighted as the funeral scene darkens.*)

GOVERNOR: (*Looking tired, worried and defeated. He now appears as one who has given in to something against his inner self.*) I wish I could see my way clearly. I've had no sleep—no rest—those telegrams—telephone calls—delegation after delegation on both sides of the issue, Shadows—ghastly mill shadows—everywhere. (*He pauses, runs fingers through his hair.*) I don't know what I am going to do—but I know whatever it is, it will be what I think is the right thing.

JUDGE: (*In a good humor and indicating that he has won his case*) Of course, John. (*Pats him on the shoulder*) Now you get some rest. I'll go back to the village and do . . . the right thing too. Good night, John.

GOVERNOR: (*Shaking the* JUDGE's *hand*) Good night, Judge. (JUDGE *goes out. The* GOVERNOR *sits in his chair, right, exhausted. He settles down, nods and goes to sleep.* CORNELIUS *appears with more telegrams, walks lightly to the table, puts them with the others, looks at the* GOVERNOR, *walks out. The* GOVERNOR *sleeps.*)

CURTAIN

ACT 4

The HOWELL-ROBERTS *yard in the waning light of a winter afternoon. It is December 22, the day of the trial of the deputies for the massacre. Shabby furniture from the* ROBERTS *house is piled in yard—a bedstead and mattress, a baby's crib, a stack of chairs, a washboard,* JIMMY'*s guitar, books tumbled on the ground, a stone jar.* LAWRENCE *enters, picks his way through the furniture, and knocks at the* HOWELL *door.* MRS. HOWELL *comes out.*

LAWRENCE: Good evenin', Miz Howell. I come to ask you all if'n you got any more room in your house fer Miz Carver's things. We got every house full up an' three more families has been put out on the road.

MRS. HOWELL: I'm real sorry, Lawrence, but we hain't got another lick o' room. We cain't even git Miz Robert's things out'n the yard. If it comes a rain, they'll be ruint.

LAWRENCE: (*Slowly*) I don't know what to do. They put 16 families out already an' hit looks like they'll throw everybody out. (*After a pause*) An' we-uns has to go tonight too.

MRS. HOWELL: We got our notice too. The sheeriff was here to chuck us out this mornin', but Emmaline is down sick agin an' Granny wouldn't let him come near the house. I wuz afeared she'd shoot him. She stood here on the porch an' just dared him to come into the yard.

LAWRENCE: Pore ole Granny! I thought she'd left here; she told us all t'other day she was a-clearin' out.

MRS. HOWELL: Oh, she's goin'. Fred's a-comin' fer her this evenin'. She's powerful mad at we-uns. Thinks we ort-a fight it out with 'em. She's takin' the baby with her up in the hills an' swears she'll never come down to a mill village agin.

LAWRENCE: Is Josie at the court house yit? She said she'd come an' tell us as soon as the jury brought the verdict.

MRS. HOWELL: Do you reckon them deppities'll be freed, Lawrence?

LAWRENCE: Shore they will. Ever'body in court knows that. You cain't convict a deppity sheeriff in that-thar court house.

MRS. HOWELL: After them a-murderin' our men like that? An' you boys a-goin' off to the chain gang. Granny wa'ar right, the law air crooked.

LAWRENCE: As crooked as a dog's hind leg.

MRS. HOWELL: You boys air a-goin' to the chain gang jest because them women toted that-thar furniture out'n that company house . . . an' them a-killin' us too.

LAWRENCE: Oh, well, six months hain't so long. They'll have to feed us, an' we don't mind. We know what we're a-goin' fer, too. (FRED *the farmer, who appeared in the first act, comes in.*)

FRED: Howdy folks. 'Pears like ever'body's movin'. I thought Granny wuz the only one what wa'ar clearin' out.

LAWRENCE: No, we hain't movin' Fred. This is what you call *eviction.*

FRED: (*Bewildered*) What's that?

MRS. HOWELL: Havin' the sheeriff tote yore belongin's out'n the house on the road becuz the mill won't give you a job an' wants yore house for t'other workers what's bein' shipped in here to take yore place in the mill.

FRED: You-all air foolin', hain't you? They wouldn't throw you in the road like that.

LAWRENCE: Listen, Fred, you'll have to come to work in a cotton mill if'n you want to larn what they'll do. This stuff you see here is the very homes of them folks what wa'ar murdered at the mill gate. This-here is Miz Roberts' things. After Jimmy wa'ar murdered, the sheeriff what kilt him chucked his maw's belongin's out'n the house.

FRED: (*Looking bewildered at the* ROBERTS *house*) An' whar in thunder is Miz Roberts then?

MRS. HOWELL: She air in the hospital. Granny is up thar with her now. They took her yistiday.

FRED: You don't tell me they dumped a sick woman out'n her home, do you?

LAWRENCE: Shore they dumped a sick woman out'n her home, an' their own doctor knows she wuz powerful sick too. That's how come she had to go to the hospital.

FRED: Well, I swan! What's the matter with yore shot guns? Fergit how to use 'em?

LAWRENCE: We hain't fergittin', Fred. But you cain't do hit like that. They'd shoot us all down like rats. The governor'ud send all the sojers in the state in here if'n we wuz to shoot off one gun. But we're a-writin' down a lot of things in the book what'll have ter be settled some day.

(GRANNY *comes in. She is dejected and appears defeated. She steps around the furniture, notices the people, and goes up to greet* FRED.)

GRANNY: (*Without her old fire*) Good evenin', folks. Howdy, Fred. (*Shakes hands with* FRED)

FRED: Powerful glad to see you, Gran. How you bin? How's Miz Roberts?

GRANNY: Porely off, Fred, an' they has to operate on her tomorrer.

MRS. HOWELL: Any news from the court, Mother? Did you stop in?

GRANNY: Yes, I stopped in fer a spell. Couldn't set fer long though; the law wuz arguin' as how we-uns done all the shootin' ourse'ves. They reckoned we'd shoot our own men. We . . . shoot our own men. (*Turns to* LAWRENCE) These men-cowards wa'ar a-feared to tote a gun, let alone shoot one off. If'n they'd a-listened to me we'd-a shot hit out with 'em. We could-a got a few of 'em anyway.

(MRS. HOWELL *goes inside of the house and* GRANNY *starts to cover the furniture with a patchwork quilt.*)

FRED: Tell me, Lawrence, is that what you-all git fer joinin' the union? The strike's lost, hain't it? All yore bad conditions stay with you—what good is all that?

GRANNY: (*Sarcastically as she flips the quilt over the furniture*) Oh, no, Fred, hit air bin a big victory. Hain't you bin a-readin' the papers? Conditions air all fixed up. We're gittin' a sewer in this-here village. Hain't that fine? (*Bitterly*) Six of our boys murdered by that-thar mill, after they wuz blinded, an' hit pays fer that . . . by givin' us a sewer.

LAWRENCE: Now, Granny, don't get riled up. You got a bunch of us goin' to the chain gang over your bravery, hain't you?

(JOSEPHINE *comes in very slowly. She crosses the stage and sits down.* GRANNY *crosses to her.*)

GRANNY: (*Sharply*) Tell us, child. They let 'em off, didn't they?

LAWRENCE: Did they bring in the verdict? Did they free 'em?

(MRS. HOWELL *comes out of the house.*)

JOSEPHINE: (*Bitterly*) Not guilty! Everyone of 'em. All free! So they could go home fer Christmas. An' look at our Christmas! (*She goes into the house, sobbing.*)

GRANNY: (*Slowly and full of anger*) The law air the law.

LAWRENCE: Well, hit's jest what I expected.

FRED: When do you begin your sentence, Larry?

LAWRENCE: We go this evenin', I reckon. The sheeriff's roundin' up t'other boys now.

MRS. HOWELL: He wa'ar here a-lookin' fer you, too, Lawrence; had a newspaper with him an' read what the Supreme Court done; said I would tell you.

FRED: Hain't that no way you kin block hit?

GRANNY: Did you-all ever hear 'bout a pore man gettin' 'round the law? Hit's only them what's brave enough to hide as does it.

MRS. HOWELL: Why, mother, you seem downright glad the boys has got to go. You oughter be ashamed.

GRANNY: No, I'm not glad, Emmaline. (*She hobbles up to* LAWRENCE *and puts her hand on his shoulder.*) I'm not glad you air goin' to the chain gang, son . . . I'm mad . . . mad as pepper. (*Turning aside, in low tone*) An' I'm real sorry I got you-all into hit. I told the law all 'bout hit. They knowed it wa'ar us mountain women what toted that furniture out'n that-air company house. But they got you fer hit 'cause it be you they wanted. (*Affectionately putting her hand on his shoulder*) Is there anythin' I kin do fer you, son?

LAWRENCE: (*Grasping her hand*) That's all right, Gran. I'm glad you done what you done. Maybe you're right. Anyway, we don't blame you. God a'mighty, ole woman, you don't think we want you-uns to go to chain gang 'stead o' we-uns, do you? (GRANNY *turns away and stands looking at the mountains.*)

FRED: (*Not quite understanding the meaning of what* GRANNY *and* LAWRENCE *have said*) It looks like a sorry mess to me. You're all licked, everything is lost.

LAWRENCE: (*Thoughtfully but with enthusiasm*) In one way hit air all lost, Fred, but in 'nother way it hain't. We larnt a heap this summer . . . we know whar we stand now. Somethin's got in our blood, an' hit hain't out yet. Hit'll all come out again in the spring, when the sap comes up in the trees. We'll fight agin, an' diff'rent too.

GRANNY: (*Who has slowly turned to listen to* LAWRENCE *now comes up to him*) Air ye goin' to fight agin in the spring, son, real fight?

LAWRENCE: Shore we air, Gran. Do you think we kin fergit?

GRANNY: I never tole you afore, son, but . . . that mornin' down thar at the mill, when Jimmy wa'ar dyin', I wa'ar a-holdin' him in my lap, tryin' to keep his life in 'im—an' I promised him. (*Eagerly*) Do you think you'll fight in the spring, shore 'nuff?

LAWRENCE: It's so hard fer you to see, Gran. You think we're all cowards. But we kin lick 'em, an' we will, shore. Ever'thin' is so dark now. We're so licked, but we won't fergit 'em, Gran, I swear.

GRANNY: (*Coming back to her old enthusiasm*) Who'll he'p us?

LAWRENCE: A lot o' folks everywhere. Maybe there'll be a labor movement. Hit's got to come an' hit'll be wonderful, Gran, like last spring. All our parades, our songs, our fun. (*Rising*) Cain't you remember hit all? Think how—how Jimmy loved hit, an' he died fer hit. We gotter do hit fer him.

(*The* SHERIFF *appears outside the fence.* GRANNY *goes quickly into the house.*)

SHERIFF: (*Calling from the gate*) Come on, Lawrence, I've got to take you. I got the other boys. We've got to start this evenin' an' we'll have to stop at the court house fer the papers first.

LAWRENCE: (*Does not answer* SHERIFF, *but turns to* FRED *and offers him his hand*)

Goodbye, Fred. You'll take good care of Granny an' take a look-in at my woman folks while I'm away, won't you?

(FRED *shakes hands and speaks inaudibly to* LAWRENCE. LAWRENCE *walks out of the gate past the* SHERIFF, *with his head high. The* SHERIFF *follows him off the scene. Inside the house there is commotion, and* MRS. HOWELL *screams.*)

MRS. HOWELL: Mother! What you goin' to do?

(GRANNY *rushes out onto the porch with a shotgun, aiming it at the departing* SHERIFF. MRS. HOWELL *tries to take the gun away, and* FRED *runs across to help her. Between them they disarm the old woman.* GRANNY *staggers down into the yard and, after staring down the road for a moment, yanks a chair from the pile of furniture and sits down, rocking back and forth in impotent anger.* JOSEPHINE *comes out with* PINEY STRIKE, *wrapped in a shawl, and motions to* MRS. HOWELL *to give the baby to* GRANNY.)

MRS. HOWELL: Here, Ma, rock Piney to sleep. I'll go git her things ready. (GRANNY *gives a snort of disgust, but takes the baby.* MRS. HOWELL *and* FRED *go into the house, taking the gun.*)

(GRANNY'*s anger has given way to tenderness, and she rocks the baby, humming "We Are Building a Strong Union." As she realizes the import of the song she has unconsciously chosen for a lullaby, she lifts her head with something of her old determination.* FRED *comes out with a bundle of clothes and stands for a moment, looking at the old woman. He shakes his head and comes down the steps.*)

FRED: I never did see a mess like this one. I shore don't blame you for clearin' out, Granny. Time we wuz a-gittin' on. I'll tote your things out to the wagon. Hit'll be dark long a-fore we're home as it is. (*As he reaches the gate,* GRANNY *speaks, not turning her head.*)

GRANNY: (*Slowly*) Better fetch it back again, Fred.

FRED: Did you say somethin', Gran?

GRANNY: (*Her mind made up*) I hain't a-goin', Fred.

FRED: Hain't a-goin'? Why, I come all the way to fetch you. How come you hain't goin'?

GRANNY: (*Smiling ruefully*) I dunno, Fred, how come. All I know for sure is (*With rising determination*) I hain't a-goin' to leave this-here mill village—least-ways not till after the spring.

CURTAIN

THE END

In Union There Is Strength and *Pins and Needles*

Plays from the ILGWU

In 1932, a labor drama performance competition—the First Workers' Theatre Spartakiad—was held in New York City, and, by all accounts, it was an artistic and commercial failure because the performing groups did not attempt to reach beyond their own particular interests. This failure marked a change in attitude about who the potential audience for labor drama should be, and it led to an expansion of the audience to mainstream theatre-goers in order to infuse money and talent into the movement. By 1934, more than four hundred labor drama groups were in existence around the country, run by theatrical organizations, unions, and labor colleges (Cosgrove 268), and they were as varied as the Brookwood Players of Brookwood Labor College in New York; the Jewish workers' theatre, Artef; and the Theater Collective. Although labor drama troupes developed in all corners of the nation, inevitably New York City became the center of the workers' theatre movement.

Labor Olympiads and other gatherings brought together the diverse groups of workers' theatres. In fact, the only success of that first Spartakiad was its assembling of the major labor drama troupes for the competition. A typical program might look like what follows from the Labor Festival at the New School in New York City, 20–21 April 1935: the International Ladies Garment Workers Union players performed five short plays, including *Who's Getting Excited, All for One,* and *Strikebreaker.* Rebel Arts, a group of New York actors and directors with labor interests, performed their own works: *The Worm Turns, American Satire,* and *A Play of 1935.* The Brookwood Labor Players performed *Model 7A, Shop Strife,* and *With Both Fists,* as well as leading the audience in mass recitations and giving puppet shows for the children. Meanwhile, the Young Circle Players performed two labor dramas for children, *Big Wind* and *In the Factory*.[1] The subjects of these plays are fairly uniform—workers unite for various reasons to overcome their bosses—but the diversity of groups ethnically and geographically represents the reality of the workers' theatre movement in the 1930s.

To overcome what seems to have become a stale genre with the same plots recycled over and over, an anonymous article in the movement's journal *Workers Theatre,* titled "We Must Write Plays," calls on writers to create plays for the labor drama movement that have something definite to convey for workers, "not the bourgeoisie." In general, the author says, the type of theatre being produced must be defined by social and economic conditions (17–18).

In the wake of *Workers Theatre* and the swift rise of labor drama and theatre, *Processional* playwright John Howard Lawson wrote several important articles about the nature of revolutionary theatre. In a series of published and unpublished documents, Lawson put forth his theory of the "the revolutionary drama." In 1934, he wrote that the "living quality" of a labor drama is that it "smashes the barrier of the footlights and forces the audience to actually take an emotional part in the events." For Lawson, the essence of revolutionary drama was its "ability to create partisanship in the audience, to establish vital contact between the actor and the observer," something impossible to create in the bourgeois theatre ("Straight" 11). In a later article, Lawson became more emphatic, stating that the revolutionary drama should "circumvent" escape and catharsis from the situation, that the plays should be filled with "authenticity and terror," and that a play was successful "in proportion to its ability *to force* partisanship upon the audience" ("Few" 1, emphasis mine).

In essence, then, a revolutionary playwright must move his or her audience toward an understanding of the need for revolution. Lawson and other writers saw the transformational effect on the broadest audience possible as the greatest potential achievement of workers' theatre. Further, Lawson saw the "*reality* of this sort of art" as the actors' reflection of the audience's life ("Few" 14). As Margaret Larkin of the ILGWU Education Department wrote in 1935, the "natural interplay" between audience and actor that occurs to some degree in every theatre is heightened in the workers' theatre ("Building" 2).

The involvement of the ILGWU, which represented many women in the garment industry, led to a greater emphasis on the actions of female workers in the union and in strikes. The female characters in these plays take on more radical, involved roles than in earlier plays, and this new portrayal

1. This information is taken from a pamphlet advertising the festival (The Billy Rose Theatre Collection, the New York Public Library of the Performing Arts).

reflects both the changing union image of the woman and the actual evolving role of women in the labor community.

This shift in focus occurred for several reasons. Historically, in the wake of the stock market crash of 1929, more women and minorities joined unions, and unions saw membership rise to levels not seen since the Espionage and Sedition Acts of 1917 and 1918. Women, however, were for the most part organized only in those industries in which they were a majority, such as in garment factories and fabric mills (Kessler-Harris 120–21). The ILGWU saw membership double (after a post-Crash dip) from 105,000 to more thn 200,000 between 1920 and 1934 (Seidman 198). Local organizing experienced the same kind of boom, with, for instance, the Amalgamated Clothing Workers adding 25,000 workers to their rosters in Pennsylvania in 1933 alone (Hardy 180). In an example that illustrates how women's issues made their way into industrial culture, the garment worker industries began debating the place of women and the question of whether the concerns of women should be addressed separately. Should the union continue to pursue the interests of workers in general? The Amalgamated Clothing Workers sought to develop women's culture within the union, sponsoring programs and events specifically for its workers, while the Educational Department of the ILGWU, under the direction of Fannia Cohn, saw this strategy as deleterious to the goals of the movement (Hardy 129–31). As a result, because women were still being left out of leadership positions, labor colleges and educational departments developed specifically to "educate women to become labor organizers" (Wong 45). This goal affected the varying styles of writing in labor dramas as well as the narrowing of dramatic representation to that of labor organizing and union action.

In the 1920s and 1930s, as women joined the industrial workforce in larger numbers, the labor and popular press continued to present images of labor women "insistently maternal and familial" (Melosh 3). And while the numbers of women in the workforce rose, the jobs available to them continued to be lower-paying domestic and industrial positions that guaranteed eventual dependence on a spouse (Scharf 86; Milkman 77). Still, gender representations "insistently denied men's and women's separate interests," according to Melosh: "A recurring configuration [in visual art] showed men and women side by side, working together or fighting for a common goal" (4). While seemingly emphasizing equality, this configuration of the sexes problematically denies gender difference. Melosh calls this the "comradely ideal—a trope for citizenship," which addressed at least to a small degree the specific problems of women workers, while reassuring "faltering manhood" in the wake of the Depression (5). Women's issues could be included as long as they did not disrupt the dominant male role in the unions and in industry.

This particular cultural representation of the comradely ideal, at least from a labor perspective, is surprisingly accurate historically. As women had taken on larger roles in the work community, they had joined unions in large numbers and, during strikes, made up a large percentage of the picketers. Because of their new industrial role, more consideration for women workers was given, at least nominally. In 1933 alone, in Detroit, two thousand out of six thousand striking autoworkers were women, who, in the strike agreement, won wage gains for women in addition to the gains for workers in general. In another action, women made up 40 percent of the strikers in a textile strike from Maine to Mississippi (Foner 268). In Philadelphia, a strike against Philco netted an agreement that gave men a 10 percent wage hike and women 15 percent to make up for past disparities. Some strikes were exclusively by women. In 1927, fourteen hundred female pecan-shellers, mostly African American, went on strike in St. Louis and were joined by their husbands on the picket line. Black-owned businesses brought meals to the strikers. When strikebreakers were brought in, the Jewish community and the ACLU wrote to the press on behalf of the strikers (Strom 363–64; Foner 314–18). Women workers thus organized themselves both alone and with male workers. Once again, as the labor movement progressed, it strove to allow the widest possible working-class community participation on some scale, and the theatre reflected this history, representing ways in which the labor community organized itself to include women.

The ILGWU's Cohn had organized a drama division within its Educational and Recreational Department in 1934, initially with other unions, but finally on its own, and eventually created the Labor Stage with amateur players doing workers' theatre (Denning 296). Many of the plays of the ILGWU were simplistic agit-prop, like the one-act *In Union There Is Strength,* which is reproduced here. In that play, by Irwin Swerdlow, and many others, the plot is a discussion among the characters, usually friends or families, over whether it would be better to join the union, with the pro-union side obviously winning. These plays served as recruiting tools and entertainment at meetings.

However, Louis Schaffer, the head of the drama division, "wanted to produce a musical revue: workers, he argued, went to the theater to be entertained, not 'just because it is a labor theater' " (Denning 296). Schaffer met with Harold Rome, a Catskills resorts musician and songwriter, and writer Joseph Losey, and they began collaborating to create the revue, eventually titled *Pins and Needles.* The process involved other writers from the workers' theatre movement, including Marc Blitzstein, whose musical about union organizing, *The Cradle Will Rock,* was undergoing its controversial treatment by the Federal Theatre Project. The cast was made up of workers from the ILGWU, and they were resistant to putting on a vaudevillian musical revue. Having been trained in the ways of workers' theatre, they wanted to do avant-garde plays like Clifford Odets's hugely successful *Waiting for Lefty.*

When *Pins and Needles* opened at the Labor Stage on November 27, 1937 it was acted by unemployed workers. It moved to Broadway on June 26, 1939, where it played for nearly a year, becoming the longest-running Broadway production until *Oklahoma.*

Jack Gould in the *New York Times* said that the original production was "a revue out of the ordinary and one which only occasionally droops to the level of the things which it is satirizing." He said that the show should be "accepted in the good-natured spirit in which it is offered" (49). In the New York *Sun,* Richard Lockridge said that the revue was more than just propaganda: "They can also laugh. And probably for the first time in labor stage history, they can laugh at themselves, as well as at their antagonists" (16). Other reviews also praised the show for being less dogmatic than other labor plays. For instance, Sidney Whipple of the *New York World-Telegram* said, "It has merriment in it which is usually not associated with 'causes,' and best of all, it has no bitterness" (7).

The satirical sketches in *Pins and Needles* were comic versions of the agit-prop street drama of the Workers' Laboratory Theatre and the ILGWU itself. Sketches like "The Little Red Schoolhouse" by Emmanuel Eisenberg parodied Brechtian epic theatre, while Marc Blitzstein's "FTP Plowed Under" attacked censorship at the Federal Theatre Project (Denning 309). *Pins and Needles* parodied workers' theatre plays, but it also took on the treatment of blue- and white-collar workers, the rise of fascism overseas, class warfare, even American blowhards like Father Charles Coughlin (Trumbull 215). As a musical revue, the show incorporates such musical forms as ethnic songs, jazz, and contemporary popular sounds in lyrics that combine workers' issues with familiar tropes. For example, in the song "One Big Union," whose title comes from the radical goal of the Industrial Workers of the World, a romance between "boys" and "girls" is put in union terms: "We'll have no lockouts to make us frown / No scabbing when you're out of town / In One Big Union for Two."

The show was so successful that Eleanor Roosevelt wrote glowingly of the production, and a troupe even gave a command performance of the play in 1938 for the Roosevelt White House (Goldman 95). Denning credits the long-running success of the show to the "working-girl songs," using Tin Pan Alley-type jazz and ethnic songs for the music, creating a new kind of "urban working-class" folk music.

> The success of *Pins and Needles* lay in its union of class, ethnic, and feminist energies, in the way it sang for young Jewish and Italian working-class women of the garment trades. Though women were only a quarter of the wage-labor force in 1940, they were a large majority of the needle trades. And though the women of the ILGWU were unable to achieve representation in the union's leadership in these years . . . they did achieve representation in *Pins and Needles.* (Denning 306)

Pins and Needles, then, connected the concerns of the burgeoning numbers of women workers with popular musical and theatrical forms. Its longevity and popularity came about because those workers saw themselves represented as part of the culture of America.

A note on the text presented here: The play was created so that sketches and songs could be added or taken out with no disruption to the show. The various forms of *Pins and Needles,* including the second version in 1939, as well as those presented by the touring companies, had a total of more than fifty pieces. Included here is the script of the original Labor Stage production from 1937, except for a dance titled "The General Unveiled."

In Union There Is Strength

A Play in One Act

Irwin Swerdlow

Based on the article "Who Should Organize Women?" by Fannia M. Cohn

Why Labor Dramatics

"In Union There Is Strength" is one of the several one-act plays prepared by our Educational Department. The importance of our plays is that they are being performed by our own members. A well-known dramatist said that the significance in the presentation was the fact that the players did not act their parts but lived them through. This is because they deal with their life, conditions, hopes, and aspirations of our members.

I.L.G.W.U. players—dramatic groups have been formed by many of our locals. While being trained by a dramatic director, they at the same time rehearse in the plays, which they then present at their entertainments.

Our one-act play "All For One" has been enthusiastically received by our members. Our own talents now provide the program for own entertainments—the dramatic group of New York, the mandolin orchestra of Union City, our Italian trio from Passaic, and group singing by local choruses. We are now completing our new one-act play "Convention Special," which deals with the recent Convention of our International. Our dramatic pageant "Marching On" is also ready for rehearsal.

We hope that I.L.G.W.U. players' groups will be organized in all centers. We have enough dramatic talent amongst our members for it.

In Union There is Strength

Characters

MR. GEORGE THOMPSON—middle aged unemployed worker.

MRS. THOMPSON—his wife, same age.

JENNY (JEN)—their daughter, 21

BETTY—their daughter, 18
BOB—their son, 20
MAC—unemployed, 19
EDNA—his sister, 20
MISS MITCHELL—union organizer
MRS. HAMMOND—old working woman

Scene 1.
Scene: Parlor of the Thompsons' home.
Time: 6 p.m., towards dinner time.

(*When the curtain rises,* MRS. THOMPSON *is discovered setting the table for dinner.* MR. THOMPSON *enters.*)

MRS. THOMPSON: Hello, George. Back rather late. Anything doing today?

MR. THOMPSON: Not a darned thing. There isn't a stitch of work for young or old.

MRS. THOMPSON: Sit down, you must be tired.

MR. THOMPSON: I'm all in. (*Sinks into armchair*)

MRS. THOMPSON: How are your feet?

MR. THOMPSON: Hell couldn't be harder on your feet than those city streets. You feel as if you were taking one step into the frying pan and one step into the fire.

MRS. THOMPSON: Take off your shoes, while I go get your slippers.

MR. THOMPSON: Thanks, Mother.

(*Exit* MRS. THOMPSON, *to reappear a moment later with a pair of house slippers.* MR. THOMPSON *proceeds to take off his shoes, revealing large rents in the front of his socks.*)

MR. THOMPSON: Oh. Did you see the fire jump out of that shoe, mother? It's burnt a hole clear through my socks.

MRS. THOMPSON: If you sawed off your big toenail, you wouldn't be ripping those holes through your socks.

MR. THOMPSON: (*His feet in the slippers, leans back in chair.*) That's better.

MRS. THOMPSON: We'll have dinner as soon as the children come home from work.

MR. THOMPSON: No rush.

MRS. THOMPSON: Here's the newspaper.

(MR. THOMPSON *takes the paper and glances hurriedly through the pages.*)

MR. THOMPSON: (*Laying down the paper*) Yep. I went to a union meeting today.

MRS. THOMPSON: What for?

MR. THOMPSON: They're organizing the mills. I'm tired of being knocked around and being outside of things.

MRS. THOMPSON: But what's the good of a union, if you haven't got a job? It's like sitting down at the table when you have nothing to eat.

MR. THOMPSON: Well, I decided to take a tip from my son, Bob. Let the young teach the old. Bob was out of work last July, but he joined the union all the same. When he went back to a job, he went back like a man, under higher wages and better conditions.

(BOB *enters, a laundry package under his arm.*)

BOB: 'Lo, folks.

MR. THOMPSON: Hello, son.

BOB: Betty and Jen come in yet?

MRS. THOMPSON: Not yet, Bob.

BOB: Here's my laundry, Ma.

MR. THOMPSON: I hope Betty and Jen aren't working overtime.

BOB: I wish my sisters would either quit that scab shop or get up enough guts to join the union.

MRS. THOMPSON: Take off your jacket Bob, and I'll give you a towel to wash up.

(*Gets towel and clean shirt from closet*)

BOB: (*Takes off jacket, hangs it on chair*) Say, that reminds me, I have some money for you.

MRS. THOMPSON: Fine, son.

BOB: (*Counting out the money into her hand*) Fifteen bucks.

MRS. THOMPSON: Thanks, son.

BOB: Thank the Cutters' Union. They got me my raise in pay.

MR. THOMPSON: I wonder whether Betty and Jen will be cheated out of some of their pay again this week.

BOB: Anything can happen in a chiselling sweat shop.

(*Rolls up sleeves, takes towel and clean shirt*)

MRS. THOMPSON: Tired, son?

BOB: Not much. I throw off the factory as soon as I get outside of it.

(BOB *goes into the kitchen.* BETTY *and* JEN *enter.* BETTY *is charming, with a chip on her shoulder.* JENNY—*thoughtful.*)

MRS. THOMPSON: Hurry up, girls, you're keeping your brother waiting for dinner.

JENNY: He can wait.

BETTY: He's no horse.

BOB: (*Re-enters, combing his hair. He has changed his shirt.*) Says who?

BETTY: 'Lo, Chief Breadwinner.

JENNY: (*To* BOB) You'll pass out from starvation, if we don't slip the feedbag over your ears, won't you?

MRS. THOMPSON: Hang up Bob's jacket, Jen.

JENNY: Yes, ma. (*Takes* BOB's *coat to bedroom*)

MRS. THOMPSON: And come and help me with the soup when you're through.

(*To Everybody*) You can sit down now.

(BOB *brings over chair from corner. The family sits down at the table.* MRS. THOMPSON *and* JEN *serve the soup and then sit down themselves.*)

MR. THOMPSON: You know, Bob, I made up my mind to try your remedy. I let a union organizer pick me up today and drag me off to a meeting.

BETTY: Listen, Dad, don't get yourself mixed up with any unions.

MRS. THOMPSON: That's what I say.

BOB: I have to keep reminding you, Ma, that you wouldn't be seeing my fifteen dollars every week, if it weren't for the Cloakmakers' Union.

JENNY: What do *you* know about unions, Betty?

BETTY: Nothing. Lily over at the shop warned me to steer clear of unions; she ought to know, she pals out with the forelady.

JENNY: Lily *would* tell you that. Why, she'd let the forelady cut her nose off for a sandwich and a malted.

BOB: This soup needs salt.

(MRS. THOMPSON *starts to rise.*)

JENNY: (*Getting up*) It's alright, Ma, I'll get it.

MRS. THOMPSON: (*To* JEN) Get some pepper, too. I never season things enough.

(JEN *goes to kitchen to fetch the salt and pepper.*)

BETTY: If you ask me, all that's wrong with Bob's soup is that it needs eating. What a crank.

JENNY: (*Returns with the pepper and salt and sits down*) I have only two objections to attending union meetings. The meetings last too long, and the halls are always far from the trolley.

BETTY: Well, I won't be taken in by any organizer.

JENNY: Did you ever hear one?

BETTY: No, and I never want to.

MR. THOMPSON: Betty, I hate to see you behaving like a chip off the old fool block.

BETTY: What do you mean?

MR. THOMPSON: For twenty years I went about with my head full of the darned fool notions that my boss put into it, the same as you.

BETTY: (*Injured*) Thanks.

MR. THOMPSON: I slaved long hours and got short pay. I've been making the rounds for two years now, looking for work. And I've had all that Charlotte Russe knocked out of my head. I owe it to my family to join the union. A worker needs the protection that only a powerful union would give him. No worker can stand alone.

BOB: Good for you, Dad. That was a swell little speech. I had time to think all that over last July when I was out of work. I came off my high horse pretty fast then. I walked around feeling like an outcast. Then I ran into a union organizer, and discovered that the union was the one organization which did care about raising the pay, shortening the hours and improving the general conditions of the workers.

MR. THOMPSON: You're darned tootin'!

JENNY: Well, the boss did it again this week.

MRS. THOMPSON: Did what?

BETTY: Aw, Jen, I thought you promised not to say anything about it.

JENNY: But I can't help it. The thing's burning me up.

BETTY: All right, shoot.

MR. THOMPSON: What happened?

JENNY: The boss cheated us out of ninety cents again this week. He seems to be making a habit of it.

BOB: I hope you let him hear from you.

JENNY: He wouldn't listen. He said the bookkeeper knew what she was doing.

BOB: You bet your sweet life. The crooks.

JENNY: I'm getting more and more discouraged every day. Cheating, low wages, long hours in a speed-up sweat shop, and rotten treatment, it's beginning to get me.

MRS. THOMPSON: The worst of it is that there's no one to complain to.

BOB: (*To the girls*) If you were a member of the International where you belong, there would be some one to complain to.

BETTY: Is that so? If the girls in our shop joined the Union, we'd have a strike right off the bat.

MR. THOMPSON: A strike is good medicine for the boss.

BOB: It brings him to his senses.

BETTY: What will we use for money meanwhile?

BOB: I think you're afraid.

BETTY: Hey, listen, cowboy, I haven't told you the half of what happened at the shop today?

JENNY: Please, Betty.

MRS. THOMPSON: Don't you start a fight, children.

BETTY: I don't care. He's spoiled my dinner, and I'll spoil his. (*To* BOB) Your big talk hasn't helped your sweetheart Edna any. She's full of your union ideas. Well, she got fired today.

MRS. THOMPSON: My god, there isn't a soul working in her family.

BETTY: Edna can thank Bob for that.

MR. THOMPSON: Why did they fire her?

JENNY: The same thing. They cheated her on pay, so she complained . . .

BETTY: So they fired her.

BOB: Why didn't you all get up and walk out?

BETTY: Yeah, with Pop out of work?

JENNY: Oh, I know, Bob. That's what we should have done. But we all sat there like dummies. They sure have bullied the life out of us.

BETTY: If it hadn't been for Lily, sticking up for us, we'd have been fired, too. The boss knew how thick Jen and I were with Edna.

BOB: Well, Edna is coming up tonight. We'll hear the rest of the story from her.

(*Throughout the previous scene dinner has been served. They have now come to the end of the meal, and are drinking their coffee.* MAC *enters. He is a happy-go-lucky.*)

MAC: Hello, everybody

(*The* THOMPSONS *acknowledge the greeting.*)

MRS. THOMPSON: Will you have a cup of coffee, Mac?

MAC: (*Sits on sofa*) No thanks, I just finished dinner. Say, you folks won't mind if I take Betty away for a couple of hours to see a movie.

BETTY: Not before Jen and I have a turn at the dishes.

JENNY: Never mind, Betty. I'll do the dishes.

BETTY: Staying home tonight?

JENNY: I guess so. I want Mother to help me cut my dress. I hope it'll fit better this time. So you run along.

BETTY: Thanks, Jen. You're a dear. Excuse me a minute, Mac, while I get my coat, and throw some powder on my face.

(*Exit.* MRS. THOMPSON *starts to clear away the dishes. She goes out into the kitchen with a pile.*)

BOB: (*To* MAC) Did your sister say anything about coming up tonight?

MAC: Edna will be up, all right.

BOB: Did she say anything at home?

MAC: Oh, so that's it? Lovers' quarrels. No wonder Edna looked so glum at dinner. It doesn't take me long to catch on to things. Say, I heard a swell new song come over the radio today. It's nifty. Sweet and crooning-like, and it just soaks up the air like a sponge. Hey, Betty, do you want to hear it?

BETTY: (*From bedroom*) Hear what?

MAC: A new song?

BETTY: Do you have to sing it?

MAC: Aw, hon, don't be like that.

JENNY: Let's hear it, Mac.

MAC: Sure. Here it goes. It's called, "It Ain't No Offense."

BETTY: Well, I hope it ain't.

MAC: (*Singing*)

"It ain't no offense
To sit on a fence
With your sweetheart by your side,
Watching the boats go by,
Watching the moon ride,
Hearing the trees sigh,
Watching the bears fight,
In the sky."

(*Ring at the door.*)

BOB: That must be Edna.

(MISS MITCHELL *and* EDNA *enter escorted by* JEN. MISS MITCHELL *is twenty-eight. She is cheerfully militant.* EDNA *is pretty and defiant.*)

EDNA: Hello, everybody. This is Ann Mitchell, organizer of the International Ladies' Garment Workers' union.

BOB: Delighted to meet you. Have a seat.

MISS MITCHELL: Thanks.

MR. THOMPSON: I guess I ought to put on my coat.

MISS MITCHELL: Not at all. Please, stay the way you are.

EDNA: You see, Mr. Thompson, that's just how we feel. Coat off, and sleeves rolled up.

MR. THOMPSON: That's mighty nice of you to say so, Edna.

MISS MITCHELL: You can guess why we're here?

BOB: Yes, and I'm damned glad you came.

EDNA: I want to get my job back again, and it's up to the girls.

MAC: Hell, Sis, you never told us you lost your job.

EDNA: I lost it today, when I wouldn't let my boss cheat me out of a dollar of my pay.

MAC: The dirty chiselers.

JENNY: Gee, Edna, you sure were grand standing up against the boss.

EDNA: I had the courage because I felt I wasn't standing up just for myself.

JENNY: We behaved like a bunch of cowards.

MISS MITCHELL: You just acted like any people who are not organized. What happened today needed united action.

JENNY: That's right. I would have gotten up and taken my place by Edna's side, if I could have been sure of the other girls doing the same.

MISS MITCHELL: Well, how could you be sure of that, unless you and the girls had come to some sort of an agreement before?

MR. THOMPSON: Don't you see, that's just the hell of being un-organized. You'll always feel that way, as long as you stay out of the union—weak and alone.

(MRS. THOMPSON *enters.*)

MISS MITCHELL: It isn't only Edna's and your problem that the Union is concerned with. It's concerned with all the problems that workers have to battle with. Women are in the industry to stay. Married women work today because the men don't earn enough to support the family.

MRS. THOMPSON: You'll be putting ideas into my man's head, Miss Mitchell.

(BETTY *comes in, greets* EDNA, *sits down on sofa.*)

MISS MITCHELL: There's no reason why you girls should have to slave both at the shop and at home.

BETTY: Well, after all, we've got to help mother. She can't do everything.

MISS MITCHELL: Of course not. I don't think your mother ought to work so hard. But your mother can have leisure only when you girls get paid well, and have enough to pay a larger share of the expenses. Then you could really quit work when you left the shop, because mother would have enough money to hire someone to help her.

MRS. THOMPSON: (*To* BETTY) And when the time comes for you to know housekeeping, you'll learn soon enough. It isn't the study of a lifetime.

MR. THOMPSON: Why, when I married your mother, she didn't even know how to burn pork chops in the stove.

BETTY: Everybody's against me.

EDNA: The Union is calling a meeting of our shops for tomorrow evening. I've been around to see most of the girls and they've promised to come. I know how Betty feels, but I'm certainly counting on your being there, Jen.

JENNY: I'll be there if I have to make father and Bob wash the dinner dishes.

MR. THOMPSON: All right, Bob, I wash them and you wipe them.

BETTY: How long will the meeting last?

MISS MITCHELL: It all depends on the attitude you bring to the meeting.

BOB: That's right. When we men attend a meeting we mean business. We know that our freedom and protection depend on it, so we're never in a hurry. We take off our coats, settle down in our seats, and light our pipes.

MISS MITCHELL: Women must learn that their union meetings are just as serious affairs. Instead, how do some women act at a union meeting? They come in with their hats jammed on their heads, grab a chair near the door, sit on the edge of their seat, so that the minute the speaker turns his head they can sneak out.

EDNA: You guessed it, all right. I've seen them do it.

MISS MITCHELL: It may sound funny, but it's sad all the same. If everybody would only understand that the union doesn't stop at getting higher wages and shorter hours for its members . . . The union wants a new life for the workers. It fights not only to abolish poverty and unemployment, and give the worker security and protection—it wants to open a whole world of interests to him. The work of our Educational Department is to make life happier and more interesting, so the workers can think and understand more about what's happening in the world.

MR. THOMPSON: And believe me, there's *plenty* going on today.

MISS MITCHELL: The worker must learn his own importance. He's got to realize that he's a power in this world, and that he can change it for the better.

BETTY: It sounds like the real McCoy to me, all right. I'm going to the meeting tomorrow night.

EDNA: That'll be swell, Betty.

MAC: But you have a date with me tomorrow night, Betty.

BETTY: You can help me up the steps of the trolley-car. I'm going to the meeting.

CURTAIN

Scene 2
Scene: The same.
Time: Three months later. After dinner.

When the curtain rises, MRS. THOMPSON *is discovered cleaning off the table. An ironing board stands in the center of the room, and* MRS. HAMMOND *is finishing up the pressing.* MRS. HAMMOND *is an elderly woman.*

MRS. HAMMOND: Have you heard from Betty, Mrs. Thompson?

MRS. THOMPSON: We received a card from her today.

MRS. HAMMOND: And what does she write?

MRS. THOMPSON: That she's having a grand time. She loves Chicago, and she's crazy about the Convention of the International.

MRS. HAMMOND: Who'd have thought it of Betty? She was dead set against unions all the time.

MRS. THOMPSON: It all happened that night Miss. Mitchell, the organizer, came down here. She sort of converted Betty. And when the strike came along the following week, Betty threw herself into it with all the fire she's got.

MRS. HAMMOND: A regular spitfire, I heard tell.

MRS. THOMPSON: She was arrested twice for picketing. After they won the strike, the girls in the shop loved her more than ever. So when the Convention came along, they sent her on to Chicago.

(MR. THOMPSON *enters from bedroom fixing tie.*)

Hurry up, George, you haven't got much time left.

MR. THOMPSON: I'll be ready soon, mother.

MRS. THOMPSON: (*To* MRS. HAMMOND) We're going to a meeting arranged by the Educational Department of the International.

MRS. HAMMOND: I have heard tell those meetings of the Educational Department are most interesting. Singing and acting and everything.

MR. THOMPSON: I wouldn't miss one for the world.

MRS. HAMMOND: (*Folding the last piece*) There. That's about finished. Now I guess I'll go and look after my own husband.

MRS. THOMPSON: Thanks, Mrs. Hammond. And I wish you'd come and help me with the windows on Thursday.

MRS. HAMMOND: I'll be glad to, Mrs. Thompson.

(JENNY *enters.*)

JENNY: Hello everybody. Gee, those things look nice and pressed. Thank you, Mrs. Hammond.

MRS. HAMMOND: You're welcome, my dear. Well, I was just going. Good evening, everybody, and have a good time.

(*Exit*)

MRS. THOMPSON: What have you got in that package, Jen?

JENNY: Oh, I splurged and bought a new dress for $7.95. But first let me tell you what happened at the shop today. It's a scream. The forelady walks over to me, friendly-like, you know, but I could see that she was itching all over for a fight. "Jenny," says she, "Let's change jobs." "Let's," says I. "I mean it," says she. "You wouldn't kid me, missus, would you?" I answer. That made her sore. "The trouble with you and your friends in the shop," she says, "is you earn too much."

MR. THOMPSON: Why didn't you offer her half your salary?

JENNY: Wait, you haven't heard the half of it. "You girls finish up here too early every day," she says. I could see she was getting angrier by the minute. "You leave the shop in broad daylight. It's all the fault of the damned Union." "Thanks", says I, "that's the greatest compliment you can pay our union."

MRS. THOMPSON: You made her eat her words, all right, the hussy.

JENNY: I made her feel she was one against thousands.

(MAC *enters.*)

MAC: Hello, everybody, any news from Betty?

MRS. THOMPSON: A postal card saying she'll be back any minute now.

(JENNY *off to bedroom with package*)

MAC: Swell. Do you know what the singing instructor of our Educational Department told me today?

MR. THOMPSON: What?

MAC: That I don't have much of a voice, but I know how to use it.

BETTY: (*Singing outside*)

East side, West side,
Sweatshops all around,
With Union recognition
No more sweatshops can be found.

MRS. THOMPSON: Why, that's Betty singing.

JENNY: (*Enter in a new dress*) Betty's back from the Convention.

(BETTY *bursts in.* BOB *and* EDNA *follow behind her with her luggage. Great rejoicing.*)

MR. THOMPSON: Did you have a good time?

BETTY: I had a swell time.

JENNY: Tell us about the Convention.

BETTY: I wouldn't tell my own mother about it before the meeting. I have a whole brief case full of notes, so if you want to hear all about the convention, come to our special meeting. Until then, mum's the word. Say, what are you all dressed up for?

MRS. THOMPSON: We are going to the Educational meeting.

BETTY: Fine. I'll go right along with you.

EDNA: Aren't you tired, Bett?

BETTY: What do you think the trains have sleepers for? What's the program for tonight's Educational meeting?

MAC: The I.L.G.W.U. players are giving a play called "In Union There Is Strength".

MRS. THOMPSON: Who's in it?

MAC: Well, I know I'm in it.

BETTY: (*Ready to go*) That's swell. This work sure fills you with courage, but there's so much more to be done yet. The world must be made a better place to live in for all the workers, but they'll have to do it through their organization.

EDNA: Well, we won our strike, didn't we? And we're organized.

BETTY: One battle is won, but that isn't enough. We've got to push unemployment and poverty overboard. We've got to hold on to the things we won, and make more gains.

(*Sings*)

One Battle is won,
But the fight's just begun,

(*All join in.*)

And the union flag's unfurled;
United we're strong,
Let us march toward the dawn
Of a brave new workers' world.
Oh, Union of the Garment Workers.
Etc.

(*The audience joins in singing.*)

CURTAIN

Pins and Needles

1. First Impression — *Lyrics by Harold Rome and Charles Friedman*
   Music by Harold Rome
2. Why Sing of Skies Above! — *Music and lyrics by Harold Rome*
3. Mussolini Handicap — *Sketch by Arthur Arent*
4. Public Enemy Number One — *Music and lyrics by Harold Rome*
5. The General is Unveiled — *Staged by Benjamin Zemach*
   Ballet music by Harold Rome
6. We'd Better Be Right — *Sketch by David Gregory, lyrics by Arthur Kraemer*
   Music by Harold Rome
7. The Little Red Schoolhouse — *Sketch by Emanuel Eisenberg*
8. Sunday in the Park — *Music and lyrics by Harold Rome*
9. Dear Beatrice Fairfax — *Music and lyrics by Harold Rome*
10. Economics I — *Sketch by Charles Friedman*
    Music and lyrics by Harold Rome
11. Men Awake — *Music and lyrics by Harold Rome*
    Conceived and staged by B. Zemach
12. Lesson in Etiquette — *Music and lyrics by Harold Rome*
13. Vassar Girl Finds a Job — *Music and lyrics by Harold Rome*
14. FTP Plowed Under — *Sketch by Marc Blitzstein*
15. What Good is Love? — *Music and lyrics by Harold Rome*
16. One Big Union for Two — *Music and lyrics by Harold Rome*
    Dance routine by Gluck Sandor
17. Four Little Angels of Peace — *Music and lyrics by Harold Rome*
18. Slumming Party — *Music and lyrics by Harold Rome*
    Dance by Gluck Sandor
19. We've Just Begun — *Lyrics by Harold Rome and Charles Friedman*
    Music by Harold Rome

"First Impression"

ALL:

We're not George M. Cohans or Noel Cowards
Or Beatrice Lillies or Willie Howards
We've never played in stock or studied at the playhouse
And the only line we've ever said in a Broadway house
Is—which way to the gallery?
As you see we're not tragedians or comedians
Or show girls or kick-in-row girls
Or troupers or even supers
We're plain, simple, common, ordinary
Everyday men and women who work hard for a living
We're from the shops.
Dressmakers, cloakmakers, cutters, underwear workers,
Knit good workers, neckwear makers, embroiderers, stampers,
Checkers, examiners, graders, pressers, trimmers, binders, pinkers
All of us—from the shops!

"Why Sing of Skies Above" ("Social Significance")

ON CUE:

(Honeymoon soon is due,
Love's around the corner,
I'm just nuts about you.)

(*Girl goes into dance. On first steps,* STAGE MANAGER *interrupts.*)

STAGE MANAGER: (*Shouting to girl*) Hey you, hey! Stop that! (*To Pianist*) Boys, you shouldn't be doing that you know! (*To Audience*) Ladies and Gentlemen, I'm really very sorry for this interruption, I don't know how it could have occurred. (*To* STRAY) Say, what are you doing on here anyway?

STRAY: My number!

STAGE MANAGER: Number! We can't have trash like that on this stage. This stage is for plays of social significance only. Who let you on? (STRAY *points.*) Felix! Felix!

DOORMAN: (*Off*) Yes, sir! (*Enters*)

STAGE MANAGER: Felix, did you let this young woman on the stage?

FELIX: Yes, sir. But you see . . .

STAGE MANAGER: Get her out of here at once. You know as well as I do that this stage is for plays of social significance only. Now get her off. (*To* PIANISTS) Boys, I'm surprised at you. (*Exit.*)

DOORMAN: You see! I told you you couldn't do this.

STRAY: Who is he, anyway?

DOORMAN: Who? He? He's my assistant. What did he say?

STRAY: No social significance.

DOORMAN: That's the trouble. That's what this whole show's about.

STRAY: How do you get it?

DOORMAN: How do you get it? Why it's everywhere. Look, here it is in the paper: Manufacturers monopolize industry; See? And here, Consumers protest high cost of living!

STRAY: Gee, you know an awful lot, don't you.

DOORMAN: You don't think I've been stage doorman all these years without getting some good ideas, do you?

STRAY: You got any?

DOORMAN: Have I? I've got a swell idea worked up all by myself. And it's better than anything in this show. Plenty of social significance.

STRAY: What's it all about?

DOORMAN: Well, it shows the rotten setup of our economic system. It shows the relationship between the bankers, the manufacturers, the wholesaler, the retailer, and the consumer, who always gets the dirty end of everything.

STRAY: Say, can't we do it?

DOORMAN: NO. They won't let me put it on. Besides, it needs actors and things.

STRAY: Actors! What do you think I'm doing here? And I'll get you some more. This place is full of them. Hey! Boys! Come out here. (*Enter five, one dressed as a banker.*) Look! I'm a member of the ILGWU and so are you and I want to be in the show but they won't let me. But he's got a marvelous idea. It's colossal. Go on, tell them . . .

DOORMAN: This is swell . . . You're just dressed for the part of the banker, you're just dressed for it. (*One actor interrupts: "NO." Others: "But there's a show going on. We can't do that, etc.".*)

GIRLS: You don't have to croon about blue moons.

BOYS: What's the matter with the good old tunes?

GIRLS: If you want to make us, you will have to wake us with a brand new style.

BOYS: What new style?

GIRLS: All you have to do is look around.

BOYS: Are there any better subjects to be found?

GIRLS:

If you must keep singing
Keep your voices ringing
With songs worthwhile.

BOYS: What's worthwhile?

GIRLS: Sing of workers' rights.

BOYS: Sing of sit down fights.

GIRLS: Sing of things you know.

BOYS: Things we know?

What of Labor Agitation?
We can give you information
On the C.I.O.

GIRLS: Now you know.

Sing the end of war.

BOYS: Sing of five to four.

1ST COUPLE: Sing us of kings

2ND COUPLE: And of revolutions.

3RD COUPLE: Sing us

4TH COUPLE: Of social trends.

5TH COUPLE: Sing us of old

6TH COUPLE: And new constitutions.

7TH COUPLE: What's to be done with 'em?

ALL:

We want it in rhythm.
Sing us a song
With Social Significance
There's nothing else that will do
It must ring true
With social view

GIRLS: Or we won't.

BOYS: Oh, please!

GIRLS: No we won't

BOYS: Oh, please!

GIRLS: No we won't

BOYS: Oh Hell!!

GIRLS: Love you.

GIRLS: Sing dictators lies

BOYS: Now we're getting wise
GIRLS: Sing of oily politicians
BOYS: And the men who make munitions
GIRLS: Open up your eyes
BOYS: And realize.

BOYS:

We'll sing a song
With Social Significance
All other tunes are taboo
We'll get a song that's satirical
Putting the "mere" into miracle.
We'll sing a song
With Social Significance
We'll get a song that will do,
Entirely fraught with social thought
Tell us, will that do?
We'll sing of wars
And conferences martial
Tell you of Mills and Mines
Sing you of courts
That aren't impartial
Dress our economics
In the best harmonics.
We'll sing a song
With Social Significance
There's nothing else that will do
It will be tense
With common sense

GIRLS: Then we will love you.

BOTH:

Sing us a song
With Social Significance
All other tunes are taboo
We want a song to make history
Robbing the great of their mystery
Sing us a song
With Social Significance
Or you can sing 'till you're blue
It must get hot with what is what
Then we will love you.

"Mussolini Handicap"

At open discovered: MUSSOLINI, *center, hand raised in Fascist salute; Four prize winners, two on either side.*

MUSSOLINI: Friends! Romans!! Countrymen!!! You have just witnessed the awarding of prizes in the greatest contest of its kind in the history of the world—The All-Italy Maternity Sweepstakes. Behold before you, the prize winners: fertile, uncompromising prolific in their Motherhood. (*He turns and points to* WOMAN right of center) Behold Number One . . . Winner of the Sardinian Marathon Endurance . . . in sixteen years, nineteen bouncing bambinos . . . (*Prize-winners start to dance and sing "Chiribiribim".* MUSSOLINI *stops them. He points to* WOMAN *left of center*) Number Two . . . Winner of the Roman Regatta . . . We are proud of her five year record: 1933–1938—children, 12; male, 7; female, 5; husbands, 4; all dead . . . (*Women again begin to dance and sing "Chiribiribim".* MUSSOLINI *stops them and points to* WOMAN *left*) Number Three . . . Winner of the Sicilian Round-Robin Handicap . . . open to Sailors' Wives only . . . (*Women start to dance the "Hornpipe."* MUSSOLINI *stops them.*) This woman—a bright example of Fascist virtue—has established an all-time high for Sicily . . . In three years, two male quartets, and they all sing bass. (MUSSOLINI *starts to sing "Chiribiribim" and is stopped by the women. He looks at them, regains his composure, and raises his chin.*) Ahhhhh. Number Four! Winner of the King Emanuel Fertility Cup. Women of Italy!! You may well envy this Neapolitan Super WOMAN, whom Italy is proud to honor today . . . Record 1934–1938: a single, a double, a triple, and a home-run . . . (*Women start to dance and sing "Finiculi".* MUSSOLINI *stops them.*)

Four runs, four hits, no errors . . . And she can't wait until next year. And now, bring on Public Enemy #1 . . . (PUBLIC ENEMY *is pushed on. Women run to Prompt.*) And there, cowering in the corner as well she may, is an example of what Italy does not want—the mother of but one child. A WOMAN who does not give to her country. Women of Italy!! Profit by the example before you . . . This! (*to prize winners*) . . . and not this!! (*to* PUBLIC ENEMY). The voice of the nation cries: "Pro-DUCE! Pro-DUCE!! And Repro-DUCE!!! . . . Let your motto be: "Multiplication For the Nation!" (*Women march out, bowing to audience and snubbing* PUBLIC ENEMY.)

MUSSOLINI (*follows, giving Fascist salute at Exit.*) "PUBLIC ENEMY NUMBER ONE"

GIRL: (W*alks to center on apron and curtain closes behind her*) Although a girl is cute she

Must follow what Il Duce
Commands, but it's no use—
I simply can't produce.

I'm sure that Mussolini
Thinks I'm an awful meany
No matter how I try
I cannot multiply
Gee, even twins for me would be sublime
But no matter how I try,
I just get one each time.
I feel quite bitter 'cause dogs have a litter
And the best I can do is just one.
I envy the rabbits with their plural habits
They know how the thing should be done.
Old kangaroos have them by threes and twos
Turtles are fertile by the score.
Mr. A. Moeba is a mighty conceiver
He keeps getting more and more.
You never did see a pod with one pea
A pod with one pea's not much fun
And every cow mudder has lots in her udder
But I've only womb for one.
Oh, how I try for a bigger supply
But I guess that it just can't be done
The neighbors are scornful—they make my life mournful
'Cause the best I can do is just one.
Senora Margaret Sanger would view with great anger
The things that I'm trying to do
I'm so patriotic—I'm getting neurotic
And here I can't even get two.
I feel quite futile when I look at a poodle
They get at least four and that's fun.
With pigs in the sty—the limit's the sky!
But I . . . I . . . Oh, Oh!!

(*She bursts into tears and runs off stage.*)

"The General is Uunveiled"

A dance piece with no dialogue or lyrics

"We'd Rather Be Right"

At open 1ST *100% American is discovered sitting at left of table center, pouring a drink from whiskey bottle.* 2ND *100% American enters from left and stops just on-stage.*

1ST 100%: (*Rising and turning to* 2ND 100%) Hello, hello, hello!

2ND 100%: And how is our worthy brother publicist today?

1ST 100%: 100% American, thank you. (*They both give the salute.* 2ND *crosses to seat at right of table and sits;* 1ST *sits at left.*) I've just been pouring over the Constitution.

2ND 100%: Oh, pour me one too.

1ST 100%: (*Pouring a drink for the* 2ND) Have you seen the Boss lately?

2ND 100%: Yes, and he doesn't look so chipper.

1ST 100%: He must be having some more ism trouble.

2ND 100%: I've got ism . . . you've got ism . . .

1ST 100%: Don't make light of the matter, Tom. We have all been too carefree. Thank goodness we're meeting with the boss—a real conservative—a real leader.

2ND 100%: Amazing what he sees and hears. Only yesterday he put down a new dangerous element, had their headquarters raided and found two copies of "Little Red (*Gags & slaps himself before he can go on*) Riding Hood". They call themselves "The Daughters of the American Revolution" and they couldn't even recite the amendments.

1ST 100%: He's a real patriot. Nothing escapes his eagle-eye— . . . bald American eagle-eye, I should say.

2ND 100%: (*Raising his glass for a toast*) A man of steel.

1ST 100%: Republican steel preferred. (*They drink a toast and they are interrupted by* 3RD 100% AMERICAN *who enters left, singing: "My Country 'Tis of ME!". He stops and they all salute.*)

3RD 100%: (*As he crosses to above table*) Men, we're facing a crisis.

1ST & 2ND 100%: (*Sitting and looking at each other*) We view with alarm.

3RD 100%: It's men like you who are the boneheads . . . I mean the backbones of the nation.

1ST & 2ND 100%: (*Facing audience and pointing to themselves*) We point with pride.

3RD 100%: Our committee is getting unpopular. The time has come for us to make America "Bigoted and Better". Boys, you'll have to go to work. (*Sits*) We've got to campaign against these lefts who know what our right hand is doing, and we haven't even got a slogan.

1ST 100%: How about using Herbert Hoover's slogan, "Rugged Individualism Will Save the Starving"?

2ND 100%: Nobody starves. That's known by all good (*Gags*) Americans. (*They all rise and give the salute, then sit.*)

1ST 100%: How about an expose on: "First Lady Plans to be First Lady-Dictator"?

3RD 100%: That dictator stuff has been dragged out too often—even Congressmen don't believe it. We've got to get a more liberal slogan. I've got spies working in Heywood Broun's cellar, and they'll either find a slogan or else . . .

1ST 100%: How about, "Make the World Safe for Democracy"?

3RD 100%: I hope that's the kid with the lunch. I'm due in Jersey City at four o'clock for a book burning.

(BOY *enters with tray.*)

BOY: (*Crossing to* 3RD 100% *and placing tray on table, removing cloth*) Allo Boss. All-American spash' coming up. Nick say no more Betsy Ross Anti-Picket Pudding. He's send a Roosevelt Salad wit side order apple sauce.

3RD 100%: Roosevelt!! Damn! What's in that salad?

BOY: Planty New Dill Pickles. (*Starts out*)

3RD 100%: Wait a minute. What's that G.O.P. comeback dessert Nick has been selling?

BOY: That's the apple sauce.

3RD 100%: (*Rising to* BOY, *who runs out*) Get out of here before I see red!!!

1ST 100%: Careful, Boss. Mustn't say the naughty word. Treason, you know . . .

3RD 100%: (*Sitting down*) We'd better watch that boy. Did you notice he was left handed?

2ND 100%: Yes, and only the other day I heard him say something about his (*Gags*) red blooded ancestors.

3RD 100%: (*Gets tangled up with* 1ST 100% *over goulash cover*) You boys pardon me for a minute. I'm so hungry, I don't know what I'm doing.

1ST 100%: Boss, isn't that Hungarian goulash? What a shame. (*Throws plate of goulash in the waste basket*)

2ND 100%: What a shame.

3RD 100%: Thanks, boys. I'd rather read the Wagner Act than eat that.

2ND 100%: French Toast!!! (*Throws it in the waste basket and "tut-tuts"* 3RD; 1ST *also "tut-tuts"* 3RD, *and* 3RD *answers him.*)

3RD 100%: Thank Goodness, there's a sandwich left and a bit of lettuce.

1ST 100%: (*Taking piece of cheese from sandwich and throwing it in basket*) Sorry, Boss. Swiss cheese, you know. Too bad.

2ND 100%: Too bad.

3RD 100%: Too damn bad. (*Grabbing rest of sandwich*)

2ND 100%: Just in time . . . (*Grabbing half of sandwich*)

1ST 100%: Russian dressing!!! (*Grabbing other half of sandwich. They throw it in the basket.*)

3RD 100%: (*Spitting out tea and pushing back his chair*) Yah!! Japanese tea!!! What do you call this anyway, I'm starving.

1ST 100%: Nobody starves. That's Un-American.

2ND 100%: There's our slogan . . . "Call It Un-American".

ALL: If you find you can't reply to your opponents, why don't you try to

Call Them Un-American.
If a radical idea gives you nervous diarrhea,
Call It Un-American.

1ST 100%: If some idiot would regulate the traffic in munitions.

2ND 100%: Or advises that we socialize our surgeons and physicians.

3RD 100%: Or suggests that trade unions better working men's conditions.

ALL: Call Him Un-American.

(*They start to march and salute wildly.*)

ALL: If you find no sound objection to a Liberal's election.

Call Him Un-American.
Though his speeches are confounding,
if his name is foreign sounding
Call Him Un-American.

2ND 100%: When the gravy that you're getting keeps the taxes mounting higher

3RD 100%: When you thunder, "I'm the Law" and people answer, "You're a Liar".

1ST 100%: Simply throw a few red herrings and with patriotic fire.

ALL: Call It Un-American.

When progressive-minded senators decide to tax the riches
That you lifted from the pockets of the public's tattered britches
Never stoop to contradict the Socialistic sons of————

They rumble the drum and exit to the O.P. side.

"Introduction to 'Little Red Schoolhouse'"

STAGE MANAGER: Ladies and Gentlemen: A year or so ago, an otherwise admirable institution, the Theatre Union of New York, startled audiences with production of a form of theatre which had only been written about, but had not actually been performed in this country—the Epic Theatre of Brecht. The play in question was, "Mother."

In it Brecht gave concrete expression to his theory of the perfect form of Workers Theatre. Among other ideas, he contended that the Theatre was a classroom to which Workers' audiences came to be taught; that the ideas and images should be simple and presented with such disarmingly simple devices as chants and ditties, in order to make the fundamental political ideas more palatable.

We will now give you our impression of the Epic form of Theatre when it is carried to its logical conclusion in the performance of a typical Labor play.

"Little Red Schoolhouse"

At open, four workers are sitting on a bench sewing in unison

SCHMALTZ: (*Rises and takes two steps forward*) My name is Herman Schmaltz. I'm thirty-two-years-old and married to a girl named Rosie. She leads me around by the nose. I work for the La Dame Chapeau Company. L-A-D-A-M-E-C-H-A-P-E-A-U-C-O-M-P-A-N-Y period. There's the sign in case you didn't hear me. (*Pointing to sign which isn't there.* BOY *comes on left with sign, discovering mistake and walking back to place.*) There's the sign in case you didn't hear me. I'm a finisher of Ladies' Hats. In season I knock down thirty bucks a week. When it's slack, I'm lucky if I make ten. Right now I feel terrible—but who doesn't?

BERNADOTTE: (*Rises and takes two steps forward*) My name is Antonio Salvatore Piedro Bartolomeo Pacciagaluppi Bernadotte. If you think I spell it out for you, you're crazy.

MILDRED: Oh Lena, I'm too shy to go out and talk to all those people. (*Girls rise and* LENA *drags* MILDRED *into line with men.*)

LENA: Now Mildred, you must pull yourself together and get used to going out into the world. Nobody's going to hurt you. They're all just dying to have us join them.

BERNADOTTE: What shall we do about our small earnings that are not enough to live on?

ALL: Struggle.

> The way for workers to triumph is through struggle.
> We do not wish crumbs of bread, but a full loaf.
> We do not wish slack seasons but always busy ones.
> We do not wish to talk our demands but chant them.

This is what we have to say to the La Dame Chapeau Company, and incidentally to (*Pointing to the audience*) you.

BERNADOTTE: There must be a way out of our agony.

LENA: I know a way, but first we must discuss it.

SCHMALTZ: A discussion????

ALL: A discussion!!!!! (*They get into a circle and ad lib, furiously wheeling right in circle.* LENA *turns away,* SCHMALTZ, *and finally* BERNADOTTE *leaves group which follows him.*)

BOSS: What are you all doing away from your work? Talking to that gang of agitators out there? (*Pointing to audience.* WORKERS *line up and take four full steps to the Boss, speaking on 4*TH *step.*)

WORKERS: Boo!!!!!

SCHMALTZ: (*Leaves others and steps to* BOSS) Mr. La Dame, there's something I've been wanting to say to you for a long time, but excuse me just a minute. (*To audience*) I am now about to act the part of the shop spokesman and tell the boss just how we feel about things around here. You may have come to this conclusion yourselves at one time or another, but we're not taking any chances on your intelligence.

MILDRED: (*Joining* SCHMALTZ) Who knows if there is so much as one brain among you?

LENA: (*Joining* MILDRED) As far as we're concerned, this is a classroom and you're all dopes.

BERNADOTTE: (*Joining* LENA) Me too!

BOSS: What is the meaning of all this anyway a strike?

LENA: Strike! What do you mean strike?

BOSS: A strike is a mov . . . (*Interrupted by workers who point to audience.* BOSS *turns to audience.*) A strike is a movement on the part of all or some of the workers in a given establishment to call a halt to work in an effort to force the employers to grant them superior conditions in hours and wages . . . . (*Out of breath*) And I bet I know who instigated it all. Probably one of those union men out there. (*Pointing to the audience*)

MILDRED: Union? What is a Union?

BOSS: A Union is an orga . . . (*Interrupted by* WORKERS *who point to audience.* BOSS *turns to audience.*) A Union is an organization of militant and class-conscious workers who band together in order to protect themselves against the exploitation by ill-meaning or irresponsible employers . . . (*Out of breath*)

SCHMALTZ: (*Crosses to* BERNADOTTE) Say, don't you think we ought to flash that definition on a screen so the audience can memorize it?

BERNADOTTE: Yeah, but how we know they can read?

LENA: (*Steps to Boss*) Listen, Mr. La Dame, don't ask us for any decisions now. First we have to make up a chant about our problems. (BOSS *leaves.*)

ALL: Now that we have found out about a strike

Now that we have found out about a union
We want to go on record as thinking that both are just dandy.
Maybe it will give us full loaves of bread
Maybe we can give up chanting
Maybe this play will come to an end at last.

WANGLER: (*Enters*) I am the man from the Union.

LENA: Name please?

WANGLER: My name is . . . (*Interrupted by* WORKERS)

LENA: Tell it to the audience. (WORKERS *point to audience*)

WANGLER: (*To audience*) My name is Morris Wangler. I'm twenty-nine going on ninety . . . I . . . I . . .

SCHMALTZ: I think you'd better come in again.

WANGLER: Yeah, yeah!! (*Runs off right*)

ALL: Maybe this play will come to an end at last.

WANGLER: (*Enters*) I am the man from the Union.

LENA: Name please?

WANGLER: My name is . . . (*Interrupted by the* WORKERS)

LENA: Tell it to the audience. (WORKERS *point to audience.*)

WANGLER: You all know who I am . . . (*To audience*) I represent the Ladies Hat Finishers' Union. I'm here because . . . because . . . (*Looks at* WORKERS; *they shrug their shoulders.*) because the script calls for it.

BERNADOTTE: We all want to join the union.

MILDRED: (*Crossing to* WANGLER) And we want to go on strike immediately.

WANGLER: Fine! What are your demands?

MILDRED: (*To audience*) Fifty percent increase.

BERNADOTTE: (*To audience*) Twenty hours a week.

LENA: (*To audience*) Three weeks vacation with pay.

SCHMALTZ: (*To audience*) Pay for Sundays and Holidays.

WANGLER: Not bad at all. Maybe you'll get half. You two act as a committee and see the Boss. (LENA *and* SCHMALTZ *run off left.*) But do you know what a strike is?

MILDRED & BERNADOTTE: (*Moving to center*) A strike is a movement on the part of all or some of the workers in a given establishment to call a halt to work in an effort to force the employers to grant them superior (LENA *&* SCHMALTZ *run back on.*) conditions in hours and . . .

SCHMALTZ: Where's John L. Lewis?

WANGLER, MILDRED, & BERNADOTTE: JOHN L. LEWIS!!!!!

LENA: The Boss sat down!

"Sunday in the Park"

FATHER *and* MOTHER *are seated under tree; also on stage are:* BALLOON MAN, SISTER, COP, GIRL #4. GIRL #4 *crosses and exits;* COP *crosses and exits;* SISTER *runs to family;* BALLOON MAN *goes center;* SISTER *gets rope;* GIRL #1 *crosses and exits out;* FIGHTER *crosses, looks at* GIRL #1, *bumps into* SISTER; *exits;* BALLOON MAN *crosses behind tree and exits;* SHINE BOY *crosses in front and then behind tree and exits.*

FATHER:

All week long I work in the shop,
I work and work and never stop,
Get up at six and go to bed at nine.
But the day I think is the best
Is Sunday—that's my chance to rest,
The only day that you might say is mine.
We leave our hot and stuffy flat.
There's one place that we know.
And subway to the Public Park,
Oh, that's the place *to go* . . . On
Sunday in the Park
All week long we keep on looking forward to
The happy things *we do*
It's such a lark.
On Sunday in the Park.

ALL ON STAGE:

Sitting in the sun
With the trees and grass and flowers
Everywhere
And lots of room to spare
We have such fun
On Sunday in the Park
Rich folks go away to the country, *you know.*
When the days get hot.
But we all decided that we wouldn't go,
We prefer this quiet spot—On
Sunday in the Park.
It's our summer home where we can play
and sport,
Our fashionable resort,
Until it's dark.
On Sunday in the Park.

BROTHER: Can I climb the tree?

FATHER: If you do I'll give you so you won't forget

A monkey you'll be yet,
Sit quiet, please.

MOTHER: On Sunday in the Park!

SISTER: Mama, look at me

COP: Hey you, kid, be careful! Can't you read that sign?

MOTHER: A hundred dollars fine! (MOTHER *smacks* SISTER, *and turns to* BROTHER *who is in tree.*)

In jail you'll be! Get down!

BROTHER: On Sunday in the Park!

SISTER:

Pa, I want a hot dog with mustard and pop.
Aw, I'm hungry, please
Can I have a co-ne with choc'late on top?

FATHER: You think that money grows on trees?

VENDOR: Ohh—get your frozen ice!!

Cherry, pineapple, strawberry, lemon, lime
It's three cups for a dime
And very nice (You like it, huh?)
On Sunday in the Park.

BOY and GIRL: Sunday in the Park

BOY:

And for hours maybe not a cop will pass
To say "Keep off the Grass!"

GIRL: Wait 'till it's dark.

BOY and GIRL: On Sunday in the Park.

MAN WITH CARRIAGE:

That's the very spot, where I met a
Girl—we took a little walk,
And had a little talk—-
Look what I've got!!
On Sunday in the Park.

LONESOME GUY:

I put on my best clothes and slick
down my hair, careful as can be

But the only thing that I get is—
The Air! I don't know.
What's wrong with me???
All I do is look—Just keep sitting
here and watching girls go by,
Not one gives me the eye—
I read a book.
On Sunday in the Park.

PARK ATTENDANT:

Sunday in the Park
There's so much to do my hair is
turning gray, I'm picking up all day.
How my dogs bark!
On Sundays in the Park.

SISTER: Ain't it time to eat?

BROTHER: Where's the sandwiches and pickles that we brought?

MOTHER: The cake that Mama bought!

FATHER: It's such a treat.

FAMILY: On Sunday in the Park.

RADICAL: Look! He reads a novel—Eh, heh, "Hearts of Flame"—Opium for the Masses

LONESOME: Aw, go mind your business.

RADICAL:

Young man, be ashamed! You must learn
The struggle of the classes; and what it
Means to be in the forefront of the Labor
Movement and the C.I.O.

FIGHTER: Why don't you stop?

RADICAL: Here it says exactly down in black and white.

FIGHTER: Shut up!!

(FIGHTER *and* RADICAL *start to fight.*)

BROTHER and SISTER: Look, Ma, a fight!!

PEOPLE: Hey, call a cop!!!

(*During fight,* GIRL *#2 runs to* COP, *who follows her to the fight which he starts to break up. There is a bedlam on stage until the music reaches the last chorus; then everyone on stage sings the last chorus, no matter what business they may be doing.*)

Sunday in the Park
All week long we keep on looking forward to

The happy things *we do*
It's such a lark
On Sunday in the Park.
Sitting in the sun
With the trees and grass and flowers everywhere
And lots of room to spare
We have such fun.
On Sunday in the Park.
Rich folks go away to the country, you know.
When the days get hot.
But we all decided that we wouldn't go.

(*Thunder and lightning*)

We prefer this quiet spot—On
Sunday in the Park

(*Family huddles under the tree.*)

It's our summer home where we can play and sport,
Our fashionable resort,
Until it's dark.
On Sunday in the Park.

"Dear Beatrice Fairfax"

I want men that I can squeeze
That I can please, that I can tease
Two or three or four or more
What are those fools waiting for?
I want love and I want kissing
I want more of what I'm missing
Nobody comes knocking at my front door
What do they think my knocker's for?
If they don't come soon there won't be anymore!
What can the matter be?
I wash my clothes with Lux, my etiquettes the best
I spend my hard earned bucks on just what the ads suggest
Oh dear, what can the matter be, Nobody Makes a Pass at Me.
I'm full of Kellogg's bran, eat Grape-Nuts on the sly
A date is on the can of coffee that I buy
Oh dear, what can the matter be, Nobody Makes a Pass at Me.
Oh Beatrice Fairfax, give me the bare facts
How do you make them fall?
If you don't save me, the things the Lord gave me

Never will be of any use to me at all.
I sprinkle on a dash of Fragrance de Amour,
The ads say "Makes Men Rash," but I guess their smell is poor
Oh dear, what can the matter be, Nobody Makes a Pass at Me.
I use Ovaltine and Listerine, Barbasol and Musterole,
Lifebuoy Soap and Flit—
So why ain't I got it?
I use Coca-Cola and Marmola, Crisco, Lesco, and Mazola,
Ex-Lax and Vapex—
So why ain't I got sex?
I use Albolene and Maybelline, Alka—Seltzer, Bromo—Seltzer
Odorono and Sensation,
So why ain't I got any fascination?
My girdles come from Best, the Times ads say they're chic
And up above I'm dressed in the brassiere of the week
Oh dear, what can the matter be, Nobody Makes a Pass at Me.
I use Ponds on my skin, with Rye Krisp I have thinned,
I get my culture in—I began with *Gone With the Wind*—
Oh dear, what can the matter be, Nobody Makes a Pass at Me.
Oh Dorothy Dix please, show me some tricks, please
I want some men to hold.
I want attention and things I won't mention
And I want them all before I get too old.
I use MUM everyday and Angelus lip-lure
But still men stay away—Like Ivory soap I'm
Ninety-nine and forty-four one-hundredths percent PURE
I don't know!!!!

"Economics I"

People think that love is blind
And though I may sound unkind
I think love affects the mind.
I'm nutty, batty, utsnay, crazy,
Slightly daffy, too.
My mind's a blank, my senses hazy
That's what love can do.
Hi—de—hi
Ask me why
All my skies are so blue
Love's around the corner
I'm just nuts about you

Ho—de—ho
Now I know
All my dreams will come true
Love's around the corner
I'm just nuts about you.
You're sweeter than a fresh potato latka
Your kisses burn me like a drink of vodka
Ha—chadka!
Hay—de—hay
Lucky day
Honeymoon soon is due
Love's around the corner
I'm just nuts about you.

"Men Awake"

At open, group is discovered on ramps and platforms upstage.

ALL: We are the immigrants

THE WOMEN: The immigrants

ALL: The immigrants.

(*During the next section, each group marches down center and then to right or left and at end, entire group forms large semi-circle.*)

ALL:

We are the ones who left Dark Ireland's shore,
and Poland's plain,
and England's grassy lea.
From Russia's steppes came we,
From sunny slopes of Spain,
From Italy,
From France,
From Germany,
From Greece.
From East, from West, from North, from
South we came—to build a homeland of
the Free.

(*Group moves around slowly into place in the smaller groups.*)

POOR WHITES: We are the Poor Whites, fooled and pushed apart.

FARMERS: We are the Farmers, bondsmen to the soil—Bondsmen.

WORKERS:

We are the workers sold to the machine
We are the workers sold to the machine
sold to the machine
sold to the machine
machine, machine

YOUNG ONES: (*Running to downstage center and then upstage left*)

We are the Young
Ones, the Young Ones, the Young Ones—
full of strength and hope—strength and hope,
and finding only the same old stupid plan

MAN WORKER: of dog eat dog
POOR WHITES: of mighty crush the weak,
MAN YOUNG ONE: tangled in that ancient, endless chain of
WORKERS: profit
POOR WHITES: profit
WOMAN YOUNG ONE: power
WOMAN YOUNG ONE: gain,
FARMERS: of grab the land
WORKERS: grab
POOR WHITES: grab, of grab the gold
WORKERS: grab
FARMERS: grab,
WORKERS: of work the men
WOMAN WORKER: of take the pay,
ALL: take, take,
WOMAN YOUNG ONE: of owning everything
ALL: for one's own greed.

(*As dancers start, entire group whispers "Men Awake" loudly four times. One singer comes from the* FARMERS, *another one from the* POOR WHITES, *and the third from the* YOUNG ONES. *They walk to downstage center and then to downstage right, where they finish the number.*)

SINGERS:

Workers all! Heed our call!
You who toil and sweat and slave,
From the cradle to the grave,
You who strive with hand and brain,

You who live in fear and pain,
You who slumber, countless number,
You in mines and factory stalls,
You within the sweat shop walls,
You in Life's forgotten heap,
You who sell your souls for keep.
Men Awake!!
Heed the warning.
Men Awake!!
The day is dawning.
Break the chains that keep you bound
And trample to the ground
The barricades that hem you round.
Men Awake!
Wheels are humming.
Men Awake!
The time is coming.
See, the signs are everywhere
So brothers now prepare
There is no time to spare, Awake!!!
Can't you see
Life can be what you make it?
Life that's new, Life that's free,
If you take it?
Put away yesterday and its sorrows—
Men unite we must fight for a new tomorrow
Wake!! Fates are drumming.
Men Awake!! The time is coming.
Men look up! A world that's free
Is yours if you can see
For you've the powers that be
AWAKE!!!

"Vassar Girl Finds A Job" ("Daisy Chain")

GIRL *is discovered stage right, hidden behind a torso figure; a gray drape covers both the girls and the figure.* GIRL *moves arm and unveils. She then steps away from the figure, places the drape inside the figure and taking a feather duster out of the figure, dusts it.* GIRL *walks center on ramp.*

When I was young, I studied hard and thirsted after knowledge
And often burned the midnight oil so I could get to college

They told me my fine education
Would help improve my situation
So then I crammed and crammed 'till I was almost in a coma
And thesised and examed until I got me a diploma
"Aha" they said, "Now comes admission
into a very high position".
So out I went and looked around
And Macy's is the place I found.
I filled my blanks and applications
And went for my examination.
They took my weight and took my height
And tapped my chest and tested my sight
Examined my head, took prints of my toes
Looked at my teeth and up my nose.
Examined my throat, measured my hips
And even took prints of my finger tips,
They made me say "Ah", they told me to grunt
Examined my back, examined my front.
Then they tested my "I.Q."
And asked what I'd like to do.
And when that exam was through
What there was to know Macy's knew—
So I got the job.
Life is a bitter cup of tea
Now I'm just a sales-girl 73
I used to be on the Daisy Chain
Now I'm a Chain Store Daisy.
Once I was given the honor seat
Now I stand up with pains in my feet
I used to be up on the Daisy Chain
Now shoppers drive me crazy.
I sell smart, but thrifty, corsets at $3.50
Better grade, $4.69
I sell bras and girdles at Mauds and Myrtles
To hold in their plump behind—this counter
Once I wrote poems put people in tears
Now I write checks for "Red Star" brassieres
I used to be on the Daisy Chain
Now I'm a Chain Store Daisy.

(GIRL *moves upstage to counter center and pantomimes customers.*)

Oh yes, Madam
Oh no, Madam

I guess, Madam
That's so, Madam
Oh of course, Madam, that's the very best
Exactly the kind that's worn by Mae West.
For you, Madam?
That's true, Madam
We do, Madam
In blue, Madam?
That one is $19.74
It ought to be expensive—it's the largest in the store.
Once I had a yearning for all higher learning
And studied to make the grade
For subjects pedantic, I shunned the romantic
And look at the kind of grade I made.
I'm selling things to fit the figure
Make the big things small and the small things bigger
I used to be on the Daisy Chain
Now I'm a Chain Store Daisy.

"Federal Theatre Project Plowed Under"

MR. BUREAUCRASH *enters right between columns right and center sighs with relief. Immediately there is a fanfare and a guard jumps from behind a column.* BUREAUCRASH *runs to table and sits in second chair. Guard goes behind column.*

MR. ZEALOUS *enters right below column, goes upstage and looks behind columns. There is a fanfare and two guards jump out.* ZEALOUS *goes to table and sits in first chair. Guards go behind columns.*

MR. STALLALONG *enters rapidly left above columns and comes through between right and center. A fanfare stops him, and two guards jump out. He scuttles to fourth chair and sits. Guards disappear.*

MRS. CLUBHOUSE *enters rapidly from right above columns. As she gets between center and left column, three guards jump out, and she runs to third chair and sits.*

On tag, as guards exit, all look around stealthily, then sit down.

CLUBHOUSE: Are they gone?

ZEALOUS: Shhhhh . . . .

STALLALONG: Take a look.

ZEALOUS: Wait a minute.

CLUBHOUSE: Look and see . . . .

ZEALOUS: . . . Out of sight. (*Goes to columns and looks around*)

BUREAUCRASH: Not a sign?

ZEALOUS: Not a sign.

CLUBHOUSE: Can we start?

STALLALONG: Let's start.

ZEALOUS: Coast is clear.

BUREAUCRASH: Let's begin. (*They rise.*)

CLUBHOUSE: Mr. Zealous (*They shake hands.*)

ZEALOUS: Mrs. Clubhouse

BUREAUCRASH: Mr. Stallalong (*They shake hands.*)

MR. STALLALONG: How are you, Mrs. Clubhouse? (*They shake hands.*)

CLUBHOUSE: Good morning, Mr. Stallalong.

ALL: (*Taking hands and facing front*) The Washington office of the Federal Theatre of the Four Arts Project of the W.P.A. is about to commence the arduous duties of another day—Ready?. . . . Go! (*They sit down.*) Oh, surrounded by officials with military signs, and governed by initials on many dotted lines, we sit here having visions and making great decisions for Drama, Music, and Art. The Theatre we have craved at last is to be saved for poets and creative bards surrounded by the military guards.

So give a happy, happy cheer again for Theatre productions when you are leaning on the government. Oh, it's a great relief, a joy in short, to know you have the full support of both Houses and the President.

We confess our New York section keeps us worried underneath, they do just the plays we disapprove and fling them in our teeth, and it gets a bit embarrassing when the press bestows a wreath, when we are leaning on the government. (ZEALOUS *leaps to columns, looks around, returns and signs all O.K.*)

Oh, consider the composers, the people who write plays, they've waited all these years to get a minimum of praise, their moment is at hand—they're going to wow the land. The government proclaims it to be true. For we'll produce their piece—at least what little piece is left when our Directors and our Board of Supervisors have got through.

So give a modulated cheer again for Theatre productions when you are leaning on the government. If we find a worthy script, then we insist upon its liberty, and won't compromise with its intent.

If a part should get blue-penciled, or a section is red-lined, then you mustn't be offended, you must only keep in mind. (*Rise*) We've got Senators in front of us and Congressmen behind when we are leaning on the government.

When we are leaning, sort of careening
Sort of careening,
Nevertheless leaning on
The government. (*They collapse.*)

CLUBHOUSE: Help! The guards!!

GUARD: (*Enters*) Paper for you to sign. (*To* BUREAUCRASH, *who signs. Guard exits.*)

BUREAUCRASH: I wish that man would let us know when he is coming.

ZEALOUS: It's like a time-bomb; I keep waiting for something to explode.

STALLALONG: Now what do you expect to explode in here, Mr. Zealous?

ZEALOUS: Nine out of ten projects, Mr. Stallalong.

BUREAUCRASH: I haven't been the same since we got that bad review in the "Times" . . . What was that I signed?

ZEALOUS: Didn't you notice?

BUREAUCRASH: I forgot to read it.

ZEALOUS: Could it have been a pink slip for me?

BUREAUCRASH: (*Slapping* ZEALOUS *on the back*) Brace up, man. After all, we're still Supervisors!! (*Fanfare.* GUARD *enters.*)

GUARD: Guy named Hippity Bloomberg wants to see you. (GUARD *exits.*)

STALLALONG: Who's Hippity Bloomberg? A Congressman?

BUREAUCRASH: A Congressman!! Good God—what have we done now?

ZEALOUS: Or a picketer from the rank and file?

CLUBHOUSE: Oh, no. I couldn't bear that.

BUREAUCRASH: Maybe the President sent him?

STALLALONG: Maybe Jim Farley sent him?

CLUBHOUSE: Maybe he wants to sell us a book?

ZEALOUS: Maybe he only wants our autograph.

(BLOOMBERG *enters.*)

STALLALONG: Whoever he is . . . .

(BLOOMBERG *removes his hat.*)

BUREAUCRASH: O.K. He's no Congressman.

CLUBHOUSE: Have you an appointment, or are you an anarchist?

BLOOMBERG: I should think it perfectly obvious that I am here by appointment.

ZEALOUS: Well, no rank and file.

(BLOOMBERG *sits in chair right.*)

STALLALONG: Sit down strike!!!

CLUBHOUSE: Oh, no, Mrs. Stallalong, I think not.—(*She rises.*) You're just sitting down, you know, aren't you? (BLOOMBERG *gets up.*) Oh, no. Please do sit down. (BLOOMBERG *sits again.*) Let me see now, where is my appointment book? It seems to me . . . (*All four look wildly among papers.*) Ah, here it is. The same one I used as secretary of the New Orleans Delinquency Aid—it used to feel so good helping delinquency in New Orleans when I . . . (BUREAUCRASH *motions to* BLOOMBERG.) Oh, yes. What's the name?

BLOOMBERG: Mr. Hippity Bloomberg. (*He rises.*)

CLUBHOUSE: Oh, but it can't be.

BLOOMBERG: Can't be?

CLUBHOUSE: Why no—I have Hippity Bloomberg down for Friday. This is Saturday.

BLOOMBERG: Saturday?

CLUBHOUSE: So you must be somebody else. (*She sits down.*)

BLOOMBERG: Somebody else??

BUREAUCRASH: Come, sir. Don't stand there repeating everything like an assistant supervisor.

BLOOMBERG: I beg your pardon.

STALLALONG: Hold on—it's not Saturday at all—it's Friday.

CLUBHOUSE: Saturday!!

STALLALONG: Friday!! I ought to know. I used to make fancy calendars.

ZEALOUS: Then he is Hippity Bloomberg, just like he says.

BUREAUCRASH: Certainly!

CLUBHOUSE: Hippity Bloomberg . . . (*Rising*)

BLOOMBERG: Yes.

CLUBHOUSE: Playwright . . .

BLOOMBERG: Yes.

CLUBHOUSE: (*Crossing to* BLOOMBERG) I wrote you . . .

BLOOMBERG: You did.

CLUBHOUSE: A wonderful playwright—but divine!! Gentlemen, he's come to read us his play—the most interesting young man and with such experience of Life!! You've lived with the people, haven't you?

BLOOMBERG: With some of them . . .

CLUBHOUSE: Modest.

BUREAUCRASH: (*Rising*) But this is topping. Mr. Bloomberg, do you realize we've planned to give your play the most thoughtful and elaborate production—

ZEALOUS: (*Crosses to* BLOOMBERG) Nothing spared, absolutely nothing—We have endless resources . . .

CLUBHOUSE: A huge cast . . .

STALLALONG: (*Crosses to* BLOOMBERG) Two hundred principals minimum—and fifty extras . . .

BUREAUCRASH: (*Crosses to* BLOOMBERG) And a chorus—there must be a chorus . . .

ZEALOUS: Oh, my, yes. Lots of music . . . a huge orchestra . . . one conductor . . . three assistant conductors . . . two rehearsal pianists, let me see, that makes fifty-two . . .

STALLALONG: And scene changes. We've got twenty-eight stage hands lined up, and the entire crew of electricians—

BUREAUCRASH: And the costumes . . . Oh, the costumes!! . . .

CLUBHOUSE: Wait!! Couldn't we have a revolving stage? Or, I know—one of those elevator stages, so we can have a flashback from the past on the second floor, and where we are is the present tense, and our hero's future is waiting to come up from down in the basement.

ALL FOUR: Now tell us what the play's about!!!

CLUBHOUSE: I hope it's dramatic.

ZEALOUS: I hope it's abstract.

BUREAUCRASH: I hope it's colossal.

STALLALONG: I hope it's good.

ALL FOUR: Mr. Bloomberg, the Federal Theatre is about to produce you!!!!! (*Fanfare and gaurds enter. Four sink onto their chairs.*)

GUARD: Sign this. (BUREAUCRASH *signs and guards exit.*)

ZEALOUS: Now where were we? (BLOOMBERG *coughs.*) Oh yes, your play.

BUREAUCRASH: What's it called?

BLOOMBERG: Ah, the title . . . "Workers Also Love" . . .

THREE MEN: Ugh!

CLUBHOUSE: Yes, but that can be changed.

BUREAUCRASH: Mr. Bloomberg, don't you think the term "worker" a bit inflammatory, just now? Controversial and all that?

BLOOMBERG: It works three ways, you know . . . "WORKERS Also Love", "Workers ALSO Love", "Workers Also LOVE". I thought it good.

CLUBHOUSE: You can just forget anything so trivial as a title, when you remember the production we're going to give you—the musicians—the sets—

STALLALONG: The title is out!

(BLOOMBERG *tears out a page.*)

BUREAUCRASH: Please go on.

BLOOMBERG: Well, it's about a boy and a girl . . .

ZEALOUS: Now don't tell me SEX rears its ugly head!

BUREAUCRASH: Not on taxpayers' money.

CLUBHOUSE: The kiddies, you know.

ZEALOUS: Couldn't you change it to a boy and a dog?

BUREAUCRASH: Or a boy and a horse?

STALLALONG: Or a boy and a box of Cornflakes?

CLUBHOUSE: (*Rising*) What is it they do—the boy and the girl?

THREE MEN: MRS. CLUBHOUSE!!! (*She sits down. Fanfare and* GUARD *enters to* BUREAUCRASH.)

GUARD: Paper for you to sign. (GUARD *exits.*)

CLUBHOUSE: You were saying?

BLOOMBERG: The boy and the girl go on a picnic in the woods . . .

CLUBHOUSE: Gentlemen, couldn't we be bold, just this once? After all, a peoples' theatre the facts of life, you know, a picnic in the wood . . .

BUREAUCRASH: Well, I don't know . . .

STALLALONG: Maybe—

CLUBHOUSE: Just this once, the picnic you were saying—

BLOOMBERG: It's sunset—there's a brook—

ZEALOUS: Ah! I was a boy and a girl myself once. (*Bureaucrash knocks Zealous' arm off the table.*) I mean . . .

BLOOMBERG: They're wading in the brook—they remove their shoes and stockings—

ZEALOUS: Remove their—?

STALLALONG: AH! Strip tease . . .

BUREAUCRASH: Not on our stage.

CLUBHOUSE: The clergy! What would they think?

BLOOMBERG: But not really, I—

CLUBHOUSE: You're not going to object to a cut there, surely? Remember, fifty-two musicians . . .

ZEALOUS: The elevator stage, and the lighting and costumes . . .

BUREAUCRASH: Come be reasonable—

STALLALONG: Wading in the brook—is out! (BLOOMBERG *tears out another page.*)

BLOOMBERG: Now there's a dance—

BUREAUCRASH: Mr. Bloomberg, the dancers on our project are peculiarly uncooperative. They are, I may say, the troublemakers. They go on hunger strikes, they sit down in theatres all night, they protest, they picket, they do Heaven knows what else. So if it's all the same to you, I would suggest . . .

BLOOMBERG: I never did like that dance, anyway. (*Tearing out another page*)

ZEALOUS: Is there a strike?

BLOOMBERG: Yes.

STALLALONG: The strike is out!!

(BLOOMBERG *tears out another page.*)

BUREAUCRASH: Is there a radical?

BLOOMBERG: Yes.

STALLALONG: The radical—is out!!!

(BLOOMBERG *tears out almost all the rest of the pages.*)

BLOOMBERG: Saves time!!

CLUBHOUSE: Now you mustn't be discouraged—remember our elaborate production.

BLOOMBERG: But look—my play! (*Pointing to script on floor. Fanfare. Three guards enter.*)

GUARD: All these papers you signed O.K.'d by the chief. (*To* BUREAUCRASH *and exit all three*)

BUREAUCRASH: (*Reading*) "Pink dismissal slips for 3,000 actors," "Forty-five hundred musicians fired," "All but three stage-hands dismissed," "Entire office force out by March 4TH." Well, that doesn't leave an awful lot, does it? And I seem to have signed them all.

ZEALOUS: Did I get a pink slip?

BUREAUCRASH: Certainly not, the heads of the departments will still carry on.

BLOOMBERG: What about my play?

ALL: Oh, yes??? (*They all ponder the situation.*)

CLUBHOUSE: Why it works right in, Mr. Bloomberg. No actors, no stage hands, no musicians, and—next to no play. It all fits. We will simply have a very intimate production of—practically nothing.

BLOOMBERG: Why don't you keep the public out, than it would all cancel perfectly.

ALL FOUR: (*To front*) A secret performance. (*To each other*) That's an idea. (*To each other*) Very novel. (*To* BLOOMBERG) Very unusual indeed.

BLOOMBERG: I don't want to appear carping, but I was told I'd find no censorship in the Federal Theatre.

ZEALOUS: (*Rushing to* BLOOMBERG) Censorship! Censorship!! There's no such thing about here. Now of course, if you were to write about someone who wants to change the Constitution of the United States—

BLOOMBERG: But I haven't.

STALLALONG: (*Rising*) Fine—then that stays in.

BLOOMBERG: What stays in?

STALLALONG: Silly! The part where nobody wants to change the Constitution.

CLUBHOUSE: (*Rising*) You have it in your hand.

BLOOMBERG: All I've got left is: "The Curtain Rises".

BUREAUCRASH: (*Rising*) Now why can't our play open SMACK like that? Do we have to have a curtain? (BLOOMBERG *faints.*)

"What Good is Love"

Girl is discovered center, in a pin spot of light.

Everywhere I go, I hear about sweet songs about the moon
Songs about the stars above and songs of love in June
Songs of hearts that beat as one to some sweet lovers' tune
But they're not songs that sing for me.
Songs about the dreams that lie within a lover's eyes
Songs about the cloudless skies in lover's paradise
Songs about the joys of love and lovers' lullabies
But they're not songs that sing for me.
What good is love, if you haven't got
Even a thing worth giving?
What good is love, if you haven't got
Even a life worth living?
Let your poets sing of "skies above"
And "endless love" and "hearts that dance"
Where is my chance—for the call of romance?
What good is love, if you have to face
Cold hungry days and sighing?
What good is love, when life's just a race
To keep your heart from crying?
You can keep your little songs that sing
Of all the joys that love can bring
What good's Romance? What good is Love to me?
Blue Moon, don't speak to me of a lover
For I'd much rather discover
Where I'm to rest my head
Blue skies, shining for me
Tell me where I'll get my daily bread.

Love may be the newest thing, the oldest and the latest thing
The thing that can make life complete.
Love may be the truest thing, the finest and the greatest thing
But I want a job and something to eat.
What good is love, if you have to face
Cold hungry days and sighing?
What good is love, when life's just a race
To keep your heart from crying?
You can keep your little songs that sing
Of all the joys that love can bring
What good's Romance? What good is Love to me?

"One Big Union"

As the lights come up, seven boys walk on downstage left. As soon as they're on, seven girls come on downstage right. Both form a single line across stage.

BOYS: (*To girls*) We've decided the only way we can woo you is to take a hint from the A.F. of L. and the C.I.O.

GIRLS: Now you're talking, perhaps we might listen to you. We don't say that we'll say "Yes", but we don't say we'll say, "No".

BOYS: Then it's not too late to negotiate?

GIRLS: Oh, well—we'll see.

BOYS: Perhaps we can agree.

BOY #1: I'm on a campaign to make you mine.

BOYS: We'll picket you until you sign.

BOY #1: In One Big Union for Two. No court's injunction can make us stop, until your love is all closed shop.

BOYS: In One Big Union for Two.

BOY #1: Seven days a week

BOYS: We want the right

BOY #1: To call you mine

BOYS: Both day

BOYS: And night

BOY #1: The hours may be long—but—

BOYS: Fifty million union members can't be wrong.

BOY #1: When we have joined up, perhaps there'll be a new recruit

BOYS: or two

BOYS: or three

BOYS: For that's what teamwork can do In One Big Union for Two.

GIRL #1: We've got some demands, you'll have to wait.

BOYS: Perhaps we can negotiate

GIRLS: Maybe—

GIRL #1: Let's see—Just what our terms will be. Promise to boycott non-union ties

GIRLS: And we might try to organize

GIRL #1: In One Big Union for Two. We want no check-off upon your heart, no rules to keep us both apart

GIRLS: In One Big Union for Two.

GIRLS: Will they pay their dues?

GIRL #1: They're very light.

GIRLS: A kiss each day

GIRLS: A kiss each night

BOYS: We think we'll get along—for—

BOTH: Fifty million union members can't be wrong.

GIRL #1: Make up your bye-laws so there can be

GIRL #2: A girl for you

GIRL #3: A boy for me

GIRLS: And maybe we'll see it through

BOYS: Oh, Boy!

BOTH: In One Big Union for Two.

GIRLS: We won't have sit-downs inside our gate

BOYS: We'll never need to arbitrate

BOTH: In One Big Union for Two.

BOYS: We'll have no lockouts to make us frown

GIRLS: No scabbing when you're out of town

BOTH: In One Big Union for Two.

BOYS: We can have a lot

GIRLS: A union flat

BOYS: A union dog

GIRLS: A union cat.

BOTH: Our life will be a song—Fifty million union members can't be wrong.

BOTH: We'll work together in unity

BOYS: Who knows what our results will be?

GIRLS: Well that depends on you

BOYS: And on you, too—

BOTH: In One Big Union for Two (*They dance. During dance, boys and girls stop and sing tag: "Fifty million Union Members can't be wrong". Dance ends with couples in original positions.*)

BOY #1 & GIRL #1: Now that we've signed up, let's make the grade

BOY #1: And add a member

BOYS & GIRLS: Union Made!

BOYS: (*To partners*) Who'll look like you

GIRLS: (*To partners*) And like you

BOYS: Looks like us, too

BOTH: In One Big Union for Two

(*All fall in a heap.*)

Introduction to "Slumming Party"

STAGE MANAGER *walks onto apron between curtains.*

STAGE MANAGER: Ladies and Gentlemen, as you are probably well aware, at this season of the year in ——, many fashionable receptions are being held. A party of exceedingly well dressed people has just come backstage. They have heard of our revue and would like to take this opportunity to present their point of view.

So with your kind permission, I would like to introduce: Mrs. Eugene Delacroix Dalyrymple III.

(*Curtain opens on "kind permission". Stage Manager walks in with Mrs. Dalyrymple. The "Reactionaries" are revealed. There are many variations necessitated by performances in various cities—the idea however, is to make the "Reactionaries" as fashionable and plausible as possible.*)

"Doing the Reactionary"

It's darker than the dark bottom
It rumbles more than the rhumba
If you think that the two step got 'em
Just take a look at this number
It's got that certain swing
That makes you 'bout to sing
Don't go left, but be polite
Move to the right
Doing the Reactionary

Close your eyes to where you're bound
So you'll be found
Doing the Reactionary
All the best dictators do it
Millionaires keep stepping to it
The four hundred love to sing it
Ford and Morgan swing it
Hand up high and shake your head
You'll soon see red
Doing the Reactionary

ALL:

So begin it
Get in it
It's smart, oh so very
To do the Reactionary
Hands up high, and shake your head
You'll soon see red
Doing the Reactionary

MRS. D:

If the steps seem rather vague
Watch Mayor Hague
doing the Reactionary

NEPHEW:

Union men put me in rages
Asking right and decent wages
They're all devils—sons of Satan
Always agitated

ALL:

Goose-step back with all your might
Step to the right
Doing the Reactionary
So begin it
Get in it
It's smart, oh so very
To do the Reactionary

"Four Little Angels of Peace"

At open, MUSSOLINI *is discovered posing in the center of the heart;* HITLER *is posing at his left, and a* JAPANESE GENERAL *is posing with bow and arrow at right.* MUSSOLINI *turns slowly and sees someone. He calls the others' attention to it and jumps down. They fight for the bow and finally decide by lot—the* JAP *wins.* JAP *gets arrow from* HITLER *and aims off right,* HITLER *is holding him steady,* MUSSOLINI *reaches around and tickles the* JAP *under the arm,* JAP *stamps his foot which lands on* HITLER'*s foot, he in turn stamps his and lands on* MUSSOLINI'*s. They change and* MUSSOLINI *supports the* JAP, HITLER *watching from just behind.* JAP *shoots the arrow and as it lands off right, there is a great scream and* CHAMBERLAIN *walks on right with an arrow fixed into the seat of his gown.* MUSSOLINI, JAP, *and* HITLER *pretend they know nothing about it and all sing the first general chorus.*

Four little angels of peace are we
Loving our neighbors so peacefully
There's really no harm
If we do not disarm
For we're always in close harmony
Four little angels of peace are we
There is one thing on which we agree
With foe or with friend
We will fight to the end
Just for peace, peace, peace.

(CHAMBERLAIN *walking left, salutes the others as he passes; they steal pistols from his pockets and aim at him but discovers he has them covered with a gun, which he takes from his hat.*)

CHAMBERLAIN:

Tho' we *butchered* the
Boers on their own native shores,
And *slaughtered* the Irish no end *upon horde,*
We were playing the part of a friend.
Yes our arms we increase, but we're really for peace.
Except in the case of a crook.
Tho' we conquered both spheres, now we're up to our ears,
Just trying to keep what we took.
Three Angels: Three little angels of peace are we
Living together so *blissfully*
Oh, we never *fight* unless we're in the *right.*
But we're always in the right, you see.
Three little angels of peace are we
There is one thing on which we agree
Until we are wrecks

We'll break each other's necks
Just for peace, peace, peace.

(*They pinch* JAP*'s cheeks; they smack* JAP *in the stomach; he smacks them in the stomach;* JAP *grabs them by the neck; they grab him and shake him.* JAP *looks at* MUSSOLINI *who scowls, then at* HITLER *who sneers. He motions front to* MUSSOLINI, *who returns the gesture; then to* HITLER *who does likewise.* JAP *shakes his head, folds his arms, and prepares to stay in place—when the other two pick him up by the arms and throw him to the footlights.*)

JAPANESE GENERAL:

In Japan we delight in our Generals' might,
But the Emperor knows peace is finer.
It isn't our fault, it's a case of assault,
We're picked on and bullied by China
Oh, how we deplore the mere mention of war,
We're a nation of poets and thinkers.
Tho' we bomb without pity and destroy every city,
It's because all the Chinese are stinkers.

(HITLER *and* MUSSOLINI *bang him on the head and he falls. On interlude,* MUSSOLINI *dances over to* HITLER *left, they join and do an Apache dance to downstage right, where* HITLER *shakes* MUSSOLINI *and throws him to the floor.* MUSSOLINI *rises,* HITLER *dances to him and they dance another Apache left, where* MUSSOLINI *shakes* HITLER *and throws him.* HITLER *recovers, returns center, thumbing his nose, which develops into the Nazi salute as he goes downstage center for his lyric.*)

HITLER:

Tho' I fall for the urge of a nice bloody purge
And leave in my wake piles of carrion.
Tho' I clean up my shmutz with a real Nazi putsch,
It is all for the sake of the Aryan.
My ambitions are small, I want nothing at all
My plans couldn't be any littler.
New Sudetens are Nazi, it would be hotsy-totsy
To put the whole world under Hitler.

(MUSSOLINI *swings at him, but is guarded off by* HITLER's *raised hand.*)

MUSSOLINI:

Now I know that war is a thing to abhor
And that peace will fill our *cornucopia*
With love from the start, I just did my part
To civilize dear *Ethiopia.*
Tho' you call me sadistic, imperialistic
My armies require a *quarry,*
And tho' we may slay hordes of Spaniards each day
After all, don't we say that we're sorry?

MUSSOLINI and HITLER:

Two little angels of peace are we
Living together in *a*—mity
We'll sign any pact saying we won't *attack*
But that's just a mere *formality.*
Two little angels of *peace* are we
There's just one thing on which *we* agree,
We try to keep *calm* as we gas and we *bomb*
Just for peace, peace, peace.

(HITLER *bangs* MUSSOLINI *over the head and* MUSSOLINI *apparently doesn't feel it —to* HITLER'*s despair. They get into a fight as they sing last part, socking on underlined words and sinking to floor on the last "peaces".* CHAMBERLAIN *and* JAP *get up, crawl over and bang them on the head, falling in a heap on top of them.*)

Reprise

On into, HITLER, MUSSOLINI, *and* CHAMBERLAIN *dance on, waving one hand, the other behind them;* JAP *dances in front of them and very fast, fanning himself.* HITLER *grabs him and he gets into place at left end of line.*

ALL:

Four little angels of peace are we
Reeking with odor of sanctity
Tho' we slaughter the meek
We confer every *week*
And we talk it over peacefully.
Four little angels of peace are we
There is one thing on which we agree
With shot and with shell, we'll give each other Hell!
Just for Peace! Peace! Peace!

(*Hands behind each other's back and discover machine guns, which they place on apron.*

They dance around shaking hands, and smiling at each other. They grab machine guns and mow each other down.)

"We've Just Begun"

(*Curtain opens, disclosing Company on ramp center.*)

ALL: Go hire a hall!!

SPEAKER: Yeah—Tammany Hall!

ALL: Peddle your papers somewhere else We'll stand by what we have to say. And do it in our own sweet way. So now let's finish up what we've begun.

SPEAKER: Well, our work is almost done.

ALL:

Oh no, we've just begun!
Together now we know the song to sing
The words are ours—ours is the tune
We're the ninety-one percent
We're the many and the strong
In the future to be built
We intend to have a voice.

GIRL: There are millions of us.

ALL: Yes, we'll have something to say!

CURTAIN

Works Cited

Altenbaugh, Richard J. *Education for Struggle: The American Labor Colleges of the 1920s and 1930s.* Philadelphia: Temple University Press, 1990.

The American Labor Year Book, 1919–1920. Edited by Alexander Trachtenberg. New York: Rand School of Social Science, 1920.

Atkinson, Brooks. "The Play: *Processional.*" *New York Times,* 13 January 1925, 17.

——. "*Singing Jailbirds* Called Propaganda." *New York Times,* 5 December 1928, 34.

Clark, Barrett H. "*Processional* and Some Others." *Drama* 15 (1925): 129–30.

Coit, Eleanor. "Progressive Education at Work." *Worker's Education in the United States.* Place N.A.: Brameld, n.d., 153–78.

Cosgrove, Stuart. "The Political Stage in the United States." In *Theatres of the Left, 1880–1935: Workers' Theatre Movements in Britain and America,* edited by Raphael Samuel et al., 259–352. London: Routledge, 1985.

Denning, Michael. *The Cultural Front: The Laboring of American Culture in the Twentieth Century.* New York: Verso, 1997.

Dubofsky, Melvyn. *We Shall Be All: The History of the Industrial Workers of the World.* 2nd ed. Urbana: University of Illinois Press, 1988.

Feuerlicht, Roberta Strauss. *America's Reign of Terror: World War I, the Red Scare, and the Palmer Raids.* New York: Random House, 1971.

Foner, Philip S. *Women and the American Labor Movement: From World War I to the Present.* New York: Free Press, 1980.

Goldman, Harry Merton. "*Pins and Needles:* A White House Command Performance." *Educational Theatre Journal* 30 (March 1978): 90–101.

Gould, Jack. "The Play." *New York Times,* 29 November 1937, 18.

Gutman, Herbert. *Work, Culture, and Society in Industrializing America: Essays in American Working-Class and Social History.* New York: Knopf, 1976.

Hardy, Jack. *The Clothing Workers.* New York: n.p., 1935.

Haywood, William. "On the Inside." *Liberator,* May 1918, 45. Rpt. in Kornbluh, 334–37.

Johnson, Donald. *The Challenge to American Freedoms: World War I and the Rise of the American Civil Liberties Union.* Lexington: University of Kentucky Press, 1963.

Kessler-Harris, Alice. "Problems of Coalition Building: Women and Trade Unions in the 1920s." In *Women, Work and Protest: A Century of U.S. Women's Labor History,* edited by Ruth Milkman, 110–38. London: Routledge, 1985.

Kornbluh, Joyce L., ed. *Rebel Voices: An IWW Anthology*. Ann Arbor: University of Michigan Press, 1964.
Kornbluh, Joyce L., and Mary Frederickson, eds. *Sisterhood and Solidarity: Workers' Education for Women, 1914–1984*. Philadelphia: Temple University Press, 1984.
Kornbluh, Joyce L., and Lyn Goldfarb. "Labor Education and Women Workers: An Historical Perspective." In *Labor Education for Women Workers,* edited by Barbara Mayer Wertheimer, 15–31. Philadelphia: Temple University Press, 1981.
Krutch, Joseph Wood. "Drama: Jazz of the Spirit." *Nation,* 28 January 1925, 99–100.
——. "Melpomene on a Soap Box." *Nation,* 4 November 1928, 528.
Lanza, Aldo. "Teatro Operario e 'Labor Chautauquas' a Brookwood Labor College." *Movimento Operario e Socialiste* 3 (1980): 199–220.
Larkin, Margaret. "Building a Social Theatre." Unpublished essay, 1935.
Lawson, John Howard. "The Crisis in the Theatre." *New Masses* (December 1936): 35–36.
——. "A Few Words About *Stevedore*." Unpublished essay, 1935.
——. Introduction to *Ten Days That Shook the World,* by John Reed. New York: International, 1967.
——. *Processional.* New York: Thomas Seltzer, 1925.
——. "Straight from the Shoulder." *New Theatre* (November 1934): 11–12.
Lockridge, Richard. "*Pins and Needles,* Leftist Revue, Opens at the Labor Stage." *New York Sun,* 29 November 1937, 49.
Melosh, Barbara. *Engendering Culture: Manhood and Womanhood in New Deal Public Art and Theater.* Washington, DC: Smithsonian Institution Press, 1991.
Milkman, Ruth. "Women's Work and the Economic Crisis: Some Lessons from the Great Depression." *Review of Radical Political Economics* 8 (1976): 73–97.
Muste, A. J. *The Essays of A. J. Muste.* Edited by Nat Hentoff. New York: Simon, 1967.
Norton, Helen. "Drama at Brookwood." *Labor Age* (May 1926): 18–19.
Payne, Elizabeth Anne. *Reform, Labor, and Feminism: Margaret Dreier Robins and the Women's Trade Union League.* Urbana: University of Illinois Press, 1988.
Ransdell, Hollace. Untitled article. *Labor Drama* (Feb. 1936): 1–2.
——. "The Soap Box Theatre in Workers' Education." Pamphlet. Affiliated Schools for Workers. April 1935.
Ross, Steven J. "Struggles for the Screen: Workers, Radicals, and the Political Uses of Silent Film." *American Historical Review* 96 (1991): 333–67.
Scharf, Lois. *To Work and To Wed: Female Employment, Feminism, and the Great Depression.* Westport, CT: Greenwood, 1980.
Seidman, Joel. *The Needle Trades.* New York: n.p., 1942.
Skinner, R. Dana. "Jazz and Lighter Things." *Independent* 86 (1925): 114.
Slaughter, Jesse. "Does Drama Belong?" *Brookwood Review* (December 1927–January 1928): 3.
Strom, Sharon Hartman. "Challenging 'Woman's Place': Feminism, the Left, and Industrial Unionism in the 1930s." *Feminist Studies* 9 (1983): 359–86.
Taft, Philip, and Philip Ross. "American Labor Violence: Its Causes, Character, and Outcome." In *Violence in America: Historical and Comparative Perspectives,* edited by Hugh David Graham and Ted Robert Gurr, 187–242. Rev. ed. Beverly Hills, CA: Sage, 1979.
Tippett, Tom. *Mill Shadows.* Katonah, NY: Brookwood Labor College, 1931.
Trumbull, Eric Winship. "Musicals of the American Workers' Theatre Movement—1928–1941: Propaganda and Ritual in Documents of a Social Movement." PhD Diss. University of Maryland, 1991.
The Use of Plays in Club Work. New York: Women's, 1930.
"We Must Write Plays." *Workers Theatre* (April 1931): 17.

Whipple, Sidney B. "The Rich Cleverly Satirized: *Pins and Needles* on Labor Stage Has Critic's Approval." *New York World-Telegram,* 30 December 1937.

Wong, Susan Stone. "From Soul to Strawberries: The International Ladies' Garment Workers' Union and Workers' Education, 1914–1950." In Kornbluh and Frederickson, 37–74.

Young, Stark. "*Processional.*" *New Republic,* 28 January 1925, 261.

Acknowledgments

The research for *Staged Action* began as part of my dissertation more than a decade ago, so I would like to begin by acknowledging my committee at the University of Tennessee-Knoxville: my dissertation director, Stanton E. Garner Jr.; Mary Papke, whose remark in a graduate American literature survey course, "Labor unions used drama to recruit members," put me on the case; Chuck Maland; and Tom Cooke.

I also thank the many research librarians around the country who assisted me in compiling a collection of dozens of workers' theatre plays.

Several students were responsible for making digital documents out of the various forms of manuscripts: Kimberly Rose DeJesus, Nicole Catalano, and Jessica Socol. Your aching typing hands and tired eyes are much appreciated.

And special thanks to: Michelle Philippin, for her inspiration and belief in this project; Mark Creter, Eric Lassiter, and Cate Marvin, for their support and friendship; Marcus Duskin, for his help with making sure that all the pieces of *Pins and Needles* were there; and, finally, Frances Benson of the ILR Press, who has been extraordinarily patient and helpful in ushering this book through the editorial process.